Structural A[djustment] & Agriculture

Structural Adjustment & Agriculture

THEORY & PRACTICE
IN AFRICA & LATIN AMERICA

Edited by
Simon Commander

OVERSEAS DEVELOPMENT INSTITUTE · LONDON

in collaboration with

JAMES CURREY · LONDON

HEINEMANN · PORTSMOUTH (N.H.)

Overseas Development Institute
Regent's College, Regents Park, London NW1 4NS

James Currey Ltd
54b Thornhill Square, Islington, London N1 1BE

Heinemann Educational Books Inc
70 Court Street, Portsmouth, New Hampshire 03801

British Library Cataloguing in Publication Data

Structural adjustment & agriculture: theory &
   practice in Africa & Latin America.
   1. Developing countries. Foreign assistance
   by developed countries
   I. Commander, Simon
   338.91'1722'01 724

   ISBN 0–85255–115–0 (James Currey)
   ISBN 0–85255–114–2   pbk (James Currey)

   ISBN 0–435–08034–2 cloth (Heinemann Inc)
   ISBN 0–435–08037–7 paper (Heinemann Inc)

Library of Congress Cataloging-in-Publication Data

Structural adjustment & agriculture: theory & practice in Africa & Latin America / edited by
   Simon Commander.
      p.   cm.
   Includes bibliographies and index.
   ISBN 0–435–08034–2 (Heinemann).—ISBN 0–435–08037–7 (Heinemann: pbk.)
      1. Agriculture—Economic aspects—Africa.   2. Agriculture—Economic aspects—Latin
   America.   3. Africa—Economic conditions—1960–   4. Latin America—Economic
   conditions—1982–.
   I. Commander, Simon.   II. Title: Structural adjustment and agriculture.
   HD2117.S78   1989
   338.1'096—dc19   89–1968
                                                                                           CIP

Typeset in 9/11 pt Mallard by Colset Pte Ltd, Singapore
Printed in England by Villiers Publications, London N6

Contents

PART THREE: Country Studies

PART FOUR: An Overview of Adjustment Experience

List of Tables
& Figures

TABLES

FIGURES

List of Contributors

Tony Addison, School of African and Oriental Studies, University of London; formerly Overseas Development Institute, London.

Robert Bates, Duke University, USA.

Gervasio Castro de Rezende, Instituto de Planejamento Economico e Social, Rio de Janeiro, Brazil.

Simon Commander, World Bank, Washington DC; formerly Overseas Development Institute, London.

Ajay Chhibber, World Bank, Washington DC.

Lionel Demery, University of Warwick; formerly Overseas Development Institute, London.

Reginald Herbold Green, Institute of Development Studies at the University of Sussex.

John Howell, Overseas Development Institute, London.

Omotunde Johnson, International Monetary Fund, Washington DC.

Jonathan Kydd, Wye College, University of London.

Ousseynou Ndoye, ISRA, Dakar, Senegal.

Ismael Ouedrago, ISRA, Dakar, Senegal.

Per Pinstrup-Andersen, Cornell University, USA.

David Seddon, University of East Anglia.

Wayo Seini, ISSER, University of Ghana, Legon.

Paul Streeten, World Development Institute, Boston University, USA.

Vinod Thomas, World Bank, Washington DC.

Preface

This volume owes its origin to a conference organised by ODI on the Design and Impact of Adjustment Programmes on Agriculture in London in September 1987. All the chapters – bar Chapters 4 and 14 (Chhibber and Commander) – were first presented, in some cases in rather different form, at this conference.

The costs of the conference were covered through the generosity of a number of institutions. The Ford Foundation, the Overseas Development Administration (ODA) and Barclays Bank all provided significant financial assistance for which both the editor and ODI are most grateful. In particular, John Gerhart at Ford and Linda Lewis at Barclays were very considerate and helpful.

The Ford Foundation office in Dakar provided full research funding for the joint ODI/ISRA project, one of whose results was Chapter 9 (on Senegal). The Ghana case study, which came out of collaboration between ODI and ISSER at the University of Ghana, was funded by CIDA (Canada). The editor and his collaborators are particularly grateful to Richard Horovitz at Ford in Dakar and Roger Ehrhardt of CIDA in Accra for their support on these projects.

The editor would also like to thank Patricia Scotland, Lee Dianda and Jennifer Dudley for their work in organising, most successfully, the ODI conference. Margaret Cornell has, as is usual at ODI, played a key role in preparing the manuscript for publication, casting aside redundant ideas and sentences; but done so sweetly that the experience always seems painless. John Howell was a good guide and a great colleague.

Introduction

Simon Commander

Despite some significant country and regional variations in economic performance the 1980s have largely been characterised by low growth, persistent balance-of-payments disequilibria and high levels of domestic imbalance. To adjust to a largely hostile external environment, commonly compounded by domestic policy inadequacies, a growing number of developing countries have had to have recourse to a range of lending instruments, largely involving quick-disbursing assistance, that the major donor agencies have evolved over the course of the last decade.

In the case of the IMF this has only partly been the case. The traditional Stand-By agreement has only recently been complemented by the Structural Adjustment Facility (1986) and the Enhanced SAF (1987) with their emphasis on the highly indebted and low-income economies of sub-Saharan Africa. However, in the case of the other Bretton Woods institution, the World Bank, the growth in adjustment lending since 1979/80 has been positively hectic. By 1988 adjustment lending comprised around 10 per cent of the World Bank's portfolio and roughly 25 per cent of its annual lending. Though this trend has not been mirrored in quite such an extreme way in the case of the bilateral donors, the share of resources directed to policy-based lending or within the framework of adjustment lending has also risen at a rapid rate.

The use of policy-based lending has been accelerated by the presence of high interest rates, declining terms of trade and growing indebtedness among developing countries. The need for quick-disbursing balance-of-payments support has grown almost exponentially and, perhaps most significantly, shows little sign of waning. Moreover, while it is very clear that only a relatively small share of this financing demand can be met by multilateral agencies and bilateral donors, offsetting finance from private commercial banks will be available for only a very limited range of creditworthy countries or for cases where private bank exposure is already sufficiently high. Even so, recent writing-off of debt and other parallel measures raise doubts over the level of finance that will be available over the medium term from this source. One consequence is that adjustment lending by donors will not decline and is likely to rise as a share of total developing country external financing as well as in terms of the portfolios of the donors.

If initial expectations of a five-year horizon for adjustment lending have now become obsolete, a range of associated questions arise with regard to the instruments for dealing with profound, non-transitory economic imbalances. In this respect two particular questions are highly apposite. The first concerns the suitability of classic stabilisation programmes, with their almost exclusive emphasis on reducing aggregate absorption, and the second relates to the appropriate ways of attaining structural adjustment through supply-side responses. These issues arise with specific force in both the sub-Saharan African context and for the Latin American economies where a combination of institutional and market rigidities as well as high external debt and domestic inflation levels pose particularly acute problems for both stabilisation and structural adjustment programmes.

The relatively limited duration of most adjustment programmes makes assessment of their impact difficult. However, simply contrasting the performance of economies with adjustment programmes with those without such programmes indicates a diffuse and ambiguous set of outcomes. While exchange-rate and trade-policy measures have tended to yield growth in exports, this has – particularly for primary exporters – been offset by adverse movements in the terms of trade. Manufacturing exporters, such as Brazil or Korea, have seen the largest improvements in both balance of payments and aggregate growth terms, but this appears not to have been the case for the majority of low-income economies – particularly in Africa – as well as the more debt-burdened economies of Latin America. Furthermore, one unifying theme throughout the adjustment phase has been the sharp reduction in investment, both public and private. Clearly, this will have negative longer-term implications for growth and compounds the fact of existing low growth rates. Indeed, in the case of low-income countries with adjustment programmes, growth rates in the 1980s have been significantly below pre-adjustment levels.

If the benefits of adjustment programmes have yet to be widely and significantly translated into reality, the costs of such programmes have been both high and visible. Although it can be reasonably argued that the costs of not adjusting would have been greater and that some transitional costs are inevitable, inefficiencies in the adjustment process, deriving commonly from structural constraints and market rigidities, have tended to yield high, sustained adjustment costs. The extent of these costs has depended ultimately on the scale and rate of supply response in the economy. When adjustment is not frictionless and that response is constrained, the demand-reducing effects from reductions in aggregate absorption will tend to dominate. In that context, adjustment acquires more the character of reducing deviations from a given equilibrium path rather than the desired shift in the path itself. Consequently, phenomena such as rising underemployment and open unemployment, falling real wages and declining public services will tend to predominate. Not surprisingly, this can impose a heavy political cost on governments that in some cases – for example, in Zambia or Argentina – leads to repudiation of adjustment programmes.

The analytical core of conventional adjustment theory turns on the combination of expenditure reduction and expenditure switching resulting from a real devaluation. In the latter case, the price of all present goods rises relative to future goods but the domestic price of tradables rises relative to that of non-tradables. This induces a shift in domestic demand towards the latter goods, while also shifting relative output prices in favour of the former. By this process both external and internal imbalances are corrected (Corden, 1985).

The expenditure-switching process clearly attracts considerable significance for the agricultural sector – the main focus of this book. This is because, in most developing countries, agriculture is the principal source of tradables output. Furthermore, when, as in many sub-Saharan African countries, agricultural tradables producers have been discriminated against through pricing, marketing and taxation rules, adjustment policies have generally sought explicitly to reverse such discriminatory policies. Of particular significance in this context are measures to correct for exchange-rate overvaluation, low producer prices, declining intersectoral terms of trade and explicit protection for the industrial sector.

Despite the fact that the core of adjustment theory turns on the relative price effects under expenditure switching, the degree to which the incentive framework has been actually changed has varied considerably, as becomes clear from a reading of the country case-studies in this volume. Nominal devaluations have not necessarily been sustained as real devaluations, while the maintenance of administered pricing rules and marketing controls has diluted the impact of domestic relative price shifts. Perhaps most significantly, a large number of countries – particularly low-income SSA economies – have seen the efficacy of price reforms reduced by the presence of severe infrastructural constraints and market rigidities. Where the expenditure-reducing properties of adjustment have predominated, such constraints have tended to be exacerbated. This has primarily occurred through contraction in public expenditure, both on the recurrent budget side and also through a decline in real investment expenditures. Any expected investment response from the private sector may be held back by uncertain expectations, as well as the general low level of economic activity.

The presence of such major constraints, both domestic and external, in the implementation of adjustment programmes has increasingly led to demands for reappraisal of the design of such programmes. Criticism of the assumptions underpinning them has focused on a wide range of issues. Some commonly made criticisms dwell on the inflationary nature of devaluations and the limitations of exchange-rate adjustment in improving export performance. In the latter regard, it can be forcefully argued – and this is supported by much of the evidence presented in the country studies in this volume – that real exchange-rate depreciation is only likely to be effective when linked to complementary policies, such as public investment and sector-specific interventions (Taylor, 1987). Moreover, critics would point to the fact that public spending – generally a key target for reduction in adjustment programmes – can serve a critical role for crowding-in private investment rather than supplanting the latter, as is normally argued. This may be particularly critical if non-price constraints hold back to a significant degree the scale of supply response that, in theory, provides the core of structural adjustment. This is likely to be the case most particularly in the agricultural sector.

As yet, surprisingly little attention has been paid to the sector-specific design issues. This volume is an attempt to correct this imbalance and to move beyond the level of comfortable generality that has characterised much of the existing literature. The papers aim to address in a more detailed and extensive way the central issues that determine both theoretically and practically the place of agriculture in the adjustment process. The book is organised as follows. A series of chapters deal with the framework of adjustment and the specific incorporation of the agricultural sector in that framework. There then follows a set of country and multi-country case studies that attempt to bring out the localised consequences of adjustment measures. They attempt to do this not only with regard to the success or failure of adjustment in stimulating output growth but also with regard to the impact on welfare levels. While the general conclusions of these papers point – with some exceptions, such as Colombia – to relatively weak supply responses and major problems in sustaining and implementing adjustment programmes, this has to be attributed not only to the weaknesses in those programmes but also to the inadequacy of prior policies. The relative success of Colombia can in part be attributed to the longer-term quality of macroeconomic policy-making.

Although the evidence marshalled in the case-study chapters indicates both slow and partial improvement in economic performance at sectoral level, it is also clear that few countries have the viable option of not adjusting. Clearly the options – such as they are – further narrow with the maintenance of a hostile external environment. What this volume does, indicate, however, are some of the ways in which current inefficiencies in adjustment mechanisms can be explicitly incorporated in design terms and more effectively addressed. In the case of the low income sub-Saharan African economies, with which this volume is primarily concerned, such inefficiencies can largely be traced to the presence of structural barriers to accelerated growth. For such economies, the analytical and practical substance of adjustment remains largely indistinct from the basic issue of economic development itself.

REFERENCES

Corden, W.M. (1985) *Inflation, Exchange Rates and the World Economy*, Oxford, Oxford University Press.

Taylor, L. (1987) 'Varieties of Stabilization Experience', Marshall Lectures, University of Cambridge, April, (mimeo).

PART ONE

The Design of Structural Adjustment

1
A Survey of the Issues & Options

Paul Streeten

INTRODUCTION

The essence of development is structural adjustment: from country to town, from agriculture to industry, from production for household consumption to production for markets, from largely domestic trade to a higher ratio of foreign trade. While the advanced industrial countries also have to adjust to a changing world and to new technologies, their structures are more stable and less subject to change. In this very general sense, development is synonymous with structural adjustment and a paper on structural adjustment would be a paper on development.

For the purpose of this chapter, however, a somewhat narrower definition is chosen. In the pursuit of self-reliance, environmental protection, cultural values, countries are at times faced with major disruptions to which they have to adjust. Adjustment is then adaptation to sudden or large, often unexpected, changes, which may be favourable or unfavourable to the set of objectives pursued by government. In the case of a favourable change (for example, unexpected improvement in the terms of trade, additional foreign capital available for investment or greater benefits from the international division of labour), the challenge is to derive the maximum benefits from it; in the case of an unfavourable change, to adapt with the minimum social costs, that is, the lowest sacrifice of the objectives and the minimum of undesirable side-effects.

The adaptation to unfavourable change may be forced upon a country 'too little and too late', and therefore its social costs may be very high; or it may be anticipated and prepared for, and therefore its costs minimised. Even when the change is not anticipated, there are methods that provide for adaptability and flexibility, thereby reducing, usually at a cost, the social costs of adjustment.

Change may be small and slow or large and sudden. For slow and gradual change, the price mechanism is one of the best instruments of adaptation. It combines a decentralised system of signals and incentives, to buyers and sellers, for the allocation and redeployment of resources in response to changes in demand and supply, and it avoids some of the drawbacks of bureaucratic controls, such as ignorance, inefficiency and corruption. If, with Alfred Marshall, we think that nature does not make jumps, we shall rely heavily on the price mechanism and the market. For a large and sudden change, the price mechanism is less suited, at least by itself, and has often to be supplemented or replaced by other non-price measures.

The main issues discussed in this chapter are the implications of structural adjustment for open economies. The structural changes to which such economies have to adjust may come from the outside. Structural changes or shocks originating within the country also have repercussions on the balance of payments and require correcting actions and adjustment.

A special case is adjustment from a set of wrong policies to better policies. This comprises adjustments both for a given set of objectives that had been pursued in a misguided manner and for a set of different objectives, more in line with a reformed social welfare function. We shall call these the problems of transition.

The balance of payments of a developing country both reflects the attempts of domestic adjustments and imposes the need for adjustments to changes in the rest of the world. Thus, changing to an export-oriented strategy, an attempt to grow more food at home, a land reform, a tax reform or a redistribution of income, may lead to a temporary balance-of-payments deficit. On the other hand, the rise in the price of an important·import, global inflation, a fall in demand for a country's exports, or policy changes in other countries may also cause a deficit, to which the developing country must adjust. It is now generally agreed that the use of exchange rates to equilibrate payments at each moment ('clean floating') is not acceptable and would inflict unnecessary damage, even if effective. Large speculative capital movements can lead to 'overshooting' and be counterproductive to the adjustment process. But the exchange rate, often in conjunction with other measures, more fully discussed later, is a powerful instrument to bring about more long-term changes.

ADJUSTMENT FOR WHAT?

The first and most fundamental question to ask is: adjustment *for what purpose*? Any adjustment must have some end in view. Sometimes constraints are considered as if they were objectives of policy, and, of course, they can take the form of intermediate objectives. Thus the elimination of a deficit in the balance of payments or in the budget or in public enterprises, though a constraint, can become an overriding short-term objective. Or we may wish to adjust from a strategy of import substitution to one of export orientation, or to growing debt service, or to more food production. Or we may wish to correct other distortions in order to improve the allocation of resources. Or we may wish to reduce high rates of inflation. These are, at best, intermediate objectives.

Among the key objectives of structural adjustment are usually cited (i) the reduction or elimination of a balance-of-payments deficit, (ii) the resumption of higher rates of economic growth, and (iii) the achievement of structural changes that would prevent future payments and stabilisation problems. One of the most important purposes of structural adjustment is to make the economy less vulnerable to future shocks. This can be done by increasing flexibility and adaptability. The success of a structural adjustment programme depends largely on the absence of rigidities, but it may also be its aim to reduce such rigidities. Unless they can be removed, structural adjustment can be very costly, or altogether out of reach. Growing flexibility is therefore both a condition for and an objective of adjustment policy. Flexibility can be applied to the market for products or for factors of production, but if it is confined to products, while factors remain inflexible, large rents will arise which have no economic function.

There are more fundamental objectives, such as the elimination of hunger and malnutrition, or the alleviation of poverty, or the achievement of cultural autonomy or self-reliance or greater national strength and military power. Some would say that accelerating economic growth is also such a fundamental objective, although growth is simply the time dimension of other goals or policy such as consumption, or poverty alleviation, or reduced inequality, or more employment. Whatever the technical intricacies of the adjustment process, it is useful to bear its purpose in mind, if only because some of these objectives may conflict with one another.

ADJUSTMENT TO WHAT?

The next question to be asked is adjustment *to what*? Adjustments may be to an unexpectedly favourable turn of events, or more normally to an unfavourable turn of events.

The large literature of the 'Dutch disease' that arose from the bonanza of natural gas discoveries in Holland testifies to the fact that a large rise in the supply of foreign exchange can be, at best, a mixed blessing, and at worst a curse. The exchange rate appreciates, exports of other goods and services decline, competitive imports flood into the country, domestic employment declines while inflation rises as the demand for non-tradables increases. Income distribution may become more unequal and the poor may be particularly hard hit. The removal of the foreign-exchange and savings constraints can bring to the fore other obstacles. Adjustment policies should then be devoted to their identification and removal. Among these will be promotion of other exports and some control of imports, both possibly through a dual exchange rate, sterilisation of some of the inflowing foreign exchange, control of domestic inflation, and creation of alternative productive assets. Thus even a favourable turn of events can cause adjustment problems.

Much more common, unfortunately, is the need to adjust to an unfavourable turn of events. A widely accepted distinction is that between the need to adjust to shocks caused by external factors, such as a drastic deterioration of the international terms of trade, a reduction in the demand for export volumes, resulting, for example, from a world recession, or a rise in interest rates for countries with large debts, and those caused by domestic events or policies, such as an excessively lax fiscal and monetary policy, price distortions, losses of public enterprises, excessive protection, excess foreign borrowing or domestic upheavals, including revolutions. On the face of it, the distinction is clear enough.

Yet on closer inspection, the distinction becomes blurred. If prices of a country's exports drop and its terms of trade deteriorate, it is a matter of good policy to have foreseen this event or at least its possibility, and to be ready to move out of the declining export trade into more profitable lines. Thailand, Malaysia and the Philippines diversified their crops and raised productivity in existing crops in response to declining price prospects (for example, rubber in Malaysia), while other countries failed to do this (for example, Tanzania for sisal). To get stuck in declining export lines can be, at least partly, attributed to a failure of domestic policy. But the distinction between external and internal causes gives no clue to the source of the fault and the allocation of blame. Events originating in the domestic economy may be just as much beyond policy control as some outside events. A failure of the domestic harvest, a flood, a hurricane or an earthquake cannot be attributed to domestic management, though provision for such emergencies would be prudent. The external-internal distinction is not a useful guide for allocating fault or blame or entitlements to foreign assistance. And even if it were, unless more external assistance were in fact forthcoming in one case than in the other, it would not be helpful in determining what measures to adopt. For even faults that lie entirely outside the country have to be adjusted to, just the same as if they originated in the country.

A particular, often very difficult, type of adjustment is that to the policies of the advanced industrial countries. It is of the essence of interdependence that single nation states are, by unilateral action, capable of inflicting considerable harm on other countries. The main danger here arises from beggar-my-neighbour protectionist policies. Disguised as regional or industrial policies, even policies that go under the name of 'adjustment *assistance*' can often amount to adjustment *resistance*. Such measures affect most directly the newly industrialising countries (NICs) in search of markets for their growing manufactured exports. But the low-income countries can also be harmed. The fear that barriers will go up can be an important deterrent to investment in export industries, and this causes the false impression that supply constraints are at work.

Exchange-rate flexibility on the part of developed countries has trade-reducing effects on developing countries, and if the latter peg their rates to one major trading country this results in trade-diverting effects from the rest of the world. Both represent costs for countries attempting to increase and diversify their trade.

A difficult problem is presented to the developing countries by the impact of the US mix of monetary and fiscal policies on other industrial countries. The recent combination of loose fiscal and tight monetary policy combines the burden of high interest rates with depressed demand for exports from developing countries, as other developed countries have to put up their interest rates to avoid excessive capital outflows. The best scenario would be a continuing US expansion while the US budget deficit is brought under control. US interest rates would drop, easing the debt burden, Europe and Japan would expand with easier monetary policies, and demand for the exports of the developing countries would grow. Structural adjustment for the advanced countries, like charity, begins at home.

So far we have discussed adjustments as mainly responses to shocks, whether external or internal. But adjustments may be required as a result of more active initiatives for a change in strategy. A government may wish to change from import-substituting industrialisation to export orientation, or from excessive urban bias to more agricultural production both for home consumption and export, or from a conventional concentrated growth strategy to a more egalitarian one, or to institute a land reform, or a tax reform, or to make poverty eradication one of its principal targets. The adjustment problems that such transitions create are often inadequately treated and sometimes misunderstood. They will include sectoral imbalances in supply and demand, manifesting themselves in unemployment combined with inflation, and disturbances in the balance of payments, and will raise the time period for financing adjustments. As income is redistributed to the poor, the supply of food will be inelastic in the short run and prices will rise or more imports will burden the balance of payments. As expenditure on luxury goods is reduced, unemployment in these trades may rise. Owners of capital will try to move their capital abroad. If the reformist government replaces a repressive dictatorship, previously oppressed groups will assert their claim to higher incomes with inflationary results. There may be strikes and even coups d'état. Some of these adjustment problems are mistaken for manifestations of mismanagement, which, of course, especially for inexperienced reformist governments, may independently add to their difficulties.

Economists have been better at analysing comparative statics and comparative dynamics, than the transition path from one type of strategy to another. We lack a handbook for reform-minded Prime Ministers and Presidents, who would like to know how to manage the transition to a better society.

ADJUSTMENT OF WHAT?

Next there is the question: adjustment *of what*? In developed countries adjustment sometimes means the revival, with new technology, of old industries and at other times it means the creation of new industries at the frontiers of technological knowledge. (The textile industry is an example of both.) The question often posed is whether labour should move to the industries or capital and entrepreneurs to the labour. Developing countries have a much smaller industrial base and the question is normally a different one. Should there be adjustment of *policies*, particularly pricing policies, say from protection to freer trade or from keeping food prices down to raising them to the level of world prices, or should there be adjustment of institutions? These may refer to a land reform or to population control or to the administrative system or to education and training.

A vast amount of writing and exhortation has recently been devoted to advocating higher agricultural prices where they are below border prices. This, it is said, would stimulate agricultural production – both export crops and food for domestic consumption – and help poor rural people at the expense of the urban middle class. When it is pointed out that, quite apart from the fact that there are many poor urban and rural buyers of food who should be protected from hunger and starvation caused by higher food prices, other measures besides higher prices are needed if only to get a substantial supply response, the advocates of higher prices would agree. Yes, they would say, we need roads to get the produce to the market, technology to apply to agricultural production, irrigation, credit, efficient marketing etc. But the proposition 'other things are also necessary' is open to two diametrically opposed interpretations. It may mean that other things help, but to 'get prices right' by itself is better than nothing: it is a step in the right direction. Or, alternatively, it may mean that only if price policies are combined with non-price measures is there a supply response. Price measures by themselves can be either quite ineffective, or actually counterproductive, even if we have only total production in mind, and pay no attention to poverty or income distribution.

Let us first briefly look at the 'other things' and then illustrate the futility, in some situations, of applying only price measures. Prices come first, because they serve as incentives. Second, inputs: water, fertiliser, equipment. Third, innovation: technology, such as high-yielding varieties, irrigation etc. Fourth, information: the technological knowledge must be diffused through extension services. Fifth, infrastructure; unless there are roads and harbours to get the crops to the market, even the best incentives will not get production and sales up. And sixth, institutions: credit institutions, efficient marketing institutions that do not cream off too high a margin from the final price, and, in some cases, land reform. Many of these, particularly infrastructure and innovation, are normally carried out in the public sector.

There are some pricist fanatics who maintain that the correct prices will by themselves induce the right innovation and even the correct action by the government in the public sector. There are others, who say that all these instruments, other than incentives, are already in place in many developing countries. If these two groups of people were right, no independent public sector action would need to be taken. Unfortunately, this is often not the case. In Tanzania or Ghana, roads are so inadequate that even if farmers produced more in response to higher prices, the crops could not be transported: a failure of infrastructure. Or the marketing boards would appropriate the gains, leaving nothing to the farmers: a failure of institutions.

In addition, complex and difficult choices arise within each of the six instruments. Consider infrastructure, normally provided at least partly at public expense. There are choices between physical, legal, human, social and producer-specific types of infrastructure to be made; between centralised and decentralised types; between infrastructure for producers and for consumers, between maintenance of existing projects and new projects, and between different methods of financing infrastructure. The same is true for institutions and for information. (For example, should extension workers concentrate on a single line of conveying information or should they combine several?) All these compete for scarce resources with directly productive investment in agriculture.

Let us now illustrate how higher agricultural prices without action on the other five fronts can be ineffective or counterproductive. The illusion that higher prices by themselves will lead to a large response in supply derives from an illegitimate extension of what happens if the price of one crop rises relatively to others to the case where the agricultural terms of trade as a whole improve. All the evidence shows that supply response is much lower for total output.

Moreover, raising agricultural prices may not be capable of improving the terms of trade. In the effort to raise producer prices as an incentive to agricultural production, the benefits can be undone if the higher prices are communicated to the rest of the economy through proportionately higher money wages and higher mark-ups on industrial goods. If this were to happen, the attempt to raise agricultural prices would only set off an inflationary movement, and would not improve agricultural-industrial terms of trade or its objective of raising agricultural production, and would have undesirable side-effects.

A second example is from Bangladesh. There, a large proportion of the rural population are small farmers who produce some food for themselves on their tiny plots of land, but not enough, so that they have to work for bigger landlords and buy food with their wages. When the price of food rises, these deficit farmers pledge their plots against consumption loans. When they cannot repay the loans, they forfeit their land. We are not concerned here with the fact that these people may be driven to starvation, but only with the effect on output. Since the output per acre on large farms tends to be lower than on small farms, the transfer, caused by the initial rise in food prices, will lower total agricultural production (Ahmed, 1981).

A third example is inspired by Tanzania. Let us assume there is a scarcity of consumer goods in the villages, their prices are controlled and there is no black market. As agricultural prices are raised, the farmers can buy the limited amount of consumer goods at controlled prices for a smaller supply. If we also assume that they are interested in storing money for the future, they will produce and sell less. Their elasticity of supply becomes minus one. As supply prices rise, they reduce supply proportionately, because they need only a given total of receipts to buy the rationed and price-controlled goods. Let us further assume that foreign-exchange earnings are derived from agricultural crops and are spent on imports of consumer goods. And let us assume, not unrealistically, that a certain absolute amount of these imported consumer goods are reserved for the urban population. The reduced agricultural supply will mean reduced imports. Since a larger proportion of these are pre-empted for the towns, the farmers will get even less. Their supply will further shrink and we shall witness a contractionist spiral, fewer consumer goods leading to less agricultural supply, leading to fewer consumer goods for farmers, etc . . . (Bevan et al., 1987).

The conclusion is that correct pricing policies often (clearly not always) work best in conjunction with action in the public sector. It is rather like an attempt to go on a low-calorie diet for losing weight. Low calorie items taste best in conjunction with high-calorie items; strawberries are fine, but strawberries and cream much tastier.

Since adjustment normally means reducing expenditure somewhere, a prime candidate for this is military and defence expenditure. How many village pharmacies could we have for one tank? Many see rising military expenditure as a source that should be tapped for better purposes. But the presentation of more attractive alternatives has no impact on the military establishment. However, there is historical evidence that military expenditure and foreign aid, or military expenditure in wartime and improved domestic levels of nutrition, are positively, not negatively, correlated. If we wish to make an impact on the military establishment we shall have to convince it that growing defence expenditure can be counterproductive in terms of its own objective, viz. security. It is probably the only area in which the Laffer curve applies. Beyond a certain point, more defence expenditure reduces rather than increases national security.

Other candidates for expenditure cuts are various headings in the budget deficit and the losses of public enterprises. As we have seen, these losses constitute a major element in the budget deficits of many developing countries. The purported social purposes of many public enterprises appear to legitimise their losses, but two questions arise. First, are these social purposes actually achieved, or are the public subsidies to these enterprises not in fact counterproductive in terms of the claimed objectives? Secondly, even where the social purposes are achieved, can this not be done at lower cost, more efficiently, and therefore with smaller losses, or possibly with surpluses? One way of testing this is to calculate the precise amount of the cost of any 'social objective', to hand this amount of subsidy to the enterprise, and to ask it then to cover its total costs.

ADJUSTMENT BY WHOM? WHO BENEFITS AND WHO LOSES?

UNICEF has recently started to think about, and to urge upon the IMF, what they call 'adjustment with a human face' (Cornia et al., 1987). How can we bring about the required adjustment with the minimum harm to the most vulnerable groups, given that some cuts in expenditure are required?

In considering the impact of adjustment policies on the poor, three things should be clear to start with. First, any form of macroeconomic adjustment is bound to affect income distribution, if only because its purpose is to raise income in some sectors and reduce it in others. Secondly, what should be of main concern is the impact of adjustment on the poor, not on relative income distribution. If some groups benefit without anybody being hurt, this should be no cause for complaint, although in fact conflict over the division of benefits can be as serious as conflicts over gains and losses. Thirdly, any cut in living standards, imposed by the need to correct a balance-of-payments deficit, is bound to hit some of the poorer sections (though not necessarily the poorest or those groups, the meeting of whose needs contributes to human capital formation), if only because the poor are so numerous and average income is so low in low-income countries. This is particularly the case if productive investment that contributes to economic growth and to safeguarding future living standards is to be protected. Some austerity is therefore inevitable. In particular, employed wage-earners in the organised sector, including those in public enterprises, who are not normally among the poorest, may have to suffer. The question is whether IMF stabilisation policies inflict an undue share of the burden upon the poor, for instance by a sudden elimination of food subsidies, or by cuts in social services, or by price increases for essential goods.

A study by Norman Hicks and Anna Kubisch (1984) suggests that for the period of the 1970s and early 1980s, social expenditures were less vulnerable on average than other types of government expenditure, when total expenditure was reduced. Vulnerability is defined as a percentage reduction higher than the average. It could, of course, be argued that when cuts are made in other sectors, raising unemployment, social expenditure should be increased. And indeed, some countries, such as Brazil, Indonesia and the Philippines, increased social sector expenditure despite total cutbacks. On the other hand, other countries, such as Turkey, Guyana and Sudan, reduced social expenditure by more than the average. But the authors conclude (p. 39),

> the empirical evidence suggests that when governments in developing countries implement austerity programmes, they do not apply across-the-board reductions in expenditure. Generally, capital expenditures are reduced more than recurrent expenditures. Within both capital and current budgets, the social and administration/defence sectors appear to be relatively well protected while infrastructure and production absorb disproportionately larger reductions.

It should be noted, however, that social expenditure only catches a part of the impact on the poor. For example, cuts in food subsidies are counted as reductions in the productive sector. The question as to whether austerity programmes inflict an undue burden on the poor has to be answered with a view of the alternative. Any appraisal of stabilisation policies must compare them with a specified, hypothetical alternative situation, not with the situation when the deficit permitted living above the country's means. Comparisons with past performance are therefore irrelevant. The counterfactual for comparison can be either the probable situation without IMF assistance, or IMF assistance with Fund conditionality, or IMF assistance with different conditionality packages. While devaluation and monetary and fiscal restriction will hit the poor, had inflation continued at the old level and no adjustment occurred, higher prices of food and other necessities would also have harmed them. They have no assets whose value goes up with inflation, and their money incomes tend to lag behind price increases, especially of the goods mainly consumed by them, such as food. And if the corrections had then to be brought about by the imposition of import restrictions or violent deflation, the poor would suffer most. It should be expected that, in a regime in which income, wealth and power are unequally distributed, the poor suffer, whatever policies are pursued. On the other hand, in countries where the poor have political power, such as the Malays in Malaysia, stabilisation programmes in the 1970s protected them against severe damage by using food subsidies, exemption from credit restrictions, and other measures.

Inflation is sometimes called 'the cruellest tax' on the poor, and it is therefore not self-evident that the contraction imposed by the IMF hits the poor more than continuing inflation would. As far as the USA is concerned, recent work by Alan S. Blinder and Rebecca M. Blank has shown that the poor suffer more under unemployment and recession than they do under inflation, and that it is unemployment that is the 'cruellest tax' (Blinder and Blank, 1986). These results cannot be immediately transferred to the developing countries, but a similar approach could be used there.

It is not inevitable that stabilisation policies should hit the poor exclusively. Adjustment normally consists of two parts: expenditure reduction and expenditure switching. It is true that expenditure reduction, in a low-income country, will tend to hit the poor sections, unless they are specifically protected or compensated. But expenditure switching need not harm them. The reallocation from domestic sectors to tradables will tend to raise incomes in these sectors. If traded goods are mainly agricultural goods and if many poor are in agriculture, they may benefit from the reallocation. (On the other hand, some non-tradables, such as construction and government services, are labour-intensive, and a switch to the production of tradables may reduce employment and income of the poor). Analysis of the impact of balance-of-payments adjustments on income distribution and poverty is sometimes conducted in terms of a two-sector neoclassical model, in which tradables have different factor proportions from non-tradables. A switch to tradables then benefits the owners of the factor of production that is used more intensively in the production of tradables, not only in the tradables sector but in both sectors. It also benefits the consumers of non-tradables because their relative prices fall. But the difficulty with this type of analysis is that incomes of people do not always follow the functional lines of capital and labour, and the two-sector model is of limited use. Within each sector there may be, for example, an informal, labour-intensive sub-sector, in which producers own a little capital but operate on a small scale, and a formal capital-intensive, large-scale sub-sector, with wage employment. As expenditure is switched to the tradables sector, workers in the formal sector may benefit but the informal sub-sector poor may be harmed. If there is substantial mobility between the sub-sectors, this does not matter, for people will move from the informal into the formal sector. But if mobility is limited, the distinction is crucial. It has already been argued that more important than the impact of stabilisation policies on income distribution is the impact on absolute poverty.

The higher price of imported necessities caused by devaluation could be offset by subsidies, targeted towards the poor, and the restrictions on investment could be on luxury housing and durable consumer goods for the upper classes. In fact, however, many stabilisation policies have hit the poor hard. The price rises that follow devaluation and the removal of controls frequently affect particularly the necessities consumed by them. Reductions in government expenditures are often on labour-intensive public works, food subsidies and social services. High interest rates tend to encourage concentration of wealth if lenders are richer than borrowers (but this is not always so), though lower rates combined with credit rationing favouring the rich often do the same. Monetary and fiscal restrictions raise unemployment and reduce the bargaining power of unskilled labour. In all cases it is the poor who suffer more than they would have done in a situation of repressed inflation, where demand for labour is high, the prices of necessities are controlled, and social services are more generous.

The impact of adjustment programmes on the poor can be analysed by distinguishing between five effects. First, there is the impact on their access to productive assets: land, credit, fertiliser. Second, there is the return to them on these assets. Some productivity improvements may be passed on in the form of lower prices. Third, there is the impact on employment. Fourth, there is the impact on human capital formation: health, nutrition, education, that enables the poor to become more productive. And fifth, there are transfers of payments or of income in kind through social services, charity or the family. Only a part of these effects is caught in an analysis that confines itself to the changing demand for labour.

Although we do not have a rigorous model by which to assess the impact of adjustment policies on vulnerable groups, including children and women, it is possible to lay down certain guidelines. First, maintain a floor for minimum nutrition, health and education expenditures, and do not permit cuts to affect these levels. Second, restructure production within the productive sectors – industry, agriculture, services and foreign trade – so that the producers in the small-scale informal sectors are not discriminated against but are made to complement the organised sector (manufacturing components or spare parts, conducting repair, sub-contracting, providing ancillary services, etc.); and give them access to credit, domestic markets and sources of supply. Third, restructure the social services – education, health, water and sanitation – so that the vulnerable groups are not deprived of minimum services. And fourth, provide international support for these types of adjustment, both financial and technical assistance, and particularly ease debt-service conditions, so as to permit the flexibility and adaptability that are called for by such programmes.

A difficulty with reducing more broad-based welfare programmes to more 'targeted' ones is always that savings in government revenue are bought at the expense of excluding some of the poor. 'Leakages' can occur at both ends: excess coverage means that some non-poor benefit, but reduced coverage means that some poor do not benefit. The case for erring on the side of excess coverage is that this also raises the taxable capacity of the non-poor, so that at least some of the expenditure can be recovered, say by a tax on tobacco which helps to finance food subsidies.

Special problems of protecting the poor arise for the period of transition from bad to good policies. Consider a government that has kept agricultural prices too low and wishes to raise them so as to encourage production and raise the income of poor sellers of agricultural products. Once supply and employment in agriculture have increased and new technologies have been introduced, we may assume that most sections will benefit. If supply curves have been lowered, prices may be even lower. But in the interim, some may suffer. Keynes said 'in the long run we are all dead', but this does not mean that in the short run we are all alive. Poor buyers of food may die while the adjustment to a set of reforms takes place. In Bangladesh, for example, higher prices of rice have led to higher child mortality (Ahmed, 1981). Policy-makers embarking on a course of raising food prices must therefore pay special attention to protecting the poor in the transition.

The high cost – in terms of political constraints, such as riots most recently in Zambia but also in Brazil, Bolivia, Peru, the Dominican Republic, Tunisia and Egypt among others – and of economic and financial resources is one of the biggest obstacles to reform. One solution is to increase prices gradually, in small steps. A second is to adopt selective subsidies, concentrated on vulnerable groups. A third way is to provide income subsidies to the poor. Subsidies can also be combined with rations, so that the poor are guaranteed a minimum of food. Fiscal and administrative constraints set limits to such programmes. It is particularly difficult to reach poor food buyers, such as landless labourers, in rural areas. Experience has shown, however, that pro-grammes of subsidies targeted to vulnerable groups can be quite effective, as long as the number of poor is not too large, say less than 30 per cent of the population. It is rarely possible to cover *all* the poor, and *only* the poor, and we may have to accept some sacrifice in higher total food production in response to higher food prices for the sake of better nutritional standards for poor food buyers, safeguarded by lower food prices in the transition.

ADJUSTMENT HOW?

What means are to be employed to bring about the adjustment? It is in the nature of adjustment policies that they comprise measures additional to stabilisation, such as the reduction of tariffs, trade liberalisation, the elimination of controls on wages and prices, the creation of institutions to facilitate export credits, and improvement in infrastructure, all of which aim at increasing the capacity to export.

The analysis can be conducted in three stages.

(i)   How severe will be the adjustment problem – the disease – as registered in the balance-of-payments deficit? (A secondary, more important but more difficult calculation would be the costs imposed by alternative corrective measures, such as deflation, devaluation, import restrictions, tariffs, etc.).

(ii) What range of medicines is available? For example, exchange-rate flexibility increases the number of medicines, while pegging exchange rates reduces the cupboard by one medicine: forswearing increases in tariffs by another. The possibility of retaliation complicates matters.

(iii) How effective is any given medicine? With a more slowly growing volume of trade, demand elasticities will be lower and exchange-rate adjustments less effective. On the other hand, within a free trade area or common market, elasticities may be expected to be higher.

The task for policy is to combine financing and correcting deficits in such a way as to minimise reductions in employment, output and growth, and the standard of living of the poor (and any other objectives such as income distribution). Appropriate methods of financing deficits, combined with the right type of conditionality, do not frustrate the process of adjustment, but facilitate it, and can reduce its costs.

ADJUSTMENT – WHEN?

The time period over which adjustment should take place is, of course, partly determined by the finance available. The economic argument for slow and gradual adjustment is that it is much easier and less painful to adjust in the context of a growing economy than suddenly. Redeployment of labour can then take the form of not replacing retiring workers rather than firing them. Capital can be allowed to wear out and not be replaced. But there are political arguments against gradual and slow adjustment. A slow process allows vested interests opposed to the change to be built up and strengthened. Mancur Olson has explained the success of the Japanese and German economies by the destruction of interest groups in the defeat of the war. It is not easy to analyse this conflict very precisely. It will have to be left to judgement. The phasing and sequencing of different adjustment measures – macro- and micro-measures, for instance – raises complex questions which will not be discussed here. But the answer will partly depend upon the answer to another question: *adjustment – from what?* If the initial position is one in which macropolicies are right, a diversified pattern of foreign trade exists, and there are large foreign-exchange reserves, the phasing of measures can be very different from a situation in which macropolicies have first to be reformed.

ADJUSTMENT THROUGH THE MARKET OR GOVERNMENT INTERVENTION?

The virtue of allowing the market to bring about adjustments is that it combines signals and incentives in response to change. Nobody maintains that markets work perfectly, but then nobody maintains that government intervention can always produce the best results. We live in an imperfect world, and it is a matter for skilful judgement to decide which imperfections – market failures or government failures – are least bad. Governments can, of course, intervene in the free play of market forces by using prices as instruments of policy. Indirect taxes and subsidies can attempt to use prices and market forces for the purposes of government policy, where the free play of market forces would otherwise conflict with social objectives.

Fortunately, there are not only the much discussed market failures and government or bureaucratic failures, but also market successes and government successes. These demonstrate neither the success of laissez-faire, nor of centralised bureaucratic control, but show governments (a) that knew in which areas to intervene and which to leave alone, and (b) how to conduct interventions efficiently. The failures illustrate not only excessive government intervention, but also unwise and inefficient intervention in some areas, and inadequate intervention in others.

When adjustment is needed, for instance to a change in supply or demand for a commodity which has been produced and sold in the past, consequential price changes normally signal the right responses and produce the right incentives. In response to a fall in demand, prices, profits and investment will tend to fall, and labour will leave the activity, or new workers will be discouraged from entering. But some exceptions should be noted.

a) When workers have to be retrained for new jobs, or have to move to new locations, capital is needed to finance these adjustments. If capital markets were perfect, workers could borrow and repay loans out of their future higher earnings. But capital markets are not perfect, and there is a role for governments to finance adjustment assistance.

b) Adjustments may be impeded by lack of knowledge, or by inertia. At a minimum, government may, in such situations, have to provide information, and perhaps again some subsidies to the movers. On the other hand, the information available to the government may not be much better than that available to individual workers, or their reluctance to move may be justified because their subjective costs exceed probable benefits.

c) If real wages are sticky and do not fall in response to a decline in demand, unemployment will rise. Sometimes this may bring about the adjustment more effectively than reductions in real wages, particularly if there is known excess demand for labour in other sectors. But if this does not happen there may again be a case for government intervention.

d) One of the most common justifications for government intervention is the need to correct an undesirable impact on income distribution. As we have seen, in any adjustment process, some people are likely to gain, others to lose. If the losses of the losers are undesirable, the government will try to step in.

Price policies are not the same as free market policies. Prices can be used as an instrument of government intervention, in order to achieve public objectives. Tariffs, indirect taxes and subsidies permit prices to affect the allocation of resources by cutting the links between buyers and sellers that would prevail in their absence. If, in response to an increase in demand, an indirect tax is imposed on a product, this will reduce the demand for the product, and therefore not permit an increase in the supply, unless the revenue is spent on additional supplies. A subsidy can be used to lower the price to consumers who otherwise would not buy the product; it increases supply without raising prices to buyers. The limits to such policies are set by fiscal constraints. Direct controls do not call for taxes or subsidies, but make demands on scarce administrative capacity. Both fiscal and administrative constraints are severe limitations in most developing countries, and choices between the two are difficult.

It is sometimes said that if we always pursue efficient policies, such as those indicated by market forces, while there will occasionally be losers, in the long run everyone will be better-off. There is therefore no case for government intervention to correct for income distribution, such intervention is only likely to reduce efficiency. But this defence is untenable. First, there is no reason to believe that the gains would be spread randomly in the long run. Many forces such as increasing returns, higher savings out of higher incomes, etc., work for cumulative gains – 'unto those who have shall be given' – and the same group of people can be consistent losers. Second, in the long run the identity of individuals changes, and it is illegitimate to compare the gains of one generation with the losses of another. Even if the compensatory gains were spread over the same generation, the individuals' tastes, wants and needs will change over time and it is then not clear that a future gain is always an adequate compensation for a current loss.

FALLACIES OF AGGREGATION: THE NEED FOR A GLOBAL VIEW

One of the criticisms of the IMF and the World Bank has been the absence of a global view on adjustment policies. Not all countries can have export surpluses. New gold apart, the surpluses of some must be matched by the deficits of others. Similar problems could arise in structural adjustment. If several countries were to reduce their dependence on a single export crop, whose price is likely to fall in world markets, by diversifying into crops that are supplied by other countries, but are also in surplus, they would aggravate the deterioration in their terms of trade. Similar problems can arise for manufactured exports, against which protectionist barriers are likely to be raised if the total exceeds what other countries think they can absorb. It has often been said, for example, that the experience of export-led growth of the East Asian countries cannot be repeated by all developing countries because the additional exports would be so large that protectionist barriers would go up or the terms of trade would deteriorate.

In its simplest form, there are several things wrong with this argument. First, in principle, the foreign exchange earned by the exports of the developing countries will be spent on extra imports and, problems of composition (calling for adjustment) aside, need not give rise to protectionism. Second, the phasing of trade liberalisation and export-orientation will be different for different countries, and not all exports will be dumped simultaneously. Third, as a result of a better international division of labour, incomes will rise in the developing countries, out of which more will be spent on exports from the developed countries, as well as from other developing countries. In the context of accelerated growth, the adjustment problem of switching resources from import-competing to new export industries should be eased. Fourth, the commodity composition and the export/GDP ratios will be different for different liberalising countries. Many developing countries will continue to export primary products. The experience of the Gang of Four (Taiwan, South Korea, Singapore, Hong Kong) should not be held up as a model. These countries are labour-rich, natural resource-poor, while other developing countries, such as Brazil and Argentina, are likely to be more resource-rich and labour-poor, and will therefore export a smaller proportion of their GDP in the form of labour-intensive manufactured products, thus reducing the risk of swamping the market. According to these and other characteristics, different developing countries will export different goods (as well as at different times). Fifth, some exports would be directed to other Third World countries, whose vested interests clamouring for protection are less than in the developed countries. Sixth, as a result of trade liberalisation some counter-protectionist pressure groups in the developed countries are likely to arise or be strengthened, for example, agriculture in the USA.

In spite of these arguments there are bound to be adjustment problems in the industrialised countries if all developing countries were to liberalise their trade and adopt more outward-looking policies. These will apply with particular severity to some product groups and some countries. A lot depends on what is assumed about growth rates in the late 1980s and 1990s, and how successful industrialised countries' adjustment policies will be. The conclusion of this discussion is that, although adjustment problems in the developed countries in response to an export drive on the part of all developing countries would be serious, and recommendations along these lines suffer from some degree of illegitimate aggregation, they need not be as serious as some observers have anticipated.

CONDITIONALITY

There is, on the face of it, a double paradox in an international lending agency imposing conditions for loans that are in the interest of the borrowing country. If they are truly in the interest of the receiving country, why are the conditions not pursued by the policy-makers? And why does the pursuit of those policies require financial incentives? One would expect to pay for good advice, not to be financially rewarded for following it.

One can think of ten sets of reasons of unequal validity, some of which are well analysed in a paper by A.R. Khan (1986). First, the policy-makers may be ignorant about the causal relationships and in need of instruction. Second, their causal analysis of the links between levers and results may differ from that of the donor. For example, they may evaluate the impact of a devaluation differently, or may believe that direct controls are more effective. Third, their forecasts of the future state of the world may be different. One group, for example, may forecast a higher price of oil in ten years, the other a lower. Or the borrower may overestimate the amount of additional foreign resources that would become available, while the lender may cautiously underestimate it. Or the self-confident borrower may overestimate his administrative capacity to implement controls, while the sceptical lender may underestimate it. Fourth, the objectives of the policy-makers, open or hidden, may differ from those of the lending institutions, or, fifth, government and lender may give different weights to the same objectives. For example, the government may want to promote the interests of groups on whose support it relies, whereas the lending institution wishes to institute painful reforms for the benefit of less well represented people. The function of conditionality then is not to persuade but to exercise leverage.

Sixth, the philosophy or ideology of the two may be different. The borrower may believe that power should be given to the public sector, whereas the lender wishes government interventions to be reduced to a minimum. Or the borrower may believe that the lending institution is a tool of imperialist exploitation, while the lender believes that the borrower is the victim of an outdated ideology. Seventh, the risk aversion in adopting policies with uncertain outcomes may be different for the two sides. Eighth, they may have different time discount rates and a different time horizon. For example, the government may be eager to stay in power and be concerned with gains in the short term, while the lender has benefits in the more distant future in mind. Ninth, the policy-makers may wish to find a scapegoat for popular measures and foreign lenders are ideal victims for this role. Finally, tenth, the policy-makers may share analysis, forecasts and objectives, attitudes to risk and time horizons, but assess the costs of transition to better policies as being too high or unaffordable without extra assistance. These costs would cover both political opposition and economic, financial and fiscal resources. This last ground is the most sensible explanation of the double paradox; foreign funds have the function, not of filling resource or foreign-exchange gaps, but of adding flexibility to an economy wishing to change course from a set of bad policies to better ones.

The remedy for the first and second reasons is education, dialogue, presentation of the arguments, and humility; for the third more searching analysis. For the fourth, fifth and sixth there are two solutions. Either the donor agency supports those interest groups inside the recipient country that are most in line with its objectives (though this can be counterproductive), or designs ways of compensating, if desirable and feasible, the interests that are hurt by the reforms. Or the agency reduces its objectives to the minimum, viz. the achievement of external balance and the creation of conditions that enable the country to repay the loan, while leaving decisions on other objectives, such as inflation, unemployment, income distribution, etc. to the recipient. Another remedy for disagreements about causal analysis is for the lender to concentrate on *results* (improvements in the current account of the balance of payments) rather than on *means* (devaluation, fiscal restraint, credit restrictions). Another is to signal without conditionality, by supporting 'good' countries or potential improvers, but without making this an explicit condition for loans; the message will soon get around. The remedy for the tenth is additional resources provided by the international community that help to add flexibility and reduce the costs of the transition.

If it is agreed that economic policy-making is not a science, and operates in an area of great uncertainty, conditionality imposed by the lender should be replaced by a genuine dialogue between lender and recipient. But even if the correct policies were revealed with absolute certainty to the lender, it is sometimes counterproductive to impose them from without, because such imposition can be used to mobilise the opposing forces inside the country.

There is another difficulty with policy conditionality: policies, like resources, are fungible, and resistant governments can yield to one type of policy while pursuing their objectives by another. It would be excessively cumbersome and time-consuming to attempt to include all possible policies in an agreement and to close all loopholes. And even if it were possible at a high level, it would be impossible to implement or to monitor implementation.

Assume, however, that the conditionality is disinterested, sound, and in the interest of the borrowing developing country. The concessional or grant component in the loan entitles the creditor to impose conditions beyond those that provide the capacity for repayment of the loan. The conditions relating to macroeconomic policies are, as it were, 'bought' with the grant component. In that case the reverse of an often argued position would be true. It is often said that soft loans are inefficient and wasteful because they reduce the incentive of the borrower to apply hard-nosed criteria to the use of the loan. But on our assumptions, the adoption of correct macropolicies ensures the efficient use of the loans much better than a narrow concentration on the project would. The rationale of the soft component in the loan is that it buys more efficient policies with respect to exchange rates, budgets, money supply, operation of public enterprises etc.

Conditionality in lending policy has often been regarded as excessively intrusive. Yet, it would also be unreasonable to propose that money should be lent or given without regard to its use by the recipient. There are three possible solutions to this dilemma.

However irrelevant some aspects of Marshall Aid are to the developing countries today, the method that was used to monitor it can still teach us an important lesson. The European countries were asked to monitor one another's economic performance, thereby avoiding the heavy-handed intrusiveness of a large donor imposing performance criteria. This worked well and was widely accepted. But it may be said that

Marshall Aid is not an appropriate model even for an institutional framework for partnership and mutually monitored conditionality of aid. The Alliance for Progress initiated in 1961 is said to be a better model, and it is also said to have failed. It is true that the radical reforms envisaged were never implemented, but Latin America did advance, reduced its dependence on the USA, laid the foundations for the rapid growth of the 1970s, and conducted massive investment in human resources. Recently, there has been a widespread return to democratic government. Nevertheless, the negative lessons of the Alliance, as well as its positive lessons, should be learned.

A second method would be to appoint a small group of independent experts, experienced men and women who are trusted by both donors and recipients, and who would periodically report on progress. Such a review body would add authority and credibility to assessments and recommendations.

A third method would be the creation of a genuine transnational secretariat, trusted by the international community of both donors and recipients. The existing international institutions have not yet achieved this, partly because of their nationality quotas in recruiting staff or at least insistence on some balance in their staff as to their countries of origin, partly because of their location, partly because of their method of recruitment and training, and partly because they are intergovernmental organisations. What would be needed is a reform that would create a truly global (rather than inter-national) civil service, with loyalties only to the world community, recruited by merit, with expert training, but with sensitivity to local political, social and cultural conditions. It would operate from regional offices in the developing world, so as to gain from day-to-day contact with policy-makers, not only at the highest level but also at the middle level of technicians. The staff would take a view that would transcend national policies. They would not be afraid to participate, where desirable, in the management, as well as the financing, of projects, with the mandate to train and hand over to local managers in due course. Such a reformed global entrepreneurial and civil service, trusted by both advanced and developing countries, could make a genuine contribution to development.

REFERENCES

Ahmed, Raisuddin (1981), *Agricultural price policies under complex socio-economic and natural constraints*, Washington DC, International Food Policy Research Institute Research Report No. 27.

Bevan, D.L., A. Bigsten, P. Collier and J.W. Gunning (1987), 'Peasant Supply Response in Rationed Economies', *World Development*, Vol. 15 No. 4.

Blinder, Alan S. and Rebecca M. Blank (1986), 'Macroeconomics, Income Distribution and Poverty', in Sheldon Danziger and Daniel Weinberg (eds), *Fighting Poverty: What Works and What Doesn't*, Cambridge, Mass., Harvard University Press.

Cornia, G.A., R. Jolly and F. Stewart (1987), *Adjustment with a Human Face*, Oxford, Clarendon Press for UNICEF.

Hicks, Norman and Anna Kubisch (1984), 'Cutting government expenditure in LDCs', *Finance and Development*, Vol. 21, No. 3.

Khan, A.R. (1986), 'Policy Conditionality of Bank Lending: Some issues' Washington, DC, World Bank, Country Policy Department, February (mimeo).

2

The Agricultural Sector in IMF Stand-by Arrangements

Omotunde E.G. Johnson

INTRODUCTION

Among the more frequently heard criticisms of adjustment programmes supported by IMF stand-by arrangements is that they do not pay enough attention to output growth – that they may in fact often be adverse to longer-term growth. This apparent drawback supposedly reflects macroeconomic policies that are deflationary, short-term in focus and hamper capital formation. But to the extent that agriculture is important in the production structure of a country, adjustment programmes that favourably affect agriculture should also rebound beneficially on overall growth.

While it is fair to say that greater sensitivity to the consequences for growth has led to greater attention being paid to the impact of macroeconomic measures on particular productive sectors of the economy in Fund-supported adjustment programmes, there have also been other contributory factors. Perhaps the most important of these has been the realisation that the attainment of balance-of-payments sustainability often requires major structural reforms, including changes in the production structure, rehabilitation of some sectors, and enhancement of net investment in others. Balance-of-payments adjustment measures, in such circumstances, cannot easily be divorced from policies to improve growth performance.

This chapter is concerned with the way in which the agricultural sector has featured in programmes supported by IMF stand-by arrangements – still the most important facility under which members make use of the institution's resources. It outlines the analytical framework within which the agricultural sector is considered in such programmes. It is argued that the emphasis is on the internal terms of trade of agriculture and the supply response of producers in that sector. This leads into the rationale for the fundamental equation (E16) which specifies the marketed output as a function of variables that are often incorporated in the adjustment programmes, and a discussion of the real exchange rate as an instrument to influence agricultural exports. Since programmes usually deal directly with issues related to the efficiency of

* The author would like to thank Anthony Lanyi of the IMF for comments on an earlier draft of this chapter. He is, nevertheless, solely responsible for the views expressed.

resource use and various credit, investment and fiscal measures designed to raise private returns in agriculture, these aspects are also touched on. Both intersectoral and intrasectoral (within agriculture) efficiencies are discussed.

ANALYTICAL FRAMEWORK

Agriculture has featured prominently in Fund-supported programmes when it is believed that agricultural policies and institutions have played an important role in bringing about the balance-of-payments, growth and inflationary problems (the external and internal imbalances) that the programme is designed to tackle. In the countries concerned, the agricultural sector is generally conspicuous in several areas of the macroeconomy, viz. in employment, GDP, exports and imports, in inputs for industry, and as a source of revenue for the government budget. If agriculture is not very important in one or more of these areas, it is safe to say that adjustment programmes supported by a Fund stand-by will pay virtually no direct attention to it, even though, inevitably, the programme will have an impact on the sector.

Typically, where agriculture is important for macroeconomic performance, the sector provides employment for over half the labour force (often two-thirds or more) and accounts for over one-quarter of GDP and, often, about the same percentage or more of exports. But the agricultural sector can also be crucial for macroeconomic performance in situations where the contribution of the industrial sector to employment, exports and GDP is greater, if agriculture provides an essential linkage with industry through its supply of raw materials, for instance, sugarcane and sugar refinery. Furthermore, agriculture may also influence macroeconomic performance through the fiscal impact of subsidies to, and taxation of, agricultural products and inputs.

Fund-supported adjustment programmes have invariably been concerned with three basic interrelated issues when they have directly addressed problems of immediate relevance to the agricultural sector. The *terms of trade* between the agricultural and non-agricultural sectors is often the focus of analysis in trying to reach a decision on producer prices to be set by official marketing boards and on the magnitude of exchange-rate adjustment. At other times the agricultural sector is at the centre of broader growth and adjustment issues and the mode of analysis becomes the *supply response* of agriculture. Finally, the general question of *efficiency* in agriculture is often of great importance within the framework of a public investment programme that is itself a centrepiece in the adjustment effort.

Terms of trade

Of major interest in discussions leading to stand-by arrangements, particularly in low-income countries in sub-Saharan Africa, has been the terms of trade between the agricultural and non-agricultural sectors. In many countries public policy has resulted in adverse terms of trade for the agricultural sector.

From an analytical point of view, the terms of trade argument boils down to the hypothesis that if all prices were freely determined in open markets and if effective rates of taxation were the same for all commodities, then the value added in agriculture (VAa) as a ratio of GDP (Y) would have been much higher than is currently the case. Instead, for many years, vis-à-vis the non-agricultural sectors (industry and services), the agricultural sector was faced with negative effective protection (NEP) as compared with a presumably ideal zero effective protection (ZEP)[1].

The NEP situation has arisen, in turn, because the average public policy-induced (controlled) real price for agriculture was, during those years, kept lower than would have been realised under open markets cum equal taxation, and this disparity was not sufficiently counterbalanced by additional subsidies in the regulated regime (say $s.C_a$, where s is subsidy as a fraction of cost (C_a)) in agriculture. In brief, NEP implies

(E1) $$\left[\frac{\overline{P_{c_a} - P_{f_a}}}{P} + \frac{\overline{s.C_a}}{P} \right] < 0$$

where P_a^c is the controlled price of agriculture, P_a^f is the corresponding free market price, and P is the general price level. A bar over a variable indicates that the average (mean) over some time period (years) is being calculated. Note that the agricultural prices and subsidies being considered are those received by producers.

Fund-supported adjustment programmes will, therefore, tend to include actions directed at the agricultural sector when it is the view that agriculture is faced with negative effective protection vis-à-vis the non-agricultural sectors and that this fact is having adverse consequences for the balance of payments. The obvious policy implication – as can be seen from equation (E1) – could be a call for the raising of the controlled price in real terms (P_a^c/P), or the freeing of all markets (so that there is no disparity between P_a^f and P_a^c), or increasing the effective rate of subsidy(s). Budgetary constraints on the central government (or public sector) generally impel raising P_a^c/P or freeing markets – i.e. improving the terms of trade of agriculture.

In many low-income countries, especially in Africa, the producer prices of agricultural commodities particularly of export crops are established by a state marketing board. Such boards have come to be used as agents for taxing farmers – by paying farmers substantially less than the average sale (export) price realised by the board. Much of the effective tax is then remitted to the government, and accounts for a substantial part of government revenue. This situation has meant that, even when the choice has been made to improve the terms of trade to agriculture, by raising P_a^c/P, the mechanics involved must often take into account a government budgetary constraint. In many practical situations the consequence has been that producer prices and exchange-rate changes (currency depreciation) have been decided together.

Let Q represent the quantity of agricultural output, Gr total government revenue, G_{ra} government revenue obtained from agriculture, G_{rn} government revenue obtained from non-agricultural activities, and e the exchange rate; an increase in e would be a currency appreciation and vice versa for depreciation. As a simplified illustration of the problem we consider the changes in agricultural output and in government revenue resulting from changes in producer prices and the exchange rate with other policies remaining unchanged. Noting that

(E2) $$dQ = \frac{\delta Q}{\delta e} .de + \frac{\delta Q}{\delta P_a^c} .dP_a^c$$

(E3) $$dG_r = \frac{\delta G_{rn}}{\delta e} .de + \frac{\delta G_{rn}}{\delta P_a^c} .dP_a^c + \frac{\delta G_{ra}}{\delta P_a^c} .dP_a^c + \frac{\delta G_{ra}}{\delta e} .de$$

with target growth rates for Q and G_r – $\hat{Q}$ and $\hat{G}_r$ – it is, with some manipulation, possible to state the programme's aim as the solution of equation (E4) for $\hat{e}$ and $\hat{P}_a^c$; that is

(E4)
$$
\begin{bmatrix} \hat{Q} \\ \hat{G}_r \end{bmatrix} = \begin{bmatrix} a_{11} & a_{12} \\ a_{21} & a_{22} \end{bmatrix} \begin{bmatrix} \hat{e} \\ \hat{P}_a^c \end{bmatrix}
$$

where

$$a_{11} = \eta_e \cdot \epsilon_s$$
$$a_{12} = \eta_{pc} \cdot \epsilon_s$$
$$a_{21} = s_n(\alpha_e + \theta_e) + s_a(\eta_e \cdot \epsilon_s + \beta_e)$$
$$a_{22} = s_n(\alpha_{pc} + \theta_{pc}) + s_a(\eta_{pc} \cdot \epsilon_s + \beta_{pc})$$

and

η_i = elasticity of the terms of trade (P_a^c/P) with respect to i, with i = e, P_a^c;

ϵ_s = elasticity of Q with respect to P_a^c/P;

α_i = elasticity of real non-agricultural income with respect to i;

β_i = elasticity of the tax rate on agriculture with respect to i;

θ_i = elasticity of the tax rate on non-agricultural income with respect to i;

s_n, s_a = the share of non-agriculture and agriculture, respectively, in total tax income.

In the analytical framework represented by equations (E2) to (E4) the two questions most frequently asked are the following. First, if the exchange rate is to be lowered by some rate ($\hat{e}$) – for whatever reason – then by what magnitude should 'the' producer price be raised to attain a given Q? Second, if the producer price is to be raised by a given magnitude, by how much should the exchange be lowered in order to attain a given change in government revenue? The *a priori* view or working assumption is normally that, on the one hand, currency depreciation lowers the terms of trade of agriculture – since the aggregate price level (P) rises – while it tends to raise government revenue through the inflationary effect on nominal incomes and the substantial dependence of government revenue on (internationally) traded goods. On the other hand, producer price increases raise the terms of trade of agriculture but tend to lower government revenue.

The working hypothesis, of course, often becomes complicated by two considerations. One is that the existence of large external debt and sizeable imports – related to a public investment programme – can cause government expenditure to be so seriously affected by exchange-rate changes that the problem is better specified in terms of overall fiscal balance rather than simply government revenue. In our framework there is no particular benefit in taking into account this additional complication. The other consideration is that if the elasticity of supply of Q (i.e., ϵ_s) is greater than unity, then government revenue need not fall because of an increase in the producer price. But controlled prices are more often than not on commodities (mainly tree crops) for which the short-run elasticities are positive but less than unity.

As a first approximation it is seen, from manipulation of the basic equations (E2 and E3), that an answer to the first of the two questions is that

(E5) $$\hat{p}_a^c = \frac{\hat{Q}}{\eta_{pc} \cdot \epsilon_s} - \hat{e} \cdot \frac{\eta_e}{\eta_{pc}}$$

Hence the programme would aim at producer price increases large enough to neutralise the adverse terms-of-trade effect of currency depreciation and induce the desired quantity increase. Similarly, with regard to the second question, as a first approximation, we have

$$\text{(E6)}\ \hat{e}\ =\ \frac{\hat{G}r}{a_{21}}\ -\ \frac{a_{22}}{a_{21}}\cdot\hat{P}_a^c$$

The exchange-rate change must be large enough to neutralise any negative impact on government revenue of the exogenously determined producer price increase.

Equations (E5) and (E6) hold in equilibrium and given either $\hat{e}$ or $\hat{p}_a^c$, the other variable can be solved. But in this framework, the general solution for $\hat{e}$ and $\hat{p}_a^c$ can only come from a solution of a system such as equation (E4).

Supply response

It is evident from the above discussion that the elasticity of supply of Q with respect to the terms of trade (P_a^c/P) is a crucial parameter. Most discussions of supply response in agriculture, therefore, tend to be couched in terms of the quantity response in that sector to real producer price changes. But we shall see that in the context of (macro-economic) stabilisation or adjustment programmes it is generally more useful to conceptualise supply response in a far broader way.

a) **The basic model.** The basic model of supply response uses an essentially Nerlovian framework[2]. This model assigns a conspicuous place to the producer price primarily because it is viewed as the main policy variable in the short term to influence, directly, real quantities in agriculture.

In the basic model, output depends on acreage (A) and yield per acre μ. Both A and μ depend on expected real producer price(s) and various other factors whose effects are not captured through the producer price variable. Such other factors – e.g. the weather – are grouped into one variable, say, Z. The model incorporates the fact that it could take time to adjust acreage to its desired level so that divergences could occur between actual acreage and desired acreage. In addition, a distinction is made between potential and actual yield.

If, then, A represents actual acreage and μ potential yield, it is possible to specify that

$$\text{(E7)}\quad Q_t\ =\ Q_t\,(\mu_t, A_{t-1}, P_{at}^c, Z_t),\ \ \text{or}$$

$$\text{(E8)}\quad Q_t\ =\ q_t\,(\hat{P}_{at}^c, \hat{Z}_t, \lambda)\cdot Q_{t-1}$$

where the subscript t indicates time and P_{at}^c is real producer price.

A circumflex ($\hat{\ }$) over a variable indicates a rate of change. Equation (E8) embodies the assumption that it may require more than one time period to adjust acreage; the variable λ is an adjustment coefficient and takes account of the fact that some of the output in period t may be related to a divergence between actual and desired (equilibrium) output in period t-1. Equation (E8) also incorporates the assumption that actual yield and acreage depend on producer price(s) and the other composite variable, Z. In short, Q_t, is a multiple q_t of Q_{t-1}, with q depending on λ and percentage changes in p_a^c and Z. For any given value of λ, the greater are $\hat{P}_{at}^c$ and $\hat{Z}_t$, the greater would tend to be qt.

The basic model, even in a short-run formulation, often includes some consideration of technical progress or structural change. This can usually be done in several ways. Such changes can be thought of as embodied in Z already. Or they can be thought of as increasing the efficiency units of Z so that instead of Z in equations (E8) and (E9) one can have T.Z with T being some index of technical and structural changes. Finally, T can be included as a separate argument in the Q_t function. If the last procedure is adopted then we have

(E9) $Q_t = q_t(\hat{P}^c_{at}, \hat{Z}_t, T, \lambda). Q_{t-1}$

as a simple formulation of the basic supply response model.

b) **The more complete model.** In the framework of programming macroeconomic adjustment it is found useful, and indeed often essential, to expand and augment the above basic model in at least four ways. First, the agricultural sector can be viewed as comprising a group of households that may consume part of their agricultural goods and allocate their time between leisure, agricultural work and non-agricultural pursuits. This sort of approach, which is consistent with agricultural household models[3], also helps underscore the fact that it is the marketed surplus and not simply total output that should be the focus of analysis in the typical adjustment programme framework. Second, the agricultural sector uses bank credit, particularly in marketing operations, although often also for the purchase of inputs. Even where farmers do not themselves borrow directly from commercial banks, marketing agents and other middlemen do so, and in turn often relend to farmers. Thus bank credit plays an important role in agriculture and the effects of variation in credit on the marketed amount of produce will need to be considered.

Third, it is commonly found useful to consider explicitly some of the elements of Z, especially technical assistance and other variable inputs, such as fertilisers, that may be related to extension services of the authorities. Fourth, domestic marketing (including transportation) costs are sometimes highlighted in the programming exercise.

Consider now the agriculture sector as a set of producing and consuming households. We can write the balance sheet of the sector as:

(E10) $Q \equiv \dfrac{P_n}{P_a} \cdot X_n + \dfrac{w_a}{P_a} \cdot Lp + \dfrac{P_v}{P_a} \cdot V - \dfrac{Y_{na}}{P_a} + Xa + \dfrac{S_a}{P_a} - \dfrac{w_n}{P_a} \cdot L_{na} + \dfrac{R_a}{P_a} \cdot A$

such that, $L_p \equiv L - N + X_L + L_{na}$
where Q = real agricultural output
  P_n =   price of 'the' non-agricultural commodity
  P_a =   price of agricultural commodity ($= P^c_a$ with controlled prices)
  V   =   non-labour variable inputs, such as fertiliser
  w_a =   nominal wage rate in agriculture
  P_v =   price of other variable inputs – e.g., fertiliser
  S_a =   savings of agricultural households in financial intermediaries
  Y_{na} =   non-farm, non-labour income of farmers (e.g., interest earnings on bank savings)
  w_n =   non-agricultural wage rate (relevant for agricultural households)
  L_{na} =   labour supplied to non-agricultural sector by farmers
  L   =   total labour used in production of Q
  N   =   total agricultural household time available
  X_L =   leisure taken by agricultural households
  X_n =   agricultural households' consumption of the non-agricultural commodity

X_a = agricultural households' consumption of Q
A = physical assets (land, capital)
R_a = rental on physical assets

Equation (E10) states that the total produce of agricultural households plus income obtained by working in the non-agricultural sector plus non-labour, non-agricultural income received, is used up in purchases of non-agricultural commodities (X_n), non-family labour (L_p), physical variable inputs (V), and physical assets (A), plus consumption of their own output (X_a) and accumulation of bank assets through saving (S_a).

Define total output as the sum of marketed surplus (Q_m) and subsistence or own consumption (X_a). That is

$$(E11) \quad Q \equiv Q_m + X_a$$

Also define real value added in agriculture as the difference between total output (Q) and the real cost of purchased inputs. That is, abstracting from credit and from transportation costs,

$$(E12) \quad \frac{VA_a}{P_a} \equiv Q - \frac{P_v}{P_a} \cdot V - \frac{w_a}{P_a} \cdot L_p$$

where VA_a is nominal value added in agriculture. Now since output (Q) is a function of L, V, and A, it is possible to write the real value added as a function of output and factor prices. That is,

$$(E13) \quad Q = Q(L, V, A) \text{ and}$$

$$(E14) \quad \frac{VA_a}{P_a} = P\left(\frac{P_v}{P_a}, \frac{w_a}{P_a}, Q \right)$$

It is assumed that equation (E14) can also be written in the form of equation (E15) below. That is,

$$(E15) \quad \frac{VA_a}{P_a Q} = \psi\left(\frac{P_v}{P_a}, \frac{w_a}{P_a} \right)$$

From equations (E12) and (E13) we see that the ratio of real value added to output would decrease as the prices of inputs increase relative to P_a in a way that depends on the input coefficients in production as well as the elasticities of substitution among inputs. Equation (E15) is, therefore, quite general.

Now the basic hypothesis of the augmented model is that marketed output increases with the ratio of value added to total output and with the desire to accumulate savings on the part of agricultural households, but that Q_m tends to diminish with real wage rates outside agriculture and with real non-farm, non-labour incomes available to these households. If then we include domestic credit factors (availability and cost) and marketing costs, as arguments in the Q_m function, and make the additional assumption that savings ratios tend to increase with real interest (bank deposit) rates (at least up to a point), then it is possible to write the Q_m function as follows:

$$(E16) \quad Q_m = Q_m\left(\frac{P_v}{P_a}, \frac{w_a}{P_a}, \frac{R_a}{P_a}, \frac{P_n}{P_a}, rs, \frac{Y_{na}}{P_a}, \frac{w_n}{P_a}, \frac{Dc_a}{P_a}, i_a, m_a \right)$$

where

> rs = real interest earned on savings in financial institutions
> Dc_a = stock of domestic credit extended to agriculture
> i_a = interest rate charged on agricultural loans
> m_a = transport and other marketing cost per unit of Q_m

Equation (E16) is quite general. Not all variables included there would be considered in all adjustment programmes. Which ones are taken into account, i.e., the particular arguments of the Q_m function in a particular situation, usually depends on the institutional, political and social realities of the country concerned. The important point to note is that there are generally many instruments at the disposal of the authorities to influence Q_m. The more controlled the economy, the greater, by definition, is the impact which the authorities have over the level and rate of change of instruments.

The real exchange rate and agricultural exports[4]

In adjustment programmes supported by use of Fund resources probably the main focus of analysis is the real exchange rate. Policies are generally designed to lower the real exchange rate, that is, to reduce the prices of non-traded (domestic) goods relative to the prices of traded goods. To effect a real exchange-rate depreciation, the domestic rate of inflation need only be less than the relevant foreign rate of inflation. For this it may be possible to rely on domestic fiscal, monetary, and interest-rate policies.

Reducing the relative prices of non-traded goods by deflationary monetary and fiscal policies may be difficult, and at times even undesirable. Credit restraint can have adverse shock effects on output, while slashing budgetary expenditures and intensifying taxation might well face political impediments because of their effects on real output and income distribution. Such obstacles often impel a cautious approach to monetary and fiscal measures. In addition, the rates of wage and price increases commonly reflect inertia, and any sudden drop in monetary expansion may provoke acute unemployment. Moreover, when major structural distortions have set in, particularly between traded and non-traded goods, a prompt and sizeable alteration of relative prices may be imperative in the initial stages of an adjustment programme. As a result of such considerations it is often found useful to devalue or depreciate the domestic currency in order to lower the real exchange rate.

It is, of course, important to recall that monetary and fiscal restraint cannot be avoided even if currency depreciation is the major instrument used to lower the real exchange rate. Without the financial restraints, there will be offsetting increases in the prices of non-traded goods; the currency depreciation will then result in a rise in the absolute price level but the relative price between traded and non-traded goods will not change.

Indeed, experience with Fund-supported adjustment programmes in developing countries seems to indicate that an important factor in the failure of currency depreciation to induce an expansion in export supply is the inability of the authorities to ensure that the real exchange rate falls significantly and remains at the depreciated level for a period long enough to permit adjustment of supply. Invariably, this is due to a failure to pass on price increases to exporters – where such prices are regulated – or an incapacity for various social and political reasons to restrain budgetary deficits and monetary expansion sufficiently to abate domestic inflation.

Suppose now that in equation (E16), the Q_m function refers to agricultural export (traded) commodities and that non-traded agricultural commodities (mainly food items) are added to non-traded non-agricultural commodities. Then a depreciation of the real exchange rate for agriculture would be tantamount to a fall in P_n/P_a where P_n is now the price level of non-traded goods and P_a is the price level of traded agricultural goods. The quantity Q_m itself is now the exportable quantity. It is seen that this quantity depends on price elasticities of domestic production and on other domestic physical and financial factors that affect supply.

In analysing the price responsiveness of agricultural exports it is usually necessary to make an explicit distinction between annual crops, such as cotton and rice, and tree crops such as coffee, cocoa, palm oil, rubber and tea. The rationale has already been stated in discussing the basic Nerlovian framework; namely, for tree crops capacity increases (the acreage planted) usually do not begin to yield increments in output for many years. This lengthy gestation period for tree crops usually makes the short-run elasticities of supply substantially smaller than the long-run elasticities.

Even in the case of annual crops, capacity constraints are often an important factor in the short run because of land shortage or rudimentary technology. In certain places, the most aggressive farmers and those who are relatively more market-oriented or producing traded goods may not possess enough land to employ themselves fully. In many low-income countries the limited use of fertilisers and modern machinery often seriously circumscribes the short-run elasticity of supply to price increases. In addition, the active role of government agencies in the form of extension services and various other incentive programmes affects the supply responses of farmers to price incentives, including those emanating from real exchange-rate changes.

Of further importance are the factors represented simply by m_a in equation (E16). Indeed, domestic marketing constraints sometimes function as a disincentive limiting the supply response of farmers. As with capacity constraints, marketing constraints drive a wedge between the desired response of farmers and the actual response.

Studies within, but especially outside[5], the Fund do reveal that price elasticities of supply are generally positive, but that in the short run such elasticities can be quite low – that is, much less than one – and at times even negative. The studies also show that long-run supply elasticities are generally larger than short-run elasticties. Evidence supports the obvious perception that the other factors in the Q_m function also are important in determining agricultural output levels and rates of changes[6].

Even where the short- to medium-run elasticities of domestic supply to real exchange-rate change are significantly positive and where domestic marketing and other non-price constraints do not counteract the supply response, foreign market conditions play a role in determining the incremental sales realised from the augmented domestic supply as well as the amount of additional foreign-exchange receipts that ensue from these sales. In this regard, the foreign price elasticity of demand faced by a country, and the state of the world economy, are important, as is the nature of protection encountered in foreign markets and the requisite marketing arrangements for foreign sales, particularly the sort of contracts and contracting usual in the appropriate market[7]. With some notable exceptions, the assumption usually made is that the individual developing country faces an infinite price elasticity of demand for its product. Hence the usual procedure is to lean heavily on the commodity price forecast of the staffs of the Fund and the World Bank in making projections, except where a country has explicit contracts or highly specialised (sometimes preferential) relationships with its trading partners.

Efficiency

One of the most difficult aspects in the design of adjustment policies affecting agriculture is the exact mix of policies for improving efficiency and increasing the productivity of resources in agriculture, thereby raising farmers' response to price changes or reducing their costs per unit of output. There are two broad elements here: intersectoral efficiency and intrasectoral efficiency. Three guiding principles generally condition whatever specific approach is taken.

First, there is the optimal structure of relative prices. In general, under normal conditions for any two commodities i,j, it would be considered optimal to equalise the ratios of prices to marginal costs. Hence with P and MC being prices and marginal costs, respectively, the approach would, as a first approximation, seek to set $P_i/MC_i = P_j/MC_j$. In practice, with internationally traded goods, and with controlled prices or protected domestic markets, the efficiency criterion becomes one of equating the relative domestic prices with the relative international prices – given, of course, that the country is a price-taker in all the international markets concerned. Hence if P_w is the world or international market price in domestic currency equivalence, and if P_d is the domestic price (with controls or protection), then the optimal policy is to set $P_{di}/P_{wi} = P_{dj}/P_{wj}$. As long as only prices are controlled domestically the domestic producers will then adjust their quantities in line with their marginal costs, so that, in equilibrium, we shall have

$$(E17a) \quad \frac{P_{di}}{P_{wi}} = \frac{P_{dj}}{P_{wj}} \text{ and}$$

$$(E17b) \quad \frac{P_{di}}{MC_i} = \frac{P_{di}}{MC_j}.$$

The satisfaction of conditions (E17a and E17b) also implies that the so-called nominal protection coefficients will be equalised among commodities[8].

Second, as regards subsidies, particularly for inputs and agricultural imports, the Fund-supported programme would not only subject the subsidies to the usual financial balance considerations, but would also try to contain their distortionary effects on relative prices. Hence given similar impact on equity and budgetary balance, subsidies that do not affect relative prices (e.g. lump-sum transfers) would be considered superior to those that do.

Third, in allocating investment resources, the equalisation of the marginal social rates of return among sectors would be considered optimal. The social rate of return incorporates external economies and diseconomies. From a national point of view the social rates of return are related to sectoral or sub-sectoral incremental output-capital ratios. If y represents real output (GDP) and I real investments, then the ideal would be to equate the growth-rate effect of the marginal investment among the different sectors. Hence, for investment in any two sectors i and j, we shall have

$$(E18) \quad \delta\hat{y}/\delta\hat{I}_i = \delta\hat{y}/\delta\hat{I}_j$$

a. **Intersectoral efficiency.** Intersectoral efficiency is intimately connected with the questions of terms of trade and supply response that we have discussed above. With intersectorial efficiency, the allocation of resources between agriculture and non-agriculture is optimal, and the ratio of value added in agriculture relative to GDP is also optimal. In short, the idea is to ensure that resources go where they are most productive – that the normal neo-classical conditions for optimal use of resources are satisfied. In practical terms this has meant trying to create an environment ensuring, to the extent possible, that the values of the arguments in equation (E16) – the Q_m function – are conducive to wealth maximisation from the society's resources. It may be quite possible and easy to show how Q_m can be increased x per cent by reducing P_v/P_a or raising DC_a/P_a or lowering Pn/P_a etc. But it is usually much more difficult to demonstrate that the budgetary, relative price and other effects on the non-agricultural sectors do not then engender an overall adverse effect on economic growth.

As regards intersectoral efficiency, therefore, the aim would be to facilitate an allocation of resources between agriculture and non-agriculture such that conditions (E17 and E18) are satisfied, where one can think of agriculture as being sector i and non-agriculture as sector j. The typical approach taken in Fund-supported adjustment programmes is one of deference to the World Bank and caution in introducing direct policy measures – a sort of minimum information approach. Deference to the World Bank takes place especially in drawing inferences about the satisfaction of equation (E18); in fact, it is common practice to request an explicit evaluation by the World Bank of the public investment programmes or the capital budgets of countries seeking Fund assistance.

In general, as in other areas of Fund-supported programmes, there are usually both structural and demand-management policies involved. In the case of structural policies the emphasis has been on improvements in the functioning of markets – labour, capital and commodities; improvement in the global efficiency of public investment; better banking facilities in the rural areas, thereby encouraging rural households to save through the banking system; and making changes in the composition of budgetary revenue, thereby facilitating a more equitable structure of taxation.

On the demand-management side, the challenge has been to establish producer prices and rates of expansion of bank credit to the agricultural sector so as to mini-mise the risk of sub-optimal adjustment (from the viewpoint of neo-classical efficiency) of Q_m. Producer prices are generally set with reference to the effective taxation implied by different price schedules[9]. As regards bank credit, in practice a sort of real bills doctrine has prevailed as a guide; that is, credit programmed for agriculture is determined by expected agricultural marketed output and the anticipated price. The traditional level of credit per unit value of marketed output usually is determined at a micro level between bankers and customers; this traditional level is then used as a parameter in the macro decision process. Hence, in the working out of domestic credit ceilings, the credit available for agriculture is often explicitly taken into account in the calculations, in the manner described above – the more so as the weight of agriculture in exports increases.

b) **Intrasectoral efficiency.** The desired levels of the arguments of Q_m in equation (E16) are determined in the light not only of intersectoral efficiency of productive resources but also of intrasectoral efficiency in the use of resources within agricul-ture. As a result, it is common to find policies designed to attain five broad goals: abating waste in public investment projects in agriculture; removing transport and marketing bottlenecks; improving agricultural extension services; rationalising the pricing of agricultural inputs such as fertilisers; and enhancing the efficiency of management of parastatals in the agricultural sector.

Waste in public investment has occurred in a wide variety of projects, including crash crop programmes and projects to facilitate the attainment of self-sufficiency in certain food items, particularly involving state farms. Various land settlement schemes and integrated agricultural development projects have also manifested waste, especially the credit aspect of such programmes, with loans to numerous small farmers often being uncollectable. Moreover, capital projects such as dams and irrigation networks are sometimes made bigger or more expensive than would have been warranted if reasonable cost-benefit calculations had been made. Naturally, the waste that can be stopped or abated in the framework of a Fund-supported programme would relate to future investment activity.

Storage and transport facilities have contributed to the failure of agricultural policies in many countries. Inadequate warehouse and refrigeration facilities have, in certain circumstances, helped slow down progress in the fish, meat, and poultry industries and significantly circumscribed the extent of marketing of domestically produced grain. The transport situation often becomes troublesome at every stage – roads, vehicles and spare parts, and fuel. The construction and maintenance of trunk and feeder roads are often allowed to wane, usually due to serious constraints on both foreign exchange and the government budget, but sometimes also due to deficient operation of foreign-exchange control schemes and inefficient allocation of public resources. Modification, or rationalisation, of foreign-exchange and government budgetary allocations often emerge, therefore, as an essential element of the adjustment programme.

The questions of budgetary allocation and efficiency of resource use also arise with respect to extension services and the pricing of agricultural inputs supplied by state enterprises or subsidised by the government. In the case of extension services the desire is to ensure that the supply response of farmers to prices does not get muted by lack of knowledge or by overestimation of risk as a result of insufficient or inappropriate extension services[10]. In recent years especially, research and experimentation have been taking place to improve knowledge on the subject of reforming extension systems[11]. Fund-supported programmes have sometimes included the modification of extension systems.

Rationalisation of the pricing of agricultural inputs handled by public enterprises (or subsidised by the state) as well as methods to improve the management of public enterprises have been interrelated questions that have been tackled in Fund-supported programmes. In this regard, three types of policy measures have been included in such programmes. First, there have been policies designed to promote more 'economic pricing' of inputs and other services provided by state enterprises, partly for the beneficial budgetary consequences, and partly to improve the efficiency of use of resources. Apart from reducing the disparity between the supply price of an input or service and its average cost, economic pricing is not usually spelled out in greater detail. There is apparent reluctance, for instance, to impose a marginal-cost-pricing rule or even an average-cost-pricing rule. The undertaking to pursue more economic pricing becomes a loose rule that is interpreted and applied as follows: to the extent possible, set price equal to marginal cost, and, in any event, reduce significantly any negative difference between price and average variable cost.

Another type of policy response, and hence undertaking, in Fund-supported programmes has been to encourage privatisation, or, more loosely, a greater role for the private sector. This does not necessarily mean that the state enterprises or government departments cease operations completely in the particular area of activity concerned. It can simply mean that certain activities get subcontracted out to the private sector or that management contracts are given to the private sector to operate state-owned organisations and enterprises[12]. In the agricultural sector the two areas where a greater role has been sought for the private sector are marketing and extension services. In fact, in the case of marketing it is no longer inconceivable to call for the abolition of marketing boards.

Most frequently – and indeed this tends to be the initial reaction to inefficiency in state enterprises – the undertaking is to streamline and reorganise the state organisation so as to enhance its management capability and cut down on waste. Sometimes as part of this process new management teams are put in place, and certain units or branches are closed down. At other times decentralisation is thought to be the key to improving management. Whatever the process, it usually becomes part of the Fund-supported programme.

Investment, macroeconomic measures and private returns

Direct pricing policies and improved efficiency contribute to raising the marginal social and private returns to resources in agriculture. But various credit, investment and fiscal measures also have positive effects on marginal private returns in agriculture and hence on the Q_m function.

Various measures are generally included in Fund-supported programmes that serve to reduce the cost of credit to farmers (lowering i_a and raising DC_a). These include direct interest-rate subsidies or limits; credit guarantees on loans made to agricultural producers; and the redirection of credit from outside to inside official money markets, thereby lowering the average cost of private loans to agricultural producers.

Investment in infrastructure and in human capital (health, education) also raise returns to agriculture. The former do so mainly by lowering marketing costs, while the latter help to raise the productivity of labour in agriculture. As a result, Q_m is raised for any given w_a/P_a; also m_a in equation (E16) is reduced.

The provision by the government of various commodities and services used as inputs by farmers tends mainly to lower P_v/P_a. Value added per unit of output is raised for the farmer, tending to increase equilibrium Q_m. Preferential treatment in the area of exchange and trade policies can also effectively lower P_v/P_a. Equally, such preference can lower P_n/P_a by raising the effective producer price or lowering the effective price received by non-agricultural activities. Preferential treatment can also facilitate rapid increases in capacity or shorter gestation periods by permitting imports to be made on a timely basis. Particularly relevant are policies eliminating quotas and licensing restrictions on imported inputs for agriculture as well as preferential access to foreign exchange in a regime of tight foreign-exchange controls.

CONCLUDING REMARKS – SOME CRITICAL ISSUES

Both the general macroeconomic policies and the specific policies directed at agriculture, which are incorporated in programmes supported by IMF stand-by arrangements, are sometimes criticised on various grounds. It is not possible to do justice to the diverse criticisms here; but three are of relevance to the thrust of this chapter. The first is that Fund-supported programmes are biased towards short-run to medium-run stabilisation, and neglect longer-run development issues. The second is that the programmes give excessive weight to external adjustment, while all other welfare-augmenting goals such as output growth and income distribution are considered only as subsidiary to the primary goal. Third, in designing policies, Fund-supported programmes are thought of as being too oriented towards domestic price, domestic credit and exchange-rate measures, while downplaying other policies and factors affecting production and exports. These criticisms have been made not only in their general form but also directly with respect to agriculture. Indeed, the criticisms in the latter case become criticisms of the traditional neo-classical approach[13].

Hence Fund-supported programmes in the eyes of some critics do not display sufficient awareness of the fact that rising agricultural productivity is brought about by an interplay of forces that include price incentives, changes in the social and institutional structure, and public investments in research, rural infrastructure and technological diffusion. The implication would be that Fund-supported programmes should give more weight to institutional factors such as agrarian structures, contractual forms and the land market. In addition, such programmes should give greater weight to the implementation of investment policies.

Although it is easy to reply that reforms in some of these areas take a long time to yield substantial benefits and that among the factors taken into consideration in deriving the Q_m function must be certain institutions, the Fund does recognise, as we have seen, the usefulness of institutional reforms and of investment, in the enhancement of agricultural production and exports. Increasingly, not only do programmes supported by stand-by arrangements include such measures but also in many low-income countries, particularly in sub-Saharan Africa, more and more Fund-supported programmes tend to be those that are designed to facilitate institutional reforms, improvements in investment and technological diffusion[14].

Even ignoring longer-term influences on Q_m, there is still the problem that serious attention may not be paid to all the arguments of Q_m in equation (E16). This could result in a sub-optimal combination of instruments to alter Q_m. In particular, serious attention tends always to be given to influencing the relative price of the agricultural commodity (P_n/P_a) – particularly where prices are controlled – to the real credit to agriculture (DC_a/P_a), and to the level of the real interest rate. Much less critical analysis – in order to ensure optimal levels for them – appears to be made for some of the other variables. The reason is, partly, that such variables are often outside the direct control of the authorities (e.g., w_a/P_a, w_n/P_a, and M_a) or because the optimal levels of the variables are extremely difficult to determine (e.g. for P_v/P_a).

One advantage of general macroeconomic policies or certain structural policies directed, for example, at improving the functioning of markets, is that they tend to leave relative prices and relative quantities to be determined by taste, technology and comparative advantage. A disadvantage is that they may not facilitate the exploitation of dynamic comparative advantage. Selective intervention, in contrast, is amenable to optimal use to assure development along the path of dynamic comparative advantage; but there is always the risk of authorities selectively intervening in favour of commodities or services for which dynamic comparative advantage does not objectively exist.

One of the potential problems with the sort of policies contained in adjustment programmes supported by Fund standbys – i.e. setting instruments (or intermediate targets) such as P_v/P_a or P_n/P_a guided by short- to medium-term balance-of-payments objectives – is that the policy package can become one of selective intervention guided by static (rather than dynamic) comparative advantage and by the potential for immediate direct foreign-exchange earnings (or foreign-exchange savings) rather than by the overall long-run contribution to real GDP growth. Even when this risk is clearly appreciated, the fact remains that it is usually much easier and quicker to identify static comparative advantage and to estimate the direct foreign-exchange earnings or savings potential of specific policy measures, than it is to assess dynamic comparative advantage and overall long-run contribution to output growth.

NOTES

1 The view that the agricultural sector has been forced, by public policy, to face adverse terms of trade is quite widely held. See, for example, D. Gale Johnson (1987). See also Nashashibi (1980) for an analysis of exchange-rate depreciation in a situation in which improving the terms of trade and competitiveness of agricultural crops is a crucial element in the determination of the exchange-rate change.

2 See Nerlove (1958), Bond (1983), Ghatak and Ingersent (1984), and the references cited in those works.

3 See Singh, Squire and Strauss (1986).

4 This section relies heavily on material contained in O.E.G. Johnson (1987).

5 See Ghatak and Ingersent (1984) pp. 203–13 for a recent listing of the most important studies of supply elasticities by crop and by region in various developing countries.

6 See, for example, Bond (1983) and Rao (1986).

7 See Kirmani, Molajoni and Mayer (1984), Chu and Morrison (1986), Bond (1987), and various papers cited in those studies.

8 See Bale and Lutz (1979). The nominal protection coefficient can be specified in our framework at $\dfrac{P_{di} - P_{wi}}{P_{wi}}$ for any commodity i.

9 Let t_a represent the effective tax rate on the agricultural sector commodity. Then

$$t_a = 1 - \frac{P_a^c}{P_a^s(1 - mc_a)}$$

where P_a^s and m_a^c are the sales price and marketing costs (as a fraction of sales price) respectively, of the state enterprise (marketing board).

10 Farmers in low-income countries are often thought of as being concerned with safety-first, ie. survival or disaster avoidance, instead of profit maximization (see Lipton (1986), Shahabuddin and Mestelman (1986).

11 The current vogue appears to be the training and visit system. Here again the Fund staff have relied heavily on the expertise of the World Bank staff. See Feder and Slade (1984) and the references cited there for an introduction to the training and visit system.

12 See Berg (1982).

13 See Rao (1986).

14 In particular, in 1986 the Fund established the Structural Adjustment Facility (SAF). The members eligible to use the facility are the low-income countries that are currently eligible to receive IDA loans (see IMF 1986b; 132–45).

REFERENCES

Bale, Malcolm D. and Ernst Lutz (1979), 'Price Distortions in Agriculture and their Effects, an International Comparison', Washington DC, World Bank Staff *Working Paper*, No. 359, October.

Berg, Elliot (1982), 'Changing the Public-Private Mix: A Survey of some Recent Experiences in LDCs', unpublished, Washington DC, International Monetary Fund, 22 February.

Bond, Martin E. (1983), 'Agricultural Responses to Prices in Sub-Saharan African Countries', Washington DC, *IMF Staff Papers*, Vol. 30, December.

—— (1987), 'An Econometric Study of Primary Commodity Exports from Developing Country Regions to the World', Washington DC, *IMF Staff Papers*, Vol. 34, June.

Chu, Ke-young and Thomas K. Morrison (1986), 'World Non-oil Primary Commodity Markets: A Medium-Term Framework of Analysis', Washington DC, *IMF Staff Papers*, Vol. 33, March.

Feder, Gershon and Roger Slade (1984), 'Aspects of the Training and Visit System of Agricultural

Extension in India, A Comparative Analysis', Washington DC, World Bank Staff Working Papers, No. 656, July.

Ghatak, Subrata and Ken Ingersent (1984), *Agriculture and Economic Development*, Baltimore, Johns Hopkins University Press.

Gold, Joseph (1970), *The Stand-By Arrangements of the International Monetary Fund*, Washington DC, International Monetary Fund.

International Monetary Fund (1986a), *Annual Report 1986*, Washington DC.

—— (1986b), *Selected Decisions of the International Monetary Fund and Selected Documents*, Twelfth Issue, Washington DC, 30 April.

Johnson, D. Gale (1987), 'IMF Conditionality and Agriculture in the Developing Countries', in Robert J. Myers (ed.) *The Political Morality of the International Monetary Fund, Ethics and Foreign Policy*, Vol. 3, New Brunswick, USA and Oxford, UK, Transaction Books.

Johnson, Omotunde E.G. (1977), 'Use of Fund Resources and Stand-By Arrangements', *Finance and Development*, Vol. 14, March.

—— (1987), 'Currency Depreciation and Export Expansion', *Finance and Development*, Vol. 24, March.

Kirmani, Naheed, Luigi Molajoni and Thomas Mayer (1984), 'Effects of Increased Market Access on Exports of Developing Countries', Washington DC, *IMF Staff Papers*, Vol. 31, December.

Lipton, Michael (1968), 'The Theory of the Optimising Peasant', *Journal of Development Studies*, Vol. 17, April.

Nashashibi, Karim (1980), 'A Supply Framework for Exchange Reform in Developing Countries: The Experience of Sudan', Washington DC, *IMF Staff Papers*, Vol. 27, March.

Nerlove, Marc (1958), *The Dynamics of Supply Estimation of Farmers' Response to Price*, Baltimore, Johns Hopkins University Press.

Rao, J. Mohan (1986), 'Agriculture in Recent Development Theory', *Journal of Development Economics*, Vol. 22, June.

Shahabuddin, Quazi and Stuart Mestelman (1986), 'Uncertainty and Disaster-Avoidance Behaviour in Peasant Farming: Evidence from Bangladesh', *Journal of Development Studies*, Vol. 22, July.

Singh, Inderjit, Lyn Squire and John Strauss (1986), 'A Survey of Agricultural Household Models: Recent Findings and Policy Implications', *World Bank Economic Review*, Washington DC, Vol. 1, September.

3

Articulating Stabilisation Programmes & Structural Adjustment

Sub-Saharan Africa

Reginald Herbold Green

> It will be a sad day for Africa and for international co-operation if the Fund refuses to seek the necessary flexibility in its operations to permit it to continue playing a major role in sub-Saharan Africa – John Williamson, 1986

INTRODUCTION

For sub-Saharan Africa (henceforth SSA) both agriculture and the IMF are clearly important, even if the relationship between the two is not always evident.

In terms of household incomes, employment (including self-employment), inputs into domestic manufacturing, and export earnings, agriculture is the largest sector in most sub-Saharan African economies – the notable exception being mineral/hydrocarbon exporters with respect to export earnings. For about two decades (from the mid-1960s) the overall SSA record has been poor on all of these counts, with a handful of fairly satisfactory and a larger minority of truly disastrous results at country level (cf. Green, 1985, 1986b, 1987; Rose, 1985).

How can the trend rate of growth of per capita food production be raised? How can dependable, rising levels of inputs into domestic manufacturing be achieved? How can earned import capacity (the counterpart and basic purpose of exports) be sustained? How can increases in net farm household incomes (including self-provisioning or subsistence) be regained? How can malnutrition be reduced? How can these goals be attained in a sustainable way which neither pauperises the rest of society – thereby rending the social fabric and sowing the seeds of its own destruction – nor destroys the ecological context for its own survival? These are crucial questions, and in SSA they are probably the most crucial macroeconomic and human questions as well as those which stand out in respect of the agricultural sector.

In one sense, the importance of the IMF is just as clearcut. The Fund is a major source of short-term funds to facilitate macroeconomic adjustment by economies suffering from severe external account imbalances. Its presence in SSA is increasingly widespread. In the launching period of some present and past structural adjustment programmes (e.g. Uganda 1982, Sudan in the 1980s, Zaire from the 1960s, Zambia from the 1970s, Ghana from 1983, Somalia from 1980) it has been a major source of external finance and is now a major creditor and part of the debt-service burden.

The problem is fitting these two sets of importances together. Agriculture is primarily micro or sectoral and real, the IMF is primarily macro and monetary; agricultural policy and pay-off are primarily medium- to long-term; IMF programmes (if perhaps not aims) are (at least in intent) short-term. However, three principal reasons can be given for emphasising the importance of IMF programmes for SSA agriculture.

First, IMF interpretation of macro policy measures commonly includes crop prices, subsidies, taxes, credit levels, input prices (including interest rates), the price of foreign exchange and government spending. These measures will all affect agriculture directly.

Second, precisely because the IMF's concentration is on stabilisation and its three key balances are external account, fiscal account and domestic supply/demand account (as evidenced by price stability or instability), a real possibility exists of a mismatch with policies appropriate for the real and micro and/or the medium and long term.

Third, without a prior IMF standby arrangement it is in practice not possible for an SSA country to secure substantial concessional finance and especially not to achieve the World Bank-endorsed adjustment programme support through a Consultative Group, let alone a Paris Club debt-rescheduling package.

IMF PROGRAMMES: SOME GENERAL ISSUES

Prior to a more detailed examination of the principal features of IMF programmes as they relate to agriculture, it may be useful to outline some of the more general criticisms that have commonly been directed toward standard IMF programmes.

First, whether the IMF is ideological or not, the implicit model is not very well adapted to SSA. SSA markets are notoriously imperfect and the imperfections are multiple. Lack of faith in these markets and fears that removing one intervention of many will result in greater not less imperfection are by no means so unreasonable in many SSA economies as most IMF staff seem to believe.

Second, the global economic system is structured in ways that, at least in the 1980s, benefit the rich, the financially strong, the creditors and the producers of complex goods and services and damage the poor, the financially weak, the debtors and the producers of primary products. That system and its dynamics have done and are doing immense harm to SSA. The IMF, as one of its most visible institutions, needs to be seen to be pressing for adjustment cost sharing by the beneficiaries, not just acceptance by the victims. It may well be that the IMF has limited influence, but the problem is a real one and the IMF is too easily seen as a guardian of the *status quo*.

Third, external imbalance is normally a consequence of internal imbalance and/or exogenous shocks and as such can be a misleading starting-point for analysis as opposed to a problem which must be faced. Certainly – with a few exceptions, e.g. Ghana 1972 and Zimbabwe 1982 – imbalance has been caused primarily by supply contraction, with weather and terms of trade changes (plus capital market vagaries) the most common catalytic factors, not endogenous overheating of demand. That does not eliminate the need for adjustment but it may alter appropriate policies, sequencing, and time frames – not least if the initial shock has been followed by an extended period of economic decline (e.g. Madagascar 1960–80, Ghana 1966–82, Zambia 1976–87) or domestic stabilisation which partially succeeded but could not restore a sustainable upward dynamic (e.g. Tanzania 1982–6 and perhaps Zimbabwe 1982–7).

Fourth, the macroeconomic significance of agriculture and the impact of macroeconomic policy and performance on agriculture are indisputable. But the attempt to move primarily from macroeconomic to sectoral to micro, and to concentrate on monetary indicators and tools without an equally strong micro to sectoral to macro aggregative build-up, focusing on real magnitudes, variables and instruments, is open to very grave doubts. Furthermore, not only are agricultural results in the short term not easily and significantly influenced by policy, but the attempt to do so may lead to scarce resource misallocations which are inefficient from a long-term growth perspective.

Fifth, the emphasis on performance tends to downgrade other targets and the tools/resources devoted to attaining progress towards them. Prices are relevant to agriculture but in a complex way, and not always primarily agricultural prices. Furthermore, substantial sustained response to real relative price and/or real net income changes by agricultural producers is usually possible only in the context of other parallel changes, some of which (effective access to credit, to transport and to extension now and to research results over time) can be victimised (however unintentionally) by the standard IMF package.

Sixth, the differences in present IMF SSA programmes from classic ones – as with the current greater emphasis on stabilisation with growth – are, in general, welcome. But they do introduce a certain degree of incoherence and/or inconsistency in their present state – not least when there is (as is usual in SSA) a parallel World Bank structural adjustment package deal.

(i) IMF programmes and agriculture: a review of content

The IMF's analytical model in respect to agriculture does centre on prices – notably foreign-exchange prices (exchange rates), producer prices, user prices, taxes, input prices and interest rates. It does assume price elasticities significantly different from zero, especially in the medium to long term. But it is unfair to typify it – at least conceptually – as a tunnel-vision approach seeking to force output up simply by raising nominal grower prices. Especially in its more extended forms, it does seek to include all of the prices cited, as well as the general rate of inflation, and to take account of non-price variables, e.g. actual availability of credit, inputs, extension, transport (see Chapter 2).

There are in practice two problems. The overall macro model does not include real variables, so that the extended sectoral one cannot easily be integrated into it. Even more crucial, almost none of the variables in the extended (or even the pure price) agricultural sector model can be quantified with any pretence of precision, except the nominal prices. Therefore, in practice there is a fairly simplistic dependence on nominal price changes to achieve somewhat arbitrary quantitative goals, with a collation of non-price measures – usually liberalising or privatising in nature – tacked on without coherent linkage to the price measures.

EXCHANGE-RATE POLICIES

Moving from overvalued to equilibrium or realistic exchange rates is central to all IMF programmes. Only in principle is the possibility of external balance with an overvalued exchange rate acknowledged. In general, it is held that in many SSA economies exchange rates have been and some still are overvalued.

The IMF favours large initial devaluations which – in the absence of high domestic inflation – would bring the rate back to a realistic level at one go. A currently fashionable alternative is an auction.

The problem with large initial cuts and auctions is the danger that – at least in some cases – they may generate hyper-inflation (albeit Ghana in 1983/4 and Tanzania in 1986/7 suggest this is not necessarily so). Auctions in addition can – if not managed (as in Ghana and Nigeria) – easily go into a free fall which expectations then make irreversible (e.g. Zambia 1985/7, Sierra Leone 1986/7). Conceivably a semi-active crawling peg (Zimbabwe, post-1983, Tanzania, post-1986) with swift initial (real) devaluation, followed by automatic excess inflation adjustments and – if the over-valuation has only been reduced – a bit more, may reduce the inflation and free-fall risks which create patterns of uncertainty and do nothing for agricultural (or other) production.

What is clear is that only real devaluation which is expected to, and does, hold for at least 18 to 24 months (and preferably much longer) can allow time for the incentive effect to raise agricultural production. If – as is generally agreed – long-term elasticities of supply are higher than short, expectation of at least 36–60 months holding (or improving) of the new real rate is likely to be needed for output to benefit from them.

The direct impact of devaluation on the agricultural sector depends on whether the increased (in local currency) border prices are passed on to the producer. For exports this is usually the case, at least in part. Even the IMF has engaged in exercises which divert much of the gains to tax revenue (e.g. in Ghana with its 30 per cent grower, 35 per cent marketing, 35 per cent tax revenue split). For domestic market crops the results are altogether less certain. Non-tariff barriers will usually have prevented or limited official imports (other than food aid) and unofficial imports will have been at parallel market rates. Therefore, the impact on grower prices from devaluation may be small.

While not a sufficient condition, devaluation is likely to be a necessary one for raising agricultural export volume – or at any rate officially recorded volume. With domestic market crops the situation is much less clear. The impact of price shifts on the grower may be low and, if so, the negative price swing relative to exports may dominate and reduce marketed output. The 1970–79 record of 1.4 per cent overall, 1.8 per cent food and – 0.1 per cent export crop annual real growth in SSA owes much to sharp relative price swings to food. If devaluation reversed that shift, the results would not be unambiguously good, given the lack of surplus food production in most countries and years.

Timing is a further critical issue. If devaluation raises input prices (tools, fuel, wages, seed, fertiliser, pesticides, etc.) long before the higher prices on output are received, it can prevent output growth or even force a cutback (cf. for example, Longhurst, 1988). More generally the net real impact depends on input prices, other domestic costs and the prices of wage goods. The latter are significant, for they are, in effect, farm households' main real incentive to raise marketed output levels. These issues are, in practice, not incorporated into IMF programme dialogues and indeed tend to be ignored.

An additional gap is the failure to consider the impact on smuggling explicitly and with some quantitative estimates. For some export crops in some countries (e.g. cocoa in Ghana) smuggling has accounted for a very large proportion of marketed output (perhaps 33 per cent at its peak in Ghana). The main short-run impact of devaluation may be to claw back such exports, not to raise production (perhaps a third of Ghana's increased cocoa output between 1983 and 1986/7 can be attributed to such an effect). To conflate the smuggling and production effects is unsound. This is especially so if smuggled exports have financed smuggled imports so that a reduction of the former leads to an enhanced demand for officially received foreign exchange.

A genuine conundrum arises in the case of agricultural commodities with declining real world prices. Enough (real) devaluation can raise or hold constant their real domestic prices. But this is likely to increase their real world price falls by pushing an increased supply growth against a low global demand growth trend and a low price elasticity of demand. While most SSA producers taken separately would gain (albeit, at the net export proceeds level, this may be false more often than is supposed), for SSA's major export crops SSA as a whole would lose (Godfrey, 1985).

The other export prospects for SSA are poor, however, and it has been losing market share (World Bank, 1984b). One argument – apparently endorsed by the Fund – is that SSA economies do have comparative advantages, should push ahead and can expect higher-cost export producers in Latin America and South Asia to contract. This is too oversimplified a scenario. First, the interim costs before other exporters contracted could be very high. Second, in conditions other than full employment, absolute, not comparative, costs tend to dominate. Third, SSA's comparative cost advantage is open to doubt in, for example, cocoa, tea, palm oil. Fourth, if the other exporters choose to fight and have much greater fiscal and foreign-exchange resources, African economies are likely to lose. These dilemmas squarely face Ghana with respect to cocoa where Malaysia probably has a comparative advantage and both Malaysia and Brazil have greater financial muscle.

There are no easy or convincing answers to this problem. The main criticism of the Fund is that it does not appear to recognise its existence or, at any rate, to factor it into country programmes.

(ii) Pricing policies

The IMF's main tool is prices and the main goal of stabilisation policy as defined by it is 'getting the prices right'. Clearly if agricultural prices have been depressed by state intervention in a way which deters output overall or skews it in favour of crops which there is no particular reason to favour, then 'getting the prices wrong' has costs. However, severe empirical as well as theoretical doubts surround enshrining price – especially official producer price – as the key operational instrument for agriculture, with the possible exception of export crops and (if domestic to export shifts are desirable) livestock.

The deviation of official grower prices from border prices appears to be correlated negatively with output growth for SSA as a whole, even if a number of countries are well off the trend line. However, the correlation only accounts for 10 per cent of the observed deviations. In other words, 90 per cent appears to relate to causal factors other than official prices (Cleaver, 1985). Doubtless getting 10 per cent of the answer is progress, but it is hardly an adequate dominant programme plank.

If agricultural output were broken down into export crops, domestic industrial crops, domestic food crops and livestock, the picture might alter. The share explained is likely to be significantly higher for export and perhaps domestic industrial crops. For domestic food crops the level of correlation is likely to be insignificant.

The reason lies in the fact that domestic food crops are rarely sold through official channels if the official grower price is significantly below the market clearing price. Enforcement is rarely practical, whatever the legal and rhetorical position – some areas in Ethiopia and also Somalia for a few years in the middle 1970s stand out as marked exceptions. A rough estimate for SSA as a whole (country positions would vary widely) is that 75 per cent of domestic food is self-provisioning ('subsistence') or traded through very local, non-official channels. Of the remaining 25 per cent about 13-15 per cent relates to crops/animals for which there are generally no official prices, another 5 per cent is parallel marketed, and at most 7 per cent is directly affected by official prices. Trying to raise output by acting on 7 per cent of output (higher in surplus or good and lower in drought or bad years) is hardly likely to be spectacularly effective.

There are exceptions. If grain is imported heavily enough to allow market clearing at subsidised sales, this will deter local production and/or cause it to be smuggled to parallel markets across the border (e.g. Zambia over most of the past decade). However, given foreign-exchange constraints, such subsidisation becomes an increasingly rare case except where food aid sold on the basis of an artificially low exchange rate depresses the domestic price level (e.g. Somalia).

The claim that price elasticities of supply in SSA are positive is, with rare exceptions, correct. For individual annual crops they are frequently quite high because crops planted for sale are selected with a view to expected prices. But aggregate agricultural output price elasticities have usually been estimated at quite low levels – under 0.2 in some cases.

In fact, there are doubts as to what meaning can be set on these figures. Output estimates are very bad – and in many cases worsening. In any short series weather may dominate (unlagged grain price/output data tend to show a negative correlation for that reason). In any longer series with changes in access to inputs and transport, buyers may co-correlate with real price changes so that only a joint product elasticity can be obtained.

Data over time in some countries certainly raise doubts on any easily calculated, dominant price elasticity effect. Between 1961–7 and 1971–8, Tanzania had an annual agricultural growth rate of about 3.5 per cent. In this period there was no significant currency overvaluation. Domestic terms of trade for agriculture worsened to 1967, improved to 1970, worsened again between 1970 and 1973, improved dramatically between 1974 and 1975 and then declined gradually. As of 1978 the position was broadly similar to that which held in 1961. However, after 1967 food crop terms of trade improved relative to export crops. The one clear link is to the latter shift. Prior to 1967 food and export crop output each grew at around 3 to 3.5 per cent per annum. Thereafter, food crop output growth exceeded 4 per cent and export crop growth was negative. The only other easy linkage to be observed is with annual average weather conditions (Bank of Tanzania, 1984). Between 1978 and 1985 output growth fell sharply. Real price declines relative to wage goods (at official but not parallel market prices as far as food was concerned), improvements relative to wages, and poor to bad weather typified much of the period. Output levels did not change when real official food prices rose (with real export crop prices holding constant) but weather remained poor. There is no easy causal relationship to be found with prices.

The domestic terms of trade argument is complex both for SSA as a whole over the period 1970–85 and in particular countries over particular sub-periods. If the measure is of farmer versus wage-earner purchasing power, the correct comparison is between grower prices and wages. This is especially true during periods of falling per capita GDP when both grower prices and wages could well fall when deflated by the Cost of Living Index.

On the price/wage comparison export-crop growers have on the whole had constant or improving domestic terms of trade since 1970 in most countries. They have, however, with few exceptions had falling ones against a COL index, at least since the late 1970s and usually for longer.

For food crops there is little hard evidence on grower prices. Out-of-line low grower prices are regularly bypassed and for a majority of marketed crops and animals (which ones varies from country to country) there are no official prices. Parallel or informal market farmgate price data are notable for their limited and fragmentary nature. However, since 1970 and especially since 1979 the food component in the COL index in most SSA countries has risen at least as fast as the overall index when it has been computed on actual (not official) prices. This is true for rural as well as urban and national indices. Year to year movements have been very erratic – or rather very weather-related.

Thus the presumption would seem to be that effective grower prices for domestic food have been relatively constant in COL deflated terms and have risen sharply relative to wages. If this presumption is wrong, the most likely reason is a sharp rise in transport costs and/or distributor margins in the final price. While such a rise is likely in the case of transport, even a substantial adjustment would leave domestic food prices rising relative to export crop prices; export crop prices rising relative to real wages; all prices and wages falling relative to COL. If that is the case, output levels and trends (and international terms of trade) would appear to have played a larger role in weak agricultural performance than domestic wage and price trends.

Other than weather, what explains the remaining 90 per cent? Increasingly the short-run answer is identified as supplies of inputs, infrastructure (transport and buyers) and, less uniformly, extension and incentive goods (cf. Cleaver, 1984, Lipton, 1986). Without these, farmers cannot raise output much, whatever the price elasticities, and even if very low marketed surplus levels were augmented Michael Lipton's comment (1986) that any per cent of 0 is 0 remains valid.

In the longer term applied research is needed as well as improved transmission. Despite claims to the contrary, proven innovations now available off the shelf are few and far between (cf. Lipton, 1985a, 85b, 87). This implies a need generally for public expenditure outlays on research to rise, with, however, output gains unlikely to be substantial until a decade after the research push has begun.

Further problems arise with price changes taken by themselves. Do they get passed through to producers? If marketing boards previously had deficits, this may not occur. Nor will it happen if uncertainties, transport bottlenecks and high inflation create a speculative, monopsonistic context – e.g. Madagascar in the 1980s. Even if they do, what of input costs (also targets for increases in many IMF programmes), including transport? And thus net real proceeds?

Market liberalisation, price flexibility and domestic prices approximating border prices (import parity for imports, export parity for exports, some intermediate level for crops swinging between net imports and exports) appear to be the IMF's medium-term preferences. However, these priorities evidently raise a number of problems.

Seasonal price fluctuations are in a sense efficient; they charge carrying costs to the user. In Tanzania in 1986/7 the success of co-op marketing over the first nine months of the crop year was in avoiding the marketing board's carrying costs so that they could pay growers the same prices and – they believe – still earn a surplus. The problem is in ensuring that there is a buyer who can and does hold stocks for the latter part of the year and for inter-seasonal reserves – a role private and co-op traders with limited financial resources are often unwilling to play.

Border prices – even abstracting from the conundrums associated with swing export or import crops – have one serious disadvantage. They fluctuate widely, absolutely and relative to each other from year to year. Thus their use would give farmers no certainty (indeed no rational expectation at all) at the time of planting or tending as to prices at harvest or picking. At least guaranteed base prices known before planting or (for perennials) tending begins are normally viewed (not least by industrial economies) as crucial to providing incentives to plant and a basis for rational farm level resource allocation.

The IMF/World Bank answer to these two dilemmas seems to be emerging as a guaranteed price with a public enterprise buyer acting as stock holder and seller of last resort. This is, not entirely intentionally, the 1986/7 Tanzanian maize and rice pattern. But it is a formula which guarantees a loss to the public enterprise (unless it profiteers in drought years). Late season selling can be operated on a breakeven basis but this will not work for surplus purchases, export unloadings and interseasonal reserve holding. Much more general and contextual thinking as to optimal prices, reserves and government payments to cover socially and macroeconomically bene-ficial, but enterprise loss-making, functions is needed.

A last tangle of issues concerns uniform farm-gate and suitability bonus pricing. Both are Bank rather than Fund concepts – albeit the Bank has turned on the former as sweepingly as it once promoted it. Uniform farm-gate pricing, with marketing board breakeven on long-distance trade, redistributes locational rent from near-market to farther away growers and raises transport costs. Its effect on the total cost of a given volume of delivered crop is ambiguous (depending on actual grower supply curves), but it is likely to raise import costs (for transport). Whether it does or does not alter crop mix by area is an empirical question depending on ecology more than econometrics. In practice, it tends to become minimum guaranteed pricing, as in the period 1979–84 in Tanzania where official maize purchases were largely in far-off areas rather than the more accessible zones in which higher parallel prices prevailed.

Suitability-bonus (i.e. paying more in areas deemed suitable for a crop) pricing – a current World Bank favourite – appears to be absurd. If an area is well suited to a crop, an above-average payment is hardly needed as an incentive! The case for an unsuitability penalty (or not buying in the area) may be stronger, but is the opposite of liberalisation. Its logic is that farmers engage in gambling practices planting risky, high pay-off crops (e.g. maize instead of drought-resistant millet and sorghum) beyond the economically rational cut-off point. As the same farmers are usually perceived as risk avoiders or minimisers, the premise is doubtful.

The key issue of when farmers are paid is dealt with in the next section. It is, of course, a price issue, especially when inflation is high. Payment at harvest as opposed to six months later raises the real purchasing power of a constant nominal unit price 100 per cent if inflation is 100 per cent and 33 per cent if it is 50 per cent.

(iii) Credit policies

The two main credit policy instruments in IMF agreements are credit ceilings and raised interest rates. The aims are to reduce the growth of domestic credit/money supply and thus inflation; to increase real savings (including those held in currency); and to rationalise use of domestic credit/savings, including switching it from govern-ment to productive sectors. Relatively at least, agriculture should be a beneficiary.

The credit ceiling as a check on inflation is based on the identity $MV = PT$. As V (velocity of circulation) and T (physical volume of transactions) are not constants, the effectiveness of cutting the growth of M as a means to reducing that of P may not be very high. It may be less efficient than concentrating on – or giving equal emphasis to – raising T. It is not irrelevant to note that what broke inflation in Ghana in 1984 and what held it down (to 30 per cent despite a 360 per cent increase in the cost of foreign exchange) in Tanzania over 1986/7 was primarily a T rise – in these cases spearheaded by food production recovery with good weather. Equally Tanzania is probably right to view achieving a 10/15 per cent growth in manufactured goods production (again a T rise) as the most crucial factor in driving 1988/9 inflation down to a 20/25 per cent range.

The problems with credit ceilings are, first, in calculating what levels are attainable without choking off attainable T recovery and, second, in avoiding their triggering programme collapse in the face of exogenous shocks. Only if the ratio of working capital to output, the rates of increase of cost of the physical components of working capital, the volume of production and the amount of working capital available from sources other than bank lending can be estimated reasonably accurately can a safe domestic credit level for enterprises be estimated. Nominally the IMF does follow that approach; in practice it seems to estimate each item very conservatively and then bargain up a bit rather than trying to get the least unlikely empirical estimate.

For agriculture the potential costs of faulty estimation are very high. If the initial estimate was too low, then the amount allocated for crop (or input) marketing finance will not be adequate and payments will be delayed. If crops are well above projections, the same result will ensue. If seasonal swings are understated, the only way to stay within ceilings is deferred payments to (forced lending by) agricultural producers. This does happen because IMF teams often negotiate seasonal ceilings as matters of policy rather than seeking the best attainable estimates of the degree and pattern of seasonality as a matter of fact. Lags in processing, transport and export sales (or payment receipts) are likely, especially if output is above estimates, as both Fund and government personnel tend to underestimate such physical and institutional bottle-necks. The Hobson's choices of delaying payment to growers – for up to a year on a substantial portion of the price of Kenya coffee in 1985 and 1986 – and breaking a performance target are almost inevitable and the problem sector is most likely to be agriculture.

Interest-rate increases (to move towards or achieve a positive real interest rate) are seen by the IMF as a way to increase savings and to rationalise use of domestic credit. On the first count it can be said that the theoretical case is problematic and the empirical evidence (in SSA or elsewhere) does not suggest a strong correlation. For the latter the case is somewhat better, subject to the danger that financial strength and/or willingness to take risk, rather than underlying profitability, may be the dominant considerations in respect to seeking or doing without credit on the demand side. If they are, that pattern introduces a bias against agricultural production other than large estates and against small farming households in particular.

Interest-rate increases can be – indeed generally are – inflationary. They are a major cost element especially in distribution (including agricultural marketing). As most commercial sectors in SSA seem to work on cost-plus-markup pricing, interest-rate increases are likely to raise margins. In the case of export crops – where the higher cost cannot be passed forward – they ultimately reduce grower prices (or tax revenues). Both of these results are negative for agriculture absolutely and relative to other sectors.

Higher interest rates (even if preferential) to farmers in practice result in a transfer to other sectors, for the obvious reason that they are a cost farmers are unlikely to be able to pass forward. This is exacerbated by the fact that farmers as a group are normally large net creditors with non-interest-bearing claims on the marketing system (including its co-op and private segments) far above their interest-bearing debts to banks, merchants and specialised financial institutions.

This returns to the issue of prompt cash payment. High inflation and high interest rates make delayed payment a heavy tax on and disincentive for farmers. IMF performance criteria for credit ceilings tend to increase delays. Yet in Ghana, the action taken under adjustment that has been most welcomed by cocoa farmers has been the substitution of cashable cheques instead of the former chit system with its lengthy payment delays (see Chapter 7). Similarly in 1986 Tanzanian peasants by and large welcomed the return of procurement from marketing boards to co-ops because the latter often paid more promptly. Both in the price and the credit aspects of IMF dialogue and programmes this prompt payment theme seems to receive unduly little attention.

(iv) Fiscal policies

The standard fiscal performance clause in an IMF programme is a ceiling on government borrowing from the domestic banking system. The preferred method is usually expenditure (especially recurrent expenditure) cuts, but the Fund is normally flexible on means. The impact on agriculture depends largely on how the reduction is achieved. Within an overall ceiling, a reduction in government borrowing clears space for greater enterprise, including agricultural, credit. If the reduction results from additional soft external finance or largely non-agricultural taxes (e.g. a graduated sales tax tends to weigh less heavily on poor people and on agricultural producers, not only because of self-provisioning but also unprocessed commercialised foodstuffs are necessarily zero-rated), then the net results in respect to agriculture will be positive.

Taxes on agriculture, such as export or industrial use taxes, are a different matter. They unambiguously reduce rural income and, at least to some extent, either deter agricultural output or divert it to other crops. While in principle usually opposed to export taxes, the Fund has not been very firm in pushing root-and-branch fiscal reform in the cases where they form a high proportion of present revenue, as in Ghana or Uganda. Paradoxically, in both these cases the reconstruction of the indirect tax base could allow cuts in the relatively high export tax rates.

User fees – perhaps a Bank more than a Fund enthusiasm – seem to be backed more from a belief in using the market than from any serious evaluation of fiscal alternatives. The administrative and cost implications of millions of tiny charges – for example, standpipe monthly user fees, or clinic visit and vaccination charges – are appalling from the point of view of cost efficiency of revenue collection. On pure net revenue grounds, higher indirect taxes are almost always superior to virtually all user charges. However, with respect to agriculture the Fund and Bank have not (or not yet) advocated extension officer fees. Oddly enough, Tanzania used to charge them on a proportional basis for some products by having export crop authorities pay for their own extension staff and setting a grower price taking these costs into account – a policy reversed in 1984 to allow higher grower prices as well as to recentralise extension.

The general problem with user charges is that most are regressive (especially for basic health, primary education, communal drinking water). As most rural residents are poor the case against such charges from the point of view of most agricultural households is strong – but under some circumstances refutable. If rural (or urban) households wish to raise funds to rehabilitate or expand basic services which the state cannot provide, this should probably be encouraged. In extreme cases such as Somalia it is hard to see how else basic rural services can be recreated. But for such self-help to work well it needs to be community – or at least local service unit – levied, with *ad hoc* exemptions for the truly poor, and to be seen to provide support for specific services actually provided to the paying community. Those are tests few, if any, centralised user fee systems can pass.

Expenditure reduction is likely to harm agriculture and agriculturalists. Cuts in primary health, basic education and water supply (and in transport provisions in all ministries) fall disproportionately on rural areas. So do cuts in road maintenance. Within agricultural spending long-term functions – such as research – tend to fare worst.

In the shorter term, control on bank borrowing by means of blocking releases or delaying payment of local bills creates inefficiencies, preventing rational budgeting by any ministry. Since, in practice, it cuts back most on travel and on operating supplies, it is more damaging to agriculture and rural services more generally than to, say, general administration. Payment delays result in delays in work done, additional charges and general blockages. Ghana is a clear recent case in point. There, these problems were exacerbated as recurrent expenditure (including maintenance and much of rehabilitation) was cut more severely than capital. The combined result has been to destroy the viability of the budgetary process as an economic management tool (Green, 1987a) for the sake of marginally tighter apparent expenditure and tighter actual bank borrowing control.

Expenditure on health, education and water is not – as the Bank and, to a degree, the Fund are coming to admit – purely humanitarian. Ill-health reduces productivity now and in the future if the disease is serious; illiteracy is comparable. Finally, lack of basic services is clearly a major push factor in rural to urban migration. Despite verbal acceptance of these points (stressed in UNICEF, 1987), it is hard to feel they are seriously integrated into mainline Fund (or Bank) fiscal dialogue and programming.

Subsidies are an automatic IMF target. This seems to be independent of their share in the budget or their beneficiaries. The pressure to end food subsidies was as strong in Tanzania (where they never exceeded 2 per cent of recurrent expenditure and were *de facto* mixed consumer/grower subsidies) as in Sudan and Zambia (where they are clearly consumer subsidies and much larger). Agricultural input subsidies have not been equally high profile targets. However, the preference of both the Fund and the Bank is for higher grower prices, allowing, in theory, full cost pricing of inputs.

The case against standard food subsidies is simple. They either eat up a disproportionate share of revenue and reach most or all of the urban and accessible rural population (e.g. Sudan, Zambia) or they are fairly low-cost but actually serve a relatively small urban group (e.g. Tanzania, Mozambique). Zimbabwe phased out food subsidies of the first type with parallel minimum wage increases (which did not, by their nature, protect rural smallholder or informal sector buyers), and Tanzania dropped its food subsidies on realising that their initial broad coverage had contracted to formal-sector wage-earners in the capital city. The Tanzanian Government also raised the minimum wage in the relevant year.

In general, a good case can be made against food subsidies. Employment on public works is usually more efficient than giving away food, as is raising wages rather than subsidising food. Subsidy programmes that eat up high proportions of recurrent revenue are likely to reduce spending on rural health, education, water, road maintenance and extension services to benefit primarily urban consumers. This holds even if the subsidy is financed by food aid, in which case cash payments are generally superior to actual food delivery, except in cases such as supplementary child feeding (school or clinic) and immediate emergency relief.

The exceptions underline a more general point – while a case has to be made for any subsidy it is not safe to assume no case is valid. An example is a fungicide against a contagious disease, for example, copper sulphate to control coffee berry disease. One non-user can destroy the crops of ten users. In this case, an 80 per cent subsidy (as practised in Tanzania) may be more economically rational than full-cost pricing (as in Kenya). The most serious drawback has been that Tanzanian growers (with a 5 to 1 price differential for a high value/weight ratio product) find it all too profitable to smuggle copper sulphate to Kenya and to secure excess supplies to do this, thereby subsidising Kenya's balance of payments at Tanzania's expense.

Lastly, freer trade – a clear IMF goal – need not have fiscal effects. Revenue tariffs can readily be converted into sales taxes at point of import or manufacture. However, tariff cuts and relaxation of quantitative restrictions on agricultural products can affect growers. If the exchange rate is still overvalued or if time is not allowed for adjustment, the rural income and output effects could be severe. The relaxation of general import barriers cannot be predicted as having a uniform effect. In some cases it can result in lower prices for incentive goods. On the other hand – and this appears to have happened in Uganda over 1982–4 – it can shift imports from intermediate to consumption goods, with negative implications both for the supply of agricultural inputs (especially implements) and the basic domestic consumer manufactured goods that farmers commonly wish to buy.

(v) Investment policies

The IMF is not always concerned to reduce government investment; it is concerned with rationalising it and ensuring that it does not crowd out private investment. It is normally agreed that considerable fixed investment in the 1970s in SSA yielded derisory additions to output. The problem of low returns to large-scale investment has undoubtedly been particularly severe in SSA agriculture and agro-industry. Thus, virtually no large West African irrigation schemes are viable if the tests of covering operating costs, significant increments to net farmer incomes over the pre-irrigation position, maintenance and debt-service coverage, and a net external account gain are applied.

The IMF generally holds that gaps in basic infrastructure which constrain the efficiency of private producers call for a shift towards rapid rehabilitation-focused government investment in infrastructure ('stock capital') to support private-sector directly productive investment. At least the latter half of the premise appears hard to challenge. Its meaning in respect to agriculture varies and, in fact, the IMF in this respect usually defers to the World Bank for detailed proposals.

Both the Bank and the Fund have followed the increasingly common thrust on the part of a number of SSA governments since the late 1970s towards a higher share of agriculture in total investment. The one caveat which may arise is whether fixed capital, working capital (credit and input supplies) or recurrent (extension, statistics, research) spending are being balanced efficiently. On the face of it, non-wage recurrent expenditures (statistics, field travel, research) and working capital have been underfunded relative to fixed capital formation. Further, in the context of smallholder rainfed agriculture, it is arguable that the really key fixed capital formation by the government may well be in transport, water, marketing, storage and/or processing, not through direct investment in the agricultural sector proper. To the extent that this is true, the emphasis on agricultural fixed investment has commonly led to inefficient 'investment' in large-scale irrigation and mechanisation projects.

The IMF's hope that additional foreign private investment can be attracted is – in agriculture and more generally – unrealistic in SSA, apart from some special cases. Current and projected export crop prices and trends do not make investment attractive, irrespective of other constraints such as overvalued currencies and profit remittance. For the potential investor, Malaysia and Brazil can easily outbid SSA. Moreover, large-scale mechanised production of most domestic food crops is not cost-efficient in SSA. For Ghanaian mechanised rice production, the import content appears to exceed the cif cost of imported rice. Only with massive state subsidies, tax concessions or consumer-funded high prices and expectations that such measures would be sustained, could foreign private investment be expected to occur. The issue is not African state hostility to private investment so much as low profitability and high risk prospects which no amount of statutory codes can address adequately.

(vi) Institutional reform

Accountability, non-interference and responsiveness to market forces (seen as including competition and effective pressure for cost efficiency) are the key themes of the IMF's reform advice for agricultural and other sector institutions. For agriculture this approach has concentrated on public procurement/marketing bodies.

However, apart from the fact that accountability is meaningless without specifying to whom, one major problem has been the fact that most SSA crop marketing bodies have suffered not from a lack of autonomy but rather from a lack of effective policy control by governments. Similarly the Fund's faith in African markets and their degree of competition as well as the cost efficiency (at least from the growers' viewpoint) of private marketing is, to put it mildly, optimistic.

This is not, however, to argue (as some critics do) that the Fund's critique lacks relevance. Reform is frequently needed and needed urgently. How it should be done, unfortunately, is a question with few general answers at operational level. This is partly a data problem. Accounts are frequently so bad that even a basic cost break-down is not possible. Cost-cutting in the absence of that base is like punching a feather pillow or wielding an Alexandrine sword. Furthermore, in some cases profitability (as opposed to a reasoned net surplus or deficit target) may not necessarily be a suitable test. Providing a guaranteed price to all growers, provisioning distant areas, and holding intra-year reserves are all functions which tend to be loss-making for the enterprise even when economically efficient in sectoral or national terms.

Finally, through what kind of competition, and by means of what particular channels real resource costs are likely to be lowered nationally and (which is not necessarily the same thing) the growers' share of proceeds raised is, in practice, rarely self-evident and not uniform. The assumption that private-sector procurement and marketing gives growers a larger share is – at least in general – not proven. In the late 1920s and 1930s under a purely private marketing structure, the share of fob cocoa proceeds received by growers in Ghana varied widely but seems to have averaged under 30 per cent, roughly the level recently maintained with a public marketing board. In Tanzania in the 1960s and 1970s two wholly privately marketed staple foods – plantains and Irish potatoes – had grower shares relative to retail prices comparable to those received by grain growers on officially marketed grain. The distribution sector may have been highly profitable (and thus had lower real resource cost shares) but the impact on grower revenues cannot be predicted as being unambiguously beneficial. This suggests that any simple solution – such as private traders or co-operatives – just does not exist.

TOWARDS A MORE VIABLE ARTICULATION

This is not the place to seek to articulate a complete model agricultural sector strategy for a typical SSA economy. However, a sketch roughly parallel to the IMF programme areas surveyed above may be useful. It is divided into short (18 months), medium (to 5 years) and long time periods.

Measures are listed roughly in the same order as in the foregoing review of IMF approaches and not in order of importance (which will in any case vary from country to country and over time). No attempt is made to provide complete coverage.

1. *Exchange-rate adjustment.*

   Short – substantial movement towards a realistic rate to reduce disincentives to export production, to claw back smuggled exports and to stop monetised food aid amounting to *de facto* dumping against domestic producers.

   Medium – when the policy may begin to pay off in export volume – completion of move to viable rate and installation of a system (e.g. active crawling peg) to maintain it.

   Long – continuation of management of rate to avoid reappearance of severe overvaluation.

2. *Producer prices.*

   Short – remove major illogicalities (especially bias against exports).

   Medium – move towards guaranteed floor price procurement for a handful of non-perishable staple foods and fob-related (say with a 70 per cent of fob price rule of thumb target for grower payments) export crop prices.

   Long – complete medium-term measures.

3. *Sectoral credit*

   Short – ensure adequate allocations, especially to procurement and marketing, processing and manufacturing. Review medium- and long-term agricultural credit programmes. Institute cash or cheque payments to growers on procurement and ensure prompt procurement to end forced, non-interest-bearing lending by farmers.

   Medium – continue short-term policies. Restructure development credit – with special reference to women and to poor farmers – if appropriate.

   Long – continue medium-term policies.

4. *Recurrent agricultural budget*

   Short – begin to restore working capital provisions (e.g. credit, operating inputs for ministry programmes). Rebuild statistical, analytical, monitoring capacity. Redeploy (preferably to own account farming) surplus personnel.

   Medium – complete working capital restoration. Begin adaptation of services (including extension) to research results. Utilise statistical, analytical, monitoring base.

   Long – build on policies of medium term.

5. *Farm-level operating inputs*

   Short – begin restoring use of implements, fertilisers, seeds and pesticides of proven efficiency. Restore animal-drawn implement development and animal training if viable programme had existed; if not, commence such a programme.

   Medium – complete short-term policies. Add to coverage selectively on basis of proven research findings validated by user demand.

   Long – build on medium-term policies.

6. *Basic rural services* (health, education, water)

Short – begin restoration of previous coverage. Plan workable strategy for moving to universal provision. Assess appropriateness of content and accessibility of past provision.

Medium – complete short-term policies. Institute content revision (e.g. comprehensive immunisation, preventative component in primary health care). Begin drive to universal coverage.

Long – build on medium-term policies.

7. *Transport, storage, processing*

Short – emergency restoration of existing but debilitated or collapsed capacity. Development of priority restoration and expansion policies.

Medium – complete capacity restoration, begin expansion with special attention to gap filling. Create storage and processing systems designed to minimise cross-haulage and to even out seasonal crop, animal and input movement fluctuations, thus reducing seasonal peak transport needs.

Long – build on medium-term policies.

8. *Marketing*

Short – institute emergency cost control, devise accounting and accountability structures. Improve physical capacity and enforce prompt payment.

Medium – put accounting and cost control in place. Introduce competitive, multi-channel elements in non-export (and perhaps export) sub-sectors. Increase (or create) direct accountability to growers.

Long – build on medium-term policies. Explore shifting central government-owned marketing for key export crops as well as buyer of last resort – holder of intra-year stocks – to more competitive environment.

9. *Research*

Short – maintain and stabilise existing institutional capacity and promising projects. Learn from farmers as to their existing best techniques and innovations. Adopt and test (including for user friendliness and economic viability) known but untested innovations.

Medium – build on short-term policies. Put strategy priorities into operation and articulate further steps. Build systematic input from farmers into system.

Long – build on (and begin to reap substantial benefits from) medium-term policies.

This programmatic sketch does not in principle contradict IMF concerns. In practice it does not articulate very well with the standard 18-month Stand-by Loan.

If such articulation is to be achieved it will be necessary for IMF programmes to be modified to meet the particular constraints that exist in SSA. Below, certain lines of approach are suggested:

i)   Dialogue on sectoral, real (i.e. non-monetary) and social issues with the IMF should be broadened and deepened.
ii) Conditionality – and especially performance criteria – should be narrowed to progress towards realistic exchange rates, to government domestic bank borrowing and to overall credit expansion.
iii) Performance criteria should be determined along viable lines, an outcome that is

more likely outside a confrontational approach to negotiation, and should include flexibility in application (especially where increased agricultural output beyond expectations is a main cause of pressure on credit ceilings).

iv) A realistic view (not constrained by a 3-year or even a 5-year time horizon) of how long special external support will be needed to achieve sustainable – in both economic and political terms – structural adjustment with growth should be determined.

v) That time perspective should structure the phasing of instrumental changes and of performance criteria even if the actual stand-by programmes are of shorter duration.

vi) Fund drawings (excluding the Structural Adjustment Facility) should not exceed in total 20 per cent of annual export earnings or of total external programme support funding in any one year. Beyond that only the softer Special Facility funding should be seen to be appropriate.

vii) SSA states should create the capacity to prepare coherent, empirically sound sectoral programmes to be presented to the Fund (and, more important, to provide a basis for national political and economic strategy) with priority being given to the agricultural sector.

Annex

POLICIES INCLUDED IN IMF STAND-BY PROGRAMMES OF 1985–6 WITH DIRECT IMPACT ON AGRICULTURE

1. *Exchange-rate policies*
   Initial devaluation and subsequent adjustment to approach and hold to an equilibrium or realistic exchange rate. Intended to raise the relative prices of tradables in general and agricultural exports/imports in particular.

   a. Co-ordination of currency depreciation with producer price increases formalised more sharply.
   b. Policy changes made in various aspects of the exchange system to help bolster agricultural exports.
   c. Liberalisation of imports intended for agriculture.
   d. Increased availability of foreign-exchange resources for agriculture made possible (including retention schemes).

2. *Pricing policies*
   Raising real prices of tradables and especially agricultural exports to restore domestic price relativities comparable to those in the global market. Intended to raise and to rationalise agricultural production and to remove the need for subsidies.

   a. Producer prices set by marketing board raised.
   b. Minimum procurement prices raised.
   c. Food prices liberalised or made flexible in line with cost increases.

   d.   Prices of public enterprises in agro-industries raised (i.e. their selling prices).

   e.   Retail price of fertilisers raised.

3. *Credit policies*

Credit ceilings combined with sub-ceilings on government (and sometimes public enterprise) borrowings. Aimed at managing/restraining demand and at reducing crowding out of commercial enterprises by government (or chronic loss-making marketing board) borrowing. Real interest rates raised to positive levels to induce savings and rationalise use of credit.

   a.   Financing needs of buffer stocks met.

   b.   Seasonal credit needs of agricultural sector taken into account in setting quarterly credit ceilings.

   c.   Overdue loans to agricultural sector reduced.

   d.   Agricultural sector included among priority sectors in selective credit control.

   e.   Attempts made to improve security of loans to farmers, e.g. through guarantee fund or insurance scheme.

   f.   Attempts made to improve farmers' access to banks.

   g.   Foreign funds obtained to support loans to farmers.

   h.   Preferential interest rate on credit for food crop production and marketing increased.

4. *Fiscal policies*

Reduction of government borrowing (especially of domestic bank borrowing) including rationalisation/reduction of public services – with uneven attention to prioritisation among or within services. To reduce tax burdens, provide space for entrepreneurs, and to increase efficiency with which (and charges at which) remaining services are provided.

   a.   Import duties on fertilisers lowered.

   b.   Lower-than-average rate of taxation set for agricultural incomes.

   c.   Tax on first sale of important tree crop lowered to 50 per cent of standard rate.

   d.   Gradual reduction of export taxation on agriculture started.

   e.   Import bans on competitive products replaced by moderate tariffs.

   f.   Food subsidies to be phased out.

5. *Investment policies*

Rationalise state investment, concentrate on infrastructure and on rehabilitation, reduce directly productive investment role in favour of private (or autonomous public) enterprise. Increase efficiency of investment, enhance stock capital provision by state in support of enterprises.

   a.   Public investment programme aimed at increasing share of agriculture.

   b.   Various measures designed to improve efficiency of public investment in agriculture.

   c.   Begin to restructure technical packages to increase suitability to local conditions.

6. *Supply and structural problems*

Close bottlenecks by increasing openness of procurement and supply to the market (and to private enterprises) and by improving provision of public and public enterprise services. Create a climate increasing farmers' ability and incentives to produce.

   a.   Measures to improve the distribution and quality of inputs to farmers.

    b. Revitalisation of credit delivery, extension services, storage and milling capacity and other support services attempted.
    c. Diversification of agricultural output.
    d. Promotion of increased self-sufficiency.

7. *Miscellaneous institutional reform*
Increase accountability to market forces wherever possible (including but not only by privatisation) and to improve managerial capacity of public enterprises and services. To increase cost efficiency, to reduce need for/levels of subsidies.

    a. Introduction of measures to enhance privatisation within agriculture.
    b. Price liberalisation measures introduced.
    c. Various steps taken to improve management of public enterprises in agriculture.
    d. Measures to introduce more effective approaches to extension inaugurated.

NOTES

1 Certain policies could be included under more than one heading. Adapted from Johnson (1987) from whom seven areas and the lettered examples, but not the headnotes, are derived.

REFERENCES

Allison, C. and R.H. Green (eds) (1985), 'Sub-Saharan Africa: Getting the Facts Straight', *IDS Bulletin*, Vol. 16, No. 3, July.
Balassa, B. and F.D. McCarthy (1984), 'Adjustment Policies in Developing Countries, 1979–83: An Update', Washington DC, World Bank Staff Working Papers, No. 675.
Bank of Tanzania (1984), *Tanzania Twenty Years of Independence (1961–1981): A Review of Political and Economic Performance*, Dar es Salaam.
Cleaver, K.M. (1985), 'The Impact of Price and Exchange Rate Policies on Agriculture in Sub-Saharan Africa', Washington DC, World Bank Staff Working Papers, No. 728.
Colclough, C.L. and R.H. Green (eds) (1988), 'Stabilisation for Destabilisation, Stagnation and/or Growth? Short run costs and long run uncertainties in Africa', *IDS Bulletin*, Vol. 19, No. 3, Spring.
Commonwealth Secretariat (1983), *Towards a New Bretton Woods: Challenges for the World Financial and Trading Systems*, London.
—— (1984), *The Debt Crisis and The World Economy*, London.
Cornia, G.A., R. Jolly, F. Stewart (eds) (1987), *Adjustment With a Human Face: Protecting the Vulnerable and Promoting Growth*, Oxford, Clarendon Press for UNICEF.
Davies, R. and D. Saunders (1987), 'Stabilisation Policies and the Effects on Child Health in Zimbabwe', *Review of African Political Economy*, Vol. 38, April.
Dell, S.S. (1981), *On Being Grandmotherly: The Evolution of IMF Conditionality*, Princeton University Essays in International Finance, No. 144.
—— (1987), 'Balance of Payment Adjustment in the 1980s', special issue of *World Development*, Vol. 14, No. 8.
—— and R. Lawrence (1980), *The Balance-of-Payments Process in Developing Countries*, New York, Pergamon.
Dervis, K., J. de Melo and S. Robinson (1982), *General Equilibrium Models for Development Policy*, Cambridge, Cambridge University Press for the World Bank.
Godfrey, M. (1985), 'Trade and Exchange Rate Policy in Sub-Saharan Africa', in Allison and Green.
Green, R.H. (1983), 'Political-economic Adjustment and IMF Conditionality', in Williamson (1983).

—— (1984), 'IMF Conditionality' (review article), *Third World Review*.

—— (1985a), 'From Deepening Economic Malaise toward Renewed Development: Notes toward African agendas for action', *Journal of Development Planning*, Vol. 15, April.

—— (1985b), 'IMF Stabilisation and Structural Adjustment in Sub-Saharan Africa: Are they technically compatible?' in Allison and Green.

—— (1985c), 'Sub-Saharan Africa: poverty of development, development of poverty', IDS Seminar – Poverty, Development and Food: Toward the Twenty First Century, IDS *Discussion Paper* 218, July.

—— (1986a), 'The IMF and Stabilisation in Sub-Saharan Africa: a critical review', IDS *Discussion Paper* 216, June.

—— (1986b), 'Food Policy, Food Production and Hunger in Sub-Saharan Africa: retrospect and prospect', *International Journal*, Vol. XLI, No. 4, Autumn.

—— (1987a), 'Budget Management as Economic Management: some key concerns', in Ndegwa, Mureithi and Green.

—— (1987b), 'Ghana: Stabilisation and Structural Shifts' for World Institute for Development Economics Research (WIDER), Helsinki volume edited by L. Taylor – shorter variant in Colclough and Green.

—— D. Rwegasira and B. Van Arkadie (1981), *Economic Shocks and National Policy Making: Tanzania in the 1970s*, The Hague, Institute of Social Studies.

—— and H.W. Singer (1984), 'Sub-Saharan Africa in Depression: the Impact on the Welfare of Children' in Jolly and Cornia.

Griffith-Jones, S. and R.H. Green (1984), *African External Debt and Development: A Review and Analysis*, Dakar, UNCTAD technical assistance study for African Centre for Monetary Studies.

—— and R.H. Green (1985), 'External Debt: Sub-Saharan Africa's Emerging Iceberg' in Rose.

—— and C. Harvey (1985), *World Prices and Development*, Aldershot, Gower.

Group of 24 (1982), *Low Income Countries and International Monetary System. Report of a Group of Experts*, New York.

Harvey, C. (1985), 'Successful Adjustment in Botswana' in Allison and Green.

Helleiner, G.K. (1983a), 'Lender of Early Resort: the IMF and the poorest', *American Economic Review*, Vol. 73, No. 2.

—— (1983b), *The IMF and Africa in the 1980s*, International Finance Section, Department of Economics, Princeton, Essays in International Finance, No. 152.

—— (1984a), 'An Agenda for a new Bretton Woods', *World Policy Journal*.

—— (1984b), 'Outward Orientation, Import Instability and African Economic Growth, an Empirical Investigation' (mimeo).

—— (1985), 'Aid and Liquidity: the Neglect of SSA and others of the poorest in the emerging International Monetary System', *Journal of Development Planning*, Vol. 15, April.

—— (1986), 'The Question of Conditionality in Sub-Saharan Africa' in Lancaster and Williamson.

Heller, P.S. and J.E. Aghevli (1984), 'The Recurrent Cost Problem: an international overview' in Howell.

Howell, J. (ed.) (1984), *Recurrent Costs and Agricultural Development*, London, ODI.

Hugon, P. (1988), 'The Impact of Adjustment Policy in Madagascar' in Colclough and Green.

International Monetary Fund (1983), *World Economic Outlook*, Washington DC.

—— (1984a), *World Economic Outlook*, Washington DC.

—— (1984b), *IMF Survey*, Washington DC, September.

—— (1985a), *World Economic Outlook*, Washington DC.

—— (1985b), 'Formulation of Exchange Rate Policies in Adjustment Programs', *Occasional Paper* No. 36, August (by G.G. Johnson, C. Clement, S. Eken, R. Pownall, R.L. Sheehy, E.J. Zervoudakis).

—— (1986), *World Economic Outlook*, Washington DC.

—— (1986/7), *IMF Survey*, Washington DC.

Jaycox, E.V.K., R.I. Gulhati, S. Lall and S. Yalamanchili (1986), 'The Nature of the Debt Problem in Eastern and Southern Africa' in Lancaster and Williamson.

Johnson, O.E.G. (1987), 'The Agricultural Sector in Adjustment Programmes supported by IMF Stand-by Arrangements', Washington DC, IMF (mimeo).

Jolly, A.R. and G.A. Cornia (1984), 'The Impact of World Recession on Children', special issue of *World Development*, Vol. 12, No. 3.

Kadhani, X. and R.H. Green (1985), 'Parameters as Warnings and Guide Posts: the case of Zimbabwe', *Journal of Development Planning*.

Khan, M. (1984), 'Macroeconomic Adjustment in Developing Countries: a policy perspective', *World Bank Research Observer*, Vol. 1, No. 2, January.

—— and M. Knight (1981), 'Stabilisation Programs in Developing Countries', Washington DC, *IMF Staff Papers*, Vol. 28, March.

Killick, T. (1987), 'Unsettled Questions about Adjustment with Growth', *International Monetary and Financial Issues for the Developing Countries*, Geneva, UNCTAD.

—— (ed.) (1984a), *The IMF and Stabilisation: Developing Country Experience*, London, Heinemann.

—— (1984b), 'The IMF's Role in Developing Countries', *Finance and Development*, September.

Lancaster, C. and J. Williamson (eds) (1986), *African Debt and Financing*, Washington DC, Institute for International Economics.

Larosière, J. de (1984), *Does the Fund Impose Austerity?*, Washington DC, IMF.

Lipton, M. (1985a), 'Research and Design of a Policy Frame for Agriculture', in Rose.

—— (1985b), 'The Place of Agricultural Research in the Development of Sub-Saharan Africa', IDS *Discussion Paper* No. 202.

—— (1987), 'Improving the Impact of Aid for Rural Development', IDS *Discussion Paper*.

Longhurst, R. (1988), 'Structural Adjustment and Vulnerable Groups in Sierra Leone' in Colclough and Green.

Loxley, J. (1984a), 'The IMF and the Poorest Countries, The Performance of the Least Developed Countries under IMF Stand-by Arrangements', Ottawa, North-South Institute.

—— (1984b), 'IMF and World Bank Conditionality and Sub-Saharan Africa', African Studies Association (USA) Annual Conference (microfiche).

Ndegwa, P., L.P. Mureithi and R.H. Green (eds) (1987), *Management for Development: Priority Themes in Africa Today*, Nairobi, Oxford University Press/Society for International Development. - Kenya Chapter.

Patel, I.G. (1984), 'The Current Crisis in International Economic Cooperation', *Journal of Development Planning*, No. 14.

Please, S. (1984), 'Structural Adjustment, IMF Conditionality, and the World Bank' in *The Hobbled Giant: Essays on the World Bank*, Boulder/London, Westview.

Polak, J.J. (1957), 'Monetary Analysis of Income Formation and Payments Problems', Washington DC, *IMF Staff Papers*, Vol. 6, June.

Rose, T. (ed.) (1985), *Crisis and Recovery in Sub-Saharan Africa*, Paris, OECD Development Centre.

Taylor, L. (1985), 'IMF Conditionality: Incomplete Theory, Policy Malpractice', April (mimeo).

Topolski, J. (1988), 'Togo: a Structural Adjustment that Destabilises Economic Growth' in Colclough and Green.

UNICEF (1985), *Within Human Reach: A Future for Africa's Children*, New York.

de Vries, R. and C. Porzecanski (1983), 'Comments', in Williamson.

Wheeler, D. (1984), 'Sources of Stagnation in Sub-Saharan Africa', *World Development*, Vol. 12, No. 1.

Williamson, J. (1983), *IMF Conditionality*, Washington DC, Institute for International Economics.

—— (1986), 'Prospects for the Flow of IMF Finance to Sub-Saharan Africa' in Lancaster and Williamson.

World Bank (1983), *World Development Report 1983*, Oxford, Oxford University Press.

—— (1984a), *Toward Sustained Development in Sub-Saharan Africa: A Joint Programme of Action*, Washington DC.

—— (1984b), *World Development Report 1984*, Oxford, Oxford University Press.

—— (1985), *World Development Report 1985*, Oxford, Oxford University Press.

—— (1986a), *World Development Report 1986*, Oxford, Oxford University Press.

—— (1986b), *Financing Adjustment with Growth in Sub-Saharan Africa, 1986–90*, Washington DC.

—— (1987), *World Development Report 1987*, Oxford, Oxford University Press.

4

The Aggregate Supply Response

A Survey

Ajay Chhibber

INTRODUCTION

The supply response of agriculture in the aggregate to changes in the internal terms of trade has emerged as a critical parameter in the design of adjustment programmes. Views on its magnitude range widely and are a subject of much debate, yet surprisingly little work has been done on its empirical estimation. If the aggregate supply response is low, then a policy of taxing agriculture through lower farm prices or through overvalued exchange rates and industrial protection policies will generate resources for investment in other sectors of the economy, without significantly affecting agricultural growth. On the other hand, if it is high, then such policies will retard agricultural growth and create food and input supply bottlenecks which will eventually bring down the rate of growth of the economy as a whole.

In the formulation of agricultural policy it is not enough to know if the aggregate supply response is high (or low), but high (or low) relative to what. If farmers cannot respond sufficiently to higher prices because of constraints due to inadequate irrigation, unimaginative and inefficient research and extension services or poor transport facilities, then improvement of these goods and services may do more for agriculture than a policy of higher farm prices. No doubt the two together, i.e. higher prices and more public inputs, would be highly desirable and complementary but may not always be fiscally feasible. Nevertheless, the amount of emphasis to give to each factor would depend on the relative magnitude of the aggregate supply elasticity with respect to price and non-price factors. How much, for example, of China's recent success in agriculture is due to higher prices and how much to past public investments in irrigation, rural roads, health and education, without which the rapid increases in farm output attributed to price liberalisation might not have been so spectacular, is a subject of some debate.[1]

* The views expressed in this chapter are the responsibility of the author and are not necessarily those of the World Bank. The author wishes to thank J. Hrabovszky and D. Norse at FAO, and H. Binswanger, W. McCleary and W. Thirsk at the Bank for very useful comments on this chapter. Much of his knowledge on this subject came from the late Professor Raj Krishna, with whom he had the privilege to work on several occasions.

The purpose of this paper is to provide a review of the empirical literature on the subject, which critically examines the methods of estimation used as well as the choice of variables. On the basis of the available evidence, the review shows that the long-run aggregate supply elasticity with respect to prices lies in the range 0.3–0.9. It is not greater than 1.0, as is sometimes claimed by those who ascribe primacy to price policy, or as low as zero, according to those who view price policy effects as insignificant. It is higher around 0.7–0.9 in the more advanced land-abundant developing countries. However, in poorer countries with inadequate infrastructure facilities its value is lower, around 0.3–0.5. The supply elasticity with respect to non-price factors is likely to be much higher; around 1.0 in countries with inadequate infrastructural facilities, imperfect markets, and lack of capital and private research organisations. In the more advanced developing countries where farmers do not face infrastructural constraints to the same degree as their counterparts in the more underdeveloped countries, the output effect of additional non-price factors is smaller.

In some African countries where farm prices have been depressed in some cases by 20–30 per cent, through a combination of overvalued exchange rates and sector-specific pricing policy[2], an average aggregate supply elasticity of around 0.3–0.5 would suggest that agricultural output would have been on average 6–15 per cent higher without this discrimination. It is equally clear, however, that agricultural policy corrections would require more than just higher prices, as the impact of infrastructural bottlenecks on farm productivity may be very high. Agriculture has tended to suffer from under-investment in research, infrastructure and human capital. These discriminatory policies need to be given equal priority to price policies in efforts to raise agricultural productivity and growth, though in many poor agrarian economies successful action in these policy areas may be dependent on revenue from agricultural-based taxes.

METHODOLOGICAL AND CONCEPTUAL PROBLEMS

The quantification of benefits and costs of policies required to achieve higher long-term agricultural growth is complicated because some of the factors, like the adoption of new technology, are partially dependent on the price structure which farmers face. Higher farm prices induce greater effort and better management in farm production as well as higher use of inputs. On the other hand, many constraining factors, such as lack of large-scale irrigation and research, clearly fall into the category of 'public goods' and would not be forthcoming simply through higher relative farm prices[3]. The separation of the pure price effect from that of non-price factors, if at all possible, is therefore a complicated statistical exercise.

This point can be explained better with the help of Figure 4.1. Let D^1 and D^2 be the demand functions for agricultural products at two time periods t^1 and t_2. Let S^1 and S^2 be the corresponding short-run supply functions, indicating the response of output to price changes in the short run. Let us assume that a supply shift factor/technological change moves supply from S^1 to S^2 so that n_1 and n_2 define the observed prices and quantities. Let us also postulate that a part of the supply shift was price-induced, i.e. farmers made investments in response to a favourable price environment. Let this component be S^1S^{12}, so that the long-run supply curve is n_1n_3. The remainder of the supply shift $S^{12}S^2$ is therefore due to non-price factors, e.g. government investments, or government expenditures on research. The difficulty lies in trying to unravel the price-induced shift from the non-price-induced shift when the only available information is given by the observed points n_1 and n_2.

Another way of looking at the problem is to try and quantify policies required to achieve a normative growth in demand from Q_1 to Q_2 between periods t_1 and t_2. In other words, given a projected population growth rate and a desired increase in food intake per capita, demand should grow to Q_2 in year t_2. If the government does not pursue policies which would shift the supply function from S^{12} to S^2, both supply and demand would rise to Q_{12}, leaving an absolute gap of $Q_{12}Q_2$. With price policy alone, real farm prices would have to rise to P_2 to induce an increase in output from Q_1Q_2. At that price the consumer subsidy would have to be P_1P_2 for effective demand to be equal to Q_{12}.

The time horizon

Figure 4.1 also underscores the importance of the time horizon one is considering, because many of the supply shifters which private farmers would not invest in, such as research and medium and large irrigation projects, have long gestation lags. In the long run, reliance on price and incentive policies would not necessarily result in these investments, even though in the short run price policies may look relatively attractive. This is because farmers would be induced to move upwards along the short-run supply function S^{12}, creating another 'non-equilibrium' situation where the planned target Q_2 could not be met unless major consumer food price subsidies were granted.

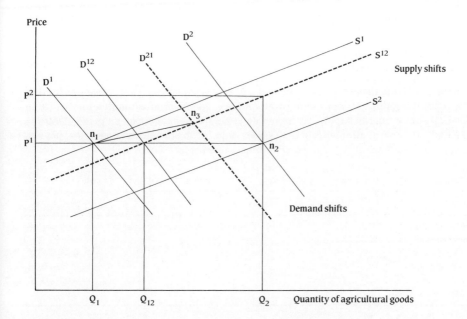

Figure 4.1 Price-induced and non-price shifts; comparative statics

Financing of policies and overall fiscal policy

Let us now introduce the problem of financing so as to enable us to place price policies in the context of overall fiscal policies. If the government desires to shift the supply function from S^{12} to S^2, it would require finance for its expenditure and investment policies. If the finance can be raised through direct taxation, and if the tax incidence falls equitably on the agricultural and non-agricultural sectors and is administratively feasible, then this can be a non-distortionary method[4] of financing government expenditure. However, in reality, administrative difficulties force governments to use indirect taxation to raise revenues, and in many developing countries the burden of such taxation falls strongly on the agricultural sector.[5]

In this case, the government must compare the cost of the consumer subsidy versus the cost of shifting the supply curve from S^1 to S^2 if it wants to evaluate alternative options for raising production and real demand to Q_2. Producers would require price P_2 to produce at Q_2 and consumers would purchase Q_2 only at price P_1. Alternatively, the government can reduce the producer price to P_1 but provide public inputs with the taxed resources such that the supply function shifts to S^2.

ESTIMATING THE RESPONSE OF AGRICULTURAL OUTPUT TO PRICE AND NON-PRICE FACTORS

In order to make a realistic assessment of the effects of different policies on agricultural growth (or the lack of them) estimates of the elasticity of aggregate supply to prices and to non-price variables are needed. The existing empirical work on the estimation of aggregate supply response can be divided into four broad categories:

(a) cross-country estimates;
(b) cross-section (farm households) estimates;
(c) inter-sectoral general equilibrium models;
(d) time series estimates.

Estimates from these four methods vary over a wide range. The cross-country and the general equilibrium approach produce the highest set of estimates for the price elasticity of aggregate supply. Comparable estimates for the long-run price elasticity of supply are also available from time series data for the developed countries, but are in general less than unity for the developing countries (see Table 4.1).

Table 4.1: *Range of previous estimates of long-run aggregate price elasticity of supply*

Method	Estimate
Cross-country	1.27 – 1.66
Time-series	
Developed	0.34 – 2.96
Developing	0.13 – 0.78
Cross-farm	–0.02 – 0.15
Inter-Sector Model	0.9

Source: Peterson (1979).

The cross-farm elasticities based on household models are either negative or not significantly different from zero. These estimates, obviously, have very different policy implications. If the long-run elasticity of aggregate supply is in general greater than unity, it provides strong validity for the argument that low real farm prices are an important reason for low agricultural productivity in developing countries. If, on the other hand, it is zero or marginally negative, a low farm price policy, for revenue or other considerations, does not necessarily conflict with the growth objective. A careful scrutiny of the methods and data used shows (a) the reasons for the wide divergence in the estimates and (b) the likely range in which the aggregate response of agriculture lies with respect to price and non-price variables.

Cross-country estimates

Peterson (1979) estimated a long-run aggregate supply function using cross-section data for 1962–64 and 1968–70 from 53 countries. A log-linear function was estimated with P, real prices received for all farm products in terms of kilograms of commercial fertiliser that could be purchased with 100 kilograms of wheat equivalents, W, a weather variable approximated by the long-run annual average precipitation, and T, a technology variable approximated by the number of research publications for each country in the sample as independent variables. Peterson concluded from his results (Table 4.2), that the long-run aggregate supply elasticity is in the range 1.27 to 1.66, and is in any case much higher than the widely accepted estimates of about 0–0.2 obtained from time series evidence. He went on to calculate the welfare costs of low price policies using his estimated meta-supply function and argued that developing countries could raise agricultural and national incomes substantially by simply raising farm prices, or by discriminating less against the farm sector.

Table 4.2: *Estimates from cross-country aggregate supply function*

Explanatory Variable		Research Included	Research and Irrigation Included
	(1)	(2)	(3)
Price	1.66	1.27	0.97
	(11.8)	(6.47)	(3.62)
Precipitation	0.303	0.290	0.369
	(2.18)	(2.19)	(2.84)
Research/ha		0.120	0.215
		(2.84)	(2.98)
D 1968–70	0.379	0.30	0.219
	(2.64)	(2.15)	(1.49)
Irrigation/ha			0.84
			(2.39)
R^2	0.612	0.646	0.71

Equations (1) and (2) are from Peterson (1979)
Figures in brackets are t-values
Functional Form: Log Linear
Estimation Method: Instrumental Variables
Data for 53 developed and less developed countries, at two time points, 1962–4 and 1968–70.
Data sources: Research/ha: Boyce and Evenson (1975), Output, Acreage, Price and Irrigated Area: FAO, *Production Year Book*: FAO Agricultural Producer Prices 1961–70.

Peterson's supply function implicitly assumes that the only major differences between the farm sectors in developed and developing countries is in the structure of price incentives and in the volume of research expenditures. Considerable evidence shows, however, that farmers in developing countries face major constraints arising either from the absence or imperfection of markets. The availability of credit, fertiliser, assured water supply, transport and communication facilities and the social and tenurial structure, in addition to geographical and ecological characteristics, are only some of the tangible non-price constraints that could not be removed simply by raising prices. In addition, a number of factors such as high-yielding seed varieties and major and some medium irrigation projects are clearly in the nature of 'public goods' whose supply can only be increased by public policy and not simply by higher farm prices. Provision of these public goods may well yield larger social returns than price increases, which would only benefit farmers who have already adopted high-yielding varieties and have access to assured water supply. These are the very farmers who do not need any further price incentives.

The importance of infrastructure facilities for raising aggregate agricultural productivity has been demonstrated strongly in a recent paper by Antle (1983). He shows in a cross-country production function that, in addition to conventional inputs, both research and infrastructure, which is measured as the gross domestic product of the country's transportation and communication industries per square kilometer of land area, are significant determinants of agricultural output. Omission of these non-price constraints from the estimating equation creates the 'missing variable' problem in econometric analysis. Such omission would lead to overestimation of supply elasticity with respect to price.

In order to demonstrate this problem empirically, three sets of empirical experiments were attempted. In the first experiment an irrigation variable (ratio of area irrigated to total area cultivated)[6] was introduced into Peterson's supply function[7]. As a result, the aggregate price elasticity of supply declined from 1.27 to 0.97, and would, in all likelihood, decline further if all structural differences across countries could be included into the analysis.

In another experiment a cross-country supply function was fitted with data from countries with yield levels less than 15 quintals of wheat equivalents per hectare. The logic behind this selection was to estimate the price elasticity of aggregate supply across countries from the same structural universe. The aggregate price elasticity of supply across this category of countries was only 0.67.

Finally, in the last experiment three country-specific shift variables which have been used successfully in cross-country production function were introduced into the supply function. Two of these variables represent natural growing conditions and are taken from a study of the potential for food production in the world by Buringh, van Heemst and Staring (1975). These are:[8] *Potential Dry Matter* (PDM) – the output in kilograms per hectare per year in roots, stems, leaves, flowers, and fruits that can be achieved if precipitation and soil conditions are optimal; and *Factor of Water Deficit* (FWD) – the ratio of actual transpiration to potential transpiration. The third variable represents infrastructure facilities in the country and is measured as the GDP per square mile in transport and communications converted into US dollars at the official exchange rate. The inclusion of these three crude cross-country shift variables again resulted in a reduction of the aggregate price elasticity of supply from 1.27 to 0.97.

Additional support for the importance of structural variables is available indirectly from other studies. Askari and Cummings (1976) analysed 320 supply price elasticities for Thailand, Chile, India and the United States for a variety of individual crops, and found that irrigation, farm income levels, and the rural male literacy rate exerted a positive and significant effect on the response of farmers to price changes.

The need for including appropriate non-price shift variables in supply functions to represent research, irrigation and other infrastructure is also evident from policy-oriented studies of Asian agriculture. Timmer and Falcon (1975) found that 85 per cent of the variations in fertiliser use in selected rice-producing Asian countries could be explained by the rice-fertiliser price ratio. But, in a carefully researched and more comprehensive analysis, David (1976) showed that with correct controls for irrigation, technology and infrastructure only one-third of the variations in fertiliser use could be explained by prices. The remainder was due to non-price variables. Studies on the 'yield gap' analysis support David's conclusions. Herdt and Wickham (1978) have attempted to determine the reasons for differences between actual and maximum attainable rice yields in the Philippines. Their findings suggest that technical factors – lack of water control, non-availability of inputs and non-adoption of new techniques – account for over 50 per cent, whereas economic factors are responsible for only 17 per cent of the 'yield gap'.

One possible solution to the problem of accounting for structural differences across countries is to include country-specific dummy variables in the supply function. Lyons and Thompson (1981) have used this approach with cross-country-cum-time series data for 13 countries to examine the effects of the corn-nitrogen price ratio on corn (maize) productivity across countries. Their results indicate that both price and non-price factors significantly explain corn productivity differences, but that the elasticity of corn productivity with respect to the corn-nitrogen price ratio is only 0.22. Using their estimates, it can be shown that prices explain only 7 per cent of the difference in corn yields between the USA and the Philippines, countries with the highest and lowest corn yields respectively, in the sample.

In a more recent study, Binswanger et al. (1987) used a sample of 58 countries for the period 1969–78 to estimate the cross-country aggregate supply elasticity. This study was unable to reproduce the high aggregate supply elasticity found in Peterson's study. It found that the aggregate supply elasticity within country (time series) with respect to the own-price is small – around 0.1–0.2 – and that the cross-country price elasticity is negative. The authors interpreted the within-country result as a short-run elasticity.

A more fundamental problem with cross-country estimation of supply functions is the establishment of the direction of causality. Supply functions implicitly assume that such direction runs from prices to output or productivity. But, recognising the importance of increased agricultural productivity for overall economic growth, it is equally plausible to argue that countries with high agricultural productivity have high per capita incomes and larger price supports for agriculture. In an attempt to explain differences in Net Protection Coefficients (NPCs) across countries, Binswanger and Scandizzo (1982) have shown that the share of agriculture in GDP, per capita income, and agricultural land per capita are all important explanatory variables. This result suggests a positive association between differences in real farm prices and productivity across countries, but the direction of causality is questionable.

Cross-farm estimates

It is important to include a review of the cross-farm estimates of the aggregate supply elasticity because the two empirical estimates using this approach show negative price elasticities of supply. Yotopoulos and Lau (1974) using a profit function, derived from a household model on farm-level data, showed that the total output elasticity in Indian agriculture was −0.15. Using the same approach with data from N.W. Malaysia, Barnum and Squire (1979) found the elasticity of rice supply to be − 0.02. Given the predominance of rice production in total agricultural output in this region, the estimates of the rice elasticity would be close to the aggregate supply elasticity.

The use of farm-level instead of aggregated data to measure the response of supply to its explanatory variables is intrinsically appealing because it measures the response of the individual agents which is cumulated to give the aggregate response. However, the method is subject to four qualifications.

First, the negative elasticities derived from this approach were attributed to the decline in agricultural labour supply resulting from higher agricultural incomes due to higher output prices. They indicate a strong revealed preference for leisure on the part of farm labour, which is unlikely at the levels of farm income obtaining in India and N.W. Malaysia.

Secondly, the models assume a closed labour market in the agricultural sector, and therefore discount the possibilities of labour flows from off-farm activities to agriculture. In a later paper, Barnum and Squire (1980) have shown theoretically that, with a sufficiently large elasticity of labour supply from off-farm sources, the aggregate supply elasticity can be positive.

Third, substitution between labour and variable capital, which is a likely outcome if farm incomes and wages increase, can overcome the shortage of labour in response to higher agricultural growth. Evidence of increased mechanisation in the green revolution economies of Punjab and Mexico points to the presence of such substitution.

Finally, farm-level price data are unreliable and difficult to collect. Moreover, poor farmers are likely to receive lower prices for their produce because they must sell immediately after the harvest. In addition, poorer farmers usually pay a higher price for purchased inputs, and also face a host of other constraints − fragmented holdings, lack of credit, lower levels of education and literacy, which are not incorporated into the analysis. As a result, differences in prices across farms may be correlated with a host of other constraining factors.

Inter-sectoral general equilibrium models

Since the aggregate supply response measures the effect of changes in the aggregate price index received by farmers relative to prices in the rest of the economy, it is logical to try and measure it in the context of an intersectoral general equilibrium model of the economy. Cavallo and Mundlak (1982) examined the effects of pricing and exchange-rate policies on Argentine agriculture with a detailed general equilibrium model of the economy. Their study showed that if agricultural prices had been higher by about 10 per cent, total agricultural output would have been about 9 per cent higher over time, implying that the long-run aggregate agricultural supply elasticity is around 0.9.

An interesting feature of this study was its ability to trace movements in labour and capital in response to intersectoral price changes. Moreover, it showed that technological change in agriculture is also retarded when agricultural prices are depressed.

This happens because technological change is embodied in capital and is therefore a function of capital formation. If price changes lead to movement of capital out of agriculture, technological change in agriculture also slows down. The aggregate response of agricultural output to price changes is therefore larger than just the sum of movements in the factors of production. In the Argentine case Cavallo and Mundlak showed that nearly half the supply response came from the technology effect. This finding was consistent with those of de Castro and Schuh (1977) regarding the effects of pricing policies on technical change in selected crops. The estimates of the aggregate supply response from a general equilibrium model should, however, be treated as an upper bound since they do not fully account for all the constraints faced by farmers in the real world.

Time series estimates of output elasticities

Two basic methods have been used to estimate aggregate supply elasticity from time series data: (a) aggregation of input demand elasticities: indirect method, and (b) supply function estimation: direct method.

AGGREGATION OF INPUT DEMAND ELASTICITIES: INDIRECT METHOD

Griliches (1959) and Tweeten and Quance (1968) estimated aggregate supply elasticity for the United States by aggregating over the product of the elasticity of supply with respect to input i (Eqz_i) and the elasticity of demand for input i ($Ez_i p$).

$$Eqp = \Sigma_i \, Eqz_i . Ez_i p$$

The same method has been used by Rayner (1970) for the United Kingdom and by Pandey, Pigott and MacAulay (1982) for Australia.

If data on inputs and input prices are available, then this method is likely to provide unbiased estimates of input and aggregate supply elasticities. But the problem is that detailed data on each significant input use are not readily available, especially in developing countries. Moreover, estimates of production functions from which one derives Eqz_i break down due to severe multi-collinearity between the different inputs.

Aggregation of individual commodity supply elasticities can also be used to obtain estimates of the sectoral supply elasticity. Herdt (1970) has used this method to calculate the aggregate supply elasticity for India in the period 1907–46 and 1951–64 and obtained aggregate elasticities of 0.42 and –0.06 for the two periods respectively. The method is again very complex and requires knowledge of the supply elasticities of each crop produced.

DIRECT METHOD: SUPPLY FUNCTIONS

Studies using supply function estimation originated from Nerlove's (1958) work on the dynamics of supply. Nerlove's model is formulated in three steps. Step 1 postulates optimal output as a function of expected prices, non-price shifters and weather.

$$Q^* = ao + a1.Pe + a2_i.Z_i + U \qquad (1)$$

where Q^* is optimal output and Pe expected prices and Z_is are non-price shift variables. The difficulty is that observed data do not give us either optimal output or the expected prices. We only have observations on the actual prices and final output reached after the producers' efforts to attain the optimal output.

In order to get around this problem, Nerlove specified a Bayesian revision of price expectations and an adjustment mechanism.

$$Q(t) - Q(t-1) = d\,(Q^*(t) - Q(t-1))\qquad(2)$$

$$Pe(t) - Pe(t-1) = r\,(P(t-1) - Pe(t-1))\qquad(3)$$

Substituting (2) and (3) into (1) gives us an estimatable reduced form from which the original coefficients can be derived.

Empirical work on the response of supply to prices has been largely based on variants of Nerlove's formulation. Attempts have been made to find suitable data for the model and to take into account other factors which impinge on production and acreage allocation decisions, such as risk, weather conditions, size of farm, tenancy, and education. Askari and Cummings (1976) have tried to explain variations in estimates of individual crop supply elasticities in these studies.

This direct method of estimation has been used in a recent detailed study of Ajmer district in India by Bapna (1980). He presents six estimates of the aggregate supply elasticity using different models of price expectation formation. Three of the six models generate reduced-form price variables with low coefficients of annual variation, and the other three produce relatively high coefficients. Two of the three price variables with low coefficients of variation show higher elasticity in the range 0.5–0.6, as against price variables with high coefficients of variation which produce supply elasticities in the range 0.2–0.25. Bapna's results are particularly interesting because they indicate that the estimates of the supply elasticity also depend on the definition of the price variable. His results, however, cannot be used for national policy formulation because they refer to the aggregate agricultural supply elasticity for a single district, which in all likelihood will be higher than the aggregate agricultural supply elasticity for the entire country.

Besides a number of Indian studies (see also Krishna, 1982), the only available estimates of the aggregate supply elasticity using time-series data are for Argentina, Ghana and Kenya. The estimates for Argentina (Reca, 1976) are very useful because they are based on a model specification which includes the intersectoral terms of trade, refer to the entire country and include two relevant non-price shift variables – credit and technology. The results indicate that the aggregate price elasticity of supply lies between 0.21–0.35 in the short run and 0.42–0.78 in the long run. These parameters are smaller than the derived aggregate supply elasticity in the intersectoral study of Argentina by Cavallo and Mundlak (1982) which, as indicated earlier, probably represents an upper bound for the supply response. Reca's estimates also provide the aggregate supply elasticity with respect to the shift variable – credit. This elasticity lies in the range 0.11–0.19.

In a more recent study Bond (1983) estimated aggregate supply functions for nine countries in sub-Saharan Africa. The Nerlovian-functional form was used. A time trend variable was introduced to capture the impact of technological change on output. A dummy variable was also used for weather shifts. The price elasticity was significant in only two countries – Ghana and Kenya – where the long-run elasticity was found to be 0.34 and 0.16 respectively.

Aggregate output response in Indian agriculture

The Argentina studies by Reca (1976) show a fairly high aggregate supply elasticity. In order to test whether that result can be generalised an aggregate supply elasticity was estimated for India. Productivity levels in India are lower, land constraints are more binding, and the role of publicly provided infrastructure, such as irrigation, much greater than in Argentina. One would therefore expect the aggregate supply elasticity to be smaller than in the case of Argentina. A Nerlovian model was applied. Irrigation was used as a proxy for non-price variables because of its importance in the use of high yielding varieties that are responsive to fertilizer.

ESTIMATES

The short- and long-run elasticities with respect to lagged prices and irrigation – the non-price proxy variables – are presented in Table 4.3. Equation 1 shows that without the inclusion of the irrigation variable the aggregate long-run price elasticity of supply is greater than 2. However, with the inclusion of the irrigation variable the long-run price elasticity is only 0.30, whereas the elasticity of output with respect to the irrigation variable is approximately equal to 1. With the dummy variable for the post-1965–6 period also included in the equation, the corresponding long-run price and non-price elasticities are 0.39–0.43 and 1.17–1.28 respectively. It can be concluded that in India in the period 1954–5 to 1977–8 the elasticity of aggregate output, with respect to non-price factors, was approximately three times the elasticity with respect to inter-sectoral prices.

A comparison of results of the equations with and without the irrigation variable is also interesting in the context of the cross-country estimates. If appropriate non-price shift variables are not included in the estimating equation with time series data, the price elasticity is in the high range of elasticities obtained from cross-country data, demonstrating the need for inclusion of non-price shift variables in cross-country estimation of supply functions.

Table 4.3: *Elasticities of agricultural output with respect to prices and non-price variables India, 1954–5 to 1977–8*

Equation Number	Elasticity with respect to	
	Terms of Trade	Irrigation
(1) short-run	0.22–0.23	
long-run	2.28–3.61	
(2) short-run	0.18–0.19	0.59–0.68
long-run	0.28–0.32	0.99–1.01
(3)	0.23–0.26	0.96–0.97
(4)	0.39–0.40	1.13–1.20
(5) short-run	0.28–0.29	0.82–0.85
long-run	0.39–0.43	1.17–1.28

* Elasticities from Equations (3) and (4) lie between the short and long runs. Empirically they are closer to the long-run elasticities.

Variables Dictionary

Equation 1: P_{-1}, W, Q_{-1}
Equation 2: P_{-1}, W, I, Q_{-1}
Equation 3: P_{-1}, W, I
Equation 4: P_{-1}, W, I, D
Equation 5: P_{-1}, W, I, D, Q_{-1}

> where P_{-1}, lagged terms of trade for agriculture; W, weather; I, percentage of area irrigated; D, Dummy equals 1 after 1965–66; Q, agricultural output.

LESSONS FOR STRUCTURAL ADJUSTMENT

Adjustment programmes usually involve major macroeconomic and sector-specific policy changes which affect the structure of relative prices in the economy. Typically, a major objective of many adjustment programmes has been to change the internal terms of trade in favour of agriculture.

The results of this survey of the aggregate supply response indicate that changing the incentive structure faced by farmers is an important, but not the only, component of a balanced policy package to raise agricultural productivity. In many low-income countries, agricultural response is often constrained by poor roads and transport facilities, unimaginative and inefficient research and extension services, lack of assured water supply and power, and poor health and education services. In this context the simple-minded notion that price adjustments will lead to the economy unconstrained, and to a higher equilibrium level of output, is not enough. The provision of public goods and services – non-price factors – must play a key role in the adjustment process.

It is important to emphasise this because adjustment operations are often undertaken during the period when public expenditure budgets are highly constrained. In this environment, cuts in the public expenditure programme are often indiscriminate and across the board, affecting the supply of critical public goods and services. The results of this survey show that if these cuts are large they can negate the expected supply response from improvements in price incentives initiated under the adjustment programme. If overall expenditure cuts are unavoidable, it is crucial to protect the most useful investments and services.

In countries in which agriculture provides the predominant tax base the issue of balance between price and non-price policy takes on an added dimension. If direct taxation of agricultural income is not administratively or politically feasible, then raising agricultural prices will reduce public revenues, requiring further cuts in public expenditures. Some of these will affect the delivery of public goods and services to farmers who were the intended beneficiaries of the adjustment programmes. The significance of such trade-offs will vary from one country to another, but should be considered in the formulation of an adjustment policy package.

These trade-offs obviously do not arise in countries in which heavy and indiscriminate taxation of agriculture has been used primarily to transfer resources to other sectors of the economy. In these countries improvements in the internal terms of trade of agriculture will obviously increase farm output. In some countries improvements in the delivery of public goods and services to farmers do not necessarily require more resources. Instead allocation within existing budgets and institutional changes can lead to significant improvements in the structural environment under which farmers operate.

NOTES

1 See Lardy (1986) and Raj (1983) for contrasting viewpoints.
2 See World Bank (1986). Chapter 4 for documentation.
3 Private research has concentrated on mechanical technology and plant protection where it is easier to extract economic returns to the new technology.
4 It is non-distortionary in the sense that it would not induce intersectoral resource shifts. It may, of course, affect the labour-leisure choice.
5 See World Bank (1986) for a documentation of the extent of indirect taxation of agriculture.
6 Irrigation facilities are partly public and partly private. Although the expansion of private irrigation facilities is dependent on public subsidies credit, the price structure may also be a contributory factor. 2 SLS estimation was used to account for the effect of prices on irrigation.
7 The author is extremely grateful to Professor Peterson for providing a copy of his data set.
8 These two variables were used by Mundlak and Hellinghausen (1982) in a cross-country production function.

REFERENCES

Antle, J.M. (1983), 'Infrastructure and Aggregate Agricultural Productivity: International Evidence', *Economic Development and Cultural Change*.

Askari, H. and J.T. Cummings (1976), *Agricultural Supply Response: A Survey of the Econometric Evidence*, New York, Praeger.

Bapna, S.L. (1980), *Aggregate Supply Response of Crops in a Developing Region*, Delhi, Sultan Chand and Sons.

Barnum, H.N. and L. Squire (1979), 'An Econometric Application of the Theory of the Farm-Household', *Journal of Development Economics*, Vol. 6.

Binswanger, H.P. and V.W. Ruttan (1978), *Induced Innovation: Technology, Institutions and Development*, Baltimore, Johns Hopkins University Press.

—— and P.L. Scandizzo (1982), 'Patterns of Agricultural Protection', unpublished paper, November.

——, M. Yang, A. Bowers and Y. Mundlak (1987), 'On the Determinants of Cross-Country Aggregate Agricultural Supply', *Journal of Econometrics*, Vol. 36.

Bond, M.E. (1983), 'Agricultural Response to Prices in Sub-Saharan African Countries', Washington DC, *IMF Staff Papers*.

Boyce, J.K. and R.E. Evenson (1975), *Agricultural Research and Extension Programs*, New York, Agricultural Development Council Inc.

Buringh, P., H.D.J. van Heemst and G.J. Staring (1985), 'Computation of the Absolute Maximum Food Production of the World', Wageningen, Holland, Department of Tropical Soil Science.

Cavallo, D. and Y. Mundlak (1982), 'Agriculture and Economic Growth in an Open Economy: The Case of Argentina', Washington DC, *IFPRI Research Report*, December.

Centre for Monitoring Indian Economy (1980), *Basic Statistics Relating to the Indian Economy*, Vol. 1, All India.

David, C.C. (1976), 'Fertilizer Demand in the Asian Rice Economy', *Food Research Institute Studies*, Vol. XV, No. 1, Stanford University.

De Castro, J.P.R. and E.G. Schuh (1977), 'An Empirical Test of an Economic Model for Establishing Research Priorities: A Brazil Case Study' in T.M. Arndt et al. (eds), *Resource Allocation and Productivity in National and International Research*, University of Minnesota Press.

Griliches, Z. (1959), 'The Demand for Inputs in Agriculture and a Derived Supply Elasticity', *Journal of Farm Economics*, Vol. 41.

Hayami, Y., E. Bennagen and R. Barker (1977), 'Price Incentives Versus Irrigation Investment to Achieve Food Self-Sufficiency in the Philippines', *American Journal of Agricultural Economics*, November.

Herdt, R.W. (1970), 'A Disaggregate Approach to Aggregate Supply', *American Journal of Agricultural Economics*, Vol. 52, No. 4, November.

—— and T.H. Wickham (1978), 'Exploring the Gap Between Potential and Actual Rice Yields: The Philippines Case', in *Economic Consequences of the New Rice Technology*, Los Banos, Philippines, International Rice Research Institute.

Indian Government, *National Accounts Statistics, Central Statistical Organization*, various issues.

Johnson, D.G. (1973), *World Agriculture in Dissarray*, New York, St. Martin's Press.

Judd, M.A., J.K. Boyce and R.E. Evenson (1982), 'Investing in Agricultural Supply', unpublished paper.

Krishna, R. (1982), 'Some Aspects of Agricultural Growth, Price Policy and Equity', *Food Research Institute Studies*. Vol. XVIII, No. 3, Stanford University.

Lardy, N.R. (1986), 'Prospects and Some Policy Problems of Agricultural Development in China', 'China in Transition', a special issue of *American Journal of Agricultural Economics*, Vol. 68, No. 2, May.

Nerlove, M. (1958), *The Dynamics of Supply: The Estimation of Farmers' Response to Price*, Baltimore, Johns Hopkins University Press.

Lyons, D.C. and R.L. Thompson (1981), 'The Effect of Distortions in Relative Prices on Corn Productivity and Exports: A Cross Country Study', *Journal of Rural Development*, Vol. 4, June.

Pandey, S., R.R. Piggott and T.G. MacAulay (1982), 'The Elasticity of Aggregate Australian Supply: Estimates and Policy Implications', *Australian Journal of Agricultural Economics*, Vol. 26, No. 3, December.

Peterson, W.L. (1979), 'International Farm Prices and the Social Cost of Cheap Food Policies', *American Journal of Agricultural Economics*, February.

Raj, K.N. (1983), 'Agricultural Growth in China and India: Role of Price and Non-Price Factors', *Economic and Political Weekly*, 15 January 1983, Special Article.

Rayner, A.J. (1970), 'The Demand for Inputs and the Aggregate Supply Function for Agriculture', *Journal of Agricultural Economics*, Vol. 21, No. 2.

Reca, L.G. (1980), 'Argentina: Country Case Study of Agricultural Prices and Subsidies', Washington DC, World Bank Staff Working Paper No. 386.

Sanderson, F.H. and S. Roy (1979), *Food Trends and Prospects in India*, Washington DC, Brookings Institution.

Schultz, T.W. (1979), *Distortions of Agricultural Incentives*, Bloomington, Indiana, Indiana University Press.

Timmer, C.P. and W.P. Falcon (1975), 'The Impact of Price on Rice Trade in Asia' in G. Tolley (ed.), *Agriculture, Trade and Development*, Chicago, Ballinger Press.

Tweeten, L.G. and C.L. Quance (1969), 'Positivistic Measures of Aggregate Supply Elasticities: Some New Approaches', *American Journal of Agricultural Economics*, Vol. 51.

World Bank (1986), *World Development Report 1986*, Oxford, Oxford University Press.

Yotopoulos, P. and L.J. Lau (1974), 'On Modelling and the Agricultural Sector in Developing Countries', *Journal of Development Economics*, Vol. 1.

PART TWO

The Impact of Structural Adjustment Programmes

MULTI-COUNTRY STUDIES

5

The Economics of Rural Poverty Alleviation

Tony Addison & Lionel Demery

INTRODUCTION

It is surely ironical, if not quite perverse, that the recent re-awakening of interest in poverty alleviation in developing countries has come at a time of general recession. But it is also understandable, bearing in mind the austerity caused by the recession itself and by the adjustment policies that it has occasioned. It has long been recognised that re-distribution is a much easier political prospect during periods of rapid growth than during prolonged recession. Herein lies a real dilemma; the sheer force of the recession in most of developing Africa and South America has rendered poverty in many of these countries life-threatening and alarming. Yet, without growth, the task of providing urgent alleviation is made all the more difficult. Not surprisingly, recent reviews of how to cope with these dismal policy dilemmas have emphasised the importance of resuming growth, as without it the prospects for poverty alleviation are grim indeed (Cornia et al., 1987).

In the present chapter this perspective is developed by emphasising the importance of increasing the *primary* incomes of the rural poor during adjustment, taking these incomes to be those that are generated through the production of goods and services. Some recent contributions (see Huang and Nicholas, 1987) have surprisingly confined themselves to examining only 'secondary' incomes such as government transfers. In our view, this limitation is both unnecessary and unhelpful. Structural adjustment programmes are designed to bring about major changes in the structure of output, and in the distribution of primary claims, so that it is perfectly appropriate to question whether poor people benefit from the changes brought about by adjustment.

In much of the recent literature, discussion has centred on how the poor have been adversely affected by adjustment, how to identify the groups who have suffered and how to mobilise transfers to tide them over these difficult times. In this chapter, we take a more positive stance, by investigating the processes through which adjustment

* This is a revised version of the paper given at the ODI conference, and was presented at a symposium on 'Poverty and Adjustment' (April 11–13, 1988) organised by the Country Economics Department of the World Bank. Financial support from the World Bank for this work is gratefully acknowledged.

programmes can actually benefit the rural poor, especially through generating increases in primary incomes[1]. Five broad approaches are distinguished:

— enhancing the rates of return on the assets they hold;
— increasing their access to productive assets;
— creating employment opportunities;
— maintaining their human capital;
— increasing income and consumption transfers.

The first four of these categories relate to primary incomes, and these will be the principal preoccupation here. Our discussion of income and consumption transfers is included under human capital-enhancing approaches, partly for convenience, but also because many of these transfers have significant effects on productivity, and can be legitimately considered as investments in human capital in their own right.

ENHANCING RETURNS ON ASSETS HELD BY THE POOR

Perhaps the most obvious means of raising the incomes of the poor is to increase the rate of return on the assets they hold. In many cases, the poor possess only their labour, so that increased incomes can only be brought about by increases in real wages or in employment (see later section in this chapter). But the poor frequently hold other productive assets. Enhancing the returns to these assets, either through increasing output prices and productivity, or reducing input costs, can be a means of achieving both the output objectives of structural adjustment and a reduction in poverty. Government provision of improved economic (or physical) infrastructure can also play an important part in raising the returns poor households derive from their assets. As we shall discuss below, recent cut-backs in state expenditures may have resulted in a deterioration in the physical infrastructure which, *ceteris paribus*, could reduce the rates of return from productive assets.

Removing price distortions

A fundamental tenet of structural adjustment is the removal of distortions in product and factor markets. Many of these distortions, such as import controls, confer significant income gains for the favoured few, mainly through the creation of rents. Insofar as this income is derived from unproductive activity, the distortions generate income transfers towards the higher-income groups. The removal of distortions may therefore reallocate resources away from relatively well-off groups and at the same time improve resource allocation.

The distributive effects of both imposing and removing market distortions are highly complex, and will differ between the short and long terms. In the short term, during which time no factor mobility is possible, the effects on incomes are likely to be greater. In the longer term, after both capital and labour reallocations are made, individual income changes are not likely to be as large. For example, pro-urban market interventions will inflict greatest harm on rural producers and confer greatest benefit to urban groups during the initial period. But this will result in rural to urban migration, which reduces the income differential caused by the distortions. Similarly the income consequences of removing distortions can be expected to vary over time.

Initially, urban groups will suffer most. But factor mobility (such as return migration responses) would tend to reduce these impact effects. The following analysis concentrates on the short-run effects of the removal of price distortions.

Agricultural prices and inequality: some issues

Much attention has been given to the distortions caused by low producer prices, especially in sub-Saharan Africa. Since the poor are predominantly located in agriculture in most developing countries, shifts in the agricultural terms of trade through the removal of policy biases against agriculture are potentially a powerful device for the alleviation of poverty. However, while there is no doubt that price-policy reforms have, in many countries, helped maintain many farmers' incomes, a number of issues have to be faced in assessing the effectiveness of this approach to increasing the incomes of the poor through structural adjustment.

The gains from producer price increases. The extent to which poor farmers gain from higher prices for food crops depends on whether they are able to produce a marketable surplus above their current consumption needs. In most countries there is an inverse correlation between the probability of a household being in poverty and the size of its marketed surplus, as, for instance, indicated by Kenyan data (Greer and Thorbecke, 1986: 131). In Tanzania Collier et al. (1986: 75) find that subsistence crops account for over 70 per cent of household income among poor groups, which is double the share of such income in the total household incomes of the non-poor. Higher producer prices will not have a significant impact on the poverty of farmers who market very little output, and who produce mainly for their own consumption. The benefits of price reform to producer incomes may thus by-pass some rural poverty groups. This is most likely to occur in sub-Saharan Africa where subsistence farming is more prevalent than in other regions. However, it is difficult to be conclusive on this point in the absence of satisfactory data on the incidence of subsistence. Pure subsistence is rare; more usually the poorest farmers have good years in which they can market some surplus after meeting their consumption needs. In the case of Tanzania cited above, the poor will gain some benefit even though the largest benefits will accrue to the non-poor. How many people move above the poverty line will depend on how low their incomes were prior to the producer price increases, and the size of those increases.

The benefits of higher producer prices to poor farmers also depend on the extent to which they cultivate cash crops in addition to staple food crops. Although recent adjustment programmes have included price reform measures for both staple foods and cash crops, the prices of the latter have tended to rise more than for food prices, reflecting the need to raise export earnings under adjustment. Whether farmers can cultivate the most remunerative cash crops partly depends on the ecological region in which they are located. Rural poverty is often highest in regions where farmers are unable to grow cash crops such as coffee and tea. Accordingly the benefits of price reforms for cash crops will often be distributed unequally across regions. This factor is particularly important in sub-Saharan Africa where ecological conditions are a major determinant of crop-mixes given the limited technologies available to farmers.

To take one example, in Côte d'Ivoire farm incomes tend to be much lower in the savanna region of the north than in the southern forest region where conditions are better suited to growing a wider range of crops. The average farm in the savanna region has an income per capita of CFAF 38,000 compared with CFAF 120,000 in the southern region. The main crops grown in the latter region are cocoa, coffee, some annual food crops (rice, maize) and tree crops (oil palm, coconut). In the drier savanna, maize is the dominant crop, followed by yams, while cash cropping is mainly limited to cotton. Food producers have the lowest incomes. Farm-level data show per capita incomes of only CFAF 34,000 in 1985 for annual food crop savanna farmers compared with CFAF 68,000 for cotton/food crop savanna farmers and CFAF 122,000 for cocoa and coffee farmers in the forest region. Both regions contain poor farmers, but the savanna region has the largest share. Glewwe and de Tray (1987) have traced how many poor households have benefited from the agricultural price-policy reforms conducted in Côte d'Ivoire over the 1980s. They find that producer-price increases for cash crops have benefited about half of the poor in the country. In the savanna region numbers of poor farmers grow cotton, but the largest improvements can be expected to occur in the south where some of the poor also grow tree crops.

Better targeted assistance to poor farmers may be necessary to help them raise their productivity. In Zimbabwe, for example, policies aimed at increasing the returns on assets held by the rural poor have been directed towards improving agricultural extension services in poorer areas. There are two distinct agricultural sectors in Zimbabwe, the commercial farms which benefit from better rainfall and use modern inputs, and the traditional smallholder sector in the so-called communal areas. These farms are not so well placed for rainfall, and their access to both modern inputs and marketing facilities is inadequate. The Zimbabwean Government is aware of the difficulties faced by small-scale farming as regards both marketing output and obtaining inputs at reasonable cost. With these farms organised in geographically dispersed small units, there are serious problems in encouraging input use and increased output. The agricultural extension service is now mainly directed towards the small-scale farmer in an effort to increase the application of inputs. Moreover, agricultural research is increasingly directed towards the needs of small-scale farmers.

In short, measures to implement price policy must be designed and administered so as to ensure that small farmers participate and benefit fully. This means that either price increases apply to the commodities produced by small farmers, or that direct micro-oriented policies are followed that encourage production switching towards those commodities receiving price support.

Rural infrastructure. Adjusting prices may not be a *sufficient* policy to enhance the output and incomes of target groups, if they lack access to supporting infrastructure. More often than not, the poor in developing countries are located in areas badly placed for transport networks, important services, such as roads and other forms of communication, agricultural services, marketing facilities, and so on. Improving prices may be a necessary condition for restoring incomes, but not a sufficient one. If farmers face real supply bottlenecks, economic infrastructural investments may be required to give these farmers the *capacity* to increase output and yields. Agricultural output is dependent on the development of rural infrastructure and support services which, especially in sub-Saharan Africa (SSA), are not always sufficient to support rapid output growth.

The emphasis of policy conditionality under World Bank programme lending in SSA has been on production switching through relative price changes, the latter being achieved through closing the gap between domestic and world prices. But the adjustments required of countries in SSA to correct their internal and external disequilibria have not only affected prices. Bond's (1983) study highlights a crucial aspect of agricultural production growth in SSA in relation to stabilisation and structural adjustment. For most countries, agricultural growth exhibited a negative time trend. This she attributes to the 'unfavourable climate for agricultural investment that has been created, the deterioration of the infrastructure and support services available to the rural farmer, and the growing lack of cash goods to the rural sector'. There have been a chronic depletion of the region's transportation, shortages of inputs into sectors servicing agriculture (for example, agro-industries) and severe budgetary constraints affecting agricultural investment.

The remarkable growth in Indonesian agriculture illustrates how incomes and employment prospects among rural communities can be improved through a combination of increased production incentives *and infrastructure development*. Agricultural growth rates have been high, even by East Asian standards, averaging 4.1 per cent over the period 1978–85. From being a major importer of rice in the late 1970s, Indonesia has become self-sufficient. Increased returns in agriculture are due to two elements of government policy. Under its adjustment programme, including the devaluations of the currency, it has raised farm-gate prices. The recent move away from non-tariff trade barriers in the industrial sector is expected to improve agriculture's terms of trade by reducing the cost of inputs into the sector. Second, the government has given a high priority to expanding rural infrastructure and support services. The expansion of irrigation and greater use of high yielding varieties, and their related production technologies, have resulted in an increase in crop area and yields.

In this context, a key issue is whether the restructuring of government investments can fully compensate for the declines in expenditure levels imposed under the constraints of stabilisation. In the case of Indonesia, the ability of the government to protect investment allocations to agriculture throughout the adjustment period has led to a favourable climate for productivity growth. In Côte d'Ivoire, the proportion of government investment directed towards agriculture rose from 25 per cent in 1983 to 35 per cent in 1985. But total expenditure has declined dramatically (from CFAF 272bn in 1981 to CFAF 88bn in 1985). Despite the re-orientation of government investment, the level of resource allocation is certain to have fallen, and the longer-run prospects of agricultural output growth to have been adversely affected. Increasing the rates of return on assets held by the poor, therefore, may require more than improved price incentives, namely fundamental improvements in rural infrastructure and agricultural services. This implies a need for more resources than are currently available.

The role of productive assets. Raising the returns on the assets held by the poor will not make large inroads into their poverty if their access to productive assets is limited. The distribution of productive assets is a powerful determinant of the distribution of marketable surpluses across households, and thus in turn of the income gains that farm households obtain from price reforms. This is most clear in the economies of South Asia. For example, in Bangladesh it is estimated that on average 77 per cent of the gross marketable surplus of rice is produced by 15 per cent of farms, reflecting the large inequality in land-holdings which prevails in that country (Ahmed, 1981: 9). An increase in the producer price of rice will offer only marginal benefits to poor farmers. While higher rice prices will raise the demand for hired labour as output expands, Ahmed (1981: 46) finds that the employment effect is small since farmers increase labour inputs by first using more family labour[2].

Furthermore, while the rural poor in South Asia may achieve only small benefits as producers, they can suffer large losses as consumers. Rice is the basic staple of food-deficit farm households, as well as landless labourers. Rough estimates show that on average the rural poor in Bangladesh and India derive 50 per cent of their calories from market purchases (Lele, 1985: 179), and short-run variations in the incidence of rural poverty are closely correlated with fluctuations in food prices.

In countries with large inequalities in the ownership of productive assets, and where the poor are very dependent on the market for meeting their food requirements, there is a real danger that raising food prices to encourage production may have detrimental effects on the rural poor. However, we do not draw the conclusion that price reforms should be abandoned for this reason. Clearly the health of agricultural economies requires that appropriate price incentives should be offered to farmers. But price reforms need to be accompanied by measures that enhance the access of the poor to productive assets, both to allow them to share more fully in the income gains generated by producer price increases, and to reduce any adverse consumption effects on them. It is to these measures that we now turn.

INCREASING ACCESS TO PRODUCTIVE ASSETS

In many developing countries, the limited availability of productive assets is a major constraint on the ability of poor people to respond significantly to the incentives generated by adjustment. Assets, in Kitching's (1977) graphic terms, get households onto upward 'income escalators'; those in possession of them are in the best position to profit once growth begins, a principle established in the literature of 'Redistribution with Growth' (Chenery et al., 1974). In reviewing the opportunities to increase the productive assets of the poor during adjustment, two aspects are emphasised: land holdings and access to credit. We have already touched on the importance of the former in the previous section, while the latter can be considered as a proxy for access to a variety of productive assets (fertiliser inputs, livestock, non-traditional inputs, capital equipment etc).

Land reform

There is little doubt about the importance of land in determining the welfare of the rural poor. For Asia, rural landlessness is a major factor in explaining rural poverty (Griffin and Khan, 1977), whilst even in Africa, where land availability is not as serious a problem, land tenure difficulties are beginning to appear. Landlessness is emerging as a serious problem in Kenya (Collier and Lal, 1986) and Malawi (Ghai and Radwan, 1983). Even traditional land tenure systems in Africa (in which the community allocates lands to individuals) are becoming less equitable (Feder and Noronha, 1987). Among landholders, the size of holding is an important determinant of real income. Greer and Thorbecke (1986) have established a robust negative relationship between landholdings and poverty in Kenya, where 70 per cent of the rural poor are smallholders. In sum, land tenure is becoming an important issue for poor households, even in sub-Saharan Africa[3].

The role played by land in determining the poverty impact of shifts in the agricultural terms of trade is highlighted by comparing India with South Korea. A recent simulation study by de Janvry and Subbarao (1986: 93) using a computable general equilibrium model (CGE) for India concludes that raising producer prices will lead to an increase in both income inequality and poverty. The money incomes of poor farmers or labourers rise, but the cost of their basic staples increases by more, and their real incomes accordingly fall. The authors contrast this result with that of Adelman and Robinson's (1978) CGE of South Korea, a country which has had comprehensive land reform,

> In that country [South Korea], the poor are principally small farmers with a positive marketed surplus. For them, improvement in the agricultural terms of trade represents a benefit and not

a cost. This is not the case in India where an exhaustive land reform has failed to occur and where 47 per cent of the rural population are net buyers of food.

It may seem surprising at first to suggest that land reform might be introduced into structural adjustment programmes, bearing in mind the political support that is required to implement such a policy effectively. Periods of recession and adjustment entail enough political difficulties without imposing a policy reform which can potentially exhaust whatever political capital a government has been able to retain. There are, however, three broad reasons why this approach merits some consideration:

— First, existing systems of land tenure and land distribution may be inefficient, so that land reform would be an effective instrument for improving resource allocation, and raising productivity growth. With most structural adjustment programmes concerned to reduce the costs of resource mis-allocation, land reform may be considered a legitimate policy instrument to achieve this objective. Much of the discussion on land reform in the Philippines, for example, has been couched in these terms; land reform is considered as one of the policy instruments under the government's economic recovery programme. Viewed in this way, land reform measures can help achieve the objectives of both poverty alleviation and structural adjustment.

— Secondly, governments in receipt of structural adjustment assistance from the multilateral agencies may be more prepared to consider fundamental policy reforms which may have been beyond discussion during better times. This 'back-to-the-drawing-board' case for introducing land reform on the political agenda may have some force in countries with limited access to international credit markets.

— Finally, land reform has already appeared in a number of structural adjustment programmes (in Thailand, Kenya, Brazil and the Philippines), and therefore merits further consideration in the future policy design.

Clearly, the role that land reform can play within the context of poverty alleviation under structural adjustment depends on the particulars of each case, and it would be foolhardy to attempt any generalisations. However, experience to date highlights two opposing considerations; on the one hand, land reform is seen to be a particularly difficult policy to implement under normal circumstances, let alone during periods of recession and adjustment. Secondly, it also appears to hold considerable prospects for improving agricultural productivity over the medium to long run, and at the same time helping to alleviate rural poverty.

The political constraints. First, very little effective land reform has been achieved within the context of structural adjustment programmes, despite a number of attempts. In the first and second World Bank Structural Adjustment Loans (SALs) for Thailand an attempt was made to introduce land reform which granted poor farmers in the north-east region 'right-to-farm' certificates for land that they had earlier been cultivating illegally (Demery and Addison, 1987). These measures, however, did not go far enough, in that they fell short of granting full legal ownership. Although the Thai Government has implemented a study of land reform in the north-east, partly as a result of this initiative, it is fair to conclude that the reforms only proceeded as far as political expediency permitted. It should be emphasised that the land concerned was entirely state-owned, so that the reform under consideration can be viewed as a relatively softer option than more typical reforms which involve transfer of land away from large landowners.

Similarly, land reform was included in the policy conditions for the 1982 SAL II in Kenya. Although the government agreed to prepare a programme for reform by March 1983, in the event nothing materialised. The reforms concerned also involved mainly state-owned land. The reasons for the failure of this initiative are undoubtedly political. Opposition to land reform proposals in the Philippines and in Brazil (over the Land Tenure Improvement Project for the north-east region) have also clouded the prospects for these programmes. Predictably, opposition from large landowners in both countries is a major factor in limiting the implementation of reforms to marginal or state-owned lands.

In short, the message of experience to date is that land reform is an extremely difficult prospect for governments to consider during periods of adjustment. This may be due to concern over its 'political-capital' effects – a concern which is undoubtedly heightened during periods of recession and adjustment. But it may also be the result of a more considered assessment of possible adverse short-run output effects caused by the disruption land reform inevitably entails.

The potential benefits. The beneficial effects of land reform on agricultural productivity and incomes among those countries that have considered such reform under structural adjustment/recovery programmes are most clearly demonstrated in the case of Thailand. In studies of the implications of the reforms in SALs I and II for farm productivity, Feder et al. (1987) found that the right-to-farm certificates had little or no effect on productivity and income levels. This was due to the fact that the farmers concerned could not use the land as collateral to secure institutional credit, since they had no legal title to it. Farmers holding the right-to-farm certificates were found to have lower levels of productivity, land improvement and input use compared with land-owning farmers who were similar in other respects. According to this study, there are considerable productivity and output gains to be obtained from effective land reform. In other words, had the land reforms gone further, and granted legal title to the farmers in the north-east, the interests of structural adjustment would have been better served. This convergence of interest of poverty alleviation and structural adjustment seems to apply also to the cases of land reform in Kenya, the Philippines and Brazil mentioned above.

Institutional credit

The example of land reform in Thailand also serves to emphasise the key role played by institutional credit in granting access to other productive assets (than land). Land-holdings were seen to be crucial in determining the access of poor farmers to credit and to the inputs which credit facilitates. The question therefore arises: can policy intervention within structural adjustment programmes improve the availability and terms of institutional credit to the poor, especially those engaged in self-employment activities – farming and non-farm small-scale enterprises (for example in the informal sector)?

Farm credit. The supply of credit to the rural poor obviously depends on the development of lending institutions in rural areas which are generally ill served by credit services. However, even with institutionalised credit generally available, the poor will have little or no access to it if they lack the necessary collateral to secure a loan. Generally, households with above-average non-farm incomes (Collier and Lal, 1984: 1015) and those holding individual land titles have much greater access to institutional credit[4]. What is obviously required is the development of lending instruments that are tailored to the needs of small borrowers, and which can spread the high risks such lending usually entails. The group-lending activity of the Grameen Bank in Bangladesh will certainly offer insights into how credit institutions can orient their lending to the small-scale activities of poorer groups without increasing the risks unduly. This issue is taken up again in the discussion on employment opportunities for the poor (see next section).

Informal sector credit. The provision of assistance to the *informal* sector can be an important area for policy intervention to help the urban poor gain better access to productive assets. A common feature of most adjustment periods is the absorptive role played by the informal sector. Workers disengaged from formal employment move into informal activities, either tradable or non-tradable. This is often simply a manifestation of low levels of labour utilisation during an adjustment phase. In this context, assistance should concentrate on those informal activities producing tradables (ECLAC, 1986: 60). This mainly implies a focus on small-scale manufactures and non-personal services.

A body of experience now exists regarding the cost-effectiveness of technical assistance to the informal sector. For example, techniques have been developed (such as lending to groups) that can reduce the administrative costs of providing credit to micro-enterprises. But this may require accommodating policy changes that can encourage micro-enterprise schemes to grow. Such policy changes include the modification of registration and other legal requirements that may be unrealistic for very small enterprises, and the liberalisation of credit markets, with special attention to reducing restrictions on lending to small enterprises.

CREATING EMPLOYMENT OPPORTUNITIES

The process of structural change set in motion by adjustment programmes inevitably has far-reaching implications for the level and composition of employment[5]. Large reallocations of human resources take place as enterprises and households shift into the production of tradables. For households which are producing units, this process may simply involve changing their output mix. For some households it may involve a change in location in order to gain access to new employment opportunities. For others, it will be necessary to seek new employment through entering the labour market. Thus the process of labour reallocation under adjustment will be widespread, and is therefore of special interest to policy-makers.

The impact of adjustment on employment

Once the process of structural adjustment is complete, and productive factors have been reallocated, employment prospects should be much better than those prior to adjustment, simply because policies that had previously reduced labour absorption will have been reformed. Overvalued exchange rates reduce the cost of imported capital and favour its substitution for abundant local labour. Low agricultural producer prices discriminate against a sector that has very high labour-absorptive capabilities. Although some non-tradable sectors are often labour-intensive (for example private and public services), most of the tradable sectors encouraged by the adjustment process should be *relatively more* labour-intensive – small-farm agriculture and labour-intensive export manufactures are important examples. In addition to these resource-reallocative effects, a successful adjustment programme would benefit employment prospects in the long term if it restored economic growth.

While we can be reasonably confident that the long-term prospects for employment are better after successful adjustment than before, difficulties can nevertheless occur during the transitional period when the economy is being restructured. If unemployment occurs among politically vocal groups, their reaction could undermine the government's commitment to adjustment. In addition, growing unemployment would have a devastating effect on the poor, since they usually lack the resource base to tide them over until employment recovers.

Transitional unemployment under adjustment is likely to occur for a number of reasons. In practice, production-switching from non-tradables to tradables is far from the smooth process implicit in many orthodox economic models. Fiscal and monetary restraint reduce the demand for non-tradables, leading to declines in labour-demand in these sectors. How this is shared between cuts in wages and employment depends on whether real wages are flexible downward. Likewise the domestic demand for tradables will fall, and it may take some time for producers to locate compensating foreign markets. In the interim they may shed labour (and/or cut wages), rehiring labour and restoring payments once foreign sales are secured.

Even with a policy mix geared towards supply-incentives, the expansion of the tradables sector will still require new investments, particularly in supporting infra-structure. In general, declining non-tradable sectors can be expected to respond fairly quickly to adverse market signals, but the expansion of tradable output can only be as fast as the expansion of capacity. If tradable activities are expanding only slowly, while non-tradables are contracting rapidly, an employment problem is likely.

These difficulties will almost certainly be greater when agents have unclear expectations about the adjustment programme, since these influence the speed at which resource reallocations are made. If the private sector believes that the programme is not *credible* – for example that policies are likely to be reversed – it will be reluctant to reallocate its resources. Moving into tradables could be an expensive mistake if adjustment is abandoned and the policy bias against these sectors is restored. Programmes are all the more likely to lack credibility if there is a past history of programme breakdown. Producers may therefore delay decisions. For similar reasons redundant workers may delay moving into tradable employment, especially if this involves migration costs for them.

Finally, employment losses are often concentrated in particular sectors, so that their labour shake-out may create special problems. Industries will be affected by the reduction in their rates of protection under trade liberalisation and reduced government subsidies. Labour retrenchments from state and parastatal enterprises are often part of a general reduction in public employment. This is necessary from both a micro-perspective – to reduce administrative inefficiency – and from a macro-perspective – to cut the government budget deficit and to move resources out of non-tradables, the latter often comprising mainly government services. At such times, large numbers of public employees may appear on the labour market.

The role of employment policy

With these observations in mind, what can governments do to minimise the employment problems of adjustment? A number of policy interventions suggest themselves.

Increasing labour mobility. First, policy can aim to increase the occupational and geographical mobility of labour, by assisting movement into activities and locations which are favoured by the adjustment process. People are often poor because their participation in the most profitable activities is restricted. The previous section has already discussed the lack of productive assets which constrains poor households, and the kinds of assistance discussed there may be needed to enhance occupational mobility. Help may take the form of land, tools and other facilities. Training is also important to help poor families acquire the new skills now in demand under adjustment. In the restructuring of education expenditures it is desirable to make special provision for such training.

One particular problem is whether assistance to the unemployed should take the form of loans. The difficulties in organising small-scale loan schemes in developing countries are well-known: low rates of repayment and the use of loans for purposes other than those agreed are common. In addition, the very poor are often excluded because they lack collateral. The Indigenous Business Advisory Service (IBAS) project in The Gambia funded by ILO and UNDP illustrates the latter problem. IBAS provides credit and training to people establishing small businesses, and redundant public employees have been referred to it. IBAS loans are geared to those with the most collateral. Past defaults on unsecured loans have led to financial difficulties for IBAS (and the Gambian banks), and it is naturally reluctant to reduce its recently raised collateral requirements. This is a tricky problem which must be faced in a number of countries because restoring soundness to their financial systems does not favour experimenting with new schemes to reach the poor. Yet some success is possible. The Grameen Bank in Bangladesh has reduced the need for collateral, and its ability to reach small farmers with low default rates has attracted much interest. The ILO is looking at the possibility of transferring this model to The Gambia, as a way of helping the poor during adjustment.

Enhancing geographical mobility is especially necessary if the urban unemployed are to move into agriculture and other rural-based activities. However, encouraging the urban poor to take up farming is not the easy solution it sometimes appears to be. Much will depend on how far the urban poor have retained their village links, whether there is land available for them, and – critically – whether they have any farming skills. Second- or third-generation urban immigrants can have very weak links with their rural kin, and may have no farming skills at all. Land constraints in Latin America and Asia can make it very difficult for the urban poor to find agricultural self-employment even if they have farming skills. Indeed, land-shortage often forced their migration to the towns in the first place. Return-migration to the country is generally easier in Africa than in other developing regions because of the nature of the urban-rural migration that takes place (which is often circulatory), and the relative abundance of land. Nevertheless there may be substantial difficulties in achieving such migration in some African countries if they are highly urbanised (for example Zambia) and if land-pressure exists (for example Kenya).   .

Where the urban unemployed lack farming skills, the resources needed to help them establish themselves in farming can be sizeable. Projects to resettle retrenched public employees in farm co-operatives are now underway in Guinea-Bissau. The co-operatives will produce food, and this will help restore Guinea-Bissau's food security, a central objective of the adjustment programme. The projects involve substantial land reclamation and infrastructural investments. The costs of this exercise are not small, and conclusions on the benefits of the schemes must await analysis of project rates of return. Moreover, while the retrenched public employees are from the lowest skill grades, and have low incomes, they are far from being the poorest and most unskilled in society. Assisting the most destitute in urban societies to relocate to rural areas, and to become self-supporting farmers, will require very carefully designed programmes.

These projects must take place in the context of an adjustment programme that is sending out clear signals that previous policy discrimination against agriculture is being eliminated. Expectations, as discussed earlier, are crucial. People who have viewed farming as an unrewarding activity for years will not rush back to agriculture. In many countries farming has a low social status. To reverse such sentiments inevitably takes time.

An example of the role of expectations is provided by the IBAS scheme in The Gambia, to which reference has been made. Of the projects selected for assistance, over 60 per cent are in retailing (mainly urban), which is overwhelmingly non-tradable. Only 20 per cent of funded projects are for farming, despite the priority of this sector for adjustment. This reflects the sector preferences of most applicants. For at least the last decade it has been urban rather than rural businesses which have been the most profitable in The Gambia, reflecting the very large urban-rural income disparity created by the policy environment. With chronic shortages of consumer goods, large economic rents have been made in retailing. While goods are now more plentifully available under the donor-backed adjustment programme, the perception still remains that urban retailing, even if it is small-scale, remains the best prospect for self-employment. With policy reforms now generating strong incentives for agriculture, and the beginning of the recovery of rural incomes, it is hoped that these perceptions will change, and that IBAS will receive more requests for urban based projects.

'Make-work' programmes. Secondly, projects can directly provide employment to target groups through so-called 'make-work' programmes. However, projects which help the unemployed to become self-supporting are superior although much more difficult to organise than make-work schemes. Accordingly, the cost-benefit calculations in weighing up the relative merits of temporary employment programmes versus self-employment projects are quite complex. In general, while the short-term costs of make-work are lower, the longer-term costs are higher than the (slower-yielding) alternative. Unfortunately governments often give more weight to the short-term than the long-term costs in their calculations, and opt for the make-work alternative (gambling that recovery will come soon). The fiscal austerity required under adjustment further encourages this approach.

If make-work programmes have to be used then there are ways to improve their benefits. The first is to focus on tradable-orientated activities, or in non-tradable activities which are essential to the expansion of tradables – construction work on roads serving export regions is one example of the latter. This will contribute to the success of the adjustment effort, thus speeding up the time that economic recovery is achieved and the programmes are no longer needed. Many of the Latin American programmes have been poorly organised and have been directed at non-tradable activities with low benefits for the adjustment effort. The second improvement is to provide some on-the-job training to participants to raise their skill levels and improve their chances of better employment. Finally, steps should be taken to devise structures of payment that reward skills, thus encouraging participants to seek on-the-job training.

This brings us to the vital issue of how assistance is to be organised given the demands placed by adjustment on the government's scarce administrative resources. Mobilising the organisational capacities of local communities, if it can be done, is one way to minimise administrative demands on central government. In Bolivia, the World Bank and other donors are assisting the Emergency Social Fund (Fondo Social de Emergencia, or FSE), which finances projects put forward by municipalities, co-operatives, NGOs, and other community organisations. These organisations act as the executing agencies for projects mainly focused on small-scale employment and income-generation. The target groups include unemployed workers (including former tin miners) and informal sector workers (particularly women). Again local and international NGOs through their work with poor urban communities provide some of the best vehicles for the difficult task of designing projects for very deprived people. OXFAM, for example, is helping poor communities – both rural and urban – to take up activities which increase their self-reliance.

Public works programmes in which the unemployed are paid a small daily stipend (normally in cash but sometimes in food) are usually a 'second-best' solution. Such programmes are generally implemented to provide 'temporary' relief for the unemployed while they search for permanent jobs. The most extensive of these measures to be implemented under adjustment are the emergency employment programmes (EEPs) run by the Government of Chile (Demery and Addison, 1987: 22). Although such programmes provide much needed help to the unemployed, they must pay a wage very much lower than the prevailing market wage in order to encourage participants to seek regular employment. Usually the stipend covers only a fraction of the household's consumption needs, leaving little possibility of saving to establish a self-supporting business. If the unemployment problem is expected to be only temporary then the fact that the unemployed do not become self-supporting may not be critical, since employment will recover. But if unemployment persists then there is little chance of the poor leaving the programme. Such programmes can end up covering large numbers of people, but conferring very little benefit to each and consuming significant amounts of public resources.

An assessment of employment policy under adjustment

We have discussed a range of policy interventions for improving employment prospects during adjustment. The best of these not only assist the target group, but also contribute to the success of the adjustment programme through encouraging employment in tradable sectors. Throughout this discussion we have emphasised the importance of careful design in devising employment projects. Too many employment projects degenerate into de facto transfer mechanisms, public-works programmes being a case in point. Transfers to the poor may well be desirable (and are discussed below), but if that is the objective then specific transfer programmes should be designed rather than letting employment programmes do the job by default. However, designing and implementing good projects takes time and resources, which are in restricted supply if adjustment has to be implemented rapidly. Donors can play an important role in providing project resources and personnel to relieve part of this constraint. But the large local commitments required must make governments even more thorough in examining the allocation of their manpower resources and budgets if they want to create space for high-return employment projects.

The reform of government interventions that impede the functioning of labour markets, and thus lead to a misallocation of labour resources, is also required. The performance of labour markets is a critical determinant of the way in which the costs and benefits of adjustment are distributed across society. Since the labour market acts as a clearing house through which human resources are allocated and reallocated, its performance has a direct bearing on the welfare of households. Yet the performance of this key market is usually far from satisfactory. Even before the economic turbulence of the 1980s, the existence of underemployment, unemployment and wage rigidities attested to problems in the operation of labour markets in many developing countries, and these will affect both the success of the adjustment programme as well as its social impact.

Finally, something must be said about the specification of priorities for employment assistance. Ex-public sector employees are not generally among the poorest in the community, although many of the unskilled have low incomes. In Africa, where the main public sector retrenchments are taking place, this group is now receiving assistance under a number of programmes. While many in this group will suffer hardship, they have benefited from the over-expansion of public employment that took place during the last decade, which has often been financed at the expense of poor farmers. Given this, there are grounds for concentrating scarce public resources on helping the very poorest to get the maximum benefits from the structural change engendered by adjustment. But whether this is politically manageable is another question.

MAINTAINING HUMAN CAPITAL THROUGH SOCIAL EXPENDITURES AND TRANSFERS

Most families often have little else but their labour endowments, and the returns that are obtained from the sale of their labour services are often critically conditioned by their human capital. Such households are faced with the difficult task of husbanding their meagre resources to meet their needs for food, health care, sanitation and education. But fluctuations in earnings, health and family circumstances all act to constrain their choices. On average in developing countries, illness disrupts normal activities for about one-tenth of a person's time (World Bank, 1984). Not only does this affect current productivity and income, but through being unable to obtain sufficient health care, human capital deteriorates, and with it permanent income. Children represent major investments for future family earnings, yet these investments are under constant threat from malnutrition and debilitating illnesses. These problems interact: meeting current health needs may require cutting back on investments in education, cutting female education leads to higher child-mortality and morbidity, withdrawing children from school provides current income at the cost of future incomes, and so on.

For these reasons, ensuring that the poor have access to health care, education and other services that protect and enhance their human capital should be a crucial component of poverty-focused adjustment programmes. In addition, the public transfers which poor people receive are often vital to their well-being, either directly as in the case of food transfers and their effect on nutrition, or indirectly when cash transfers supplement their incomes. At the same time adjustment requires the protection and enhancement of public expenditures on directly productive sectors and economic services. There exists therefore a trade-off between protecting social programmes and transfers on the one hand and crucial economic expenditures on the other.

How much room for manoeuvre do countries have?

A government's room for manoeuvre in protecting poverty-focused welfare programmes depends on two factors: first, its overall pre-adjustment development strategy, and secondly, the structure of its social and transfer expenditures.

Pre-adjustment conditions. As with the problem of employment, much depends on the country's economic circumstances before adjustment. Take the case of a country engaged in 'non-tradable'-led growth prior to adjustment. The policies behind this growth path engendered a steady appreciation of the real exchange rate and other effects which increasingly discriminated against tradables. This growth process invariably becomes unsustainable, since it is based on growing dependence on external borrowing, especially in an increasingly adverse international economic environment.

Consequently an adjustment programme to reverse the shift in output away from tradables and to cope with the trade shock is warranted, and when this eventually comes, the compression in non-tradables required to switch resources to tradables will be larger than if the economy had been more tradable-orientated to begin with. Since public expenditures on social programmes are by and large non-tradables, the *potential* compression required in these activities in the former case will be greater than in the latter. The problem will be exacerbated if the non-tradables leading the growth process have been social programmes – for example in the case of a 'populist' government which has sought political support on the basis of expanding social expenditures.

On these grounds a government has more room for manoeuvre in avoiding cuts in social expenditures when the economy is orientated to its comparative advantages in tradables, rather than when it is based on non-tradables. However, countries suffer trade shocks of different durations and magnitudes depending, for instance, on the characteristics of their exports. The most severely shocked economies will have to make large resource shifts out of non-tradables, and will have to diversify their tradable sectors, thus leaving their governments with much less manoeuvrability than in more favoured countries.

The room for manoeuvre for governments previously following a non-tradable-led growth strategy will be further aggravated on the revenue side. Recession inevitably reduces a government's tax base, and thus its ability to fund social programmes without deficit financing.

Again many of the African economies now undergoing adjustment present a particular picture of their own. As we emphasised earlier, a number of these countries have tried to avoid comprehensive adjustment by relying on controls to compress imports. Economic stagnation results as such controls eventually bite into imports of intermediate inputs. This has three effects on government's ability to deliver social programmes:

— the fall in economic activity cuts the domestic revenue base and thus public resources for programmes;
— excise duties are important sources of public revenue and these fall with import compression;
— social services are directly hit by being unable to obtain the required imports of drugs, books etc as well as by the generalised shortages of fuel.

In such situations the effective delivery of social services has almost always fallen sharply prior to the adoption of a comprehensive donor-supported adjustment programme.

If governments fail to pursue adjustment sufficiently, the economy's ability to generate sufficient tax revenues to finance social expenditures will remain weak. Without such revenues (and in the absence of external financial support) governments are forced to cut social budgets, whether they want to or not. Failure to adjust, or insufficient adjustment, reduces the government's room for manoeuvre in its budget decisions. In such situations maintaining social expenditures by increasing taxation is equally not a sustainable solution given the continued decline in the taxable economic base. Even if a comprehensive adjustment programme fails to achieve its objectives – because of a new external shock for example – the situation post-adjustment is often still superior to that pre-adjustment, because some gain will have been made in tradable output, thus allowing a larger measure of protection to social budgets than if adjustment had not been undertaken, and the additional domestic resources not generated.

In the case of severely import-compressed economies, the implementation of comprehensive donor-backed adjustment may be associated with a significant rise in social programmes since: (i) the foreign-exchange constraint on their supply is directly eased, (ii) donor commitments can be made to social programmes, and (iii) the relaxation of the foreign-exchange constraint will raise the economy's capacity utilisation from its low level, thus increasing the taxable economic base, and thereby easing the government's revenue constraint.

The structure of social programmes. In addition to the orientation of the country's overall development strategy, a government's room for manoeuvre on its welfare programmes depends on the structure of those programmes. Consider social services first, and in particular their distribution across society. Governments have more room to protect social expenditures benefitting the poor if the distribution of such services has been weighted to the rich, than if the distribution has been more egalitarian. In the former case, expenditures benefiting the better-off can be cut proportionately more or can take all of the cut-back, thus raising the *share* of the poor. In very unequally distributed systems there may even be room for raising not only the share but the *absolute* amount of services to the poor, while still achieving sizeable cutbacks in total budgets, through cutting expenditures to the better-off. Major problems arise when countries have a relatively egalitarian structure of social services prior to adjustment.

We therefore need empirical evidence on the distribution of social expenditures before being able to pronounce on the severity of the likely trade-off between social programmes for the poor and essential adjustment-related expenditures. Measuring such incidence raises conceptual and practical problems, but work is now under way in a number of agencies. A recent World Bank policy study estimates that in most developing countries 70 per cent or more of public expenditure on health is taken by urban hospital-based care (World Bank, 1987: 22). Given the large urban-rural income differentials prevailing in developing countries, this inevitably favours the better-off. Cornia et al. (1987) and the World Health Organisation have also pointed to the large inequalities that exist in public health care provision. Similarly, wealthier groups are over-represented at all levels of the public education system in developing countries, especially in Africa. Rough calculations show that 'the children of white-collar workers accumulate four to five times as much public education expenditure as do the children of rural workers', with the ratio rising to 10:1 in Francophone Africa (World Bank, 1986b: 16). These data, while highly aggregative in nature, imply that many governments do have some room for protecting poverty-focused programmes if they are forced to cut social budgets.

Transfer programmes must be considered in a similar way to establish how far their benefits reach the poor. There is much evidence that food subsidies have disproportionately benefited the relatively better-off in many countries (see for instance World Bank, 1987). The principle of 'targeting' is now well established (World Bank, 1986a and Berg, 1987), and a number of governments could make resource savings, and give more help to the poor, by replacing global food subsidies with targeted food interventions. As with other poverty-focused interventions care must be taken to ensure that food assistance does not reduce the incentive to work. In the context of adjustment it is important that such assistance does not unduly inhibit the mobility of the poor – for example by reducing the incentive of the urban poor to take up farming. In addition, food assistance makes demands on government resources and administrative capabilities, and forms of assistance which minimise these costs are especially desirable during times of budget austerity. Thus providing the poor with food stamps rather than with food itself reduces programme costs since the government is not responsible for the distribution of the food which remains an activity of the private sector (Reutlinger, 1988).

While the call for restructuring welfare programmes to favour the poor is now loud and clear, implementation raises some difficulties, even aside from the political questions involved. With regard to social programmes, the irreversibility of past investment decisions assumes great force: social capital is far from being so malleable that hospitals can be reshaped into rural clinics. Investments have been made in physical capital, personnel and administrative capacity. All of these take time to reorientate, and new investments and personnel training must be undertaken. Likewise, transfer programmes need time to be reorientated although the problems of sunk investments in capital and equipment are not so great as in the case of health. While it may take time to adjust transfer programmes, governments may find that they can achieve this sooner than for social programmes. So in the short term the protection and enhancement of the human resources of poor families may have to rely on transfers rather than major interventions through health care.

SOME CONCLUSIONS ON POVERTY ALLEVIATION UNDER ADJUSTMENT

This chapter has emphasised the importance of assisting the poor through the processes that generate their primary incomes, thus allowing the scarce public resources available for transfers to be concentrated on the most needy families. However, programmes which work through the primary incomes of the poor, and those that supplement their secondary incomes, must be carefully co-ordinated in their phasing. Critically, it may take some time for the primary incomes of the poor to improve, even if they are already in tradable sectors, since productivity-enhancing assistance (including the enhancement of human capital) takes time to implement and to deliver its benefits. Many poor families derive their incomes from non-tradable activities (such as informal services in urban areas), and their assistance will require careful appraisal and intervention. So during this period of transition – which will vary substantially across households – some targeted secondary transfers are crucial.

A key feature of all countries pursuing adjustment is the heavy strain that is placed on public resources. Budgets for both development and recurrent expenditures must meet the demands of investments in infrastructure in turn required to support price reforms. Administrative resources are under great pressure as all aspects of micro- and macro-policy come under review. If the main route to helping the poor is through the extension of public activities, then there is a real danger that poverty alleviation will be crowded out under adjustment.

Whatever the tensions created during periods of adjustment, it is clear that the trade-off between poverty alleviation and the objectives of structural adjustment (stability, allocative efficiency and growth) are complex and difficult to establish *a priori*. We are of the opinion that there is greater policy flexibility than many would have us believe. If greater emphasis is placed on creating and enlarging primary incomes of the poor, especially in tradable and supportive sectors, this will allow policy-makers room for manoeuvre. However, in many cases it will undoubtedly expose governments to political uncertainties, so that, in the last analysis, whether or not the poor are in fact protected during and beyond adjustment depends on political will.

NOTES

1 This chapter is based on an earlier contribution (Demery and Addison, 1987) in which country examples were discussed in some detail. Here, the emphasis is on the principles involved, with reference to the country cases by way of illustration.

2 In addition the increase in the rice price leads to the substitution of rice for jute in production, and this substitution effect adversely affects employment since jute is a more labour-intensive crop than rice.

3 This is even more applicable when land *quality* is taken into account. Poorer households generally possess some land, though this is frequently of poor quality.

4 Here is another example of the 'income escalator' – possessing productive land gains access to other productive assets.

5 Our discussion here will be concerned with both wage employment and self-employment, and the term 'employment' will be used to cover both. During adjustment people often move from wage employment to self-employment, so a fairly wide definition of employment is needed to describe their circumstances.

REFERENCES

Acton, J.P. (1975) 'Non-monetary Factors in the Demand for Medical Services: Some Empirical Evidence', *Journal of Political Economy.*

Addison, T. and L. Demery (1985) *Macro Economic Stabilisation, Income Distribution and Poverty: a Preliminary Survey*, London, Overseas Development Institute, Working Paper No. 15, February.

Adelman, I. and S. Robinson (1978) *Income Distribution Policies in Developing Countries*, Stanford, Cal., Stanford University Press.

Ahmed, R. (1981) *Agricultural Price Policies Under Complex Socioeconomic and Natural Constraints: The Case of Bangladesh*, Washington DC, International Food Policy Research Institute, Research Report No. 27, October.

Berg, A. (1987) *Malnutrition: What can be Done?*, Baltimore, Johns Hopkins University Press.

Bond, M.E. (1983) 'Agricultural Response to Prices in sub-Saharan African Countries', Washington DC, *IMF Staff Papers.*

Chenery, H., M.S. Ahluwalia, C.L. Bell, J.H. Duloy and R. Jolly (1974) *Redistribution with Growth*, Oxford, Oxford University Press.

Collier, P. and D. Lal (1984) 'Why Poor People Get Rich: Kenya 1960–79; *World Development*, Vol. 12, No. 10.

—— and D. Lal (1986) *Labour and Poverty in Kenya 1900–1980*, Oxford, Oxford, University Press.

—— , S. Radwan and S. Wangwe with A. Wagner (1986) *Labour and Poverty in Rural Tanzania*, Oxford, Oxford University Press.

Cornia, G.A., R. Jolly and F. Stewart (eds) (1987) *Adjustment with a Human Face: Volume 1*, Oxford, Clarendon Press for UNICEF.

de Janvry, A. and K. Subbarao (1986) *Agricultural Price Policy and Income Distribution in India*, Delhi, Oxford University Press.

Demery, L. and T. Addison, (1987) *The Alleviation of Poverty under Structural Adjustment*, Washington DC, World Bank.

ECLAC (1986) 'The Economic Crisis: Policies for Adjustment, Stabilization and Growth', Twenty-First Session, Mexico City, 17–25 April.

Feder, G. et al. (1987) *Land Policies and Farm Productivity in Thailand*, Baltimore, Johns Hopkins University Press.

—— and R. Noronha (1987) 'Land Rights Systems and Agricultural Development in sub-Saharan Africa', *World Bank Research Observer*, Vol. 2, No. 2.

Ghai, D. and S. Radwan (eds) (1983) *Agrarian Policies and Rural Poverty in Africa*, Geneva, International Labour Office.

Glewwe, P. and D. de Tray (1987) 'The Poor during Adjustment: a Case Study of Côte d'Ivoire', World Bank, Policy Planning and Research, (mimeo) November.

Greer, J. and E. Thorbecke (1986) 'Food Poverty Profile Applied to Kenyan Smallholders', *Economic Development and Cultural Change*, Vol. 35, No. 1.

Griffin, K. and A.R. Khan (eds) (1977) *Poverty and Landlessness in Rural Asia*, Geneva, International Labour Office.

Huang, Y. and P. Nicholas (1987) 'The Social Costs of Adjustment', *Finance and Development*, Vol. 24, No. 2.

Jamal, V. (1985) *Structural Adjustment and Food Insecurity in Uganda*, Rural Employment Policy Research Programme, Working Paper WEP 10–6/WP73, Geneva, International Labour Office, October.

Johnson, O. and J. Salop (1980) 'Distributional Aspects of Stabilization Programs in Developing Countries', *IMF Staff Papers*, Vol. 27, No. 1.

Kitching, G. (1977) *Economic and Social Inequality in Rural East Africa: the Present as a Clue to the Past*, Swansea, Centre for Development Studies, University of Swansea, Monograph No. 1.

Lal, D. (1984) *The Real Effects of Stabilization and Structural Adjustment Policies: an Extension of the Australian Model*, Washington DC, World Bank Staff Working Paper No. 636, March.

Lele, U. (1985) 'Terms of Trade, Agricultural Growth, and Rural Poverty', in J. Mellor and G. Desai (eds) *Agricultural Change and Rural Poverty*, Baltimore, Johns Hopkins University Press for the International Food Policy Research Institute.

Pinstrup-Andersen, P. (1985) 'Food Prices and the Poor in Developing Countries', *European Review of Agricultural Economics*, Vol. 12, 1/2.

Reutlinger, S. (1988) 'Efficient Alleviation of Poverty and Hunger: A New International Assistance Facility', *Food Policy*, February.

World Bank (1980) *Health Sector Policy Paper*, Washington DC.

—— (1984) *Towards Sustained Development in Sub-Saharan Africa: a Joint Program of Action*, Washington DC.

—— (1986a) *Poverty and Hunger: Issues and Options for Food Security in Developing Countries*, Washington DC, February.

—— (1986b) *Financing Education in Developing Countries*, Washington DC.

—— (1987) *Financing Health Services in Developing Countries: An Agenda for Reform*, Washington DC.

—— (1988) *Education Policies for Sub-Saharan Africa: Adjustment, Revitalisation, and Expansion*, Washington DC.

6

The Impact of Macroeconomic Adjustment

Food Security & Nutrition

Per Pinstrup-Andersen

Severe economic crises have made macroeconomic adjustments necessary in most developing countries during the last ten years. These adjustments have been attempted through changes in monetary, fiscal, exchange rate, foreign trade, wage, and price policies aimed at demand contractions and/or supply expansions with or without major changes in the structure of the economy. The immediate goals of these policies usually are to remedy an acute foreign-exchange deficit (usually referred to as 'stabilisation') and to stimulate long-term economic growth (often referred to as 'structural adjustment').

Until recently, and with a few notable exceptions, short-term effects on the poor have usually been ignored or given low priority in the design of adjustment programmes unless they were perceived to threaten political stability. Yet, because adjustments frequently include changes of particular concern to the poor (for example, increasing food prices, reduced real wages, and declining government expenditures on social programmes), those effects can be severe. Furthermore, disinvestment in human capital through deterioration in nutrition, health, and education will hamper future economic growth and thus counter long-term solutions. Investment in human capital must accompany investment in physical capital. Finally, policies which cause severe hardships to the poor may result in political instability which, in turn, reduces the impact on economic growth.

Thus, explicit consideration of short-term effects on the poor in the design of macroeconomic adjustment programmes is important to avoid unacceptable human suffering in the short run and to facilitate economic growth and improved well-being for all in the longer run. This chapter provides a brief synthesis of what is currently known about the short-term effects of macroeconomic adjustment policies on the food security and nutritional status of the poor, assesses the adequacy of current knowledge for policy design, and proposes action to improve the food security and nutrition effects of future adjustment programmes.

Quantitative evidence of the impact of macroeconomic adjustment programmes and policies on income distribution, poverty, food security, and nutritional status is very scarce. However, due primarily to efforts by UNICEF and collaborators in a number of countries, indicators of the main effects on these variables are beginning to emerge.

IMPACT ON MORTALITY, NUTRITIONAL STATUS, AND FOOD SECURITY

Although insufficient data and time lags do not permit a systematic assessment of the effects of specific adjustment policies, a pattern of deterioration in the nutritional status of pre-school children is apparent in the information available (Table 6.1). It is not clear whether these deteriorations are lagged results of economic recessions that led to adjustment or to the adjustments themselves. However, since most of the countries shown in Table 6.1 undertook major adjustments during the period for which data were available, it may be concluded that adjustment policies either had negative nutrition effects or were unable to counter negative effects caused by other factors. In either case there is cause for concern.

Table 6.1: *Malnutrition among pre-school children and infant mortality rates (IMR) for selected countries and time periods*

	% malnourished pre-school children		IMR (per thousand)	
	Period	First & Last Yr.	Period	First & Last Yr.
Brazil			1982–84	65–73
Botswana	1982–84	25–31	1981–86	68–65
Chile	1982–84	8.8–8.4	1981–84	27–20
Ghana	1980–84	35–54	1970s–80s	86–107
Jamaica	1978–85	38–41		
Peru	1980–83	42–68		
Philippines	1981–85	18–22	1981–84	62–58
Sri Lanka	1979–82	6.1–9.4	1978–80	37–34
Zimbabwe	1982–84	20–20		
South Korea			1979–81	38–36
Uruguay			1983–85	29–32

Source: Cornia (1987).

In many countries infant mortality rates (IMR) continued a long-term trend of improvement during the early 1980s, although at a slower pace. A considerable time lag is expected between macroeconomic policy changes and changes in IMR and a slower rate of reduction in IMR may be an indication of future increases unless something is done. Such increases have been detected in several countries – Brazil, Ghana, and Uruguay, for example.

A long-term trend of falling child mortality rates in Brazil was reversed in 1982. The increase since 1982 is more pronounced in the poorer states (Figure 6.1). The reversal was accompanied by a significant increase in the prevalence of low birth weight, an indication of deteriorations in maternal nutrition (Figure 6.2). Although the causes of the increase in child mortality rates and deteriorations in maternal (and probably pre-school child) nutritional status are not identified, it appears that large falls in real incomes of the poor may be at least partially responsible (Figure 6.2).

Evidence from several other countries where the economic recession has required severe adjustment confirms the deterioration in malnutrition and infant and child mortality rates in recent years. In Mexico, energy consumption among the poor fell by 13 per cent between 1982 and 1984, the IMR increased from 5 to 5.5 from 1981–2 to 1983 and the proportion of infant deaths due to malnutrition increased (Lustig, 1986). In Uruguay, the IMR increased from 28.6 to 31.8 between 1983 and 1985 and long-term declines in IMR in Costa Rica were replaced by a constant IMR during the early 1980s (Cornia, 1987). In Bolivia, one-third of all deaths among infants were nutrition-related in 1972, increasing to two-thirds in 1982 (Musgrove, 1987).

Small but significant increases in malnutrition occurred in both urban and rural areas of Jamaica during 1978–85 (Boyd, 1987) and nutritional wasting (per cent of pre-school children with weight-for-height less than 80 per cent of standard) in Sri Lanka almost doubled between 1975/6 and 1980/82 (Sahn, 1986). Deteriorations in the nutritional status of pre-school children in Jamaica are indicated by significant increases in the proportion admitted to the Bustamente Childrens' Hospital suffering from malnutrition/gastroenteritis (Figure 6.3).

Figure 6.4 presents a somewhat more detailed picture of changes in IMR and malnutrition in the Philippines. While IMR continued to decrease, a significant deterioration in the nutritional status of pre-school children appears to have taken place since 1982. Whether this will result in increases in IMR in the years to come depends largely on whether anything is done to avoid it.

Reductions in food consumption by the poor during periods of adjustment are now documented for a few countries. Furthermore, as shown in Table 6.2, and Figures 6.5 and 6.6, it appears that such reductions are inversely correlated with income level and that the highest income groups have suffered no such reductions.

Table 6.2: *Average daily per capita calorie consumption in Greater Santiago, Chile 1969 and 1978*

	1969	1978	% change
Poorest 20%	1,925	1,626	–16
Next 20%	2,113	1,875	–11
Next 20%	2,422	2,176	–10
Next 20%	2,830	2,504	–12
Richest 20%	3,160	3,186	0
Average	2,587	2,328	–10

Source: Raczynski (1988).

Thus, both the absolute level of food consumption by the poor and the relative distribution among income strata have deteriorated. In view of the very low levels of energy and nutrient intakes by the poor prior to the periods of adjustment, the observed reductions are almost certain to have had negative nutrition effects although households will attempt to counter the effects of adversity in a variety of ways. One such mechanism is substitution among foods in the diet towards cheaper calories. Table 6.3 illustrates such substitution by urban households in Costa Rica. The effects of decreasing purchasing power on the ability to meet energy needs were countered by shifting to foods providing cheaper energy, i.e. carbohydrates. Thus, the consumption of carbohydrates was maintained unchanged between 1978 and 1982, a period of severe economic hardship, while protein and fat consumption was reduced by 8 and 6 per cent, respectively. These reductions refer to the average urban consumption. Much larger reductions were undoubtedly found among the poor.

Figure 6.1: *Child mortality rates in Brazil by region 1977–84*

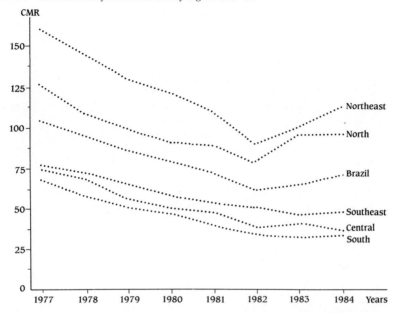

Source: Becker and Lechtig, (1986)

Figure 6:2 *Cost of fixed food basket (a) child mortality rate, (b) and low birth weight (c) in northeast Brazil 1977–84.*

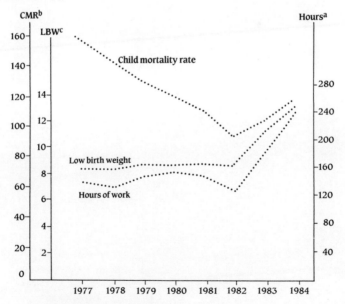

a) In working hours at minimum wages
b) CMR per 1000
c) LBW in percent of all newborn

Source: Ibid

Figure 6.3: Admissions of children below 5 years of age with malnutrition/gastroenteritis in percent of all admissions at the Bustamente Childrens Hospital, Jamaica 1978–85

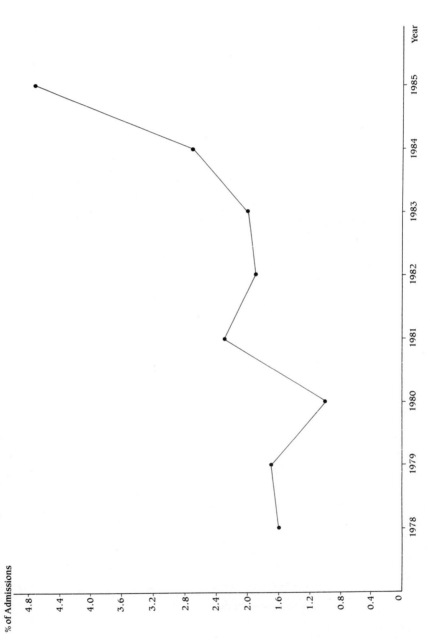

% of Admissions

Figure 6.4: *IMR and prevalence of malnutrition among pre-school children (weight/age below 75 percent of standard) in the Philippines.*

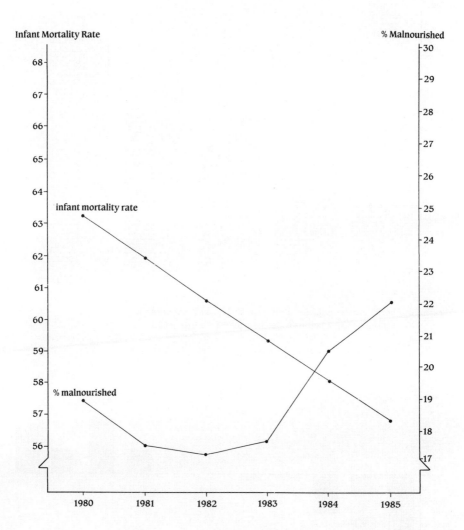

Figure 6.5: *Change in calorie consumption by income quintile in Chile 1969–78 (calories/person/day)*

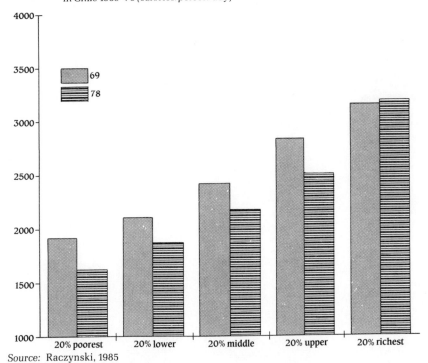

Source: Raczynski, 1985

Figure 6.6: *Percentage change in calories consumed daily per adult equivalent by income decile: Sri Lanka 1978/9 to 1981/2*

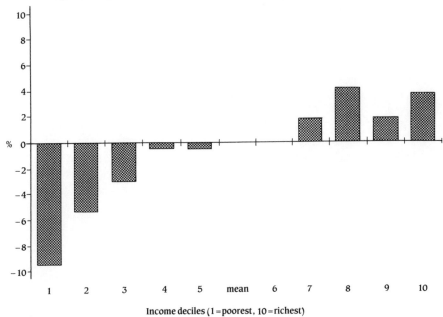

Income deciles (1 = poorest, 10 = richest)

Source: Sahn, 1986 b.

Figure 6.7: *Percentage change in total household expenditure by income strata: Chile 1969–78*

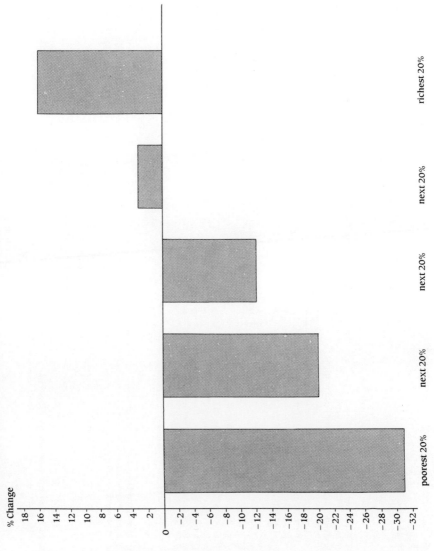

Figure 6.8: *Schematic overview of aims and types of compensatory programmes and policies*

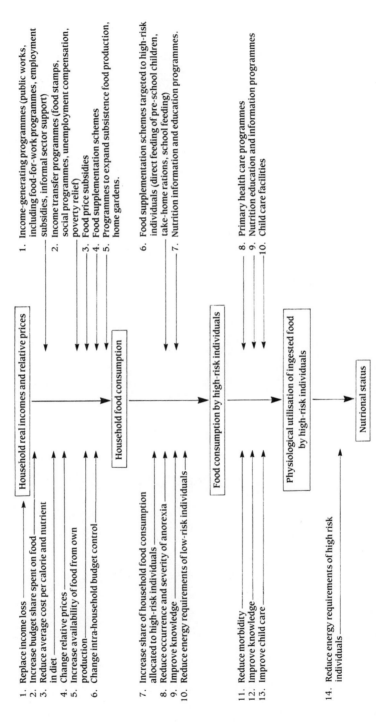

Source: Pinstrup-Andersen, (1987)

Table 6.3: *Average per capita nutrient consumption in urban Costa Rica*

	1978	1982	% change
Energy (kcal)	1,947	1,885	−3
Protein (g)	58	53	−8
Fat (g)	67	63	−6
Carbohydrate (g)	284	285	−0

Source: Pinstrup-Andersen (1987b).

IMPACT ON FACTORS CLOSELY ASSOCIATED WITH MORTALITY, NUTRITIONAL STATUS, AND FOOD SECURITY

While the evidence cited above provides strong indications that the nutritional situation is deteriorating in a number of countries where macroeconomic adjustments have been made, it tells us little about the factors that bring such deterioration about. It is important to identify these factors in order to suggest measures which will alleviate negative nutrition effects. Furthermore, monitoring changes in these factors may provide advance warning of impending negative impact on nutrition and household food security.

Household food security and nutritional status may be affected by macroeconomic adjustment in a variety of ways. A conceptual overview of the principal relationships is discussed elsewhere (Pinstrup-Andersen, 1988b) and will not be repeated here. The key factors which establish the link between macroeconomic adjustment and nutrition are the real incomes of the poor, the price of food and other necessities, and access to government services and transfers. Thus, changes in these factors are likely to be reflected in food consumption and nutritional status, although usually with a time lag.

Changes in real incomes of the poor

Real incomes are determined by nominal incomes and the rate of inflation. Nominal incomes may consist of wage earnings, incomes of self-employed, transfers, and the value of own production consumed by the household. Since the poor spend a large proportion of their incomes on food, changes in incomes provide strong indications of changes in food consumption.

Traditional stabilisation programmes generally result in decreasing real wages, at least in the short run. Real wages fell in Sri Lanka during the period 1979–84 after adjustments were made in 1977–8 (Sahn, 1986; UNICEF, Colombo, 1985). Between 1981 and 1984, real wages declined in five of seven Latin American countries studied by the Inter-American Development Bank (1985). The real wage decreases were not offset by increasing employment. On the contrary, unemployment increased in most of these countries.

Real wages in Mexico declined by 28 per cent from 1981 to 1983, with another drop in 1984 (World Bank, 1986). In Costa Rica, real wages declined by 40 per cent during the economic crisis 1979–82 but recovered after 1982 and by 1985 were back to pre-crisis levels (World Bank, 1986). Thus, developments in Costa Rica illustrate a case where macroeconomic adjustment clearly had a positive effect. In Brazil, average real wages decreased by 32 per cent during the period 1981–3 (Cortazar, 1986; 3).

Drastic falls in the real minimum wage rate in a number of countries indicate that the poor are seriously affected. Thus, the purchasing power of the minimum wage in Zaire in 1982 was only about 3 per cent of what it was in 1970 (Ntalaja, 1986). Furthermore, the Inter-American Development Bank concludes that there is evidence that a disproportionate part of losses in real incomes 'have been concentrated in the lower income strata'. The Bank further suggests that:

> to the extent that real wage containment remains a necessary element of the adjustment process, mechanisms will have to be found to shift some of the burden to the higher income groups in the interest of social justice and domestic peace (Inter-American Development Bank, 1985; 12–13).

In Mexico, real minimum wages decreased and the percentage of workers earning one minimum wage or less increased dramatically during the period 1982-5, from 13 per cent in 1982 to 29 per cent in 1983 and 1984 and 38 per cent in 1985 (Lustig, 1986). Similar developments occurred in Brazil and Chile during 1981-3 (Cortazar, 1986). In Brazil, per capita GDP fell by 14 per cent but real incomes of the poor fell by 20–30 per cent and the proportion of households below the poverty line increased from 40 to 60 per cent. In Costa Rica, the proportion of households below the poverty line increased from 17 to 29 per cent during the economic crisis 1979–82.

CASAR estimates that 150 million people were below the poverty line in Latin America in 1986, up by 20 million since 1981. The contribution made by macro-economic adjustments to this increase is not clear. Adjustments have generally increased inflation (primarily due to devaluations), increased unemployment and reduced real wages. It also appears that food prices increased more than non-food prices during the period of adjustment in many of the Latin American countries. Increasing food prices together with falling real incomes are likely to be harmful for poor consumers, as illustrated by developments in Peru where it is estimated that 70 per cent of the population had insufficient income to cover a minimum food basket in 1984, a rise from the 51 per cent level of 1972, and 62 per cent in 1980. Similarly, in Mexico the cost of a basic diet for one person increased from 8.5 per cent of a minimum wage in 1982 to 13 per cent in 1986 (Lustig, 1986).

In Chile, *both* relative income distribution and absolute poverty deteriorated between 1969 and 1978, a period of serious economic crisis and severe macro-economic adjustment. Thus, the real value of total expenditures of the poorest quintile of the population dropped by 30 per cent, while it increased by 16 per cent for the richest quintile (Figure 6.7). Similar developments occurred in the Philippines (UNICEF, Manila, 1988) and Sri Lanka (UNICEF, Colombo 1985).

In many developing countries, the poorest wage labour is found in the informal sector producing goods and services which are not exported or imported – the so-called 'non-tradables'. Since macroeconomic adjustment policies aim at improving the balance of payments, they typically increase the prices of goods and services that are either exported or imported – 'tradables' – relative to the non-tradables. Therefore, if the poor are concentrated in the non-tradables sector, they are likely to be made worse off relative to wage earners in the tradables sector. If these poor workers are able to move between sectors and thus take advantage of relatively higher wages and better employment opportunities in the production of tradables, the problem may be less severe. Thus, policies to increase the mobility of poor workers are of great importance.

It appears that urban formal sector employment has either decreased or increased less than the growth in the labour force in many of the Latin American countries during the first half of the 1980s. Thus, macroeconomic adjustments appear to have been unable to counter the unemployment caused by the crises. In some cases, demand contractions caused by stabilisation programmes have in fact further deteriorated formal sector employment. Open urban unemployment rates in Latin America increased from about 7 per cent in 1980 to 10.4 per cent in 1984 (ILO, 1987a). The result has been rapid increases in employment in the informal sector at low rates of remuneration and widespread underemployment. Thus, as shown in Table 6.4, informal sector employment in Brazil increased by more than 9 per cent annually during the period 1980–85 as compared to 2.6 per cent for the formal sector.

Table 6.4: *Selected Latin American countries: annual changes in total, urban formal and urban informal sector employment 1980–85 (percent)*

Country	Total employment	Urban formal sector employment	Urban informal sector employment
Argentina	0.8	−0.2	3.2
Brazil	4.0	2.6	9.3
Colombia	2.5	2.3	5.4
Chile[a]	1.2	−1.6	1.2
Mexico[a]	3.0	1.9	8.4
Peru[a]	1.8	−1.3	6.5
Venezuela	2.1	1.5	2.2

[a]1981–5

Source: ILO/PREALC: *Creation of productive employment: A task that cannot be postponed* (Santiago, 1986).

For the purpose of exploring how the various groups of low-income households have been affected it may be useful to make some rough classification of those with insecure access to food. A more effective functional classification can be done only on a country-by-country basis. In such a rough classification it may be useful to distinguish among the following groups:

i)   semi-subsistence farmers;
ii)   small market-oriented farmers;
iii) landless agricultural workers;
iv)   rural landless non-agricultural workers and self-employed;
v)   urban workers in sectors producing goods that are or could be exported or imported or inputs for such goods ('tradables');
vi)   urban workers and self-employed in sectors producing goods that are generally not exported or imported ('non-tradables').
vii) public-sector workers.

Available evidence suggests that the first two groups have been able to maintain their food security more successfully than any other group. Semi-subsistence farmers were at least partially protected from the erosion of real incomes through lower wages and higher prices because they produced their own food.

In-kind incomes are an important source of income for many poor households, particularly semi-subsistence farmers. The importance becomes very clear during periods of rapid increases in the prices of food and other necessities which frequently follow macroeconomic adjustments. Price increases erode the real value of monetary incomes such as money wages; thus, as food prices increase, a given wage income will buy less food. Such erosion does not occur for a given in-kind income.

Developments in Uganda during the last 10–15 years illustrate this point (Jamal,

1985). The price index rose from 100 in 1972 to 35,000 toward the end of 1984. The price of maize meal, the principal food staple, rose from about one Ugandan Shilling per kg in 1972 to 180 Shillings per kg in early 1985. The rate of increase in wages was considerably less. Thus, the index for real wages fell from 100 in 1972 to 9 in late 1984. The number of minimum wages needed to purchase the food necessary to meet minimum calorie requirements for an average household increased from 0.6 to 4.5 over this 12-year period.

However, in spite of these developments, the nutritional situation did not deteriorate greatly during the period. One explanation is that most of the rural poor obtain a major share of their food from own production, while the urban poor either increased food production for own consumption or obtained food from their rural relatives (Jamal, 1985).

Small market-oriented farmers have gained from policies such as agricultural price increases, which are frequently a part of structural adjustment. Although very little empirical evidence is available, agricultural workers would be expected to gain also from higher agricultural prices through increased labour demand. This should also be the case for the rural landless workers and self-employed who derive their incomes from producing goods and services traded locally, because farmers will spend some of the additional income on such goods and services.

Thus, in cases where structural adjustment has resulted in higher output price levels to farmers without large contractions in the demand for agricultural output and without large increases in input prices, the overall effect on the food security of the rural poor may have been positive. The picture is much less clear in cases where large relative price changes have occurred among agricultural commodities or where input prices have increased significantly. In attempts to expand the production of agricultural commodities that could be exported or used for import substitution in order to improve the balance of payments, some countries have focused agricultural price increases on commodities and regions where quick responses were expected. Food-insecure farmers are frequently found in regions with poor infrastructure and where the supply response is slower, and they may have been bypassed by adjustment-related price policies. Moreover, increasing input prices caused by devaluations, trade liberalisation, and removal of subsidies are commonly linked with adjustment programmes and the net gains to agriculture from the total programme are usually considerably less than indicated by output price changes. Finally, with regard to the rural poor and those with uncertain access to food it should be mentioned that a large share of their incomes usually comes from outside agriculture and many, if not most, are net buyers of food. Thus, while incomes may have increased either directly through higher prices for the marketed surplus, or indirectly through increased labour demand and expanded demand for locally produced non-agricultural goods and services, negative effects have been encountered through lower real wages outside agriculture and higher food prices.

As noted earlier, traditional stabilisation programmes usually result in reduced real wages. Due to changes in the relative prices between tradables and non-tradables, increased employment in the tradables or formal sector is to be expected. However, as mentioned above it appears that urban formal sector employment has either decreased or increased less than the growth in the labour force.

Thus, based on the available empirical evidence, it may be concluded that the rapid deterioration in real incomes reported earlier refers principally to low-income urban wage earners and the self-employed, in both the formal and the informal sectors. In some countries, particularly African ones, urban to rural migration has been one response to this situation. Furthermore, urban to rural remittances have undoubtedly been reduced and possibly reversed in some cases. Reductions in public-sector employment have contributed to the hardships experienced by the urban poor.

Gifts and transfers are another important source of income for the poor. Government transfer programmes take many forms, including explicit price subsidies for selected commodities such as food, housing, and transportation; food stamps; unemployment compensation; social security payments; and poverty relief payments. The importance of these transfers is illustrated by food subsidies which account for 15–25 per cent of total incomes of the poor in a number of countries (Pinstrup-Andersen and Alderman, 1988). Macroeconomic adjustments typically attempt to reduce subsidies and other transfers in order to reduce government expenditures and remove price distortions.

Food subsidies

No global estimates of government expenditures on food subsidies are available. However, data from ten countries with large subsidy programmes show a clear and significant downward trend in food subsidy costs (Table 6.5).

Table 6.5: *Government expenditures on explicit food subsidies in selected countries and change since 1980*

Country	Year	US$/Capita	Index of real cost[a] US$	Index of real cost[a] Nat. curr.
Bangladesh	1985	0.91	92	124
Brazil	1985	2.38	19	31
Colombia	1982	0.09	71	71
Egypt	1985	27.58	71	95
India	1985	0.92	71	93
Mexico	1985	14.46	73	99
Morocco	1985	11.75	68	140
Pakistan	1985	1.51	34	50
Sri Lanka	1985	4.32	42	51
Zambia	1982	2.82	38	41

[a]1980 = 100
Source: Pinstrup-Andersen, Jaramillo and Stewart (1987).

While changes in the magnitude of food subsidy expenditures may provide some guidelines for changes in the benefits derived by the poor, a number of factors, including food price changes and the degree of targeting and efficiency of the subsidy programme, influence the impact of a given subsidy expenditure on the welfare of the poor. These factors vary across countries and over time, and cuts in food subsidy expenditures need not result in negative welfare effects for the poor if appropriate changes are made in the subsidy scheme. Thus, it is important to analyse both changes in the magnitude of subsidies and changes in the design and implementation of the subsidy schemes, particularly those related to targeting and efficiency.

The observed decreases in the real value of government expenditures on food subsidies since 1980 are not primarily due to explicit policy action aimed at subsidy programmes. Falling import prices of subsidised foods – e.g., wheat, rice, and sugar – have contributed to reduced subsidy costs in dollars in many countries with little or no explicit policy action toward food subsidies. Rice prices fell from about

US$500/ton in 1980 to about US$350/ton in 1985. Wheat prices fell during the same period from about US$170/ton to about US$100/ton. The largest relative price decrease occurred for sugar, which fell from about US$60/ton to US$8/ton. The real price decreases for rice and wheat were larger than the real decreases in subsidy expenditures for six of the ten countries shown in Table 6.5.

Thus, it appears that the cost savings have not been translated into decreases in consumer benefits of similar magnitudes. In fact, the cost reductions do not preclude increases in consumer benefits in more than half of the countries studies.

In four countries – Brazil, Pakistan, Sri Lanka, and Zambia – the savings in food subsidy costs exceeded price decreases. Decreases in consumer benefits are more likely to have occurred in these countries. Evidence from other sources shows large decreases in consumer benefits in Sri Lanka (Edirisinghe, 1986; Sahn, 1986).

Explicit policy measures were taken to reduce subsidies in Colombia and Sri Lanka. In Colombia, a food-stamp programme which had been in effect since 1976 was discontinued in 1982, and a long-standing untargeted ration scheme in Sri Lanka was targeted in 1977 and subsequently converted to a targeted food-stamp programme in 1979. Cost savings were obtained initially from targeting to only one-half of the population and then by maintaining a constant nominal value of the food stamps in the face of rapidly increasing food prices.

None of the ten countries have succeeded in effectively increasing the degree of targeting food subsidies to the absolute poor since 1980. Furthermore, there are no indications that the efficiency of the subsidy programmes has improved. Thus, opportunities for cost savings and increased benefits for the poor through targeting have not been exploited.

For developing countries as a whole, the percentage of government expenditures allocated to transfer programmes, excluding food subsidies, stayed constant during the period 1976–82 (IMF, 1985). Some countries show drastic decreases in the real value of transfer programmes during periods of adjustment. Thus, the Sri Lankan expenditures on such programmes fell from 20 to 12 per cent of total government expenditures from 1976 to 1982 (IMF, 1985, and UN, 1982). Furthermore, the value of the food subsidy programme fell from 16 to 3 per cent of current government expenditures from 1977 to 1984 (Sahn, 1986). By 1982, the real per capita value of transfer programmes in Sri Lanka had been reduced to about one-half of the real value in 1978, a dramatic change which is almost certain to have caused severe hardship among the poor.

Changes in government services

Government expenditures on health care in developing countries as a whole decreased from about 4.3 to 4.1 per cent of total government expenditures during the period 1976–83 (IMF, 1985, and UN, 1982). The decrease during the early 1980s was particularly severe in Latin America (Table 6.6).

These cuts are direct consequences of severe macroeconomic adjustments made during that period. Severe cuts were observed in several African countries, including Ghana where real health expenditures in 1982 were 23 per cent of what they had been six years earlier.

Large cuts in health-care expenditures would be expected to have serious effects on the health and well-being of the poor unless they (a) occur primarily in the services used by the better-off population groups, or (b) are accompanied by improvements in programme targeting or efficiency. The distribution of the cuts among types of health

Table 6.6: *Changes in health expenditures in selected countries 1980–84 (percent)*

Bolivia	−78 (1980–82)
Guatemala	−78
Dom. Republic	−47
Surinam	−44 (1980–83)
El Salvador	−32
Chile	−24
Barbados	−21
Jamaica	−19
Costa Rica	−17
Honduras	−15
Argentina	−14
Uruguay	−13

Source: Pinstrup–Andersen, Jaramillo and Stewart (1987).

services varies among countries and the available evidence does not provide general guidelines regarding the extent to which the poor are affected.

In several countries, including Chile and Jamaica, capital investment in the health sector was reduced more than recurrent costs. It is likely that capital investment has been biased toward the better-off population groups because they tend to use more capital-intensive health care, such as hospitals and special equipment, while recurrent costs may be biased towards the poor, e.g. primary health care. If this is correct, the poor may have been at least partially protected.

In Brazil, there was a major shift in relative expenditures on curative versus preventive health care during the 1970s and 1980s (de Ferranti, 1983). The latter decreased from about 40 per cent of total health expenditures in 1970 to about 15 per cent in 1982. A similar, although less rapid, relative shift took place in the Philippines between 1978 and 1982, where the share of total health care expenditures used for field health services stayed constant at about 28 per cent while expenditures on hospitals increased from 48 to 54 per cent (de Ferranti, 1983). If preventive health care is primarily focused on the poor while expenditures on curative health care are biased towards the better-off population groups, the shifts in Brazil and the Philippines are likely to have been adverse for the poor. In Brazil, this may have been at least partly offset by large increases in food transfer programmes for the poor initiated during 1985–6.

ADEQUACY OF CURRENT KNOWLEDGE FOR POLICY DESIGN AND PROPOSED ACTION

As illustrated above, deteriorations in the nutritional status, as well as the absolute and relative level of food consumption by the poor, are rather dramatic and deserve serious attention by policy-makers. However, the causes are not fully understood. Are the deteriorations caused by the adjustment policies that were introduced in these countries or by the crises that made the adjustments necessary? What would the situation have been if the crises had been permitted to continue or if a different set of adjustment policies had been used? Answers to these questions must await further research.

However, even though very little research that firmly establishes and quantifies a causal link between specific adjustment policies and food security and nutritional status has been completed, available evidence suggests that there is a high risk of deterioration in nutritional status as a consequence of traditional macroeconomic adjustment programmes. Scattered evidence of nutritional deterioration, alongside considerable evidence on falling real wages, rapidly increased food prices, reductions in transfer programmes to the poor, and reduced government expenditures on primary health care and education, should not be ignored just because solid causal links have not yet been established. Enough is known about the effect of food price increases and real wage decreases on food consumption by the poor to conclude that the nutritional status of those most at risk has deteriorated. While the causal links are being studied and the estimates of nutritional impact refined, explicit attention should be paid to avoid negative, and enhance positive, nutrition effects in the design of macroeconomic adjustment programmes.

In principle, governments can do one or both of two things in order to incorporate nutritional considerations into the design of such programmes. They can design new, or modify existing, adjustment policies to accommodate such nutritional concerns, or they can introduce separate policies and programmes to compensate the poor for any adverse effects caused by the adjustment programme.

The preference for compensatory measures over modifications in the adjustment programmes is appropriate if the programme is expected to contribute to improvements in the nutritional status in the long run, as, for example, through higher incomes for the poor, with short-run negative effects expected to be transitory. Although the record is mixed, this is an argument frequently made in support of traditional adjustment programmes. If, on the other hand, it is unlikely that the long-run nutrition effects of the traditional programmes will be positive and sufficiently large, compensatory measures would be less appropriate than changes in the programmes themselves. In many such cases, structural changes in the economy and reorientation of the development strategy are likely to be needed.

Figure 6.8 lists the possible aims and certain types of compensatory programmes and policies. These programmes and policies are discussed elsewhere (Pinstrup-Andersen, 1987a) and only a short summary is provided here. The principal opportunities for compensation are embodied in programmes and policies to: (i) enhance the income-generating ability of the poor through: a) employment generation in the public or private sector, b) increased productivity of the poor by means of larger investments in primary education, vocational training, skill development, c) improved access by the poor to productive assets such as land and d) expanded programmes for credit, technical assistance, modern technology, and other inputs for the low-income self-employed in the informal and agricultural sector, (ii) increase income transfer, whether in cash, food, or other form to the poor by improved targeting of existing programmes or design of new ones, and (iii) expand the benefits obtained by the poor from health and related programmes through improved targeting and efficiency of existing programmes, changes in the composition of current public health expenditures, and the introduction of user fees for the non-poor.

The above programmes and policies may be pursued without large additional government outlays, partly through gains from income generation (which may be partially captured as revenues) and partly through savings from improved efficiency and targeting of existing programmes.

Modifications in conventional adjustment programmes that may improve the effects on nutrition and food security include the following:

i)   seeking stabilisation and adjustment over a longer rather than a shorter period of time. Solutions to very severe foreign-exchange problems have frequently been attempted over an unrealistically short period of time using policy measures that have had severe disruptive effects on the economy and caused excessive hardship for the poor.

ii) placing more emphasis on supply expansion and growth than on demand contraction. Orthodox stabilisation and adjustment tend to emphasise demand contraction, in part because of likely lags in supply expansion. However, drastic cuts in domestic absorption can result in very severe hardships for the poor.

iii) focusing adjustment programmes on the selective removal of market and institutional distortions in the economy rather than single-minded pressure for market liberalisation. While institutional rents may be reduced, the latter frequently result in rapid accumulations of wealth among a small number of people because of imperfections in markets and institutions. Removal of certain distortions in input and output markets, asset ownership, and a series of other institutional and market distortions that are adverse to the poor would allow for a much broader participation in the benefits.

iv) emphasising strengthening the capacity of the poor to generate income. This implies a focus on policies and programmes which will result in increased employment, higher labour productivity and higher real wages among the poor. While full wage indexation for all is likely to contribute to the economic crisis, opportunities for wage indexation for the lowest wage earners, using price indices most relevant for their expenditure patterns, should be explored. This would include, but not necessarily be limited to, full indexation of institutional minimum wages.

v) paying special attention to measures which will enhance the productivity of the self-employed in the informal sector, many of whom lack secure access to food. Credit programmes, technical assistance, market development, training, and skill development are some of the possible measures to be considered.

With respect to the agricultural sector, a number of issues need to be considered. First, while a significant part of structural adjustment, the importance of price policy has been grossly exaggerated as a tool to achieve rapid increases in total agricultural output and food security in many developing countries. Poor rural infrastructure, lack of appropriate production technology and modern inputs, seasonal labour bottlenecks, and land and marketing constraints result in low supply response in total output. However, changes in relative prices, a common feature of adjustment programmes, have been very successful in changing the output mix. This has resulted in surpluses for some commodities, countries, and time periods, and deficits for others. The contribution of such relative price changes to the achievement of adjustment and food security goals varies among countries and time periods and no consistent picture has emerged. What is clear, however, is that higher food prices result in reduced food security for those poor who do not derive their income from food production, i.e. the urban and many of the rural poor.

If, as mentioned above, total output responds in a very limited way to price increases, further price increases will transfer incomes from consumers to producers in proportion to the amounts purchased and sold. In the case of a large number of low-income consumers and concentration of the marketed surplus on a small number of large farmers – a rather common scenario – such transfer will result in lower food security. Unit-cost saving measures such as enhanced access by farmers to appropriate technology and modern inputs as well as greater marketing efficiency are much more appropriate for achieving the combined goals of stabilisation and food security.

From the point of view of food security one of the key modifications needed in structural adjustment programmes is a change from the goal of maximisation of agricultural supply expansions to that of maximisation of real incomes of the poor. The former leads to policies and programmes which are likely to benefit larger, better-off farmers who control better production environments, while food-insecure farmers may be ignored because the short-run potential for expanding the marketed surplus is lower. Consumers with low purchasing power will gain from such policies and programmes only if prices are permitted to fall. However, the opposite usually occurs, because higher prices are used to bring forth additional supplies. When such policies are taken to the extreme, as in some African countries during the last 5–6 years, surplus stocks of commodities for which prices were increased are accumulated at prices that exceed export parity prices and consumer purchasing power. Parallel with the stock build-up, food insecurity and malnutrition among urban and many rural people increase because of food price increases. In cases where total output responds little to price increases, the surplus stock of one commodity is accompanied by reduction in the production of other commodities. The price of these commodities is therefore likely to increase, adding to the negative effects on the food security of poor consumers and non-producers. Moreover, since a large share of the rural poor, particularly in South Asia, lack access to land, policies and programmes allowing for self-sustained income generation in rural areas, including labour-intensive rural infrastructure, are desirable. Examples of programmes in this area were mentioned earlier.

Because of the relative failure of many of the rural development programmes in the past, there is currently a strong tendency not to enter into such programmes. Rather than shying away from rural development as a concept, it is now time to regroup and search for innovative ways of facilitating rural development without repeating past mistakes. Attempts to improve food security in rural areas where a large proportion of the poor do not have access to land cannot be successful if they are based solely on the goal of maximising agricultural output. While drawing lessons from past successes and failures, ways must be found to develop rural areas so as to benefit the rural poor both within and outside agriculture.

The design of adjustment programmes and compensatory programmes and policies must take into account the social, economic, and political environments of the country for which they are intended. Therefore, in order to facilitate the explicit consideration of the expected nutrition effects at the time when adjustment programmes are being designed, it is essential that national decision-makers have access to the relevant information, particularly information about the expected impact of various adjustment and compensation options on specific population and household groups at risk of malnutrition. The generation of such information should be pursued through the establishment of functioning research and data collection systems.

REFERENCES

Addison, Tony and Lionel Demery (1986), *The Impact of Liberalization on Growth and Equity*, Geneva, International Labour Office, International Employment Policies, Working Paper No. 4.
—— (1985), *Macroeconomic Stabilization: Income Distribution and Poverty: A Preliminary Survey*, London, Overseas Development Institute, Working Paper No. 15.
Becker, A. and A. Lechtig (1986), 'Increasing Poverty and Infant Mortality in the Northeast of Brazil', *Journal of Tropical Paediatry*.
Biswas, Margaret and Per Pinstrup-Andersen (eds) (1985), *Nutrition and Development*, Oxford, Oxford University Press.
Boyd, Derick (1988), 'The Impact of Adjustment Policies on Vulnerable Groups: The Case of Jamaica, 1973–85', in Cornia et al.
—— (1986), 'Stabilization Policies and Poverty: The Case of Jamaica', Overseas Development

Institute/International Development Research Centre, Mona, Jamaica, University of West Indies, Department of Economics (mimeo).

CASAR (1986), *National Food Programs in Latin America and the Caribbean: A response to the economic crisis*, Buenos Aires, Comite de Accion para la Seguridad Alimentaria Regional.

Centro de Estudios del Trabajo (1986), *Impacto de la Crises en los trabajadores Mexicanos*, Mexico, Congreso del Trabajo, 9–11 December.

Cline, William R. and Sidney Weintraub (eds) (1981), *Economic Stabilization in Developing Countries*, Washington DC, The Brookings Institution.

Corbo, Vittorio and Jaime de Melo (eds) (1985), 'Liberalization with Stabilization in the Southern Cone of Latin America', *World Development*, Vol. 13, No. 8.

Cornia, Giovanni Andrea (1987), 'Economic Decline and Human Welfare', in Cornia et al.

—— Richard Jolly and Frances Stewart (eds) (1987), *Adjustment with a Human Face:* Vol. I: *Protecting the Vulnerable and Promoting Growth.* (1988), Vol. II: *Ten Country Case Studies*, Oxford, Clarendon Press for UNICEF.

Cortazar, René (1986), *Employment, Real Wages and External Constraints: the Case of Brazil and Chile*, Geneva, International Labour Office, International Employment Policies, Working Paper No. 8.

—— (1980), 'Distribucion del Ingreso, Empleo y Remuneraciones Reales en Chile, 1970–78', *Coleccion Estubios CIEPLAN* 3, Santiago, Chile.

de Ferranti, David (1983), *Background Information on Analysis of Financing and Resource Allocation Issues in Health Sector and Project Work*, PHN Technical Notes, Gen. 23, Washington DC, World Bank.

—— (1986), *Financing Health Services*, Washington DC, World Bank.

Dethier, J.J. (1986), 'Macroeconomic Adjustment Policies and Human Nutrition: The Macroeconomic Relationships', prepared for ACC/SCN, Washington DC, International Food Policy Research Institute, (mimeo).

Edirisinghe, Neville (1986), 'The Food Stamp Program in Sri Lanka: Costs, Benefits, and Policy Options', Washington DC, International Food Policy Research Institute, (mimeo).

Foxley, Alejandro and Dagmar Raczynski (1984), 'Vulnerable Groups in Recessionary Situations: The Case of Children and the Young in Chile', in Jolly and Cornia.

Helleiner, Gerald K. (1985), 'Stabilization Policies and the Poor', Working Paper No. B.8, Paper prepared for a conference on Government Policy and the Poor in Developing Countries, 25–26 April.

—— and Frances Stewart (1987), 'The International System and the Protection of the Vulnerable', in Cornia et al.

Inter-American Development Bank (1985), *Economic and Social Progress in Latin America. External Debt: Crisis and Adjustment*, Washington DC, Inter-American Development Bank.

International Labour Organization (1987a), *Tripartite Preparatory Meeting on Employment and Structural Adjustment*, Geneva, ILO, 27–29 April.

—— (1987b), *World Recession and Global Interdependence*, Geneva.

International Monetary Fund (1985), *Government Finance Statistics Yearbook*, Vol. IX, Washington DC.

—— (1986), *Fund Supported Programs, Fiscal Policy, and Income Distribution*, Occasional Paper No. 46, Washington DC.

Jamal, Vali (1985), *Structural Adjustment and Food Security in Uganda*, World Employment Programme Research, Geneva, ILO.

Johnson, Omotunde and Joanne Salop (1980), 'Distributional Aspects of Stabilization Programmes in Developing Countries', *IMF Staff Papers*, Vol. 27, No. 1.

Jolly, Richard and Giovanni Cornia (eds) (1984), *The Impact of World Recession on Children*, Report prepared for UNICEF. New York, Pergamon Press.

Killick, Tony (ed.) (1984a), *The Quest for Economic Stabilization: The IMF and the Third World*, London, Heinemann.

—— (1984b), *The IMF and Stabilization: Developing Country Experience*, London, Heinemann.

Lustig, Nora (1986), 'Economic Crisis and Living Standards in Mexico: 1982–1985', Mexico City, El Colegio de Mexico (mimeo).

Montes, Manuel F. (1986), 'Macroeconomic Adjustments and their Impact on Living Standards in the Philippines', Washington DC, International Food Policy Research Institute.

Musgrove, Philip (1987), 'The Economic Crisis and its Impact on Health and Health Care in Latin America and the Carribean', *International Journal of Health Services*, Vol. 17, No. 3.

Nelson, Joan M. (1984), 'The Political Economy of Stabilisation: Commitment, Capacity, and Public Response', *World Development*, Vol. 12, No. 10.

Ntalaja, Kalonji (1986), 'The Short-Term Social Impact of Adjustment Policies in Zaire: Some Explanatory Results', Washington DC, International Food Policy Research Institute (mimeo).

Overseas Development Institute (1986), *Adjustment to Recession: Will the Poor Recover?* ODI Briefing Paper, November.

Pinstrup-Andersen, Per (1986), 'Macroeconomic Adjustment Policies and Human Nutrition: Available evidence and research needs', *Food and Nutrition Bulletin*, Vol. 9, No. 1.

—— (1987a), 'Nutrition Interventions', in Cornia et al.

—— (1987b), *The impact of economic adjustment on people's food security and nutritional levels in developing countries, and the role of multilateral agencies*, paper prepared for the World Food Council and WFC/UNICEF/ILO consultation, Rome, 11–12 May.

—— (1988a), 'Food Subsidies: The Concern to Provide Consumer Welfare While Assuring Producer Incentives', in John W. Mellor and Raisuddin Ahmed (eds), *Agricultural Price Policy for Developing Countries*, Baltimore, Johns Hopkins University Press.

—— (1988b), 'Assuring food security and adequate nutrition for the poor during periods of economic crises and macroeconomic adjustments: Policy options and experience with food subsidies and transfer programs', in David Bell and Michael Reich (eds), *Health, Nutrition and Economic Crises: Approaches to Policy in the Third World*, Dover, Mass., Auburn House Publishing.

—— (1988c), 'Macroeconomic Implications of Consumer-Oriented Food Subsidies', in Pinstrup Andersen (ed.), *Consumer Oriented Food Subsidies: Benefits, Costs, and Policy Options*, Baltimore, Johns Hopkins University Press.

——, Mauricio Jaramillo and Frances Stewart (1987), 'The Impact of Government Expenditures', in Cornia et al.

—— and Harold Alderman (1988), 'The Effectiveness of Consumer-Oriented Food Subsidies in Reaching Rationing and Income Transfer Goals', in Pinstrup-Andersen (ed).

Raczynski, Dagmar (1985), 'Politica Social, Pobreza y Grupos Vulnerables: Situation de los Ninos in Chile', UNICEF (mimeo).

—— (1988), 'Social Policy, Poverty and Vulnerable Groups: Children in Chile', in Cornia et al.

Richards, P.J. and R. van der Hoeven (eds) (1986), *Stabilization, Adjustment and Poverty*, Geneva, International Labour Office, International Employment Policies, Working Paper No. 1.

Sahn, David E. (1986), 'Changes in the Living Standards of the Poor in Sri Lanka during a Period of Macroeconomic Restructuring', *World Development*, Vol. 15, No. 6.

Stewart, Frances (1987), 'Supporting Productive Employment among Vulnerable Groups', in Cornia et al.

UNICEF, Colombo (1985), *The Social Impact of Economic Policies During the Last Decade*, a Special Study, Colombo.

—— Accra (1988), 'Adjustment Policies and Programmes to Protect Children and Other Vulnerable Groups in Ghana', in Cornia et al.

——, Manila (1988), 'Redirecting Adjustment Programmes Towards Growth and the Protection of the Poor: The Philippines Case', in Cornia et al.

United Nations (1982), *Demographic Yearbook*, New York, United Nations.

Vellutini, Roberto (1986), 'Macroeconomic Adjustments, Agricultural Performance and Income Distribution in Brazil after 1985: Overview', Washington DC, International Food Policy Research Institute.

World Bank (1986), *Poverty in Latin America, the Impact of Depression*, Washington DC.

World Food Council (1985), *Improving Access to Food by the Undernourished*, Report by the Executive Director to the Eleventh Ministerial Session, Paris, 10–13 June, (WFC/1985/4).

—— (1987), 'Consultation on the impact of economic adjustment on people's food security and nutritional levels in developing countries', Report by the WFC Secretariat for the 13th Ministerial Session, Beijing, 8–11 June.

PART THREE

Country Studies

7

Ghana

1983–7

Simon Commander, John Howell & Wayo Seini

INTRODUCTION

Since 1983 the Ghanaian Government has pursued an extensive set of policy reforms designed to reverse the economic decline that had marked the previous two decades. These measures have been supported to a significant extent by external donors. Following the announcement of the government's Economic Recovery Programme (ERP 1), annual concessional assistance between 1983 and 1986 rose to roughly double the level for the four preceding years. Support from the major multilateral agencies has been particularly pronounced, largely in the form of programme aid. In 1985 and 1986 multilateral aid commitments amounted to nearly two-thirds of total commitments, and the strong support given to ERP 1 and its second stage, ERP 2 (1987–9), by both the World Bank and the IMF has enabled a growing level of aid pledging in recent years (World Bank, 1987b)).

The scale of donor support and participation in the design of economic policy has made Ghana something of a model case, an example to other African governments of the virtues of managed adjustments. This chapter reviews this adjustment phase, focusing, in particular, on the impact of the ERP and donor interventions on the key agricultural sector. Data generated by a survey of one of the core cocoa regions – Ashanti – are presented as part of the analysis of the micro level impact of producer and input pricing policy changes. The chapter further concentrates explicitly on the role of public sector agencies in the delivery of goods and services to the sector and attempts to evaluate the options open to government for improving these services, as well as the feasibility of transfer to the private sector.

BACKGROUND TO ERP 1

Despite a relative affluence in natural and human resources, Ghana's economy deteriorated steadily from the early 1960s, with the pace of decline accelerating in the 1970s. National income fell by around 0.5 per cent per annum between 1970 and 1982

* The authors wish to thank Roy Cole for excellent computational assistance.

with *per capita* income falling by over 30 per cent in the same period, (ibid). Agricultural output also declined at a rate of 0.3 per cent per annum through the 1970s, and in 1982 and 1983 drought and fire damage contributed to an output decline of over 6 per cent for each year, with an equivalent fall in overall GDP. Adverse climatic conditions thus compounded an established downward trend for all major economic indicators.

This adverse longer-term trend can be attributed in part to external factors. Between 1970 and 1984 the terms of trade declined by around 1.1 per cent per annum. However, major domestic policy shortcomings remain the principal explanatory factor behind weak economic performance. The links between macroeconomic policy and agricultural sector performance are particularly clear in the Ghana case. With the latter sector contributing over half of GDP, around 65 per cent of average export revenues and about 55 per cent of the labour force, macroeconomic policy acquires considerable significance.

The most striking link concerns the recent evolution of the real exchange rate. Between 1969/71 and 1981/3 the cedi appreciated in real terms by over 90 per cent – by far the highest appreciation rate in sub-Saharan Africa. Naturally, this trend was heavily biased against domestic tradables producers and this bias was further compounded by the high implicit taxation rates levied by successive governments on the producers of the principal export commodity, cocoa. Between 1960/65 and the early 1980s Ghana's international market share fell from a peak of 36 per cent to around 17 per cent. The enormous wedge between official and parallel exchange rates consequent upon the rapid appreciation of the currency likewise stimulated the growth of smuggling to neighbouring countries. Apart from the fact that by 1982 cocoa growers were receiving under 17 per cent of the 1960/63 price in real terms, producer prices were below 50 per cent of the level sustained in neighbouring Togo and Côte d'Ivoire. One estimate suggests that between 8 and 12 per cent of cocoa output was marketed outside of Ghana through the 1970s (May, 1985).

The trend in the exchange rate not only diminished export earnings but was also associated with a reduced tax base and an expanded budget deficit. A fixed exchange rate did not result in fiscal discipline but was primarily financed through domestic money creation. Inflation rates soared so that between 1976 and 1981 the average annual rate of inflation approached 80 per cent (World Bank, 1984). However, the exceptional overvaluation of the exchange rate that existed did not lead to a large current account deficit. The latter averaged no more than 1.5 per cent of GDP in the same period, with restraint being engineered through acute rationing of official foreign exchange. But as foreign-exchange reserves declined, so too did the ability to import. This was associated with rapidly falling capacity utilisation and investment in domestic industry.

By the early 1980s, the Ghanaian economy was thus marked by rampant inflation, abnormally low investment levels and a highly reduced access to foreign borrowing. The negative consequences cut across all sectors. Output from the core agricultural sector was constrained not only by inappropriate pricing and taxation policy but also by inadequate levels of public investment in the sector. Agriculture's share of total fiscal expenditure remained constant at around 9 per cent, but allocations to the economic infrastructure declined so that by the end of the 1970s its share was no more than 7 per cent – a marked decline from the 20 per cent level attained between 1953/4 and 1959/60 (Akoto, 1987: 246). Transportation and other infrastructural constraints further held back the ability of the economy to generate export revenues. Producers shifted increasingly into non-tradables production but because of marketing constraints this was further associated with low levels of market releases and high absolute price levels for basic wage goods.

MACROECONOMIC POLICY AND PERFORMANCE UNDER ERP I

The ERP initiated in 1983 was regarded as the first phase of a long-term process of economic rehabilitation. The so-called 'stabilisation' phase was aimed at halting the decline in the tradables sectors and at re-establishing the conditions for higher overall growth. Its main actions have involved: (i) exchange and trade policy reform; (ii) prices and incomes policy, aimed at establishing realistic relative prices and incomes in the context of the large movements in the exchange rate; (iii) fiscal and monetary policy, which sought to recover revenues and to restructure expenditure programmes in favour of essential rehabilitation expenditures; (iv) reduction in external payments arrears; (v) sector-specific programmes, prepared to rehabilitate key export industries and the supporting infrastructure needed to ensure an adequate supply response; and (vi) an effort to improve the climate for private investment (Republic of Ghana, 1985).

Exchange-rate reform has been a priority. Between 1982/3 and 1987 a nominal depreciation of c. 6000 per cent has occurred and, in real terms, the cedi depreciated by around 90 per cent over this period. At the same time, a shift from a fixed rate to a unified auction rate was achieved. With restrictions on consumer goods imports being relaxed by the end of 1987, the auction market accounted for around 25 per cent of non-oil imports.

The restructuring of the exchange-rate system and the massive devaluations that have occurred since 1982, when linked to tighter monetary and credit control policies, have not stimulated domestic inflation rates. Indeed, these have been lowered in the adjustment period to a current annual average of between 25 and 30 per cent. This can be attributed to conditions of rationing prior to devaluation. The latter actions thus reduced the substantial rents deriving from import quotas without materially affecting the aggregate price level or domestic demand. However, neither exchange rate nor monetary policies have been able to address the persisting problem of a high absolute domestic price level, deriving in large part from the price of basic wage goods. Moreover, devaluation and tight monetary policy have led to a sharp liquidity squeeze in the economy.

This can be explained by a number of factors. Firstly, recent frequent exchange-rate adjustments have required progressively larger amounts of cedis to back up limited foreign exchange. High domestic interest rates and a chronic lack of confidence between the banks and their clients have compounded the credit squeeze imposed through IMF conditionality. Rising input costs have created particular problems for enterprise liquidity in the industrial sector, but have also had an adverse effect on counterpart funding for projects and hence on actual aid disbursements.

Emphasis has also been placed on the restructuring of public finances. The budget deficit, when measured as a share of GDP, has declined from a level of just under 6 per cent between 1981 and 1983 to around 4 per cent between 1984 and 1986. Under IMF conditionality domestic deficit financing has been radically curtailed. Revenue collection from both export taxes – a function in part of exchange-rate policy – and direct and non-tax revenues has increased. In 1983, the trough year, revenues amounted to under 5 per cent of GDP. By 1987 they were expected to exceed 16 per cent. In the case of budget expenditures, these had collapsed to under 8 per cent of GDP by 1983. By 1986 they had reached around 18 per cent of GDP and were projected to rise to 23 per cent for 1987. The continuing massively sub-optimal level of expenditure on both recurrent and capital accounts has meant that for the period 1987/9 total expenditure is projected to double as a share of GDP when compared with the previous three years (World Bank, 1987b).

This view is reinforced by an examination of the composition of government expenditures. Capital expenditures which had averaged around 21 per cent of total expenditure between 1974/5 and 1979/80 had fallen to nearly 13 per cent between 1982 and 1986. Capital expenditures throughout the first phase of the ERP have been consistently cut in real terms, being defined for the most part as a residual financeable through external resources. In 1985 when foreign net financing fell short of estimated targets by around 35 per cent, this was reflected in a 21 per cent reduction in the capital budget (Republic of Ghana, 1985). Consequently, between 1982 and 1987 capital expenditures and net lending have comprised on average no more than 2 per cent of GDP.

Within this aggregate, allocations to agriculture comprised around 10.5 per cent of total capital expenditures. Allocations to economic infrastructure fell below 10 per cent over the same period. When expressed as a share of total budgetary expenditure, however, allocations to agriculture were significantly below levels achieved through the 1970s, while for infrastructure the share was rather higher. Moreover, recurrent expenditures as a share of GDP averaged between 8 and 9 per cent. These have risen to around 11.5 per cent for the period 1985–7 but, even with this increase, declining real wages, inadequate budgeting for supplies and maintenance and the virtual collapse of health facilities have continued to compromise any sustained development effort. Thus, the combination of highly constrained capital and recurrent public expenditures has meant that basic infrastructure remains in very poor condition, while the operational capacity of government services has been badly affected by the very limited resources made available under the recurrent budget.

The continuing restraint exercised on the economy by the collapse of infrastructure and the highly depressed levels of public investment has had implications for Ghana's ability to improve its current account position. Movement of cocoa – the main tradable – has been held back by the collapse of the transportation network, particularly in the largest cocoa-growing region – the Western Region. Nevertheless, export earnings have continued to rise, although at lower than projected rates, in part as a consequence of downward pressure on the cocoa price (see Table 7.1). The acute import strangulation that existed prior to 1983 has been relieved to some extent, as capital inflows have risen. This has allowed for higher levels of imports and some weakening of the import constraint. But given the significant disjuncture between aid pledges and disbursements, the extent to which this has been achieved has remained more limited than was intended. Even so, the principal financing source for the current account deficit has been concessional assistance. For, despite undoubted growth in export earnings from cocoa, sustaining higher volume and revenue levels over the medium term remains problematic, given current market conditions for Ghana's main export commodities.

Table 7.1: *Ghana: balance of payments 1980–89 (per cent of GDP)*

Balance of Payments	1980/83	1984	1985	1986	1987	1988	1989
					- - - projected - - -		
Exports	4.5	8.0	9.9	15.8	21.7	22.2	22.7
Imports	−5.4	−10.7	−12.9	−18.5	−28.6	−30.0	−30.5
Resource Balance	−0.9	−2.7	−3.0	−2.6	−7.0	−7.7	−7.8
Current Account	−1.6	−2.8	−4.2	−3.7	−8.6	−8.8	−7.9
Overall Balance	−1.0	−1.6	−1.7	−1.1	2.8	3.0	2.5

Source: World Bank, (1987b).

The adjustment programme has not been without severe social and economic costs. Although the economy has grown at around 5 per cent per annum for the past three years, *per capita* incomes – particularly for urban inhabitants and non-cocoa farmers – have continued to fall. Unemployment has continued to rise, accelerated by the substantial lay-offs that have occurred in the public sector. Between 1986 and 1988, one of the conditions for the World Bank Structural Adjustment Credit has been the retrenchment of a further 15,000 public sector workers per annum. To add to these problems, real allocations to both health and education fell substantially during the first phase of the ERP (Cornia, 1987, 1988).

The stabilisation phase of the ERP has thus registered some progress in removing the key constraints on the economy, primarily through a significant inflow of external resources. As with most other sub-Saharan African economies, private financing has been almost non-existent. In the case of the IMF Stand-by Loans and Compensatory Financing Facilities taken by Ghana since 1983, repurchases have already begun and will soon result in a net outflow of resources to this source, even if partly offset by agreement on an Extended Financing Facility and Structural Adjustment Facility over the next three years. At a wider level, the growth in external borrowing has ratcheted up the debt-service ratio. Already by 1987 debt-service payments as a share of exports of goods and services exceeded 61 per cent.

At present rates of economic growth, it seems unlikely that Ghana will be able to sustain such high relative debt levels without consistent rescheduling or debt for-giveness. Yet the need for external financing remains acute, given the limited progress that has been managed over the past four years. This is very clear when looking in more detail at agriculture – the core productive sector.

AGRICULTURAL SECTOR POLICIES AND REFORMS

The main feature of recent agricultural policy has been the increase in output prices, with particularly sharp increases in cocoa relative to other crops. There has also been broad agreement between the government and the major donors on the reduction of input subsidies, particularly for fertiliser, pesticides and farm equipment, but less practical commitment by the government to shifting the functions of input distribution to the private sector. In the more general area of reform of public agricultural institutions, the main initiative has been in reducing the budgetary costs to the government of the large parastatal sector and a drastic redundancy programme for the Ghana Cocoa Marketing Board (GCMB). The GCMB, which at its peak in 1980 accounted for nearly 20 per cent of wage employees (for institutions with over ten workers), has shed around 16,000 workers (plus a further 25,000 ghost workers) in an attempt to reduce marketing costs.

But the main thrust has been on pricing policy, and a number of the more complex issues of private sector involvement and institutional reform have been held over, in effect, to ERP II and more directly targeted project interventions (see below).

Cocoa pricing

Unlike the major food crops – maize, rice and cassava – the cocoa market remains largely characterised by monopsony. This implies that, to a considerable extent, price determination by government is a key feature, even if, under certain circumstance, producers have circumscribed official markets. Thus, during the 1970s as real cocoa producer prices fell sharply, in relation both to earlier levels and to price levels obtaining in neighbouring countries, producers had recourse to parallel markets and smuggling. Consequently, a key feature of the ERP has been the attempt, first, to raise producer prices closer to border price levels as a means of engendering a supply response and, second, to achieve a higher level of market release through official channels.

The emphasis on cocoa price reform can be attributed not only to the importance of cocoa in export revenues but also to the punitive levels of implicit taxation embodied in pre-1983 farmgate prices. The new policy has meant that between 1984 and 1987/8 nominal cocoa prices increased by five times – a rate of increment substantially in excess of that for food crops, such as maize or rice, where the government has attempted to establish floor prices. Although it can be argued that such divergence in the rate of price adjustment would lead to resource transfers away from food crops, thereby diminishing the supply of the latter, raising prices and hence appreciating the exchange rate, this pitfall has not emerged, as yet, in the Ghanaian context. This can be attributed, first, to the peculiarly low level of cocoa prices prior to the ERP; second, to the fact that all sub-sectors are operating significantly below capacity; and, third, to the fact that actual market prices for food crops have consistently exceeded the minimum prices established by the government. Upward adjustment of the cocoa price has been undertaken with a view to establishing a medium-term output level of around 300,000 metric tons per annum.

However, it ought to be noted that it was not until 1985/6 that the real cocoa producer price increased significantly. By 1986/7 that price fell to below 30 per cent of the international price and was only a third of the price obtaining in neighbouring Côte d'Ivoire. Under 1987/8 prices of 150,000 cedis/ton these shares have increased to around 42 and 57 per cent respectively, and under the Structural Adjustment Credit of the World Bank the government has agreed to aim for a producer price of 55 per cent of the international price by 1988/9 (World Bank, 1987a:17).

Relative agricultural prices

Despite the fact that the main focus of government policy under the ERP has been to revive cocoa production through higher farmgate prices, the relative shift in favour of cocoa producers carries a number of other implications. In the first place, cocoa producers are concentrated regionally, in the West and Central Regions of the country. In the historically backward northern savannah region, cocoa is not grown at all (Ewusi, 1984). Thus, emphasising cocoa relative price shifts has clear distributional implications within the agricultural sector. Second, in the absence of a food producer price series and using the national food price index as a proxy, it appears that, save for the drought years of 1982 and 1983, food prices remained roughly constant between 1978 and 1984 but have subsequently declined significantly. This decline has been very pronounced relative to cocoa, as can be seen in Table 7.2. As regards the inter-sectoral terms of trade, however, it appears that for food producers the terms of trade fell by around 50 per cent between 1982 and 1987. By contrast, in the same period the terms of trade for cocoa improved dramatically – by around 80 per cent – over manufactured products.

Falling relative real prices for food crops have obviously had beneficial implications for the inflation rate and can be mainly attributed to higher output levels associated with reasonable climatic conditions. However, given the fact that, at present consumption levels and trends, the economy will be marked by significant food deficits by

Table 7.2: *Relative prices of agricultural crops, 1977–87*

Year	Consumer Price Index	Consumer Price Index (Food)	Real Food Price Index	Nominal Cocoa Price Index	Real Cocoa Price Index	Intrasectoral Terms of Trade
1977	100	100	100	100	100	100
1978	173	159	92	200	115	125
1979	267	258	97	300	112	116
1980	401	393	98	300	75	77
1981	869	829	95	900	103	108
1982	1,062	1,125	105	900	85	81
1983	2,357	2,755	117	1,500	64	55
1984	3,304	3,059	93	2,251	68	73
1985	3,647	2,718	75	4,246	115	153
1986	4,523	3,269	72	6,414	141	195
1987*	5,400	3,841	71	11,253	214	301

* January 1987.
Source: Compiled from the Statistical Services Newsletter No.A3/87 and Records of the GCMB.

the turn of the century, the maintenance of low producer prices for food crops relative to competing tradables would tend to constrain growth in area and productivity.

Output performance

Associated with the pronounced shift in relative prices in favour of cocoa, Table 7.3 shows that by 1985 and 1986 cocoa output had recovered to levels roughly equivalent to those attained between 1980 and 1982. However, between 1984 and 1986 cocoa output reached only 80 per cent of its targeted level – a level that would have restored output to broadly that maintained in the second half of the 1970s. A significant proportion of the increase in cocoa output since the trough year of 1983 can be put down to a return to official marketing channels. This has in part been a result of higher real prices, but also other improvements, such as a more rapid payment of growers through the Rural Banking system.

Table 7.3: *Ghana: output of key crops, 1970/74–1986 ('000 tons)*

Year	Cocoa	Maize	Rice	Cassava	Total cereals[a]	Total starchy staples[b]
1970–74	403	452	62	2,817	812	6,628
1975–79	312	300	90	1,936	664	4,380
1980	258	382	78	2,322	674	4,349
1981	225	378	97	2,063	725	4,114
1982	179	346	36	2,470	544	4,431
1983	159	172	40	1,721	308	3,649
1984	175	574	66	4,065	965	6,150
1985	219	335	80	3,075	780	4,891
1986	230	495	80	3,040	905	5,005

[a]Includes maize, rice, millet, sorghum.
[b]Includes cassava, cocoyam, plantain and yam.
Source: Ministry of Agriculture and GCMB.

For cereals and starchy staples production, output trends, despite recent price movements, have been more strongly positive. For the period 1984–6 total cereals output was significantly higher than the levels attained even in the early 1970s, and this was even more pronounced in the case of cassava. For the main food crops, output has fallen only very slightly below targeted levels post-1984. Most of this output effect can be attributed to an area response. Thus, for maize and cassava the sown area in 1984 and 1985 was between 15 and 20 per cent greater than the average area planted to the crop in the 1970s. This can be attributed in part to a combination of response to severe drought and food shortages in 1983 and better climatic conditions. Nevertheless, output for both cocoa and the major food crops still remains below the peak levels of the late 1960s. Moreover, there is no evidence of any underlying upward trend in productivity.

Input Subsidies

Under adjustment, input subsidies have attracted considerable attention from donors, not only on account of their supposed distortionary implications, but also for budgetary reasons. Major donors, such as the World Bank, have argued that input subsidies cannot be justified on classical 'infant-industry' arguments. Rather, such subsidies have tended to favour larger producers, primarily of rice, at the expense of the bulk of small-holders (World Bank 1985a). At the same time, in a context of severe import compression and rationing, the subsidy policy has allowed for diversion of significant rents to distributors, thereby invalidating the justification for the subsidy in the first place. A further consequence has been the stimulus to the export of subsidised fertiliser to neighbouring states.

Under ERP 1 the government agreed to phase out input subsidies. This was largely achieved in 1984. The combination of a bumper maize crop, food imports and a massive price increase (from 45 cedis to 295 cedis per 50 kg bag) choked off demand for fertiliser (FAO, 1985). To draw down existing stocks, the price was held constant in nominal terms, so that by 1986 the subsidy element was of the order of 37/44 per cent. In mid-1986 fertiliser prices were raised by 80 per cent, with a small subsidy still remaining. Fertiliser imports have declined sharply, but this is unlikely to have had a strongly adverse impact on productivity. This is because, firstly, cocoa producers do not apply fertiliser; for them, pesticide use is more important. Second, in the recent past, barely 5 per cent of the cultivated area has been fertilised, with only 15 per cent of the maize area undergoing fertiliser application (Kapusta, 1986). Most of this area has been in the Northern and Upper Regions where larger rice and maize farms predominate.

Lastly, the government has also agreed, though it has still to implement, the transfer of fertiliser imports to the private sector. As elsewhere in sub-Saharan Africa, the principal issue remains one of feasibility, given the sharp variability in demand and the legacy of price-fixing by the government. At current input/output price ratios and according to previous cultural practice, it seems unlikely that demand for inputs will become more buoyant.

AGRICULTURAL POLICY UNDER ERP 2

Under the second phase of the adjustment process, the government has chosen to emphasise the increase in cocoa producer incentives, largely through reduction in

GCMB overhead costs as well as the overhaul of the extension system. These priorities have been expressed through two substantive projects – the Cocoa Rehabilitation Project, financed by the International Development Association, the government and other donors, and the Agricultural Services Rehabilitation Project, again financed by IDA and a mix of other donors. Taken together these projects represent a detailed attempt to chart the future course and structure of government interventions in agriculture. They imply going beyond the largely price-related reforms that marked the first phase of the ERP.

Agricultural Services Rehabilitation Project (ASRP)

Measures agreed in 1987 to rehabilitate Ghana's agricultural services include a number of items similar to earlier, if less purposeful, attempts to assist the Ministry of Agriculture. For example, there are financial commitments to new policy and planning units, to agricultural research facilities, to veterinary and irrigation services and to existing extension programmes.

Three main components are less familiar, however. First, support for a programme of divestiture of publicly-owned agricultural enterprises (through liquidation, sales and conversion to joint ventures) and large reductions in subventions to remaining enterprises. There are 18 enterprises currently under the Ministry. Among those proposed for joint-venture operations is the Ghana Seed Company which is the main source of improved planting material on which much of the current extension effort rests.

The second main new component is the privatisation of certain Ministry services, most notably fertiliser supply and tractor hire but extending also to some areas of animal health. Tractor hire organised by the Ministry does not, in fact, constitute a significant share of the total mechanisation services available and the main impact is likely to be in staff redundancies. But in fertiliser supply, there are major consequences for a change in policy. This is because privatisation will be preceded by the elimination of price subsidies and the replacement of uniform pricing by an unregulated market. The five-year programme involves, first, retail trade privatisation, followed by wholesale trade, followed by importation.

The third important new area for the ASRP is the reorganisation of extension services. The reorganisation itself is not an immediate root-and-branch exercise. It consists of a series of pilot projects which leave open difficult questions such as the merger or otherwise of cocoa and non-cocoa extension services. But there is one major assumption behind future national reorganisation, namely, acceptance of the view that extension staff should be largely confined to technical advisory work and should cease to be directly involved in the supply of production requirements.

Cocoa Rehabilitation Project (CRP)

Several of these concerns are also evident in the CRP, but the project (which has yet to be given final approval) is an even more radical initiative towards privatisation and contains more explicit commitments on producer prices and margins. The main assumptions behind the project are that the cocoa industry has declined because of poor prices, weak services such as disease control and research, and inefficient farm input supply and marketing under the GCMB.

As regards pricing, the government's intention of moving the producer price to around 55 per cent of the international price will be met partly by squeezing GCMB shares of cocoa revenues to around 15 per cent of fob from a current 30 per cent level. Investment in services is primarily in research, with plant breeding and disease control as the main activities. There is also the intention to reorganise the extension work of the Cocoa Services Division, with many of its current functions, such as distributing inputs, being dropped. The withdrawal of these CSD services will be accompanied by an elimination of subsidies and the 'progressive privatisation' of GCMB commercial input supply functions.

The privatisation programme is also intended to extend to cocoa marketing, starting with the purchase and collection of cocoa from producers. This is currently the responsibility of the Produce Buying Corporation (PBC), a GCMB subsidiary. It is recognised by donors that the objective of privatising the cocoa trade has wider ramifications for Ghana, and there has been no immediate pressure to instigate action. However, emphasis has been placed on improving the operational efficiency of PBC, largely through retrenchment and the closure of under-utilised buying centres.

The Implementation of ASRP and CRP: Field Reactions

Following the compilation of the results of a survey of four villages undertaken during 1987 (see below), a series of inspections and interviews with field-level officers in the Ministry of Agriculture and the GCMB was undertaken. A number of points arose which indicate possible implementation difficulties and which also question some of the assumptions behind parts of the agricultural adjustment programme.

First, there is the issue of alleged over-manning of agricultural field services which is part and parcel of the efforts both to retrench public sector employment levels and to improve public service efficiency. In the case of the GCMB, it is evident that the current operating costs of the Board are difficult to justify, given the substantial decline in trading operations over the past decade. Moreover, there has been chronic over-manning at headquarters and regional levels. In its field operations the Cocoa Services Division has also acquired a large labour force for farm-level operations which is largely under-employed and has been undertaking many of the tasks that could be done by casual wage labour.

Against this, however, the extension services themselves (in the CSD and in the Ministry) are clearly not over-staffed, given their current range of responsibilities; and in the case of the PMB (which is also under pressure to retrench) the staffing levels of the buying centres appear to be appropriate to their levels of business. For example, in one of the surveyed villages – Tetrem – the buying centre handled the produce of 250 growers with one Produce Clerk, supported by a single labourer and a watchman. In another village, Ofoase, the Produce Clerk now manages two centres on an itinerant basis. At the level of farmer services, therefore, 'over-manning' may not be the key issue.

Arguments in favour of privatising cocoa purchasing also revolve around the alleged inefficiencies of the PMB. Field-level evidence in the survey area does not bear out these assumptions. For the 1987 season all the registered growers contacted had sold their crop and been paid. Credit recoveries on seasonal loans for cocoa growers were close to 100 per cent; losses in storage were very low and delivery to buying centres had not been difficult, even for smaller growers with farms some distance from the nearest centre.

A final area of interest concerns extension services and their role in input supply. Apart from the feasibility constraints, mentioned above, of greater private sector involvement, there also remains the question of consistency in donor policy. While World Bank support for the ASRP stresses a more technically oriented service, other donor assistance in the survey area is clearly committed to a more familiar pattern of extension investment based upon extension-fertiliser-seed packages and inputs on concessionary terms to encourage 'demonstration' farmers. An EEC financed project in Ofinso, for example, has been providing vehicles and stores to assist in the public supply of fertiliser, while Global 2000 (a private US charity) has also been promoting fertiliser-based extension in all four villages.

In the cocoa sector, extension work is even more closely bound to input supply. In fact the main function of CSD extension service is in ensuring plant protection measures and supplying seed. Field Assistants hold stocks of insecticides, fungicides and mistblowers for sale as well as organising machinery repairs. In some respects, the CSD acts as an inspectorate, as much as an advisory service, and even if private suppliers took over parts of its work it is difficult to envisage a separation of input supply activities and advisory services for cocoa farmers.

THE IMPACT OF ADJUSTMENT POLICIES: MICRO-ECONOMIC EVIDENCE

In this section a detailed attempt, using cross-section data collected in a four-village survey in 1987, is made to evaluate the impact at farm level of the major reform measures – primarily related to pricing policy – that have been instituted since 1983. The principal concern is to estimate the level of area response by farmers to relative price shifts and, in particular, the substantive real increases in cocoa prices. While, given the limitations of the data, it has not been possible to estimate econometrically the short-run supply response, the data that have been collected allow for more limited estimation of the planting response, as well as mapping the impact of relative price shifts on the size and composition of farm income from crop production. The results confirm much of the available evidence from cocoa supply models based on national-level time-series. One such model points to an immediate price elasticity of supply of 0.14, a short-run elasticity of 0.71 and a long-run elasticity ranging between 0.95 and 1.25 (Gbetibouo, 1987. See also Akiyama and Bowers, 1984). Ghanaian cocoa producers therefore appear to respond, with the usual lags associated with a tree crop, to improved returns to cocoa achieved by raising real farmgate prices.

The Survey Area

The survey, using a random stratified sample, was carried out in March-June 1987 in part of the old core cocoa area, the Ashanti Region. In the past as much as 84 per cent of the total cultivated area in this region has been allocated to cocoa, but this share has fallen as has the region's share of aggregate output. In 1985 Ashanti cocoa production amounted to around 25 per cent of total national output – a decline from a 36 per cent level in 1980/81. Nevertheless, the region remains strongly based on cocoa and therefore provides a reasonable measure of the degree of responsiveness to price changes at farm level. Data were collected in four villages, the basic characteristics of which are summarised in Table 7.4. The villages display a reasonably wide spread of characteristics in terms of population and access to infrastructure.

Out of a total listing of 622 cocoa farmers, 151 were ultimately sampled randomly. This amounted to just under a quarter of the total cocoa producer population, albeit

Table 7.4: *Basic village characteristics and sample frame*

| | | Villages | | | Total |
Characteristics	Dwease	Ofoase	Poano	Tetrem	Av./%
Population: 1970	654	454	1,737	2,893	5,738
1984	882	662	2,680	3,699	7,923
Population Growth Rate,					
1970–84 (%)	2.5	3.3	3.9	2.0	2.7
Cocoa Farmers:					
Total by Village:	103	78	149	292	622
Total Sample Size:	18	15	54	64	151
% of Total	17.5	19.2	36.2	21.9	24.3
% of Sample Size	11.9	10.0	35.7	42.4	100.0
Non-Cocoa Farmers:					
Total Sample Size:	5	3	14	18	40
Village Facilities:					
Distance from: Main Road	5	10	0.5	0.5	–
(in miles) Post Office	0	5	0	0	–
Rural Bank	13	5	9	20	–
Commercial Bank	7	14	9	20	–
Market	7	25	9	20	–
Hospital/Dispensary	0	5	9	20	–

with a significant bias towards the larger villages, Poano and Tetrem. In addition, 40 non-cocoa farmers were purposively selected as controls. The assembled data concern the 1986/7 cropping season. Sampling occurred at the end of the main cocoa purchasing season when farmers' memories were still fresh.

All four villages had roads which were accessible throughout the year. All, except Ofoase, had Post Offices but other basic facilities were available only at some distance. Again, all except Ofoase had a resident Agricultural Field Assistant and a Produce Buying Centre with a purchasing clerk.

Some Basic Sample Attributes

While it is clear that infra-marginal land scarcity has already begun to emerge in parts of the more densely populated and cultivated forest zones, such as the region in which the survey was carried out, Ghanaian agriculture remains for the most part characterised by under-utilisation of land, if not by actual surpluses. This comes about in part because of constraints on land ownership and the presence of a limited land market. In this regard, labour rather than land constraints tend to be more binding.

A further feature of Ghanaian agriculture is a surprisingly high level of skewedness in land-holding distribution. The last national survey – in 1970 – suggested that 68 per cent of holdings fell below 6 acres but controlled under 21 per cent of the land area. By contrast farms of over 20 acres controlled nearly 46 per cent of the total area (Agricultural Census, 1970). However, it ought also to be noted that by 1980/81 only 12 per cent of the total area was under arable or permanent cropping, while nearly 38 per cent was still classified as forest or woodland (FAO, 1985).

The 1987 survey, though demonstrating some variation by village, throws light on both these issues. In the first place, of the total sample, just over half held below 10 acres, with under a quarter holding over 20 acres. Skewedness was, however, far more pronounced among cocoa farmers than non-cocoa farmers. In the former case, larger farm holdings of above 20 acres controlled 60 per cent of total land and nearly 65 per cent of cultivated land.

As regards land use, it is interesting to note that extensive fallowing, a marked characteristic of Ghanaian agriculture, still occurs. For cocoa farmers a third of their land holdings are kept fallow in any one year. Moreover, land utilisation rates tend to be lowest for the smallest farms. The latter were also marked by low aggregate family size relative to other farm size classes. This can be attributed to the greater importance of non-farm labour and migration. Lower land use directly reflects lower on-farm labour attributes. In the case of non-cocoa farmers, the situation was rather different. Almost all held below 10 acres, with fallow land on average comprising around 15 per cent of total land. Moreover, while almost no cocoa farmers rented land, 28 per cent of non-cocoa farmers rented, with around a quarter of their total area being leased from other households. To that extent, cocoa farmers with land of more than 5 acres tended to rent out land, and this was strongly positively correlated with farm size. Although the rented-out area comprised, on average, no more than 6–7 per cent of total area, 22 per cent of cocoa farmers were actually renting out land in 1986/7 (see Table 7.5).

The survey data thus conform with much of the existing information: capacity utilisation remains relatively low, but increasing; land holdings distribution is marked by significant inequalities (although it was not possible to correct for land quality attributes); there is a modest land rental market and tenanted land tends not to be cultivated with tree crops such as cocoa (see also Feder and Noronha, 1987). The distinction in this area between cocoa and non-cocoa farmers is less related to choice of production than to tenancy constraints and other farm attributes. In this last regard, it should be noted that non-cocoa farm households were significantly smaller than their cocoa counterparts.

For cocoa-producing households, the dominance of that crop was striking. For all farm size groups, nearly 80 per cent of the cultivated area (excluding fallow land) was under cocoa and this dominance was especially pronounced for the larger farms over 20 acres. The remaining cultivated space was devoted to a mixture of other tree crops – oil palm, plantain and citrus, as well as food crops – maize, vegetables, and starchy staples such as cassava and cocoyam.

Cocoa Production and New Plantings

Given the emphasis placed by the government on raising the relative return to cocoa production, an explicit intention of the survey was to estimate the level of response as measured through recent replanting. This was particularly pertinent, given the sharp real producer price increases post-1985. Any increase in the cocoa area through new planting would be a reversal of earlier trends which had seen continuing decline in the cocoa area and a parallel failure of cocoa production projects, such as Suhum and Ashanti.

Despite recent price increases, it was recognised by donors that until 1985 higher prices might lead to some rehabilitation but would not engender replanting (World Bank, 1985). In other words, there would be better capacity utilisation rather than capacity expansion. Recent output data only partially clarify whether this has been

Table 7.5: Ashanti: farm size distribution and basic attributes

Farm Size (acres)	Observations	Total Cultivated Area (acres)	Total Area Harvested 1986/7 (acres)	Total Area (acres)	No. of Cases renting land	No. of Cases renting out land	Cocoa Area (acres)	
0–5	16	67	51	181	0	0	44	
5–10	45	376	250	599	1	9	235	COCOA
10–20	45	670	498	1,081	1	8	447	FARMS
20–30	28	653	444	934	0	9	470	
>30	17	1,410	1,125	1,877	0	7	1,285	
Total	151	3,176	2,368	4,672	2	33	2,481	
0–5	22	68	61	78	6	0	–	
5–10	15	110	88	136	5	2	–	NON-COCOA
10–20	2	28	28	39	0	0	–	FARMS
20–30	1	30	26	38	0	0	–	
Total	40	236	203	291	11	2	–	

Source: ODI/ISSER, Ashanti Survey, 1987.

the case. For although the underlying production level may be of the order of 300/310,000 tonnes, with current output below 250,000 tonnes, the latter level of market release may merely represent a clawing-back by official marketing outlets of produce previously sold on the parallel market. At the same time higher output could be a function of improved cultural practices as well as enhanced application of pesticides and fertiliser top dressing.

Information from the survey area clearly supports the view that officially marketed output has risen. Officially marketed cocoa was over 60 per cent higher in 1986/7 than in 1985/6 in the four survey villages. In one village, Tetrem, the quantity marketed through the GCMB more than doubled in this period.

While this short-run growth can be attributed to a number of factors, longer-term expansion of productive capacity will obviously require significant new planting. Cocoa takes between three and six years to start producing pods (hybrid and amelonado, respectively); hence one would expect a considerable lag before the effects of improved prices and marketing arrangements would filter through. In order to capture the level of replanting, the survey data distinguished between cocoa fields in terms of their position in the productive cycle. Table 7.6 presents this information.

Table 7.6: *Ashanti: Cocoa production: composition of stock (as share of total cocoa area)*

| | | | | | Proportion of households with | |
Farm Size acres	Area planted in 1986/7 %	Area too young to Produce* %	In Full Production %	Near End of Production %	New Plantings in 1986 %	Cocoa too young to Produce %
0–5	20	30	57	13	56	63
5–10	25	36	49	15	58	76
10–20	21	28	52	20	78	82
20–30	27	31	51	18	89	92
>30	14	17	47	36	82	88
Total	19	24	49	27	72	81

* Column includes area planted in 1986/7.
Source: Ibid.

It is evident that significant planting has occurred in the recent period and that this has been almost uniformly the case. It is only the largest farms (of over 30 acres) that show relatively low levels of planting. Moreover, it is interesting to note that nearly 80 per cent of this planting occurred in 1986/7, suggesting that the real price increases of that year and the series of prior increases were required to elicit a shift of resources. Nevertheless, the area that has recently been planted is still less than the area under cocoa at the end of the productive cycle. If the largest farms with low new planting are excluded, however, then over 30 per cent of the cocoa area is under plants too young to produce as against 18 per cent under old trees. Moreover, even despite relatively low area response on the part of large farms, just under 90 per cent of those households had some planting, with a level of over 80 per cent for the entire sample. This indicates that even with domestic cocoa prices at between 20 and 28 per cent of international prices (using parallel and official exchange rates), there has been a significant level of planting and rehabilitation.

It can also be noted that, alongside cocoa, new plantings of plantain were found to be significant. Over a third of the plantain area was newly established, with almost all new planting occurring in 1986/7. This has been associated with cocoa expansion since plantain tends to be a complementary crop, with plantain leaves providing shade for young cocoa seedlings.

Although, at present relative price levels, returns to oil palm have been substantially superior to those for cocoa, in the survey area oil palm did not emerge as a major competing tree crop. The acreage under the latter was less than 4 per cent of that of cocoa, even though new plantings accounted for nearly two-fifths of that relatively limited area. But of the total area newly planted to tree crops, oil palm accounted for under 3 per cent.

Inputs Use, Marketing and Access to Services

It has already been mentioned that, despite a good agronomic case for using fertiliser as a top dressing, Ghanaian cocoa farmers, unlike their Ivoirien counterparts, do not apply fertiliser. This was amply borne out in the survey. Only 2 out of 151 cocoa farmers applied any fertiliser. Moreover, the use of pesticide was restricted to only two-thirds of cocoa growers, comprising around 11 per cent of total inputs cost. This can be attributed in part to continuing supply problems, not just of pesticide but of fuel for the mistblowers, as well as the sharp recent increases in retail prices for pesticide. Between 1982/3 and 1986 the price of pesticide more than quadrupled in nominal terms, while that of mistblowers has risen from 700 cedis in 1984/5 to 23,000 cedis in 1986/7. The reduction of subsidy has been associated with some reduction in pesticide use.

The relatively restricted use of fertiliser and pesticide for all crops meant that hired labour and, in the case of food crops, seed inputs, comprised the major shares of production costs. For cocoa, nearly 90 per cent of farms hired some labour and labour costs amounted to 75 per cent of total production costs. Use of hired labour was, moreover, positively associated with farm size and was far more significant for tree crops than for food crops. For the latter, less than 10 per cent of growers used any hired labour.

For the other major input, seed, at least two-thirds of cocoa growers received hybrid seedlings from the Cocoa Services Division of the GCMB. There appears to be no parallel market, despite the fact that four-fifths of the farmers who had obtained hybrid seedlings complained of difficulty in securing the seedlings, let alone their timely delivery.

As regards marketing, marketed releases were, as expected, high for traditional cash crops – largely tree crops – across farm size. In the case of food crops, principally cassava, maize and cocoyam, roughly 50 per cent of households that grew these crops marketed some share of their output.

It would appear that the share of households, as also the share of aggregate output marketed among non-cocoa growers, was higher than for cocoa-growing households. For the total sample, it emerges that around a third of aggregate output for cocoyam and cassava – the two starchy staples – was marketed, with just over half of the total maize output being sold. This points to higher levels of marketed release for food crops than has been commonly supposed (see Table 7.7 for disaggregated data). Moreover, the information gathered on marketing outlets indicates that, while the GCMB was the effective monopoly buyer for cocoa and local oil mills the dominant buyers of oil palm, in the case of food crops, local traders were the purchasers in a third of all cases, with itinerant traders accounting for the remaining two-thirds. This suggests that marketed food crop output was largely directed toward urban markets.

Table 7.7: *Ashanti: share of households and output marketed, 1986/7 season (per cent)*

| | | FARM SIZE (acres) | | | | | | | | |
| | | 0–5 | | 5–10 | | 10–20 | | 20–30 | | >30 | |
Crop	Category	A	B	A	B	A	B	A	B	A	B
Plantain	C	72	79	78	78	56	71	63	67	57	47
	NC	54	40	82	98	50	50	–	–	–	–
Oil Palm	C	–	–	100	95	100	99	100	87	–	–
	NC	–	–	100	100	100	100	100	100	–	–
Cassava	C	31	13	63	28	41	31	38	19	40	11
	NC	52	44	85	75	100	38	–	–	–	–
Cocoyam	C	23	24	50	33	37	25	41	31	33	13
	NC	33	22	69	77	100	45	–	–	–	–
Maize	C	57	71	44	38	50	50	50	43	57	41
	NC	64	39	86	71	–	–	–	–	–	–

Category: C = Cocoa Grower.
             NC = Non-Cocoa Grower.
A = Proportion of households growing crop that market some share of output.
B = Share of total output marketed.

Source: Ibid.

Farm Income: Size and Composition

As an explicit aim of the ERP has been to raise rural incomes, both absolutely and relatively, the impact of price adjustments on farm income levels is clearly a key matter. While in general it can be argued that the intersectoral terms of trade have shifted in favour of cocoa-growers, this has not been the case for households producing primarily food items.

Table 7.8 provides some information concerning average household and *per capita* income levels, as well as breaking down income by source. It should be noted that income is used here to define net crop income after deducting aggregate production costs. However, no shadow wage has been estimated for family labour inputs, on the assumption of a low opportunity cost. Moreover, what is referred to as household income is only crop income. Data on other income sources – including wage employment – proved scanty and unreliable.

Table 7.8 clearly demonstrates, first, the importance of cocoa in household income, an importance that is strongly and positively associated with farm size and, second, that a very significant spread exists between household and *per capita* incomes across farm size. For cocoa growers, average *per capita* incomes for the largest farms were nearly ten times those for the two smallest farm size classes. However, although the smallest non-cocoa farm size category had average income levels significantly lower than for cocoa growers, income for the 5–10 acre category was superior, this being attributable to far higher levels of market release for both food and tree crop products. This suggests that, while an absence of cocoa might commonly be linked to lower income levels, this was not always the case, given the buoyant market in food commodities.

Further analysis of the data on cocoa incomes indicates that returns to cocoa were positively related to farm size. Net income per acre for the two largest farm size groups was nearly 60 per cent higher than for the two smallest farm size classes. Analysis of

Table 7.8: Ashanti: Crop income 1986/7

Farm Size (acres)	(Observations)	Average Household Income (cedis)	Per Capita Income (cedis)	Shares in Household Income (%)			
				Cocoa	Other Tree Crops	Food Crops	
COCOA GROWERS							
0–5	(16)	25,982	6,759	49.7	28.7	21.6	
5–10	(45)	29,798	5,601	65.6	23.8	10.6	
10–20	(45)	85,400	12,555	67.9	25.5	6.6	
20–30	(27)	132,260	18,017	91.0	6.1	2.9	
>30	(17)	500,569	59,592	99.0	–	1.0	
NON-COCOA GROWERS							
0–5	(22)	12,818	3,578	–	46.4	53.6	
5–10	(15)	79,067	17,543	–	49.7	50.3	

Source: Ibid.

the range of cocoa incomes indicates that the top 11 per cent of landholders (those with over 30 acres) controlled over 48 per cent of total cocoa income. By contrast, the 70 per cent of households with holdings of below 20 acres controlled under a third of total cocoa income. This cautions against any over-simplified view that raising producer prices will have a uniformly beneficial impact on farmers. Given existing land distributions and control over assets, the principal gainers have been the larger farms.

CONCLUSIONS

The adjustment programme in Ghana has been marked not only by its recent start but also its concentration on a relatively limited range of policy instruments. In the latter regard, the main emphasis has been placed on exchange-rate reform and the restructuring of domestic relative prices. As would be expected, the primary emphasis has been put on reviving the cocoa sub-sector.

The survey results presented in this chapter indicate that recent producer price increases for cocoa have indeed called forth a supply response. However, with the usual lags, this response will not become apparent in output terms until the end of the present decade. With favourable climatic conditions, output of food crops has also continued to rise, despite the relative price decline vis-à-vis cocoa. The survey data indicate that marketed releases of food crops have been higher than was commonly supposed and have consequently comprised – for non-cocoa growers – a major share of monetary income. This may, in part, explain the significant deceleration in the rate of food price increases relative to the general price index over the period 1983/6.

The emphasis now being placed on institutional reform under the second phase of the ERP remains more problematic. In the first instance, it is by no means clear that the private sector will be willing to take over the importation and distribution of basis inputs, particularly given the thin demand consequent upon the elimination of subsidies. Secondly, while the GCMB and the Ministry of Agriculture have been characterised by over-manning and inappropriate skill composition – a recent survey of MOA staff demonstrated that roughly one third were labourers and a further 38 per cent clerks or typists (FAO, 1985) – inadequate attention has been paid to improving the performance of the field-level services. Evidence from the Ashanti survey indicates that at this level there was not acute over-manning nor the apparently high levels of inefficiency in the provision of services to farmers that have been commonly cited by donors. Nevertheless, the survey results confirmed weak performance as regards distribution of pesticide and seedlings. Possibly the single most important shift in practice has been the move away from the much-abused chit system of payment to payment of cocoa growers by cheque through the rural banking system. All cocoa growers in the survey were paid within two weeks of delivering cocoa to the PBC centre. This is likely to have been one important factor behind the recent increase in cocoa planting.

As regards the performance of the economy as a whole under adjustment, it is evident that, despite some growth in the minerals sector, Ghana's external trade profile remains worryingly dominated by cocoa. In recent years, faced with relatively flat demand and increased competition from new producers, such as Malaysia, export unit prices for cocoa have fallen. Despite a projected annual growth of 8 per cent in export volume for the period 1987–90, falling cocoa prices and a necessary increase in imports will result in a deterioration in the current account (World Bank, 1987b). Consequently, worsening external terms of trade, relative lack of export diversity and limited scope for further import compression have made the Ghanaian economy highly dependent on concessional aid flows. But this imposes its own cost in terms of a rapidly growing debt overhang.

The continuing existence of a strong external constraint has been matched domestically by the collapse of government expenditures for both recurrent and capital accounts. This has compromised the ability to sustain a longer-term development effort. Recurrent expenditures amounted to no more than 9.5 per cent of GDP between 1983 and 1986, while capital outlays have collapsed to less than 2 per cent of GDP over the same period. The consequences have been various but have included falling real wages and further deterioration in basic infrastructure. In the social sector, ERP 1 was marked by a particularly sharp contraction in resources directed to health and education. *Per capita* expenditure on the former was at less than a quarter of the 1975 level and at half the 1979/80 level (Cornia *et al.*, 1987). Although under ERP 2, explicit emphasis has been placed on revising these priorities, considerable increases in public outlays on infrastructure, as much as for the social sector, will be required if the output gains from the elimination of the grosser external and domestic price misalignments are to be sustained. Despite major progress since 1983, achieving these ends will remain difficult, given on unfavourable external trading environment, limitations on concessional transfers and strict IMF-supervised constraints on domestic deficit financing.

REFERENCES

Akiyama, T. and A. Bowers (1984), *Supply Response of Cocoa in Major Producing Countries*, World Bank Working Paper 1984–3, Washington DC, World Bank.

Akoto, O.A. (1987), 'Agricultural development policy in Ghana', *Food Policy*, August.

Cornia, G. et al. (1987 and 1988), *Adjustment with a Human Face*, Vols 1 and 2, Oxford, Clarendon Press for UNICEF.

Ewusi, K. (1984), *The Dimensions and Characteristics of Rural Poverty in Ghana*, ISSER Technical Publication 43, Legon, University of Ghana.

FAO Investment Centre (1985), *Ghana, Agricultural Sector Rehabilitation Credit*, Identification/Preparation Mission Report, Rome, November.

Feder, G. and R. Noronha (1987), 'Land rights systems and agricultural development in Sub-Saharan Africa', in *World Bank Research Observer*, Vol. 2, No. 2.

Gbetibouo, M. (1987), 'Cocoa Production in Ghana and Export Prospects', World Bank, November, (mimeo).

Kapusta, E.C. (1986), 'The fertilizer system in Ghana', IFDC, June, (mimeo).

May, E. (1985), *Exchange Controls and Parallel Market Economies in Sub-Saharan Africa: Focus on Ghana*, World Bank Staff Working Paper No. 711, Washington DC.

Republic of Ghana (1985), *Progress of the Economic Recovery Programme, 1984–1986 and Policy Framework, 1986–1988*, Accra, October.

Rourke, B.E. (1974), 'Profitability of cocoa and alternative crops in Eastern Region, Ghana', in *Economics of Cocoa Production and Marketing*, Legon, University of Ghana, ISSER.

Tabatabai, H. (1986), *Economic Decline, Access to Food and Structural Adjustment in Ghana*, ILO, World Employment Programme Working Paper, WEP10–6/WP80, Geneva, July.

World Bank (1984a), *Ghana: Managing the Transition*, Washington DC.

—— (1984b), *Ghana: Policies and Program for Adjustment*, Washington DC.

—— (1985a), *Ghana: Agricultural Sector Review*, Washington DC.

—— (1985b), *Ghana: Towards Structural Adjustment*, (2 vols), Washington DC.

—— (1987a), Report of the President of I.D.A. on a Proposed Development Credit to Ghana for a Structural Adjustment Programme, Washington DC, March.

—— (1987b), *Ghana: Policies and Issues of Structural Adjustment*, Washington DC.

8

Zambia in the 1980s

The Political Economy of Adjustment

Jonathan Kydd

INTRODUCTION

This chapter provides a case study of the linkages between macroeconomic policy and policies for the agriculture and food sector in Zambia during a period of extremely demanding adjustment to an external environment which deteriorated dramatically after the mid-1970s. It is shown that slow progress in agricultural/food sector reforms, in particular in the reduction in maize subsidies, was a critical factor in the breakdown in relations with the Washington institutions which occurred in May 1987. The broad conclusions do not deny the synergy between macro- and sectoral-level reforms, but do suggest that insufficient emphasis was given to agricultural reforms. If the strong political pressure for relatively cheap food in urban areas is taken as given, then the poor performance of food production and marketing can be regarded as perhaps the most important internal constraint on the adjustment programme. Yet government officials and members of the donor Consultative Group were slow to get to grip with these problems.

OVERVIEW OF THE ECONOMY

The economic inheritance and post-independence policy

For more than 60 years, Zambia's economy has been driven by mining. Political independence came in a decade when copper prices were high (at nearly twice average world production costs) and Zambian production was on a rising trend. Thus the government found it possible to extract large revenues from mining. As over a third of the population was already concentrated in major urban centres (mainly in Copperbelt towns where the wealth was generated), it is hardly surprising that the development strategy focused on forms of urban development. An ambitious industrialisation programme was undertaken and there was considerable investment in urban housing, medical and educational services. Nationalisation was a major theme linking the strategy for extracting greater 'national' benefits from mining to the strategy for industrialisation. A pyramidal structure of state holding companies was established, and at the apex was ZIMCO, a corporation which owned the mines (ZCCM) and state industry (INDECO), as well as financial institutions. This ownership structure conferred on import-substituting industry a degree of protection above the already high formal structure of tariffs and quotas, because it created great latitude for hidden cross-subsidies.

Overall, the country's agricultural development policies must be judged a failure[1] and, by the early 1980s, Zambia had become dependent on food imports while export volumes, never very large, had fallen to virtual insignificance. But there were some agricultural successes, notably the increase in the share of marketed food supplies accounted for by small- and medium-scale African farmers (from about a third to two-thirds), and there were large maize exports in 1973, 1974 and 1978. An efficient sugar industry was established which, by the 1980s, had an exportable surplus over domestic requirements. Moreover, in the early 1980s quite large areas of the country suffered severe drought, which even the best conceived agricultural policies could not have withstood.

POLICIES AFTER THE COPPER BOOM

Zambia's recent economic history is discussed more fully elsewhere[2] and for the purposes of this chapter it can conveniently be considered in four phases:

(i)   The first phase, from 1975 to the end of 1982, in which the response to the collapse in copper prices was to extend controls;

(ii) the second period spans approximately two-and-a-half years from the beginning of 1983 to the announcement of foreign-exchange auctioning in 1985, and was characterised by preliminary liberalisation;

(iii) third, the 19 months during which a foreign-exchange auction system operated, from the beginning of October 1985 to the end of April 1987;

(iv) finally, the period from the abandonment of the auction to the time of writing (early 1988), during which there has been a reimposition of many of the economic controls which had been progressively relaxed from 1983. The policies of this most recent period can appropriately be given the title used by the Government – the Interim National Development Programme (INDP).

The extension of controls, 1975–82

In 1975, the price of copper collapsed, and Zambia's terms of trade index fell by 49 per cent in a single year. For the rest of the 1970s, prices remained around this new low level and, then, in 1980, began to slide again. Although there have been a few short-lived recoveries, copper prices have continued to fall, reaching an all-time low in real terms in early 1987. (By early 1988 the copper outlook was a little more hopeful, as the recovery from the 1987 'low' was showing rather more strength.)

The general tenor of the response to the copper price fall was to accelerate the move towards a controlled economy (which already had a political/ideological rationale prior to foreign-exchange shortages). Two highly visible measures were, first, increasingly detailed control over the allocation of foreign exchange exercised by the Bank of Zambia, and, second, price controls, which were progressively extended from staple foods to cover most basic consumer goods and some production inputs such as fuel and fertiliser.

In retrospect, it can be seen that policy during this period had the effect of protecting aggregate consumption levels, while sacrificing investment. Over the period 1975–80, investment declined at an annual rate of 11 per cent per annum, and over 1981–84 the annual rate of decline was about 20 per cent[3] (Kydd, 1986: 235-6). Infrastructure fell into disrepair, and industrial capacity shrank owing to shortages of spare parts. The aid agencies did not help matters by, in the main, continuing to direct their resources to new projects.

By the end of the 1970s, shortages of foreign exchange were becoming serious, but the government (perhaps hoping for a recovery in copper prices) preferred to allow the queue of applications for foreign exchange to lengthen, rather than to take measures to dampen demand for imports. The exchange rate of the kwacha was maintained unaltered against the SDR until 1983 (see Table 8.1). The familiar consequences of protracted shortages and rationing of foreign exchange were experienced: capacity under-utilisation, a decline in investor confidence, capital flight and inflation.

The collapse in copper prices had placed diversification of the export sector on the agenda, and the government quickly embraced this as a formal goal. There was general agreement that most of the promising export opportunities would be in the agricultural sector, because of Zambia's substantial endowment of relatively well watered land, and because its landlocked situation made labour-intensive manufacturing for export unattractive. But there was little progress in diversification (apart from the fact that price changes made cobalt a more important by-product of copper mining), and agricultural exports actually declined.

Aware that the economic environment was increasingly unattractive to business, the government brought in a number of compensatory measures. Foreign-exchange retention schemes were introduced as a reward for 'non-traditional' exports (a category which included all agricultural exports). Faced with maize deficits from the beginning of the 1980s, the government offered foreign-exchange bonuses to commercial farmers for 'above-target' supplies into the domestic market. The foreign-exchange rationing system was operated to give relatively generous allowances for 'diversification investments', and for agriculture generally. This probably kept farm production at a higher level than would otherwise have been the case, but it induced some investments which were far from congruent with Zambia's underlying resource endowments (e.g. in capital-intensive systems for the domestic high income market, such as irrigated wheat mechanically harvested, and refrigerated storage for vegetables).

Preliminary liberalisation 1983–5

In the early 1980s, pressure to pay attention to the critics of its policies in the IMF, World Bank, and the more right-wing Western governments became progressively more difficult for the government to resist. At the end of 1982, external debt was 3.2 times its 1974 level in dollar terms, despite write-offs by a number of bilateral development agencies. The balance-of-payments deficit could not be financed without debt rescheduling, and successful rescheduling required IMF support. An Economic Reform Programme was announced in December 1982, which received the imprimatur of a new IMF Stand-By facility, (which did not in itself bring in large net additional resources – see Table 8.1). The programme was supported by a donor Consultative Group (CG) which first met in Paris in 1984, and provided a framework within which debts were successfully rescheduled with private banks and bilateral official lenders.

Table 8.1: Basic data on the Zambian economy

	1979	1980	1981	1982	1983	1984	1985	1986
National income								
GDP at 1980 prices (millions of kwacha)	2,973	3,064	3,253	3,161	3,099	3,058	3,070[a]	..
Growth rate of GDP per capita (%)	..	-0.3	2.8	-6.2	-5.4	-4.7	-3.0	..
Shares of GDP (%)								
government consumption	23	26	28	28	24	25	19	..
gross fixed capital formation	17	18	18	17	15	12	10	..
change in stocks	3	5	2	0	0	2	2	..
trade balance (exports – imports)	8	-4	-13	-9	-1	4	7	..
private consumption	50	55	65	64	63	56	62	..
Exchange rate								
(SDR per kwacha)	.98	.98	.98	.98	.78	.46	.16	.11
IMF position (millions of SDRs)								
Quotas, SDRs, reserve psn	270	270	270	270	270	270	270	270
General dept credit	320	308	628	576	636	712	693	675
International transactions (millions of kwacha)								
Exports (fob)	1,090	1,023	937	950	1,052	1,231	2,475	..
(of which copper %)	(83)	(98)	(93)	(92)	(88)	(84)	(79)	
Imports (fob)	594	877	924	930	893	1,107	1,610	
(of which petroleum)	(10)	(14)	(8)	(17)	(25)	(23)	(26)	

	1979	1980	1981	1982	1983	1984	1985	1986
Prices and production (index numbers, 1980 = 100)								
Consumer prices	90	100	114	128	153	184	253	384
Industrial production	97	100	98	100	97	91	106	..
Mining production	97	100	92	96	95	86	80	..
Interest rates								
Discount rate	6.5	6.5	7.5	7.5	10.0	14.5	25.0	25.0
Monetary developments (% change on previous year)								
Domestic credit	..	15	17	28	15	21	83	27
(of which:)								
claims on government	..	19	5	32	15	23	115	30
claims on private sector	..	5	52	19	14	16	11	19

[a] Rough estimate from World Bank sources.

Intellectual leadership of the CG resided effectively with the World Bank, partly because of its financial resources, but also because it was the only agency with the capacity to undertake the detailed staff work. (For this reason the term 'World Bank – CG' is used below.) Development agencies came to accept that Zambia had an urgent requirement for programme aid, and preparations were put in hand for three major, multi-donor, programme aid packages, which were conceived of as 'sector rehabilitation loans', covering the industrial, mining and agricultural sectors.

In the short term, the Economic Reform Programme (Government of Zambia, 1984a, 1985a) aimed to achieve what may be called 'rescue and stabilisation', i.e. conventional stabilisation, to which were added injections of foreign exchange sufficient to raise capacity utilisation substantially in what was, by now, an import-starved economy. In the medium term, the intention was to improve the efficiency of import-substituting industry and central government, and to induce 'diversification along lines of natural comparative advantage'. The 'World Bank – CG' believed that these medium-term objectives could only be achieved by policies which rolled back economic controls: the subject was to liberalise as many sectors of the economy as possible, and to break up the monolithic structure of state-owned industries. It was also deemed necessary to cut back government spending, especially on subsidies.

Knowing the direction in which they wanted to push Zambia, the main intellectual problems for the 'World Bank – CG' were those of (i) sequencing and (ii) carrying through the necessary sectoral studies to arrive at detailed plans. But in practical terms, their greatest challenge was the problem of how to use aid resources to persuade the government to commit itself to policies about which it was sceptical, if not hostile.

The first stage in the adjustment sequence was the outcome of the government's negotiations for debt rescheduling, and for IMF support. A fairly conventional stabilisation package resulted. Although this brought about a 60 per cent nominal depreciation of the kwacha against the dollar (40 per cent effective depreciation) between January 1983 and September 1985, foreign-exchange rationing and the payments pipeline remained. Interest rates were nudged up few points, but to nowhere near market-clearing levels (see Table 8.1). The most substantial change during this period was the abolition of many domestic price controls, announced in December 1982, which left maize and fertiliser as the only commodities subject to formal control in domestic transactions.

The domestic impact of this package was moderate. The devaluation certainly benefited the mining industry, which, with low copper prices, domestic cost inflation and a fixed exchange rate, had become chronically unprofitable[3]. To the extent that the mining industry financed government expenditure, the benefits were more widespread. But the exchange rate was still far from any plausible equilibrium, and the systemic damage caused by massive excess demand for foreign exchange therefore continued. A related, but separate, problem was the fact that the exchange rate was still well above a level which made agricultural production for export an attractive proposition. Price decontrol allowed the removal of a number of subsidies, and gave industry a more sensible framework within which to operate. But with state-controlled organisations dominant in industry and agricultural marketing, informal controls remained, and there was only slow movement towards greater competition.

The introduction of the foreign-exchange auction

The reforms of the 1983–5 period seemed, at best, to be laying the foundations for a very slow recovery. Although it could be argued that industry had been saved from imminent disaster, the structure of the economy, and the philosophy of economic management, had made painfully slow progress towards a system which could induce greater efficiency and attract new, export-oriented, investment.

Over 1983-5 the World Bank and other CG members had been discussing with the government a series of sectoral reforms, linked to the rehabilitation loans. In agriculture, the leading edges of the proposed reform package were to be the abolition of 'equity pricing', the liberalisation of agricultural marketing and the elimination of the maize subsidy. In industry, the thrust was towards a lower and more rational structure of protection (through a tariff commission), a new Investment Act to encourage private (and especially foreign) participation, and the reorganisation and partial privatisation of state-owned concerns. For the mining industry (which was competently managed at the technical level), the priority was to inject aid funds to compensate for inadequate maintenance.

The IMF, meanwhile, was discussing more radical moves, namely the simultaneous liberalisation of the current and capital accounts on the balance of payments, and the liberalisation of domestic financial markets. A plan was evolved whereby a system of auctioning foreign exchange was to be introduced, while interest rates were to be allowed to find their 'market level'. The auction was to be supported by most CG members with programme aid, which would be used to augment the supply of dollars into the auction. Fiscal and monetary targets were to be set which, it was hoped, would cause the exchange rate and interest rates to stabilise at 'tolerable' levels.

Through the first half of 1985, the government tried to hold this plan at bay. But it was steadily hemmed in, as important CG members made clear their support for the proposals. The government's fundamental weakness was that it failed to propose a plausible alternative. It could probably have avoided the imposition of the auction with a very large 'once-off' devaluation, but there was strong resistance to this within the upper echelons of the Party.

A chronology of the auction, October 1985 to April 1987

In the 19 months of its existence, the auction went through a number of phases, as the government wrestled with IMF resistance to altering the system in such a way as to reverse the continuing depreciation of the kwacha. The system set up a 'single-tier auction', under which firms and individuals requiring foreign exchange were required to submit bids through their commercial bank, these bids having to be covered by kwacha deposits with the Bank of Zambia and either import licences (for current account transactions) or Bank of Zambia approval (for capital transfers). The understanding was that authorisations would be granted liberally. At the first auction, the kwacha fell from the previous official rate of K2 = $1 to K5 = $1, and, within three weeks, was down to K7 = $1. After this, the rate appeared to settle down, but this was only achieved by considerable support by some CG members (through the supply of foreign exchange to the Bank of Zambia). From the end of the first quarter of 1986, the kwacha began to fall again, and increased criticism of the system began to be voiced by the press and in parliament, probably reflecting the concerns of the anti-devaluation majority in the Party Central Committee. President Kaunda reacted in April 1986 by transferring the two senior negotiators of the agreement (the Minister of Finance and the Governor of the Bank of Zambia), and replacing them with two of the system's critics.

The new financial team introduced various changes, none of which had more than short-lived effects. The auction was finally suspended for two months in January 1987, after the rate had reached nearly K15 = $1. When it was restarted in early April 1987, a two-tier system was tried. The rate of K9–12 = $1 was set for government transactions, debt service and agricultural inputs, while the rest of the economy had to bid in a 'second window'. In the second-window auctions, the kwacha went into a free fall, and, by the third of them, had fallen to K21 = $1. At this point, the government announced the abandoment of the system, and a return to the administrative rationing of foreign exchange at the rate of K8 = $1.

By early 1987 the dispute between the government and the IMF had become broader than simply about the maintenance of the auction. The IMF was concerned that government expenditure was out of control, and that without strong measures to rein back spending the kwacha could not be expected to stabilise. As reported by the Prime Minister[4], other key points of difference were as follows:

(i)   Although the IMF accepted that the existing level of nominal expenditure on maize subsidies could remain, it had insisted that the in-season increase in marketing costs (i.e. the unbudgeted, and customarily unfunded portion – discussed further below) be passed on to consumers.

(ii)   The IMF had demanded that fertiliser and fuel prices be raised by very high multiples (113 and 75 per cent respectively), in order to protect the cash flow of the fertiliser company and of the oil refinery and oil distributors, and to prevent the emergence of implicit subsidies which would have been the consequence of the alternative, i.e. of credit extended to these companies to keep them in business.

(iii) The IMF wanted a 'positive interest-rate policy', which seemed to imply nominal rates slightly above the rate of inflation, currently in the 50–60 per cent range.

(iv)   The IMF and the World Bank had insisted that the mineral sector was overtaxed, and should be allowed to retain a higher proportion of its earnings to finance rehabilitation and regular maintenance. The government could not accept the revenue loss.

(v)   It was the IMF view that the maximum possible pay award to government workers was 10 per cent, while the government felt it had to pay a higher award.

Appraising the auction

In pushing the auction experiment, the IMF placed its reputation on the line, and for this reason, if no other, it can be expected that this chapter of Zambia's economic history will eventually be well researched. At this stage, it is only possible to note and comment on some of the explanations which have been offered.

First, there are suggestions that the IMF made a number of technical misjudgments. A senior IMF official has admitted that it was too sanguine about trends in copper prices[5]. Another allegation against the IMF's competence is that it took insufficient account of the effects on the auction of the 'forgiveness' offered to Zambian residents with illegal external holdings of foreign exchange (much of which had been generated by various forms of smuggling and bribery). This measure was quietly brought in at the time of the auction, on the ground that it gave Zambia access to free foreign exchange which could be used to finance imports. In the event, it seems that substantial quantities of this foreign exchange may have been used to finance imports, which were then sold into a decontrolled market which had been import-starved, a situation which allowed very large kwacha profits to be realised. These profits were then, so it is argued, recycled into the auction, to finance a further round of imports.

Second, most bilateral donor members of the CG were slow to release resources pledged to the auction, and this, reportedly, has been the subject of some acrimony between them and the IMF and World Bank. Each bilateral donor has its own procurement and disbursement requirements, and it is argued that the Bank of Zambia and the Ministry of Finance simply did not have the leadership and managerial competence to make much headway through this maze of red tape.

Third, the government is blamed for failing to keep within agreed fiscal and monetary targets, and, in particular, for failing to get a grip on the maize subsidy and marketing inefficiency problems, which were the main factors in driving government expenditure off-target. The government may also be faulted for its lukewarm support of the auction, which influenced expectations in such a way as to drive the kwacha down. After the events of April 1986, shrewd observers would have concluded that the risk of the auction system collapsing had risen markedly, and this would have increased pressure on the kwacha, by stimulating capital flight, and through manufacturers taking precautionary action to build up stocks.

The government's failures raise more substantive questions of sequencing. At issue here is the wisdom of introducing current and capital account liberalisation (and also domestic financial liberalisation) prior to making much headway (i) in solving major sectoral/structural problems such as agricultural subsidies and agricultural marketing and (ii) in altering the government's ideological attachment to the kind of controlled economy which had been developing in Zambia since the colonial period.

Presumably, the answer to these questions depends on the nature of the positive and negative interactions between the processes mentioned. On the negative side, it can be pointed out that, when 'everything happens at once', there must be an overloading of political leadership and of managerial and analytical capacity. During the time of the auction, the government was frequently in a state of panic-induced inertia, with such urgent problems looming on all fronts that it was impossible to concentrate on any defined set of issues. Would it not have been better to have first tackled a narrower set of defined problems (such as agricultural marketing, subsidies, state-owned industry and government spending generally), within the more 'reassuring' context of a more controlled economy?

A second negative point stems from the ideological/political question raised above. To some extent, the auction was a subterfuge, by which the IMF, and its few sympathisers in the Zambian Government, were able to get round the government's commitment against a large 'one-off devaluation'. The introduction of the auction did not alter the fact that there remained a large 'anti-devaluation' majority in the Party Central Committee and in the Cabinet. The supporters of the auction calculated that its immediate benefits (improved capacity utilisation in domestic industry, and greater profitability in the mineral sector) would cause it to pick up support as it proceeded. Indeed, this happened: not only did the auction receive the almost universal acclaim of private industry and of ZCCM officials, but it was also defended by the leadership of the Zambia Trades Unions at their November 1986 congress (because the devaluation – and linked access to foreign exchange from programme aid – was favourable to employment in mining and certain import-substituting industries). But the coalition of groups which perceived themselves to be losers from the auction was much more powerful. Among the economic losers were the Party elite and similar groups in the upper ranks of state industry and the government service, who, accustomed to considerable foreign travel, suffered the humiliation of a collapse in the dollar value of their salaries and perquisites. Their concerns converged with those of the urban masses, who were fearful of much increased maize prices, a danger which they perceived, quite correctly, to be somehow tied up with the IMF and the auction.

The Zambian experience also suggests that the setting in train of a debate about how the economy works, and about what its future might be, ought to have been recognised by the CG members and the IMF as a major challenge. Zambia's public debate on economic issues, while open and entertaining, has been on the whole ill-informed. The IMF and CG members made only desultory efforts to articulate to the Zambian political elite the intellectual basis of their prescriptions.

The Interim National Development Plan (INDP)

The salient features of the INDP were announced at the time of the break with the IMF. The exchange rate was to be fixed (though it was stated that it might be adjusted from time to time), debt service was limited to 10 per cent of export earnings, and price controls on basic consumer goods, fuel, fertiliser etc. were re-imposed. Bank lending rates were capped at 20 per cent. As of the beginning of 1988, no detailed statement of the INDP policies had appeared, but an interim report in November 1987 admitted that it had yet to have any significant effect on the economy[6].

The government is unlikely to have achieved more than temporary room for manoeuvre by the break with the IMF. While it will gain some relief through its default on payments due to multilateral institutions, this has to be balanced against the fact that some CG members have already suspended programme aid, and that others are likely to follow. (In November 1987 the Budget Office reported that it had received only one-quarter of its reckoning of donor pledges of external grants)[7]. Even if it turns out that Zambia is left with a higher level of net external resources, the current approach to economic management gives little ground for hope that additional resources will be used for anything other than consumption.

Nevertheless, in late 1987, a dialogue had restarted between the government and the Washington institutions. A World Bank team arrived in Lusaka to discuss how 'the World Bank might help in the implementation of INDP' and was told by President Kaunda that the break with the IMF was 'not a confrontationist or isolationist move' but was motivated by a concern 'to reduce the shocking figures for malnutrition'[8]. Immediately following these discussions with the World Bank the Governor of the Bank of Zambia was changed[9], an action which the President probably hoped would placate Zambia's creditors. In January 1988 there were talks over Zambia's $16m. of arrears to the World Bank[10] (which had caused the suspension of all existing World Bank loans), amid rumours that some sympathetic bilateral donors would step in to clear this debt. A few days later came the President's announcement that maize subsidies would be cut, and that new proposals were being put to the IMF[11]. The 1988 Budget, presented at the end of January, appeared to be designed to keep the door open for a resumption of IMF support. An important measure was the abolition of mineral taxation (the mining companies will still pay normal company taxation)[12]. The provisional 1987 estimates for the trade balance gave grounds for some qualified optimism – a 1986 deficit of kwacha 1,447m. having turned round into a surplus of kwacha 2,528m.

THE IMPACT ON AGRICULTURE

Basic problems of the agricultural sector[13]

Looking back on agriculture in the early 1980s, a number of features stand out:

(i) An inefficient spatial location of production had developed, mainly because, over the 1970s, the government had implemented a policy of uniform producer prices for most crops (equity pricing). In the more remote areas, producers were subsidised by: (a) direct government subventions to the marketing agencies and (b) cross-subsidies from locationally favoured producers. Calculations by Dodge, later elaborated by the World Bank, showed that the costs of this policy were high, in terms of production forgone and of government subsidies (Dodge, 1977; World Bank, 1984b).

(ii) More generally, there were scant signs of dynamism in the sector (with the exception of sugar). The cotton and tobacco industries, in which Zambia's resource endowments suggested it should have a comparative advantage, had difficulty in meeting domestic requirements. The large farm sub-sector, in which Europeans continued to play a major role, showed little interest in producing for export, and when the more enterprising firms in this sub-sector brought in new activities these were almost exclusively aimed at the local market (e.g. wheat, soya, vegetables and fruit, livestock, poultry). This lack of dynamism cannot be attributed to a lack of access to credit. Most large farms, and also smaller farmers within government schemes, could obtain access to credit for these export crops. The main factors holding back agriculture seemed to be:

(a) a continuing rise in the real exchange rate, which was only checked by the introduction of the auction;

(b) the fact that the volume of exports had, historically, been so low that marketing channels were under-developed;

(c) from the mid-1970s, difficulties in remitting funds abroad discouraged existing European farmers, and also new foreign investment;

(d) substantial protection was available for import-substitution (IS) enterprises, and this, together with easy access to credit, and relatively easy access to foreign exchange to import capital goods, attracted the dynamic larger farmers out of maize production into new IS activities;

(e) special schemes for small farmers were badly managed, but some important improvements have been observed in the last few years (e.g. LINTCO – the parastatal with responsibility for cotton development).

(iii) Marketing infrastructure and institutions had expanded rapidly since independence, in some cases bringing marketing services to areas which previously had been isolated. But the system was extraordinarily inefficient (Kydd, 1988). At the beginning of the 1970s, the government had begun to consolidate responsibility in a monopoly parastatal, NAMBOARD. By the later 1970s, aware that NAMBOARD was performing badly, under pressure to seek more 'socialist' solutions, and encouraged by two Scandinavian aid agencies, the government transferred NAMBOARD's provincial assets and monopoly status to a structure of provincial and local co-operative societies. Most co-operatives were new organisations and, as decentralised and nominally democratic organisations, they fell under the control of small local elites, whose behaviour was often venal. Masked by a generous flow of aid funds, it took some years for it to become apparent that the performance of the co-operatives was, in most respects, inferior to that previously provided by NAMBOARD. In January 1985, the government reacted to mounting public criticism of the co-operatives with a hasty decision to transfer overall marketing responsibilities back to NAMBOARD. Prior to this announcement there had been no planning at a technical level, and the process of implementing the decision added to the confusion and demoralisation in the marketing system.

(iv) The government became committed to consumer subsidies almost by accident. In the mid 1970s, the subsidies paid to the marketing agents were seen as instruments which achieved more than one goal, i.e. that there were elements of producer and of consumer subsidy. The size of the subsidy did not become a serious problem until the early 1980s. By then the main factors were the renewed slide in copper prices, pressures to contain inflation and wages, and the decreasing efficiency of the food system (due to costly marketing and an inefficient spatial location of production). From 1984, the government tried to contain the growth of the subsidy by raising food prices and by using reductions in the budgeted level of subvention to put pressure on the marketing agents. Thus the maize subsidy spiralled out of control, moving from 55 per cent of the into-mill price in 1984/5 to 131 per cent in 1985/6 (Kydd, 1988).

The maize subsidy and the IMF programme

The maize subsidy issue provides an excellent example of the macro-micro linkages which need to be analysed to gain a fuller understanding of the impact of adjustment policies on the agricultural sector. In the Zambian case, several policy problems connect at the point of the maize subsidy, and it has become a Gordian knot, the cutting of which could relieve multiple constraints on the progress of the economy.

The government's weak control over the level of subsidy arises from the fact that it has experienced compelling political pressure to maintain the availability of maize flour at a fixed price, while it has little influence, in the short term, over the costs of the marketing system. The government perception is that it has no option but to ensure that the marketing system has sufficient liquidity to buy maize from farmers and transport it to mills: it faces the threat that any prolonged liquidity shortage may result in a drying-up of supplies. In recent years, the government and the marketing agencies have played a game of brinkmanship. As a gambit to put downward pressure on the costs of the marketing system the government has set the budgeted subsidy at an unrealistically low level in relation to the actual costs of the system. Marketing agencies therefore tend to run out of liquidity in the middle of the purchasing season, thus precipitating a crisis which can only be resolved by injecting more finance into the system. The political imperative is to get the harvest into safe storage before the next rainy season. A further problem is that the atmosphere of continuing financial crisis vitiates actions to improve the management of the marketing system, and provides fertile ground for corruption.

The maize subsidy is at the root of massive inefficiency within the food system. One major distortion is the bias it creates against on-farm storage and localised trade (i.e. localised storage and circulation). This certainly leads to a considerable amount of unnecessary haulage (over poor roads with scarce fuel and even more scarce vehicles!). The evidence for the effects on the overall costs of storage and milling (i.e. on the unit costs of village storage versus silos and other large-scale storage technologies, and of village processing versus capital–intensive mills) is less clear-cut. Even if there are efficiency gains from these sources, they are unlikely to compensate more than marginally for the additional transport costs.

The haulage distortion works as follows. Small farmers can gain access to the subsidy only on that portion of their maize harvest which is sold into a marketing chain which is able to collect the subsidy. In the past, this has meant selling to a parastatal or co-operative agency, but, with the liberalisation of the past two years, it is now only necessary to sell into a chain of intermediaries (public or private) which is eventually going to deliver to a large-scale milling operation, because this is the point at which the majority of the subsidy is applied. Some milled flour is then transported back into rural centres, where it is sold at the official retail price (thereby attracting the additional component of the subsidy, namely, the cost of back-haulage to the rural centres, for which co-operatives are recompensed directly by the government). Some flour is then marketed into villages at a mark-up on the official price, which, over distances which take in substantial populations, is less than the cost of locally stored and milled flour. Although it is cheaper to the consumer because of the subsidy element, nevertheless, taking into account the full resource costs, this system is socially and economically inefficient.

It is possible to think of a 'subsidy shadow' surrounding those rural centres which receive regular supplies of subsidised food, dark at the centre and fading towards a boundary which is defined by points at which the official retail price plus mark-up is equal to the costs of locally grown, stored and milled flour. To the extent that rural households are sheltered within the darker areas of a 'subsidy shadow', and have the money to buy the flour, they benefit from some degree of subsidy, and are able to cut out some of the labour-intensive activity of processing maize by village technology. Of course, the margins of the shadow fluctuate according to such factors as the regularity of deliveries of subsidised food, the size of local stocks and the quality of the local transport network. Many rural residents do not benefit: they may lack the available funds, may perceive the process to be too risky or may live outside a 'subsidy shadow'. The rural poor probably gain least, except, perhaps, where their livelihoods are based mainly on permanent labour for commercial farmers.

Another distortion is excessive production of maize as against other grains and tubers, which may be better adapted to specific agro-climatic conditions[14]. That this may be an important source of inefficiency in the agricultural sector is suggested by the fact that, in the recent past, rising subsidies have coincided with the rapid advance of maize production in certain areas (e.g. parts of the Northern Province), where maize previously had a minor role. In places where maize has recently been a 'colonising crop', it has normally been cultivated with the use of chemical fertiliser, which has received an explicit subsidy and a plethora of implicit subsidies[15]. As the competing grains and tubers (i.e. millet, sorghum, cassava) are generally cultivated with little or no chemical fertiliser, it is likely that a sizeable part of the 'excessive maize' distortion is represented by excessive use of fertiliser.

What of the urban beneficiaries of the subsidy? That the benefits are substantial is demonstrated by the potency of political action in defence of the subsidy, notably the riots which, in December 1986, caused the government to backtrack on a fairly mild measure, designed merely to contain the subsidy bill, not to reduce it[16]. The government's inability to make this measure stick cost it dearly. The additional bank credit required to keep the marketing system supplying adequate quantities at 'politically tolerable' consumer prices violated the credit ceiling agreed with the IMF.

There is now broad agreement that rapid phasing out of the subsidy would cause widespread distress in urban areas, jeopardising the nutrition of families in the informal sector and in the lower paid part of the formal sector. By mid-1986, the World Bank had modified the position it had first taken in 1983, namely, that the subsidy should be phased out completely over three years; it now accepts that subsidies on lower-grade maize flour will be required for much longer.

In summary, the food subsidy question is an extreme case of the classic policy dilemma. Substantial progress in reducing the subsidy may induce the gains indicated, i.e., enhanced fiscal and monetary control, the possibility of some increases in other categories of government spending, and potentially large gains in the efficiency of the food system. In the longer run, the efficiency of the food system is probably the most important of these considerations because, if the food system is able to make progress, real food prices will fall, and *cheap un-subsidised food*, available across the country-side as well as in the towns, can provide a more promising and stable framework within which Zambia's nutrition problems can be tackled.

Finally, a somewhat brutal point should be made: that the urban focus of the food subsidies inhibits the urban-rural population movement which is integral to the wider strategy for enhancing the agrarian sector. The poorest groups in the towns, though desperately under-employed in the informal sector, still, on the whole, appear to perceive the possibility of joining the rural labour force (as wage workers or subsistence farmers) as even more unattractive than their present circumstances. There is little popular enthusiasm for 'rural resettlement schemes', while commercial farmers complain of labour shortages (with urban unemployment estimated at over 50 per cent) and the President and Party are openly discussing the possibility of amending the constitution to enable forced resettlement[17].

Agricultural reforms

The thrust of the World Bank's 1983–5 analysis of Zambian agriculture was to demon-strate some of the deficiencies of existing policies, and to convey some notion of what the agricultural sector might look like, in terms of crop mix, with less distorted (i.e., more free-market) policies. But this critique, which focused on an assessment of the structure of protection for each crop, shed only limited light on the question of appro-priate policies. The dimensions lacking were institutional and political-economic analysis. Recommendations on such factors as the exchange rate, subsidies, tariffs and quotas were useful, but left unresolved the issue of how to deal with the marketing system, and the pressures on the government to keep food prices down. On these latter two points, the World Bank harboured the general notion that solutions could be found in policies of liberalisation and a greater role for the private sector, which it was hoped would make a large enough contribution to cost reduction to take pressure off the subsidy bill.

In the event, the first phase of reforms, from December 1982 to September 1985, consisted of the decontrol of prices and marketing for all commodities except maize and fertiliser. These moves were important in raising the morale of commercial farmers and in stimulating investor interest in the agricultural sector. But the impact was limited for three reasons:

(a) It excluded the system supplying food to the majority of the population – the NAMBOARD/co-operative network remained in place, and in receipt of subsidies large enough to discourage unsubsidised competitors.
(b) The 40 per cent real devaluation which occurred over this period was not enough to make production for export profitable.
(c) The government had the capability to influence the prices of import-substitution crops (e.g. wheat) through trade policy, and it exercised this power in an unpredictable manner.

The foreign-exchange auction brought in the next phase of agricultural reforms – a concentration on stimulating export production. To ensure that the hoped-for invest-ment surge would not be held back by a shortage of capital goods or inputs, the World Bank and USAID made programme funds available to the auction, which were ear-marked for agriculture. The exchange rate looked attractive to potential exporters, and there was a much increased interest on the part of both local businessmen and foreign companies in the possibilities of investment in export enterprises. But the immediate benefits were only moderate. Partly this reflected the lead times involved in appraising and deciding on investments. Foreign investors appear to have brought few resources into Zambia, presumably waiting to see if the devaluation gained acceptance. Reportedly, demand for agricultural inputs in the auction was well below expectations.

A major factor affecting local farmers was the hike in interest rates (see Table 8.1). Although these were never more than mildly positive, and had become strongly negative by the end of 1986, this added a further element of risk for a group of businessmen who had grown to distrust the government's ability to manage the economy.

The problems of the public sector marketing system came into focus in 1986, when a consulting firm, Landell Mills (LM), was contracted to examine the problem. The essence of the LM recommendations was that NAMBOARD should undertake a staged retreat from its current role, to concentrate on two functions:

(a) to maintain a strategic food reserve;
(b) to act as market intervention agency to maintain producer confidence and to protect consumers.

LM recommended that the co-operatives should not be abolished and should be allowed to compete, unsubsidised, with an emergent private sector. It seems probable that the LM proposals will be held in reserve, if for no other reason than that they require substantial funds for their successful implementation (for capitalising NAMBOARD's intervention fund, and for providing credit to new private sector operators).

Summing up the impact on agriculture

The best construction that can be put on present circumstances is that the reform programme has lost most of its momentum. There is precious little to show for five years of detailed involvement by CG members in assisting the identification and implementation of policy changes. The inefficiency in the food system remains unresolved, as does the question of the maize subsidy. It seems improbable that either local or foreign investors will be attracted by the environment of the INDP.

If the reform programme can be brought back on track within the next two years, then the intellectual work, and preliminary policy changes, may not have been in vain. The agricultural policy changes brought in up to 1987 were mainly a clearing of the undergrowth – necessary, but not sufficient, conditions for self-sustaining agricultural growth.

LESSONS OF THE ZAMBIAN EXPERIENCE

To conclude, some more general implications of Zambia's experience may be noted:

(a) It underlines the central role of macroeconomic management in determining what happens in the agricultural sector. Of course, a host of sector-specific factors are also important, as are trade policy and deeper structural factors. Nevertheless, agricultural sector specialists should give more attention to macroeconomic factors.

(b) It provides food for thought on the question of the sequencing of reforms. In this connection four points can be made:

(i) In ambitious liberalisation programmes, in which 'everything happens at once', there is a danger of spreading scarce human resources too thinly.

(ii) It is important to tackle ideological/intellectual differences head-on. The costs of not doing so result in problems when a government implements a policy it neither believes in nor understands. This is *not* a call for a crude propaganda campaign, but for more emphasis and more care to be given to the policy dialogue.

(iii) Following on from this point, in the transition to market-based systems, weight should be placed on the credibility of government policy to market participants. This consideration is likely to argue for caution where staged programmes of liberalisation are being designed.

(iv) Producers who have previously been operating in tightly controlled sectors may initially be cautious about making investments in capital goods on the basis of judgments about markets in which resources are costed at their full scarcity price. (This is an interpretation of Zambian commercial farmers' vociferous complaints about interest rates and other input costs.)

(c) Where there are major inefficiencies in the food system, as was the case in Zambia, then the social costs of adjustment can be reduced by actions which are effective in raising its efficiency. The Zambian experience was actually more powerful than this: inefficiency in the food system was central to the government's inability to control the subsidy bill. The sequence in which Zambian agricultural reforms were tackled may be questioned. After four years of reform, solutions to the problems of the food system were still under debate, while measures had been implemented to tackle problems which were, in the short term at least, of lesser importance.

NOTES

1 The classic discussion of post-Independence agricultural development policies is Dodge (1977). A more recent interpretation is provided by Kydd (1988).

2 For a version of the government's analysis see Government of Zambia (1984a and 1985a). For World Bank views see World Bank (1984a and 1985a). For academic analyses see Daniel (1985) and Kydd (1986 and 1988).

3 There are some respectable arguments *against* devaluation as a remedy for the problems of the mining industry, based on the observation that this will not (in the short term) alter the foreign-exchange revenues from copper exports. The potential benefits of a devaluation lie in the fact that, at least in the very short term, it reduces the real costs (i.e. in terms of foreign exchange) of the domestic resource component in mining costs. It is perfectly true that costs might be reduced by other means (e.g. if the government were to reduce mineral royalties – as actually happened in the 1988 budget – or if the mine companies were to cut employment and pay). The arguments for and against devaluation then turn on the relative efficacy and political feasibility of devaluation versus other possible packages of measures.

4 Evidence of the IMF's conditions for the continuation of support in the first quarter of 1987 comes from the Prime Minister's briefing of diplomats shortly after the break with the IMF, reported in *Times of Zambia* – 6 May 1987.

5 Ahmed Abdalla, Director of the IMF's Africa Department, (quoted in *Times of Zambia* – 19 and 20 June 1987). From the standpoint of early 1988 – following several months of rising prices – the IMF's projections appear less embarrassing.

6 *Times of Zambia*, 24 November 1987.

7 Ibid.

8 *Times of Zambia*, 13 November 1987.

9 *Times of Zambia*, 26 November 1987.

10 *Times of Zambia*, 14 January 1988.

11 *Times of Zambia*, 22 January 1988.

12 *Times of Zambia*, 30 January and 1 February 1988.

13 As already noted, the classic critique of the post-Independence performance of Zambian agriculture is Dodge (1977). More up-to-date additions to this literature include Kydd (1988) and two World Bank studies (1984b and 1985b).

14 The argument here being that, in the absence of subsidies, more food crops other than maize would be grown (and maize production reduced), the non-maize crops being preferred at the margin because of their lower production costs and/or lower risks of failure.

15 These included an overvalued exchange rate, and subsidies to the local manufacturer.

16 The measure was the doubling of the price of the higher-grade flour known as breakfast meal, but the price of the coarser grade, but widely used, roller meal was not adjusted.

17 The most recent estimate of unemployment, which has to be regarded as an extremely broad guess, is 2 million, in a total population of about 7.2 million, given by Ben Zulu, Minister of State for Youth (*Times of Zambia*, 28 July 1987). The observation of labour shortage on commercial farms comes from the author's fieldwork in July 1985 and April and November 1986. The disappointing response to voluntary resettlement programmes was commented on by President Kaunda in July 1987, in a speech in which he raised the possibility of amending the constitution to permit forcible repatriation of the unemployed (*Times of Zambia*, 13 August 1987). At the end of 1987 the proposed constitutional amendment was on the agenda for discussion at the UNIP National Council. (*Times of Zambia*, 19 December 1987).

REFERENCES

Bond, M.E. (1983), 'Agricultural Responses to Prices in Sub-Saharan African Countries', Washington DC, *IMF Staff Papers*, Vol. 30.

Chivuno, L.S. (1987), Text of 'Opening Address' delivered at the *International Conference on the Auctioning of Foreign Exchange*, held in Lusaka, 29 June–3 July.

Cleaver, K.M. (1985), 'The Impact of Price and Exchange Rate Policies on Agriculture in Sub-Saharan Africa', Washington DC, World Bank Staff Working Papers, No. 728.

Daniel, Philip (1985), 'Zambia: Structural Adjustment or Downward Spiral?', *IDS Bulletin*, Vol. 16, No. 3.

Dodge, D.J. (1977), *Agricultural Policy and Performance in Zambia: History, Prospects and Proposals for Change*, Institute of International Studies, Berkeley Research Series, No. 32.

Fry, J. (1979), *Employment and Income Distribution in the African Economy*, London, Croom Helm.

Government of Zambia (1981), Food Strategy Study (Drafts), Lusaka, Ministry of Agriculture and Water Development, Planning Unit, Annexes on: – 'Food Crop Production'; – 'Socio-Regional Framework'. (Final Report released 1983).

—— (1983), *Financial Report for Year Ended 1982*.

—— (1984a), *Restructuring in the Midst of Crisis*, (Background Papers for the Consultative Group for Zambia meeting in Paris, May), *Volume I: Development Policies and Objective: Volume II: The Expenditure Programme*.

—— (1984b), *Annual Agricultural Statistical Bulletin*, Lusaka Ministry of Agriculture and Water Development, Statistics Section, Planning Division.

—— (1984c), *Financial Report for Year Ended 1983*.

—— (1985a), *An Action Programme for Economic Restructuring*, Consultative Group for Zambia, Lusaka, 4–5 June.

—— (1985b), *Economic Report, 1984*, National Commission for Development Planning, Presented to National Assembly, January.

IDS, Sussex (1985), *Sub-Saharan Africa: getting the facts straight*, Issue title of *IDS Bulletin*, Vol. 16, No. 3.

International Labour Organisation (1981), *Zambia: Basic Needs in an Economy under Pressure*, Addis Ababa, (Jobs and Skills Program for Africa).

Kydd, J.G. (1986), 'Changes in Zambian Agricultural Policy since 1983: Problems of Liberalization and Agrarianization', *Development Policy Review*, Vol. 4, No. 3.

—— (1988), 'Zambia', in Charles Harvey (ed.) *Agricultural Pricing and Marketing in Africa*, London, Macmillan.

Landell-Mills Associates/Ministry of Agriculture (1986), *Zambia: Agricultural Marketing and Input Distribution Study*.

Lipton, M. and C. Heald (1984), 'The EC and African Food Strategies', Brussels, Centre for European Policy Studies, Working Document No. 12 (Economic), December.

NAMBOARD (1984), *Annual Report and Accounts, 1983*.

Timmer, C.P., W.P. Falcon and S.R. Pearson (1983), *Food Policy Analysis*, Baltimore, Johns Hopkins University Press.

United Nations (E.C.A.) (1963), *Report of the UN/ECA/FAO Economic Survey Mission on the Economic Development of Zambia*, 'The Seers Report', Ndola, Falcon Press.

Vickery, K.P. (1985), 'Saving Settlers: Maize Control in Northern Rhodesia', *Journal of Southern Africa Studies*, Vol. 11, No. 2.

Wood, A. (1984), 'Food Production and the Changing Structure of Zambian Agriculture', unpublished ms, Rural Development Studies Bureau, University of Zambia.

World Bank (1984a), 'Zambia: Country Economic Memorandum. Issues and Options for Economic Diversification', Washington DC, Eastern Africa Country Programmes Dept I, Report No. 5000-ZA, April.

—— (1984b), 'Zambia: Policy Options and Strategies for Agricultural Growth', Supplementary Volume on Methodology and Commodity Analyses, Washington DC, Eastern Africa Projects Dept, June. (no document number).

—— (1985a), 'Report to the Consultative Group on Zambia on Progress towards Economic Restructuring', Eastern and Southern Africa Regional Office, April.

—— (1985b), 'Zambia: Agricultural Pricing and Parastatal Performance', Eastern and Southern Africa Projects Dept, Report No. 5556–ZA, June.

9

Senegal

1979–88

Simon Commander, Ousseynou Ndoye & Ismael Ouedrago

INTRODUCTION

Little that is heartening can be extracted from a survey of Senegal's recent economic history. Since independence in 1960, the rate of economic growth has been extremely low by even sub-Saharan African standards, averaging under 2.3 per cent per annum and for six of the years between 1970 and 1984 showing a negative trend, particularly in the primary sector. Although agriculture now contributes around 22 per cent of total value added, economic performance remains strongly determined by that sector whose output level is, in turn, strongly conditioned by climatic factors, which from 1973 onwards have been distinctly unfavourable. Between 1965 and 1984 growth in value added in the primary sector declined from an average rate of 3 per cent in the 1960s to around 1.7 per cent between 1979 and 1984. With population growing at over 2.6 per cent per annum over much of this period and at a current rate of 2.9 per cent, per capita output trends have been largely negative. Real incomes have fallen although there may have been some increase for the rural sector since 1981 (see Table 9.1).

Changes in the external trading environment have compounded the insecurity and volatility of domestic production. In the two years 1973–75 Senegal experienced a short-term boom in export earnings from phosphates. As a member of the Communauté Financière Africaine, the Senegalese Govenment could not use the exchange rate as a policy variable. The phosphates windfall was thus associated with a 20 per cent appreciation of the real exchange rate by 1975. However, this proved to be only short-term and the trend in the real exchange rate cannot be deployed as the principal explanation of the origins of the economic crisis of the late 1970s. Nor is it clear that Senegal was faced with a particularly adverse trend in the terms of trade until the second oil price increase. However, the principal constraint for the current account was

* This chapter is an outcome of a joint ODI/ISRA project on 'Structural Adjustment and Senegalese Agriculture' which was funded by the Ford Foundation, Dakar. The authors are grateful to Richard Horovitz and Jacques Faye for their help and advice. The views expressed in the chapter do not reflect the official position of ISRA. The chapter has drawn extensively on background papers prepared by Matar Gaye, Michel Havard, Hyacinthe Mbengue and Fadel Ndiame of ISRA.

Table 9.1: *Senegal: per capita income trends: rural and urban sectors, 1970–83*

	Urban	Rural	National Average	National Index
1970	100.3	17.2	42.1	101
1971	104.1	13.8	41.5	100
1979	66.5	16.1	35.0	84
1980	70.0	12.3	34.5	83
1981	73.0	11.2	35.6	86
1982	65.2	15.1	35.4	85
1983	63.3	14.5	34.8	84
		1960/63	*1969/73*	*1979/83*
Rural Per Capita Income as Share of Urban Per Capita Income:		15%	16%	20%

Source: Duruflé et al. (1985).

quantitative, emanating from the diminished production of the main tradable, groundnuts.

The phosphates boom was directly associated with a rapid expansion in domestic, particularly public, consumption. Between 1970 and 1975 the resource gap grew at under 4 per cent per annum but between 1975 and 1980, as GDP growth stalled at around 0.6 per cent per annum, it increased to nearly 19 per cent per annum, with public consumption growing at over 6.7 per cent. The fiscal effort declined and the deficit rose substantially from 3.5 per cent of GDP in the 1970s to nearly 9 per cent in 1980/81. Furthermore, declining export income from groundnuts and phosphates coincided with a sharply rising oil import bill and a relatively unrestrained growth in manufactured goods imports, in particular. By 1978/9 the current account balance was negative to around 8 per cent of GDP.

Unable to finance such imbalances, the Senegalese Government developed a medium-term economic recovery plan in 1979 which was followed in 1980 by agreement with the IMF for an Extended Fund Facility (EFF), as well as a Structural Adjustment Loan (SAL) from the World Bank. Since then Senegal has continued to rely heavily on IMF and World Bank programme lending. By 1987 the government had drawn down five IMF Standby Loans and has also taken a three-year Structural Adjustment Facility from 1987; the third SAL/SAC from the World Bank began in mid-1987. In addition, it has been able to call upon substantial assistance from bilateral sources, particularly from France, though this has, at least in part, been contingent on its reaching accord with the multilateral institutions. Since 1983 the government has fulfilled all lending conditions satisfactorily. Indeed, it is commonly held up by donors as a model case of adjustment.

THE ADJUSTMENT FRAMEWORK

The IMF programme adopted in 1980 aimed at restricting domestic aggregate demand while, at the same time, reducing net foreign liabilities contingent upon the substantial balance-of-payments deficits. With major disequilibrium in public finances, an explicit aim was to reduce the size of the deficit and, hence, of government arrears to the economy. In most respects, the IMF strategy contained the usual ingredients – expenditure constraint, reduction of arrears, improved fiscal effort, stricter controls over monetary and credit levels as well as domestic pricing reforms. The principal short- and medium-term aim was to reduce aggregate absorption, in large measure by restraining the growth in public consumption, while raising the domestic savings rate and stimulating export performance through relative domestic price shifts. At the same time, the programme aimed to reduce the rate of growth in imports by price increments linked to credit controls. In short, the IMF programmes implemented since 1980 have been largely deflationary.

Complementing the IMF lending have been the three World Bank Structural Adjustment Loans/Credits (cf. World Bank, 1985; 1986; 1987a). The first SAL, adopted in January 1981, contained a wide range of objectives, including elimination of the budget deficit, reduction in the share of wages in total public expenditure, a freeze on expenditures for materials and supplies, the repayment of government arrears and increased financing (10 per cent increase over three years) of public investments by net public savings. In addition, restructuring of the investment programme, the application of financial controls over the parastatal sector (through the selective use of 'contrats-plans') and limited privatisation were further components. The exchange rate was accepted as non-negotiable, but the SAL sought to simulate a devaluation effect by means of an export subsidy on certain items and an increase in import duties from 5 to 15 per cent. Some tentative attempts were also made to rationalise the substantial parastatal sector and agricultural sector institutions in particular. Subsequent SALs have maintained this emphasis on price reform and parastatal restructuring, with the latter becoming an increasingly more pronounced component.

However, before examining the specific nature of the agricultural sector reforms that have been introduced, it is desirable to examine recent developments with regard to the primary objects of adjustment, the current account and the budget deficit.

BALANCE OF PAYMENTS AND EXTERNAL DEBT

The widening current account deficit that emerged at the end of the 1970s has been sustained at high levels through the 1980s. By 1981 it amounted to nearly 26 per cent of GDP, testimony not only to weak trade performance but also to falling net capital inflows. With gross official reserves exhausted, this deficit was financed by recourse to the IMF and increased indebtedness to the French Treasury. Table 9.2 shows that between 1980 and 1985 it averaged 18.5 per cent of GDP, falling in 1986 to just under 10 per cent. Since 1980 there has been some improvement in export performance, both in volume and value terms, largely reflecting trends in the groundnut sub-sector which has continued to account for around 10 per cent of total export revenues. However, groundnut export receipts have been highly variable, a direct function of output variability and the overwhelming importance of climatic conditions. Other major exports, fish, phosphates and petroleum products, have also followed an erratic course and, at present, the latter two commodities are faced with relatively poor market prospects.

Recent improvements in the resource balance have also been attributable to a falling level of imports, a direct consequence of adjustment measures. In addition, favourable price movements for oil and certain food products have lowered import costs. Domestic policy measures resulted in a lower volume of demand than had prevailed in the early 1980s. Nevertheless, as elsewhere in sub-Saharan Africa, the main mechanism for

Table 9.2: *Senegal: current account deficit and trade balance 1979–86*

Year	Current Account deficit	Share of GDP	Total Exports	Total Imports	Resource Balance
		1979 prices – (billions CFAF)			
		%			
1979	−75.8	13.0	185.2	244.7	−59.5
1980	−109.3	19.3	148.8	236.7	−87.9
1981	−139.0	25.9	192.4	303.4	−111.0
1982	−105.8	19.7	201.7	290.1	−88.4
1983	−118.4	19.5	221.4	300.9	−79.5
1984	−103.0	17.3	205.3	273.0	−67.7
1985	−115.1	17.6	179.2	254.3	−75.1
1986	−67.4	9.8	214.8	262.1	−47.3

Source: World Bank and IMF.

reducing the current account deficit has been to drive down the level of imports. Export performance has improved but the underlying trend remains ambiguous, partly on account of the continuing dependence on groundnuts. Moreover, this has been in a period when the terms of trade have been broadly favourable.

Although Senegal's capital account has been relatively stabilised, this has partly been through additional borrowing and debt rescheduling. Total disbursed external public debt rose from around 40 per cent of GDP in 1980 to nearly 90 per cent by 1986. The debt-service ratio as a share of GDP remained the same – 20 per cent – but this was possibly only through substantial rescheduling; without it the debt-service ratio would have exceeded 30 per cent by 1986.

While this ratio remains reasonably low by current sub-Saharan African standards, the longer-term prospects are not bright. Senegal has had diminishing access to private financial markets. At the beginning of the 1980s around a quarter of its total external debt was owed to commercial financial institutions. By 1985 this had fallen to 9 per cent. As expected, the share of total debt owed to official bilateral and multilateral institutions had increased appreciably, with concessional credit comprising around 35 per cent of the total (World Bank, 1987b). Secondly, the nature of the borrowing and its subsequent utilisation suggests that *de facto* financing of consumption rather than investment has continued. This is obviously heightened by the growing predominance of programme over project lending. Thirdly, current repayments to the IMF have meant that even with the new SAF there has been a net outflow of resources in 1987. Fourthly, continued debt rescheduling may not be a ready option. Senegal's request to the Paris Club in 1987 for a three-year rescheduling was rejected and a period of only eighteen months granted instead. Consequently, despite having lower debt-service levels at present than a number of other West African economies, such as Côte d'Ivoire, Ghana, Guinea-Bissau and Sierra Leone, Senegal is faced with similar problems in the longer-term management of its debt and in its capacity to service that debt. Given the fact that there has been no underlying improvement in the overall performance of the economy – GDP grew by under 2.5 per cent between 1979 and 1986, a level roughly comparable to the average for the previous twenty years – it is difficult to argue that the adjustment programme has yet achieved a series of shifts in economic performance which could satisfactorily sustain the growing debt overhang.

PUBLIC FINANCE

A key feature of the adjustment process has been the attempt to restrain domestic aggregate demand and, in particular, to reduce the public deficit. Although the economy has been characterised by historically high levels of consumption – aggregate absorption averaged around 90 per cent in the period 1960–78 – by 1979/ 81 this had risen to over 116 per cent of GDP. Since then total government expenditures have declined as a share of GDP in the adjustment period. For the period 1984/6 total expenditure in the economy averaged just under 110 per cent of GDP. This reduction has mainly occurred through contraction in real private consumption and in investment.

The control of government expenditures was prompted by the sharp increase in the fiscal deficit at the end of the 1970s/beginning of the 1980s. In 1980/1 the fiscal deficit amounted to around 9 per cent (cash basis) of GDP. By 1987/8 this had fallen to under 3 per cent with a surplus projected for 1989/90.

The shift towards fiscal balance has largely occurred through expenditure reduc- tion. In 1980/81 total expenditure fell from nearly 32 per cent of GDP to under 22 per cent. This was primarily achieved through a 45 per cent fall in real capital expendi- ture. Current expenditures declined by around 6 per cent in real terms, with the main brunt falling on materials and supplies (Shafik, 1986). The share attributed to wages and salaries fell from 12 per cent of GDP in 1980/81 to 10 per cent by 1985/6. Reduction of this component was an explicit feature of IMF lending and flowed from the belief that the 1970s had seen an unacceptable increase in government employ- ment. The reduction has largely come about through real wage cuts, since the size of the civil service has actually continued to increase. By mid-1987 the number of employees in the public sector was put at around 68,000, a 50 per cent increase over the 1980/81 level and a 56 per cent increase over the 1975 level[1]. However, the real wage rate appears to have fallen by at least 25 per cent from the 1980 level and for the lower income brackets in the civil service the decline has been even greater.

Though expenditure reduction has undoubtedly been achieved, progress towards recomposing expenditure has been limited. Moreover, the contraction has fallen largely on non-personnel costs and on the investment budget. Analysis of government expenditures classified by function and expressed in 1979 prices demonstrates that defence, public order and safety as well as health, education and social welfare have sustained their allocations in real terms and as a share of total expenditures. How- ever, allocations to housing and community services were halved in the period 1981/2–1983/4 and 1984/5–1986/7, while that for transport and communications declined by 35 per cent. Significantly, agriculture's share fell by nearly 24 per cent in real terms. When broken down in terms of ministry budgets the anomaly is even more striking. In 1986/7 the Ministry of Rural Development's allocation was less than 25 per cent of that for Interior, 18 per cent of that for the Armed Forces and around 10 per cent of the total allocation to the Ministries of National Education and Culture. These priorities reflect not only political realities and relative bargaining strengths but also the Senghorian legacy of promoting education and training.

The continuing apparent neglect of priority sectors, such as agriculture, must be put in the context of trends in both the composition of the recurrent budget and the relative balance between that budget and capital expenditures. In the first place, operating expenditures remain strikingly dominated by personnel costs. For 1986/7 these amounted to over 56 per cent of total operating costs, with materials accounting for a further 14 per cent and maintenance a mere 1.8 per cent. Secondly, there has been a very sharp fall in the capital budget. Between 1980/81 and 1985/6 capital expenditures were halved when measured as a share of GDP. Moreover, they have largely been financed by extra-budgetary resources, and by external donors in particular. By 1986/7 nearly 87 per cent of the investment budget was financed by donors and over 80 per cent of the counterpart contribution was mobilised through external borrowing.

The recent trend reflects a number of pressures. First, the government has chosen to cut the fiscal deficit mainly through reductions in investment and supplies. A further index of this has been the sharp fall in public investment in gross fixed capital formation as a share of GDP from around 30 per cent in 1981 to less than 23 per cent by 1984. Secondly, until the 1986/7 budget and the elaboration of a public investment programme for the period 1987/8–1989/90, the capital budget had not consolidated its external and domestic financing components. This meant that investment resources were defined largely as residual and conditional on the availability of external financing. Thirdly, investment efficiency has been compromised by the lack of adequate project preparation and, to some extent, of adequate donor co-ordination. Fourthly, the growth in programme lending has reduced the resources available for productive investment. While the current public investment programme is attempting to develop a more viable and selective shelf of projects, it must be noted that capital expenditures as a share of GDP are projected to remain at below 2.9 per cent until 1989.

On the revenue side, the structure continues to be characterised by the predominance of import duties. These have declined in real terms as a result of the overall weak performance of the economy and of the specific measures to reduce import levels. Revenues from income taxes have similarly stagnated partly as a result of the severe deflationary policies pursued by the government. When measured as a share of GDP income tax fell from around 4.5 per cent between 1980 and 1982 to around 3.6 per cent by 1985/6 and total revenues declined by 0.6 per cent in the same period. This fall would have been more pronounced in the most recent period without the surpluses generated from the oil refining company as a consequence of the refusal to pass on the recent fall in world oil prices to local consumers, as well as the profits of the CPSP (Caisse de Péréquation et de Stabilisation des Prix) from rice importation and transfers under STABEX to compensate for losses in groundnut marketing. These 'windfall' gains have, at least temporarily, disguised the fact that there has been a declining overall domestic tax effort since the early 1980s (World Bank, 1987c).

In summary, expenditure reduction appears to have occurred on a relatively arbitrary basis in which the parallel need to restructure public outlays has been avoided and cuts have fallen on the more accessible – and by implication, politically more feasible – areas. Short-run crisis management has obviously been unable to address the more structural constraints operating in the economy. These constraints can, in particular, be seen to be operating in the critical agricultural sector. The following sections examine the performance of that sector in the adjustment period.

THE AGRICULTURAL BACKGROUND

At present the agricultural sector generates less than 20 per cent of GDP. Yet with around 10 per cent of industrial sector output originating from oil milling and over 70 per cent of the labour force employed primarily in agriculture, its dominance in the Senegalese economy remains pronounced. Moreover, despite considerable regional variations in both ecology and cropping patterns, agricultural production itself remains dominated by the Groundnut Basin and by the groundnut/millet crop mix that has been its most marked feature. From the 1930s around 90 per cent of the annual cropped area has been devoted to either groundnuts or millet, though in recent years the area under maize and niebe (cowpeas) has increased, while in the Casamance and Fleuve regions rice cultivation has become more important. The only other cultivation of note is cotton which is grown in the east of the country, Senegal Oriental, and has been stimulated by the activities of a specific parastatal agency, SODEFITEX (Société de Développement des Fibres Textiles).

The importance of groundnuts and the Groundnut Basin remains pronounced. By the early 1980s around 77 per cent of the total cultivated area was located in the Basin, half the population lived in the region and nearly 85 per cent of groundnut production originated from this area. However, it is important to note that the share of total public investment directed towards the region has declined from around 33 per cent under the Fifth Plan (1977/8–1980/81) to under 15 per cent for the period 1981/2–1984/5 (République du Sénégal, 1985). In part, as we shall see, this reflects the view that the long-run potential of the region remains limited, on account of climatic and ecological constraints.

The wide fluctuations in overall economic performance can, in large measure, be attributed to primary sector output volatility. This is to be expected in the case of a largely Sahelian country where irrigated agriculture generates a very small fraction of total output. Regressing groundnut and millet yields on rainfall and time indicates that nearly 60 per cent of yield variation over the past thirty years can be attributed to rainfall[2]. Moreover, rainfall has declined significantly since the early 1960s. Further, when compared with the preceding thirty years, rainfall in the Groundnut Basin for the period 1976–84 was on average barely 65 per cent of that for the earlier period and in the north of the country – around St Louis and in Louga – about 50 per cent.

Given the absence of major technical changes in production, this trend in rainfall has obviously held back productivity increase. Between 1960 and 1979 groundnut yield growth rates remained broadly similar to those for millet at just under 3 per cent per annum. Between 1979 and 1984 both crop yields declined by over 10.6 per cent. This has had major implications for both value added from the sector and government revenues, given the importance of groundnuts in overall exports.

The adjustment programme pursued since 1980 has thus had to contend with a major structural impediment to raising the economic growth rate. The entire agricultural sector has been characterised not only by adverse climatic conditions but also by a falling area allocation for the traditional tradable, groundnuts. Groundnut products, which comprised nearly three-quarters of export goods earnings in the 1960s, fell to 42 per cent in the 1970s and to around 17 per cent between 1980 and 1986. Similarly, groundnut production's share of GDP in the latter period was half that of the 1960s.

Table 9.3 indicates the direct and indirect financial effects of groundnut production for the period 1980–84. Apart from the extreme fluctuations in value added, the principal sufferer has been the state. This can also be seen from the operating losses of the CPSP's groundnut and refined oil sales account.

The deficits registered by the CPSP have continued to escalate since 1984, because of the diverging trends in domestic and international groundnut prices. The 33 per cent real price increase for groundnut producers introduced in 1985 coincided with a sharp fall in international prices for groundnut oil, Senegal's main export. By 1986 the price of unrefined groundnut oil was around 45 per cent of its 1984 level and less than a third of the 1980 level in real terms. For the crop year 1986/7 the effective price support offered amounted to CFAF 11 billion, which was part-financed by the oil mills through profits on sales of imported vegetable oil, the remainder being borne by the CPSP (Price Equalisation and Stabilisation Fund).

Table 9.3: Senegal: financial effects of groundnut production 1980–84 (CFAFm.)

	1980/81	1981/82	1982/83	1983/84
Producer Revenues	18,573	45,440	59,080	23,160
Salaries	8,371	11,307	12,168	10,834
Financial Institutions	1,248	3,821	5,104	1,531
Enterprises	8,638	12,669	22,218	9,667
Government	–14,769	–18,560	–7,556	–6,436
Total Value Added	22,061	54,677	91,014	38,756
Exports	8,699	49,319	75,756	52,785
Induced Imports	15,703	18,333	16,344	25,541
Balance	–7,004	30,986	59,414	27,244
CPSP Account (Groundnuts Sector and Local Oil Sales)	–15,788	–21,776	–10,471	–8,585

Source: Agel and Thenevin, 1984.

The pressure on the groundnut sector derives not only from falling international prices and the dominance of one market – France – and one trading enterprise – Lesieur, but also from the structure of domestic costs and, in particular, the overheads associated with the state's interventions in groundnut marketing and processing. In the first place, capacity installation in the milling sector has enormously exceeded actual utilisation. Over the period 1978–85 maximum capacity utilisation did not surpass 78 per cent and average utilisation fell below 40 per cent. This has been sustained by the state's subsidisation of any differences between actual capacity and a guaranteed level of 600,000 tons per annum (Jammeh, 1985). Secondly, the share of fixed costs in total processing costs has remained very high at around 95 per cent. Again, this can be largely explained by inefficiencies generated through the system of state income guarantees to the oil milling companies.

The loss of export revenues from groundnuts has clearly hampered the government's attempts to stabilise its finances. However, the issue is made more complex by developments on the import side, where rice and wheat imports have remained buoyant. Senegal, in common with a number of other West African economies, is thus faced not only with the problem of a weak and unstable export base but also with a rising import burden deriving from a shift in consumption away from traditional coarse grains, such as millet, towards imported commodities like rice and wheat. Given the strong constraints on import capability, the question of relative crop area allocations and pricing has become a critical factor in the present policy stance towards the agricultural sector.

AGRICULTURE IN THE ADJUSTMENT PROCESS

The deteriorating performance of the agricultural sector in a significant number of sub-Saharan African countries has been attributed to the pursuit of inappropriate pricing, marketing, taxation and trade regime policies by governments. These themes have surfaced in the debate over agriculture policy in Senegal. Unlike, for example, Ghana, where the taxation of tradables producers has been the key issue, Senegalese agricultural sector policy-making has been primarily driven by budgetary considerations. Producer price policy has been largely guided by trade considerations and, in particular, the pressure to reduce the share of food items in the overall import bill. The current account constraint has effectively regulated domestic agricultural price policy. Secondly, Senegalese policy-makers have been faced with a set of rigid constraints in agriculture. At present, Senegal lacks comparative advantage in any agricultural output. This inhibits the application of incentive systems that could favour the production of selected tradables. In these respects, the Senegalese case cautions against the application of an oversimplified model of discriminatory trade and domestic pricing regimes as the explanation of the weak performance of the agricultural sector.

If the colonial hallmark – groundnut production – remains imprinted on the core of the economy, other features have been radically revised. Perhaps most significant has been the growth in the parastatal sector. Their functions ranged from credit through to marketing, inputs supply, extension, agricultural research and the diffusion of new technology. The institutions charged with these functions themselves underwent change, the history of which is well told elsewhere[3]. What requires emphasis in this context is the fact that through ONCAD (Office National de Coopération et d' Assistance pour le Développement), its successor agency, SONAR (Société Nationale d' Approvisionnement Rural) as well as the Regional Development Agencies such as SODEVA (Société de Développement et de Vulgarisation Agricole), SAED (Société d' Aménagement et d' Exploitation des Terres du Delta), SOMIVAC (Société de la Mise en Valeur de la Casamance) and SODEFITEX, the state intervened in principle in almost all spheres. This was obviously most pronounced for the groundnut sector. For other crops, actual interventions were limited. Official prices for millet, for instance, have always diverged significantly from market prices, while the maintenance of floor prices, through bodies such as the CSA (Commissariat à la Securité Alimentaire), has remained largely fictional. Nevertheless, the nature and range of public interventions in the agricultural sector by the end of the 1970s probably exceeded those in most other sub-Saharan African countries. Not surprisingly, the role of the parastatals became a key issue in the adjustment programme.

The agricultural sector components in adjustment have primarily been organised around the three World Bank Structural Adjustment Loans and the government's general policy orientation – the Nouvelle Politique Agricole (NPA) – that was elaborated in 1984. In addition, IMF Standby programmes have contained conditionalities with direct relevance for the sector. The main themes that have been a consistent feature of such lending have concerned the role and financial position of the parastatals, the liberalisation of domestic markets, particularly for cereals, the reduction in budget support for inputs such as fertiliser, seeds and agricultural implements as well as the restructuring of relative prices. In this latter regard, an important feature has been the reduction or elimination of subsidies to, principally, urban consumers for major food items.

The unifying strand in recent public policy towards agriculture has been the attempt to reduce the burden of rural parastatals on the budget, and the associated withdrawal of the state from certain key functions. It began with the abolition of ONCAD in 1980 and its replacement by a smaller agency, SONAR. At its dissolution ONCAD had accumulated debts of over CFAF 94 billion (c.$295m.) and a labour force of around 4,300 people. Most of this debt was owed to the domestic banking system and to the state-owned banks, in particular. Settlement of these arrears has been a specific IMF conditionality but at current levels of repayment, CFAF 9 billion per annum, the ONCAD debt alone will not be paid off until 1998. SONAR, which was charged with a more limited range of functions, principally the collection and distribution of groundnut seed, was itself abolished in early 1985. The government has also taken measures to reduce the functions, staffing and budgetary cost of other parastatals. As yet, for the rural sector, this has not involved any privatisation measures, but all the major Rural Development Agencies have now drawn up 'contrats-plans' with the government. By 1987, they had suffered significant reductions in state funding and in the case of SODEVA – the extension agency for the Groundnut Basin – there were substantial cuts in personnel, particularly extension agents, and in operating budgets.

Reduction of government transfers to the parapublic sector had emerged as a key issue by the end of the 1970s. Between 1962 and 1977 the number of public enterprises had nearly quadrupled (from 21 to 83) with those in agriculture more than doubling. Between 1977/8 and 1980/82 government operating subsidies to the parapublic sector more than doubled and for agriculture increased by 75 per cent in real terms. Disaggregated figures for the principal agricultural sector institutions – the extension agencies – for the period 1981–84, show that in real terms the net subsidy in 1984 remained over 40 per cent higher than in 1981 but had slightly declined from 1982 and 1983 levels. Since 1984 it has been further reduced. Moreover, actual expenditures for the extension agencies by 1985/6 were less than 40 per cent of their 1981/3 levels in real terms.

This reform of the parastatal sector has been meshed in with a more general policy orientation, elaborated in the NPA, which comprises four main areas. First, the transfer of specific key functions, such as groundnut seed storage, to producers. This transfer of responsibilities has also been linked to changes in the important co-operative system. 'Sections villageoises' have been established in an attempt to strengthen village-level organisations in place of parapublic agencies. At the same time, but with an ambiguous response on the part of the government, there have been moves towards creating 'groupements paysans' that are independent of the official co-operative system. The second main feature of the NPA has been to improve the input supply system with the private sector playing the central role. This aim has been largely unrealised. The third area has concerned the restructuring of the parastatal agencies and a reduction in their specific functions. Though not yet implemented, this would appear to have particularly pronounced implications for SAED, the agency responsible for stimulating rice production in the Fleuve region. The fourth concerns pricing policy, and has emphasised not only 'vérité des prix' but also the explicit decision to grant domestic cereals production protection against imports. This latter aspect – with the emphasis on raising food self-sufficiency – has not only been an explicit feature of policies embodied in structural adjustment lending, but has been formalised in the Plan Céréalier of April 1986, which provides a detailed exposition of the main lines of government policy – policy that is implicitly, albeit with reservations, supported by the major donors[4]. It is worth elaborating in greater detail some of the critical features.

The Plan Céréalier takes as its starting point the fact that by the mid-1980s Senegal was producing only just over half of its domestic food requirements. The rest consisted of food imports (c.40 per cent) and food aid (c.8 per cent) (Ministère du Développement Rural, 1986), with a consequent negative impact on the balance of payments. The objective has therefore been defined as 80 per cent domestic food self-sufficiency by the end of this century. The means for achieving this include the maintenance of a minimum 25 per cent nominal protection rate for domestic cereals, the improved transformation of local coarse grain cereals, increases in price incentives for domestic cereals producers, continuation of market liberalisation measures for cereals and a minimum 75 per cent increase in average yields for rice, millet and maize through expanded irrigated agriculture and an increased use of yield-enhancing inputs. The Plan also envisages greater crop diversification and substitution of maize for millet in

Table 9.4: *Senegal: measures to be taken under World Bank Structural Adjustment Lending 1981–8 (agricultural sector and parapublic sector measures)*

SAL I: $56.8m: Started January, 1981, Cancelled June 1983

Parapublic Sector

  i) Return of selected parapublic activities to private sector.
  ii) Introduction of 'contrats-plans' between Government and individual PEs.

Agriculture Sector

  i) Studies regarding liberalisation of prices for domestic and export crops and fertiliser.
  ii) Studies on reform of co-operative structure.

SAL II: $70m: January–October 1986

Parapublic Sector

  i) Preparation of list of PEs to be privatised.
  ii) Finalisation of 'contrats-plans' with major parapublic institutions.

Agriculture Sector

  i) Preparation of cereals action programme.
  ii) Definition of Scale of Price Support Activities by CSA for cereals.
  iii) Maintenance of minimum nominal protection rate of 25% for domestic cereals.
  iv) Progressive disengagement of the state from importation of rice with increased involvement of private sector in rice importing.
  v) Reduction of fertiliser subsidies with elimination by 1989/90 and privatisation of fertiliser distribution.
  vi) Reduction of central seed buffer stock to 50,000 tons.
  vii) Complete liberalisation of groundnut seed distribution by 1986/7.
  viii) Finalisation of 'contrats-plans' with SONACOS and SEIB.
  ix) Restructuring and reduction in functions of RDAs.

SAL III: $93m: May 1987–June 1988

Parapublic Sector

  i) Divestiture of 10 PEs by 1987/8 and selection of further 10–17 PEs to be privatised.
  ii) Reduction of direct subsidies to PEs.

Agriculture Sector

  i) Studies on potential for agricultural diversification (Senegal Valley) and export promotion.
  ii) Studies on agricultural incentives and price support system.
  iii) Study of existing credit systems.
  iv) Audit of CSA, CNCAS and SONACOS.
  v) Maintenance of minimum 25% nominal protection rate for cereals and elimination of fertiliser subsidy by 1980/90.
  vi) Definition of Land Tenure Policy for Senegal River Valley.
  vii) Restructuring and strengthening of Ministry of Rural Development.

areas where rainfall exceeds 700mm as well as niebe for groundnuts in parts of the Groundnut Basin. In addition, under the Seventh Plan and the Public Investment Programme, agriculture's share of total investment has been raised to 14.4 per cent and 17.9 per cent respectively for the period 1985/6 to 1988/90 as compared with

11.5 per cent of total investment under the Sixth Plan (1981/2–1984/5) (World Bank, 1987c.)

The main features of government and donor policy vis-à-vis the agricultural sector can be summarised as follows. First, there has been consistent emphasis on reducing the role of the state. Secondly, despite according groundnuts considerable importance, the main emphasis has shifted to cereals production. Here the key issues are consumption preferences, relative prices and productivity. Thirdly, there has been a consistent attempt to reduce the budgetary costs of subsidies to the sector, not only with regard to operating subsidies for the extension agencies but also for fertiliser and agricultural matériel. The following sections examine in more detail the impact of these measures.

PRICING POLICY

A recent appraisal of the welfare implications of the adjustment programme judged them to be positive, even over the short term (World Bank, 1986). This was attributed firstly to the employment effect flowing from readjustment of tariffs and agricultural prices to favour domestic labour-intensive production and, secondly, to a direct redistributional effect, with the greater part of the transfer being from the urban to the rural sector. The latter was judged to have been over-taxed in the past. In short, the principal losers from adjustment would be the urban poor faced with higher food and energy prices and declining employment.

There is little doubt that this latter prognosis has proved correct. Urban unemployment has grown significantly with the great majority of the unemployed being located in the towns, particularly Dakar. Yet the assumption that raising producer prices, while also enhancing inputs costs, could elicit both a positive supply response and an outwards shift in the labour demand curve – consequences that would both result in a positive aggregate welfare effect – is not immediately obvious in the Senegalese context. Nor is it correct to assume that the agricultural sector has been penalised by unduly heavy taxation.

Most Senegalese farmers are faced with a relatively simple trade-off between growing a cash crop, like groundnuts or cotton, and a consumption crop, mostly millet or sorghum. In the case of groundnuts, the bulk of the crop is normally marketed either as shelled or unshelled nuts or as fodder. While in theory this market was monopsonistic, years of preferential prices in either the informal processing sector or in neighbouring Gambia have seen substantial sales on the parallel market, occasionally surpassing 40 per cent of marketed output (Jammeh, 1985). For millet, on-farm consumption is thought generally to be the norm. In 1980/81, for instance, it was estimated that just over 4 per cent of domestic output was marketed (SONED, 1982). This was, however, a particularly poor agricultural season and in other years marketed output may range between 15 and 25 per cent of aggregate production.

The decision whether to allocate land to millet or groundnuts should on the face of things be primarily price determined. Output and yield variability for both are very close; for the period 1965–86 output variability was between 0.28 and 0.29, and for yields 0.24 and 0.20. The ratios of the lowest output years to mean output were also very proximate. In other words, both crops face the same risk framework and appear to respond, agronomically, in a broadly similar manner. Yet the fact remains that, since the mid-1970s, the area under millet and maize has increased, largely at the expense of groundnuts, particularly in the 1980s. To what extent has this been a function of relative price shifts?

Before answering this question, one needs to establish the importance of prices in a context of high climatic variability, generally low savings (or stocks) on-farm and hence a preference for reducing consumption variability on the part of the farm household. When the general level of risk – as measured by the annual variance in rainfall, and its distribution – is raised, as in the recent period from 1972/3 onwards, one might expect the degree of risk aversion to increase as a function of declining consumption levels, particularly when the level of output variability for the normal cash crop was reflected in the lower bounds for price variability, given the semi-controlled nature of the market. However, a partial counter-weight would exist if a substitute consumption of food – such as imported rice – was available at a stable price. In addition, it can be deduced that non-price factors – such as the availability of government-distributed groundnut seed – would be a further explanatory factor.

Estimating supply response equations for groundnuts and millet is hampered by lack of data on labour and capital inputs. Reduced estimations, with prices of groundnuts and millet lagged one period and with average annual rainfall for the Groundnut Basin for the years 1961–86, yield the results shown in Table 9.5. The equation is estimated in log-linear form.

Table 9.5: *Senegal: Determinants of groundnut marketed output (all variables logged)*

Lagged Groundnut Price:	0.539	(1.255)
Lagged Millet Price:	−0.812	(−1.64)
Average Rainfall:	1.190	(3.21)
Constant:	5.319	
$R^2 = 0.55$ F = 8.64		
(T Statistic in brackets)		

As expected, the rainfall variable is significant at a 5 per cent level but neither of the price variables is significant, even though the signs are in the right direction. Other estimations that included fertiliser inputs, area under competing crop in previous year and constant prices with either area or marketed output as the dependent variable, provided no better fits. However, a specification that used the quantity of groundnut seed annually distributed and time as independent variables proved significant, with the groundnut area as the dependent variable for the period 1965–86 [5].

Examining the structure of relative prices as shown in Table 9.6 suggests that since 1979/80 the groundnut price fell in real terms between 1983 and 1985 but was roughly constant by 1986. A broadly comparable trend can be seen to exist for the weighted cereals price index. For millet, official producer prices have fluctuated less in real terms since the late 1970s; by 1986, they were around 8 per cent lower than in 1980. Since 1979/80 the ratio of groundnut to millet prices had increased from the level attained between 1961 and 1979. Thus, at recent relative prices, returns to groundnuts would be higher than for competing crops.

Increased groundnut producer prices have been a policy measure emphasised by donors, particularly the World Bank. But as Table 9.7 demonstrates, the net producer price, which ranged between 40 and 45 per cent of the unit export value of crude groundnut oil and groundnut cakes (the principal Senegalese exports) in the 1970s, has subsequently fluctuated substantially. The producer price increase of 1985 lifted the farmgate price to over 80 per cent of the consolidated unit export value, largely on account of the sharp fall in world groundnut prices.

Table 9.6: *Senegal: producer prices for agricultural output 1971–86*
(1971 constant prices)

Year	Groundnut Price Index	Millet Price Index	Cereals Price Index (weighted)	Maize Price Index	Rice (Paddy) Price Index
1972	115	97	98	99	112
1973	100	125	87	118	89
1974	111	128	106	141	143
1975	115	97	99	107	109
1976	116	112	99	106	108
1977	104	101	100	101	97
1978	101	112	108	97	94
1979	100	101	98	88	85
1980	102	94	90	82	79
1981	116	111	85	98	92
1982	99	94	91	84	79
1983	73	93	81	79	82
1984	79	91	81	86	80
1985	70	94	71	88	92
1986	99	88	88	83	91

Table 9.7: *Senegal: groundnut producer prices as share of unit export prices and international prices, 1970–85/6 (per cent)*

Year	Producer Price as Share of Unit Export Price*	Producer Price (decorticated) as Share of Border Price
1970/74	41	40
1975/9	45	34.5
1980/81	37	44
1981/2	66	35.5
1982/3	57	47.5
1983/4	26	37.6
1984/5	28	39
1985/6	82	57

* Refers to unit value of crude groundnut oil and groundnut cake exports.

At a time when groundnut prices have been falling, the government has thus attempted to raise producer prices as an incentive to farmers to maintain, if not increase, the area under groundnuts. At present relative price levels, this policy has resulted in higher returns for groundnuts than for competing crops in the core producing regions of the country. Farm budget data suggest that in 1986/7 net returns per man day for groundnuts in three states of nature and under two current technology regimes are considerably in excess (three to four times) of the return for millet, but inferior to that for maize (Martin, 1988).

The area shift towards millet and, to a lesser extent, maize and cowpeas has thus to be interpreted largely as a response to enhanced aggregate output variability and the preference for assuring that share of output destined for own consumption rather than the outcome of conscious price policy.

Table 9.8: Senegal: farm budgets for groundnut, millet, maize, rice and cotton (national averages) (net return per man-day-CFAF)

State of Nature	Groundnuts		Millet		Maize (Intensification Level)		Rice (Irrigated)*		Rice (Rained)	
	Medium	Low	Medium	Low	Medium	Low	Medium	Low	Medium	Low
Good	2,170	2,370	599	769	2,473	2,051	1,080	885	1,162	1,162
Average	1,754	1,988	436	635	2,203	1,970	840	629	767	792
Bad	870	1,003	-24	282	1,633	1,551	284	345	-1,288	-476

* Irrigated rice refers to 'riz de nappe' and both rice columns refer only to Upper and Lower Casamance.
Source: Martin, 1988.

PRICES, CEREALS OUTPUT AND IMPORT DEMAND

The issue of growing domestic cereals deficits has also been addressed largely through price interventions. Again the economic reasoning is straightforward, even if the cross-elasticities are unclear. Braverman and Hammer have estimated that a 25 per cent consumer rice price increase would stimulate an 11 per cent millet output response, albeit with a sharp presumed fall in agricultural export earnings through a millet-groundnut substitution effect. By contrast, the public deficit for agriculture would fall by nearly 25 per cent, principally as a function of enhanced import tariff revenues, a factor that is clearly the case at present with the massive surpluses accruing to the CPSP rice account (Braverman and Hammer, 1986). As already outlined, the reasoning behind the Plan Céréalier is simple. Consumption of imported wheat and rice has been stimulated by low relative prices vis-à-vis domestically produced cereals and by, at some periods, direct subsidisation of consumers. In Senegal, as for the region as a whole, this has been accompanied by a declining per capita consumption of millet. FAO data point to a 10 per cent fall between 1960/65 and 1980 (Delgado and Reardon, 1987).

Two main points can be taken from Table 9.9. Wheat flour consumption is almost entirely an urban phenomenon and has been declining as a share of total cereals consumption. The more intractable issue concerns rice, consumption of which has been growing in both urban and rural sectors and particularly rapidly in the latter. This has been a function of past policy where the retail price of imported rice has been established and where the distribution system of licensed wholesalers and SONADIS has ensured wider availability. It also emerges from survey data that the level of rice purchases in rural areas is in direct inverse relation to the aggregate level of cereals output in any given year. Even so, on average rice purchases comprise a little under half total cereals purchased and 20 per cent of total cereals availability (Benoit-Cattin, 1987). While rice purchases can also be explained in terms of an income effect – as a preferred good among higher-income households – most farm units in Senegal are deficitary with regard to own-farm cereals consumption requirements. Rice is purchased as a supplement – at least in the Groundnut Basin – to millet and as the preferred consumption for the midday meal.

Estimation of consumer nominal protection coefficients and relative nominal protection for the major cereals shows quite clearly (Table 9.10) how for the period 1970–75 and again between 1980 and 1983 rice consumers benefited from a significant

Table 9.9: *Senegal: per capita consumption of cereals (in equivalent consumable products) by kg/year/person 1977/9–82/4*

Period	Sector	Millet/ Sorghum	Rice	Wheat (Flour)	Maize	TOTAL
1977/9	Urban	25	96	41	4	166
	(share)	(15.1%)	(57.8%)	(24.7%)	(2.4%)	(100%)
	Rural	113	42	4	9	168
	(share)	(67.5%)	(24.9%)	(2.3%)	(5.3%)	(100%)
1982/4	Urban	26	110	38	5	179
	(share)	(14.5%)	(62.5%)	(21.0%)	(3.0%)	(100%)
	Rural	115	51	3	10	179
	(share)	(64.0%)	(28.5%)	(2.0%)	(5.5%)	(100%)

Source: Plan Céréalier, 1986.

Table 9.10: *Senegal: consumer nominal protection coefficients and relative nominal protection for cereals 1970–85*

Period	Millet	Rice	Wheat Grain	Rice/ Millet	Wheat/ Millet
1970/75	1.81	0.89	0.61	0.52	0.39
1976/78	2.01	0.97	1.01	0.50	0.52
1979/81	1.87	0.75	0.98	0.40	0.56
1982/83	1.89	0.87	0.98	0.46	0.52
1984/85	2.06	1.04	0.84	0.50	0.41

Source: Delgado, 1987.

subsidy (Delgado, 1987). However, as a direct consequence of increases in the domestic retail price post-1984, by 1985/7 market prices were between 25 and 30 per cent higher than the import parity price for Thai broken rice, the major Senegalese consumption. Secondly, on the assumption that millet/sorghum can be traded, domestic production generates outputs at price levels considerably higher than the equivalent import parity cost. However, it should be borne in mind that most traded sorghum is for animal feed and that an adequate substitute for millet may not exist. Thirdly, despite increased rice retail prices, the ratio of rice to millet prices has tended to decline, when measured against the ratios that obtained through the 1970s. The trend has also existed for international prices. However, despite the fact that – using finger millet (souna) prices – the ratio of the millet to the imported rice price shifted from around 0.57 between 1974 and 1978 to 0.91 between 1981 and 1985 and was broadly at parity by 1986/7, this partly disguises the fact that equivalent processed millet products – such as flour – were priced at levels ranging between 95 and 110 per cent of the retail rice price (Martin, 1986). This suggests that, even with 25 per cent protection, current processing technology cannot transform at rates that could make millet more competitive vis-à-vis rice. Fourthly, price fluctuations for rice have remained lower than for millet, with the supply of rice to urban and rural markets more assured than for millet.

INPUTS SUPPLY

Seed Policy

The abolition of ONCAD in 1980 was accompanied by the collapse of a formal credit system in the agricultural sector. However, certain functions – such as the provision of groundnut seed – were passed on to ONCAD's successor body, SONAR or to the RDAs, such as SODEVA, and later, under the broad directives of the NPA, to the oil milling companies, SONACOS and SEIB, which were already responsible (since 1982/3) for marketing the crop. For the 1985/6 season, further changes were made. The retention of a share of the producer price to cover the provision of seed and fertiliser – in effect an implicit tax, given the highly rationed distribution of fertiliser and the unequal distribution of seed – was suppressed and the net producer price was raised sharply, 50 per cent in nominal terms. Reconstitution of the groundnut seed stock was left to the farmers, with SONACOS only holding a buffer stock of 100,000 tons. Farmers were thus given the option of storing their own seed or storing it with the oil mills. In addition, they could also buy seed from the security stock, which is regarded by the government as the foundation for a higher quality seed base.

The withdrawal of seed provision – linked to credit – has been rationalised as part of the 'responsabilisation des paysans'. As with the suppression of fertiliser subsidies, it has also been guided by the need to reduce the budgetary costs associated with such interventions. Yet, apart from the sharp break with previous practices, the question of seed storage and fertiliser availability remains central to the issue of agricultural productivity.

In the case of groundnuts, the seed issue is made more complex by the high required ratio of seed to sown area. Groundnut seed's multiplicative powers are much lower than for other crops, with a ratio of output to seed of around 10, as against 45–50 for maize and millet. In other words, storage has to be at a far higher level if self-provisioning remains the aim of farming households. Before 1985/6 public provision of groundnut seed in the Groundnut Basin appears to have accounted for between 70 and 80 per cent of farmers' requirements. The change therefore seems to explain in large measure the substantial decline in the groundnut area in that year. However, it does not appear to have inhibited the resurgence of groundnuts in the 1986/7 season. A USAID survey covering 90 villages and 800 farm households prior to the 1986/7 season found that 92 per cent of farmers stored seed and that, of the nineteen departments covered, only three revealed significant shortages of groundnut seeds (Ly, 1986). However, the same survey found that virtually 80 per cent of stored seeds were inadequately protected and that the overall quality of the seed stock was low.

Further data from the Sine-Saloum area for 1986 and 1987, based on a survey of 240 households, found that groundnut seed reserves at the farm level had grown by around 10 per cent between 1985/6 and 1986/7 but that this was substantially below the level of output growth (viz.55 per cent) (Gaye, 1987). For these years, the share of total output retained as seed was no more than 14 and 10 per cent respectively. If all seed requirements were to be met from farm stocks, around 38 per cent of output would have had to be retained in 1985/6. This suggests that, despite the absence of formal credit systems, the informal credit market, as well as loans from relations and friends, managed to bridge the gap. For the 1986/7 season more than 15 per cent of farm households counted almost exclusively on credit for seed.

It would therefore appear that, for groundnuts, the withdrawal of the State from seed provision has indeed led to larger stock levels on-farm, but – given the high seed-output ratio – recourse has also been had to borrowing. Nevertheless, this does not appear to have constrained the area under groundnuts, despite a temporary fall in 1985/6. To that extent, the policy of shifting responsibility to farmers has succeeded, though it has to be noted that a considerable proportion of farmers view this shift as temporary. A longer-term issue concerns the quality of the seed base. The 1986/7 survey found that some 75 per cent of farmers had chemically treated their seed stock but that seed losses and quality remain important, unaddressed issues.

Fertiliser

Fertiliser policy – particularly the heavy subsidies borne by the State – has been an explicit condition in the Structural Adjustment Loans of the World Bank. The second SAL laid down five main conditions. No subsidy was to be financed through the Treasury, directly or indirectly, thus eliminating the 50 per cent average subsidy sustained since the mid-1970s. Secondly, temporary subsidies – such as that financed by USAID – were to be phased out by 1989/90 with any sales under such subsidy schemes being purely on a cash basis. Thirdly, imports were to be fully liberalised by 1989/90 and, fourthly, domestic marketing of fertiliser transferred to the private sector. Lastly, pan-territorial pricing was to be abolished – a condition subsequently relaxed in the third SAL.

The impact of subsidy reductions on price has been dramatic. By 1985/6 the average fertiliser price was 2.4 times its 1980 level in real terms in contrast to ground-nut producer prices which were only 13 per cent superior. The impact on demand has likewise been significant. For groundnuts and millet, which between 1975 and 1980 accounted for over 80 per cent of total fertiliser consumption, sales in 1984/5 and 1985/6 were less than 30 per cent of the former level. Apparent consumption fell from over 102,000 mt in 1980/81 to around 12,000 mt in 1986/7 (World Bank 1987d). However, it should be noted that fertiliser consumption had declined very sharply prior to the post-1983 price rises, and even with the heavy subsidies in the past, average consumption had remained very limited.

The throttling of fertiliser demand emerges clearly from the results of the earlier mentioned survey in Sine Saloum in the 1986/7 season. It was found that fertiliser use ranged between less than 2 per cent (for urea) and 11 per cent (for NPK) of desired levels. Moreover, nearly 64 per cent of surveyed households used no chemical fertil-iser in 1986/7. For those that did, roughly two-thirds was allocated to contract growers. Cash sales accounted for only a third of the very limited quantities that were used (Gaye, 1987).

The relatively limited adoption of fertiliser, even under the previous heavily subsidised price regime, can be attributed to the absence of financial viability in the fertiliser packages proposed by the extension agencies. This can be clearly illustrated with regard to millet and maize cultivation using 1986/7 prices. If ISRA-recom-mended doses of 100kg of 0–15–20 and 50kg of urea per hectare were applied, then, at unsubsidised prices, the benefit-cost ratio would have exceeded 2(2.3) only with a yield increase of around 80 per cent. A comparable benefit-cost ratio could have been attained with the USAID-financed 24CFAF per kg subsidy on the assumption of yield increments of at least 60 per cent. In the case of maize the respective yield shifts would have been of a slightly lower order, viz. c.75 and 50 per cent[6]. In the Senegalese context the likely shift effect would be much weaker, hence reducing substantially any incentive to employ fertiliser particularly at unsubsidised levels. Moreover, the Senegalese extension effort has clearly failed to link fertiliser use with improved cultural practices or optimal allocation by crop. Yet, the uncomfortable fact remains that the returns to fertiliser use may be currently so low that the actual decline in consumption may not merely be a reflection of recent price shifts but also a recogni-tion among farmers of this more binding constraint (cf. Ndiame, 1986a).

This situation has only tangentially impinged on the government's longer-term objectives, as embodied in the Plan Céréalier. Under this scenario fertiliser consump-tion by 1990 would be around 133,000 tons, rising to 220,000 tons by the years 2000. With use of improved seed and improved cultural practices, millet yields have been estimated to rise by around 25/30 per cent for rainfed millet and by around 90 per cent for rainfed maize. For irrigated maize, yields would double and for irrigated rice would increase by about 30 per cent. On the assumption that current policy condi-tionality under the World Bank SAL will hold and fertiliser will remain unsubsidised after 1989/90, these assumptions appear heroic. With unsubsidised fertiliser the yield response would have to be considerably superior to warrant adoption by farmers, and when the opportunity cost of additional labour is also taken into account, the potential for enhanced fertiliser use appears even more bleak. In this context, the government's and donors' emphasis on involving the private sector in fertiliser impor-tation and distribution appears a nebulous hope.

Agricultural Technology

Under the Programme Agricole sustained up to 1980, the substantial provision of credit and matériel to the agricultural sector through a variety of parastatal institutions resulted in a major shift in the technical basis of production (Havard, 1987). This mainly involved the introduction of animal traction and ploughs, seeders, hoes and lifters, together with horse-drawn carts for crop and other transportation. Senegal emerged as the only agricultural economy in West Africa where the use of such technology had been widely disseminated and conclusively adopted.

The principal consequence was the possibility of extensive growth. However, the distribution of machinery has almost entirely ceased since 1980, except in the cotton-growing tracts of Senegal Oriental where SODEFITEX has been functioning, in the SAED-controlled sections of the Fleuve and, to a lesser extent, in the Casamance. As regards the impact of the Programme Agricole, it appears that the impact on productivity levels has been negligible on the whole, despite the fact that farmers favour the use of animal traction in land preparation for 'timeliness' reasons. This can be attributed to the presence of more powerful contrary forces, particularly soil exhaustion and rainfall variation. Where these factors have been less intrusive, evidence suggests that more timely land preparation will be associated with better maize and groundnut yields.

Despite a consistent attempt by the agricultural sector institutions to distribute matériel, this was not associated with a shift towards better cultural practices. In general, use of equine traction and light organic and inorganic fertiliser applications have been the norm. Even 'semi-intensive' levels involving bovine traction, substantial applications of manure and fertiliser and widespread land preparation have never been achieved.

The collapse of the Programme Agricole and the formal credit system has had the effect of cutting the costs to the State but has also been accompanied by a decline in the available machinery stock. This has been despite the growth in artisanal workshops specialising in the maintenance and, occasionally, manufacture of agricultural machinery. This informal sector – largely based in Kaolack and other parts of the Groundnut Basin – has been hampered by a lack of access to formal credit and remains highly technically constrained. Machinery produced by the public enterprise, SISMAR, has been at relatively high cost, and with present, unsubsidised price levels, demand has collapsed. High import taxes – averaging over 70 per cent for production inputs and between 32 and 38 per cent for agricultural machines – have likewise ensured low levels of demand (Havard, 1987).

In common with fertiliser use, a key issue remains the degree to which the continued distribution of such agricultural machinery is desirable and, secondly, whether under the existing price regime its continued adoption by farmers is at all possible. The answer to the second question is rather easier to formulate. Using a 12 per cent opportunity cost of capital, Ndiame (1986b: 53) has estimated that over a ten-year period and with credit available, the internal rate of return would be strongly negative for the adoption of animal traction. To turn it round would require a minimum annual growth in the groundnut area of 15–20 per cent with a yield growth rate of 5 per cent as well as a 10 per cent per annum area growth rate for millet/sorghum and maize, while yields for these crops and rice would need to grow by 10 per cent per annum.

When addressing the issue of the desirability of technical change in agriculture, a range of further issues need to be considered. In the first place, land and labour endowments should determine the appropriate technical blend. The Senegalese agricultural sector is facing a mounting land constraint, particularly in the former core regions. This has already manifested itself in out-migration towards the eastern areas of the country, and infra-marginal land scarcities already exist. Secondly, despite considerable seasonal flux between rural and urban areas, as well as between rural areas, over 70 per cent of the labour force is concentrated in the sector. On the assumption that current labour force growth rates (c.2.4 per cent per annum) will be sustained, this implies that over the next 15–20 years non-agricultural employment would have to grow at between 6.2 and 6.5 per cent per annum if the agricultural labour force is to be stabilised at present (absolute) levels. This is not a level of growth that can reasonably be attained, given the already high levels of unemployment in the urban sector and the sluggish growth trend in industrial sector employment. Thus, using FAO estimates of land-carrying capacity, the agro-climatic population density for Senegal will soon fall into the high density category – a condition shared by most of the other semi-arid or arid countries in sub-Saharan Africa. These factors combined imply that the labour force in agriculture and hence the agro-climatic labour density (number of agricultural sector workers per million calories of potential output) will continue to rise sharply. Although this need not necessarily be coeval with a condition of chronic labour surplus, it does suggest that labour constraints will not be the primary constraints on production. This in turn has implications for the type of technical change that could be deemed desirable.

First, labour-saving technologies will be mostly unsuitable, except in limited contexts such as, for instance, in the Fleuve region, but even here SAED's experience with tractorisation has not been promising. However, there will remain scope for labour substitution for peak season activities. Secondly, there will continue to be a case for providing the technical means – such as animal traction and ploughs – for achieving extensive growth in those areas (e.g. Senegal Oriental) where the land frontier has not been closed. Thirdly, major emphasis will have to be given to raising the productivity of crop and fodder production – through biological research and also through better use of fertiliser and other inputs. In addition, enhancing the quality of production, through improved cultural practices and land conservation, acquires considerable significance in the Senegalese context. To achieve this will undoubtedly require a better extension effort – an effort that cannot possibly be envisaged if the current strategy towards the extension agencies is sustained. At present, all the RDAs have had their operating budgets drastically reduced with major cuts in staffing. In the case of SODEVA, around 55 per cent of the staff have already been made redundant. The majority of those who have lost their jobs have been extension agents. A similar effect – though less dramatic – has occurred with SAED and SOMIVAC. Reduction in the wage bill has come before genuine rationalisation of staffing. Fourthly, the constrained potential for productivity growth in rainfed agriculture raises the issue of investment in irrigation. Under the current public investment programme and the Seventh Plan the share of irrigated agriculture in total agricultural investment exceeds 50 per cent, with most of this concentrated in the Fleuve and Casamance. But the costs of establishing irrigated perimeters have remained high. While the construction of the Diama and Manantali Dams offers the potential for very substantial increases in coverage, the costs of developing the irrigation feeder system preclude, with present budget constraints, an expansion of more than 2–3,000 hectares per annum. Clearly, irrigated agriculture remains a long-term and regionally limited option.

The sum of constraints on agricultural sector policy imply that, while earlier policies favouring the subsidisation of 'culture attelée' cannot be sustained, nevertheless under existing conditions there is a danger that the stock of matériel will continue to decline and that, in the absence of an adequate credit and extension effort, earlier gains will be nullified. Even in areas, such as the Casamance, which have been accorded high priority in the longer-term strategy for the sector, the availability and distribution of machinery and inputs remain very significantly below optimal levels (Ndiame, 1986b).

Credit

A critical constraint remains the absence of any generalised, formal credit system. Since the collapse of the Programme Agricole, very limited amounts of credit have filtered through, either via the RDAs or – to a far more limited extent – through the organised banking system. Between 1984 and 1986 the agricultural sector's share of total short-term credit was less than 2 per cent and of medium-term credit around 1 per cent. Of aggregate private sector credit, barely 3 per cent was directed towards agriculture between 1980 and 1985 (BCEAO,*Bulletin*). Moreover, as we saw earlier, the sharp decline in the rate of growth in total credit to the economy since 1982/3 has been particularly pronounced in terms of net government borrowing. Payment of debts amassed by ONCAD has, in recent years, amounted to around half the total credit to the parapublic sector. Seasonal crop credits, which have primarily been for groundnuts and have been directed through SONACOS and SEIB, were halved between 1980/83 and 1984/7 when expressed as a share of total domestic credit.

The sharp liquidity squeeze associated with the adjustment programme, coupled with a very low domestic mobilisation of savings by the banking system, has further reduced the limited willingness of the banking sector to lend to agriculture. This has compounded the specific legacy of debt cancellation that the government established in the 1970s, when the average repayment rate for seed and other credits fell below 60 per cent. Despite the fact that the Programme Agricole required a minimum repayment rate of 85 per cent, credit was still made available. Apart from the high levels of indebtedness of the parastatals that this engendered, one further result was an undermining of repayment sanctions and the credit system itself. This also explains the strong reluctance of donors and the banking sector to venture into this field.

Indicative of the void that exists in the official credit system is the fact that the Caisse National de Crédit Agricole au Sénégal (CNCAS) was only established in 1984 and currently has only four branches. In addition, most lending has been from the Dakar office and has largely been channelled outside agriculture. In Lower Casamance, PIDAC has established, with support from USAID, a modified credit system linked to the adoption of animal traction and extension packages. Elsewhere, SODEFITEX and SAED have maintained limited credit programmes but in the Groundnut Basin there has in effect been no formal credit programme since 1980.

The recent history of massive debt default and mismanagement at the level of the co-operatives and parastatals has obviously retarded the pace at which a revised formal credit system can be established. Moreover, even where tighter controls over credit, linked to collective sanctions against defaulters, have been implemented, as with the current PIDAC programme, repayment levels for short-term inputs loans fell from around 90 per cent in 1983/4 to 54 per cent in 1984/5. Furthermore, apart from climatic disturbance, the economic content of this credit programme is problematic. Acquisition of a team of draught oxen – a prerequisite for being considered for a loan – has been estimated to involve expenditure equivalent to over 150 per cent of average annual net monetary income. With five-year repayment spreads for matériel credits, the viability of the package remains dubious (Ndiame, 1987).

Nor has the absence of a generalised formal public credit system called forth a lending response by informal rural sector agents. Evidence from a survey of 11 villages in 1982/3 demonstrates clearly that informal credit is largely for consumption purposes, with borrowing mostly concentrated in the *soudure* or hungry season between June and October. The average loan period was around 4½ months with just under half the estimated credit flows being in kind (mostly millet). No recorded borrowing was for inputs or other productive purposes (Tuck, 1983). In short, the credit market – to the extent it exists – remains highly demarcated by type of function, length of credit and – though to a surprisingly limited extent – level of interest charged on loans.

The current policy stance by government and donors towards the re-establishment of a credit system remains understandably conservative. This does little to address the current constraints on the sector. Without organised credit for inputs purchase and acquisition of animal and machine stock, utilisation will remain at the present very low levels. Secondly, increased mobilisation of domestic savings will remain impaired. Savings rates in rural areas remain, in any event, low. The absence of savings institutions, and the fact that the real interest rate on time deposits is barely positive, restricts attainment of this objective. Thirdly, the major policy documents of the government – particularly the Plan Céréalier – are posited on the development of a credit system for financing the incremental purchase of inputs and machinery required to boost domestic sectoral output. Clearly, few of these objectives can be attained without a credit system, especially given the sharp increase in the cost of such items with the elimination of subsidies.

Domestic market liberalisation

A further leading feature of the adjustment period has been the liberalisation of domestic markets for all major agricultural commodities. In the case of the groundnut sector responsibility for marketing had already been transferred from the government to the oil millers by 1982/3. However, it was only in December 1985 that the mills were allowed to make their own marketing arrangements using private traders. Moreover, from that date private traders were authorised to buy groundnuts directly from farmers, selling to the mills at negotiated prices. This marks a major change from the earlier system under which the entire marketing chain was financed by crop credits given to the oil mills and SONAR by the central bank (BCEAO).

Liberalisation for cereals has also been pursued. Prior to October 1985, only licensed wholesalers were allowed to collect locally produced cereals from producers. Such authorisation required a minimum bank deposit of CFA 3 million, as well as sufficient storage facilities. Transactions in excess of 200kg could only, in theory, be done through licensed wholesalers. At the same time, the official producer price was the reference price, even though major variance existed between official and market prices. As expected, this merely led to creative accounting practices on the part of traders; the explicit aim of reducing actual margins to traders and thereby shielding producers from unequal transactions remained largely unrealised. Rather, market controls tended to reduce competition among buyers, increased market uncertainty through the system for authorising the sale of produce and restricted the overall scope of the cereals market through controls on margins and prices.

Since late 1985 local cereal collection has been wholly liberalised, as has commerce in these commodities. The official producer price has been replaced by a floor price with margins no longer fixed by government. Guaranteeing the floor price for producers has been the responsibility of the CSA (Ndoye and Ouedrago, 1987).

Lastly, State involvement in the important rice trade has also been subject to some revision, though to a more limited extent. Since 1980 rice importation has been controlled by the CPSP, who have subsequently distributed imported rice through 'quotataires' – licensed wholesalers and SONADIS – , whose selection has been widely recognised as being based on political considerations. The reform of the rice import and distribution system has been a policy conditionality in both IMF and World Bank lending, the explicit objective of the donors being to privatise the rice trade. CPSP's monopoly on imports was to be abrogated by December 1986 with its share in total rice imports reduced by 25 per cent to an annual level of around 85,000 tons. Full privatisation was also aimed at by the end of 1987, but this has been compromised by a number of factors. Firstly, the number of traders with sufficient capital to participate in rice importation is limited. Replacing the CPSP's monopoly with three or four large importers is unlikely to result in major gains. Secondly, with the fall in imported rice costs, the CPSP's surplus on the rice account has risen dramatically. This has been explicitly used as budgetary support and for 1987/8 will amount to around CFAF 16 billion. Faced with continuing weak export performance and overall tax effort, this surplus constitutes a major government resource. Liberalisation of rice importation has therefore been shelved – at least for the moment.

Measuring the impact of market liberalisation is complicated by the wide range of factors that impinge on market decisions and by the short time the reforms have been in operation. Moreover, in the Senegalese economy, with the exception of groundnuts and rice grown in the Fleuve and controlled by SAED, marketed output remains a very insignificant part of total cereals production. Furthermore, the liberalisation policy itself has made little impact on the balance between direct state interventions – as through the CSA – and private sector involvement. The latter sector has always dominated both wholesale and retail trading, with the possible exception of outlets for imported rice distribution. Despite controls over margins and inter-regional trade, the cereals market has been historically characterised by its competitive structure and by an apparently high degree of market integration. Rural markets appear to have been well integrated both before and after liberalisation (Ndoye, 1987). There are few reasons for supposing that the liberalisation measures per se have had any major impact on this score.

Survey data collected in the Groundnut Basin for the period 1984/5–1985/6 that sampled between 166 and 170 millet producers and between 63 and 70 wholesalers in 34 markets in 1984/5 and 16 markets in 1985/6, throw some light on recent developments. However, direct comparison between pre- and post-liberalisation effects is rendered difficult by the widely differing output levels for both years. Millet production in 1985/6 was roughly double that of 1984/5. This can largely be attributed to the shift in groundnut seed policy. Thus, although the share of millet output sold by households increased significantly, it is instructuve to note that in the southern part of the Groundnut Basin (Kaolack and Fatick) where output increased far less significantly, marketed shares remained broadly constant for male producers and rose only slightly for female producers. The output effect can equally well explain the marked increase in millet traded by wholesalers. With millet production around 80 per cent above trend, market releases were correspondingly enhanced. As would be expected in a relatively glutted market, wholesalers' margins fell from an average of 6.4 CFAF per kg in 1984/5 to CFAF 5.2 in 1985/6, a real decline of around 20 per cent. Perhaps more significantly, the total volume of millet handled by the sampled wholesalers when expressed as a share of regional production only rose from 3 to 4 per cent (Ndoye and Ouedrago, 1987). However, this was accompanied by a sharp fall in the volume of rice handled by wholesalers, suggesting that in good years, rice consumption falls off in the presence of higher self-provisioning levels[7].

A further factor emerging from the survey results is the continuing preference among wholesalers for rapid turnover of stock. Stock is rarely held beyond one or two months, largely due to liquidity constraints and the high cost of borrowing from the informal credit sector. Current policy measures taken by the government are unlikely to have impinged on this situation. Indeed, this is one of the chief justifications for the role of the CSA.

CSA interventions in the cereals market have remained relatively limited. In 1984/5 CSA purchases in the millet market in the six months after the harvest amounted to no more than 1,752 tons or 0.4 per cent of total output. For 1985/6 purchases were around 13,000 tons or nearly 1.4 per cent. As such, private traders continue to play the leading role in cereals marketing. Apart from the limited resources available to the CSA for purchasing millet, evidence from the ISRA surveys in the Groundnut Basin suggests that the CSA's interventions have been hampered firstly, by its late arrival in the market and secondly, by the refusal to purchase small quantities of millet, viz. anything below 30kg. In 1985/6 the CSA began purchasing in mid-October, in 1986/7 as late as December. However, millet sales start normally in late September and it is in the immediate post-harvest period that the sharpest price fall occurs. The refusal to purchase small quantities further means that the CSA relies to a large extent on traders for primary assembly.

Apart from these operational shortcomings, the role of the CSA in maintaining floor prices would in any event be limited, given recent millet price levels. Market prices have exceeded the official or floor price – at times by significant margins – for most of the period between October 1984 and June 1987. As already mentioned, immediately post-harvest is the only time when market prices have consistently dipped below the floor price. Yet, to date, this is the period when the CSA has not successfully intervened. Nor does it appear that CSA interventions have been able to smooth consumer price fluctuations for millet. Price levels continue to be determined not only by supply factors but also by groundnut marketing and seed purchase as well as by periodic surges in food aid distribution.

In short, liberalisation of domestic markets for agricultural commodities has involved a significant disengagement by the state in marketing arrangements for some major products. This has been less true with regard to groundnuts. The parastatal oil millers remain *de facto* monopoly buyers while, for importation and distribution of rice, the CPSP has continued to play the pre-eminent role. With protection given to domestic cereals and hence a substantial tax on rice consumers, the rents from this monopoly have grown substantially over the last three years. Yet, simple solutions – such as privatisation – remain problematic. Earlier attempts at contracting-out rice imports have had a chequered history. In 1980 a private company – ARAFEMCO – was granted exclusive rights to import rice. Excessive margins were agreed by the government allowing the company gross earnings of around $12m. on 360,000 tons of rice. Likewise, a successor company – ECAMI – with the same investors as ARAFEMCO, was granted similar rights in 1982 and a further three companies that were registered in 1983 are all owned by wealthy marabouts, Mourides and associates of the administration (Waterbury, 1984).

To that extent, the message is clear. The distinction between the organised private sector and the state in Senegal is a fine one. Privatisation measures in this context are unlikely to yield efficiency gains.

CONCLUSION

In common with many sub-Saharan African countries, Senegal continues to face major economic difficulties. Yet the constraints on policy-makers are particularly restrictive in the Senegalese case.

The adjustment programme implemented since 1979/80 has been both radical and, at least superficially, successful. Using traditional IMF performance criteria, improvements in most target areas, such as the fiscal deficit as a share of GDP, have been significant. Likewise, the current account deficit has been closed to some extent, even if largely through import contraction.

Closer examination of recent trends demonstrates the limitations of the criteria used by the IMF in evaluating performance. Public expenditure reduction has undoubtedly occurred but in a relatively arbitrary manner. The sectoral distribution of expenditure has remained unmodified. Revenue performance has remained weak, partly as a function of the deflationary nature of the economic policies being pursued. Consequently, increased recourse to external borrowing, largely from concessional sources, has had to be made. Although the current debt-service ratio remains lower than for many other sub-Saharan African countries undergoing adjustment, it is important to note that already there is a net outflow of resources to the IMF and that current levels of debt servicing have been reduced through very substantial rescheduling. With no underlying improvement in the tradables sector and in the overall rate of economic growth, the longer-term implications of higher debt levels will be adverse. Senegal continues to lack creditworthiness in commercial markets and access to heavily concessional credit – such as that from IDA – remains restricted. The dominance of programme over project lending is associated with financing consumption and, to a lesser extent, investment. One measure of this – the capital budget – demonstrates an unequivocal decline in real terms over the recent past.

In theory, the case for programme lending rests both on the tasks to be addressed and the degree of conditionality that would be deemed necessary in achieving those ends. Yet, such lending obviously creates problems if the underlying trends in the economy do not prove susceptible to improvement. Moreover – and the Senegalese example substantiates this point – the emphasis on conditionality tends to skew the nature of the lending so as to generate monitorable indices. Simple examples include measures such as the fiscal deficit as a share of GDP, or the reduction of particular subsidies by a specific time or the reduction of staffing by a specific amount for a given parastatal. When it is assumed, moreover, that the basic issues are simply efficiency issues – efficiency of parastatals and of general resource use – then relatively crude conditionalities can be imposed. This is made simpler if it is also assumed that any given reduction in state activity can call forth a private sector substitution.

Such assumptions, in the case of Senegal, are not easy to sustain, particularly as regards agriculture. This is indirectly reflected in the third World Bank SAL where the underlying lack of any strategy is transparent once more accessible pricing and budgetary conditions have been stipulated. Furthermore, the very emphasis on pricing and fiscal issues reflects not only current constraints, but also the manner in which financial stabilisation measures have strict precedence. In the case of agriculture, this can be seen in the policy measures taken towards the RDAs, as also towards the elimination of inputs subsidies. Ironically, this may be the most pronounced feature of recent cereals market policy, where imported rice price increases have largely provided budgetary support.

While there can be little denying that state or parapublic interventions in agriculture have been marked by gross inefficiencies and high budgetary costs, this chapter has also tried to show that merely emphasising reductions in budgetary transfers to agriculture risks ignoring the development of an adequate longer-term strategy for the sector. For the basic issue that confronts policy-makers concerns the means for raising productivity levels in agriculture. Productivity has remained at best constant over the past 25 years. Output of the principal tradable – groundnuts – in the period 1980/87 has been significantly below the levels achieved in the early 1960s, while *per capita* cereals production has also declined noticeably. Reversing these trends, in the presence of short-run supply elasticities that do not exceed 0.2/0.3, will clearly be problematic. With limited crop diversification within regions, relative price shifts merely juggle with the balance between groundnuts and cereals, principally millet.

At present producer price levels, relative returns strongly favour groundnuts. Yet the area effect will tend to remain limited by the emphasis placed by farm households on generating a reasonable share of cereals and self-sufficiency. Current estimates suggest that on average farm households achieve no more than 65 per cent self-sufficiency, and most households need to buy in a significant share of nutritional intake. Under present relative prices, this will continue to mean relatively strong demand for imported rice, given the continuing lack of competitiveness of processed millet products with rice. Moreover, because most rural households buy in significant quantities of cereals, recent rice and millet retail price increases are likely – particularly in bad years – to have an adverse effect on consumption. Indeed, it is important to note that agricultural sector *per capita* monetary income between 1981 and 1985 was less than 70 per cent of the 1971–5 level when expressed in constant 1971 prices. This suggests that the positive welfare implications deriving from producer price increments have been exaggerated.

If low supply responses are to be expected largely on account of physical constraints, this reinforces the point that productivity-raising measures are the key issue. For Senegal, achieving these ends will be difficult. The potential for yield gains from biological research for millet and sorghum is very limited. Agricultural research resources in the country have been largely directed towards cotton and rice (Jha and Oram, 1987). But regional research activity has failed to develop methods able to reduce unit production costs. For the Sahelian zone, this option does not exist at present (Matlon, 1987). Greater potential does exist for maize, rice and niebe, however. Yet all means for reducing unit production costs imply higher levels of input use than has been the case in the past. Benefit-cost ratios at current unsubsidised prices demonstrate that use of such inputs will remain very limited. While a return to general input subsidies would be unfinanceable, a strong case can be made for directing subsidised inputs to targeted regions and crops. This would have to be linked to restructured extension and credit packages offered by RDAs.

The building-up of a functioning delivery system for inputs and other services currently plays no real role in the adjustment programme, other than as a nebulous hope for private sector involvement. The emphasis remains on reductions in claims on the budget, but has also compromised the ability of the RDAs – especially SODEVA – to function with any adequacy. Budgetary cuts have been enforced in a relatively arbitrary manner falling most heavily on actual field services.

The Senegalese experience under adjustment is instructive. Emphasis has been placed on financial stabilisation. This has yielded ambiguous and perhaps deceptive measures of improvement. It has also been accompanied by an inability to formulate adequate longer-run sectoral strategies. Because Senegal now lacks comparative advantage for any of the major agricultural outputs and has very limited other sources of export earnings, conventional trade theory provides limited enlightenment for policy. Strategies for accelerating output and productivity growth will, moreover, have to depart from the restrictive assumptions that 'vérité des prix' will yield superior welfare outcomes. Investment in agriculture and agricultural technology remains so sub-optimal that public interventions, linked to improved institutional capacity for research and extension, will necessarily be an integral part of any policy framework that looks beyond short-run stabilisation.

NOTES

1 If employment in the parastatals and armed forces was included, it would appear that by the mid-1980s the state employed around 4 per cent of the total workforce and just under 20 per cent of the non-agricultural labour force.

2 Estimated using the following specification,
   $\log Y = a_1 + a_2 \log \text{RAIN} + a_z \log \text{TIME}$, where RAIN = Average annual rainfall in Groundnut Basin and TIME = time trend with 1960 = 1. Time period for the equation was 1960–86.

3 For example, ABT Associates (1985); Caswell (1985).

4 For such reservations, see Préambule, Plan Céréalier, Ministère du Développement Rural, Senegal, Dakar, 6 June 1986 (mimeo).

5 Dependent variable: Groundnut area (logged)

	Coefficient	Standard Error	T
Groundnut seed (logged)	.4508	.0858	5.253
Time (logged)	−.1255	.0346	−3.626
Constant	8.9760		

$R^2 = 0.6032$
DW = 1.7

See also Thioune (1987).

6 Fertiliser Benefit-Cost Ratio: *Millet* (1986 prices)
   (base yield 500kg/ha)

Fertiliser Price (CFAF)			Yield			
NPK	Urea	600kg/ha	700kg/ha	800kg/ha	900kg/ha	1,000kg/ha
64	39	.84	1.68	2.51	3.35	4.19
72	47	.73	1.47	2.20	2.93	3.66
80	55	.65	1.30	1.95	2.60	3.26
88	63	.59	1.17	1.76	2.34	2.93

Fertiliser Benefit-Cost Ratio: *Maize* (1986 prices)
(base yield 850kg/ha)

Fertiliser Price (CFAF)			Yield			
NPK	Urea	1,000kg/ha	1,250kg/ha	1,500kg/ha	1,757kg/ha	2,000kg/ha
72	47	.82	2.19	3.56	4.94	6.31
80	55	.73	1.94	3.16	4.73	5.59
88	63	.65	1.74	2.83	3.92	5.01
96	71	.59	1.58	2.59	3.56	4.35

7 See also Benoit-Cattin (1987) on this point.

REFERENCES

ABT Associates (1985), 'Senegal Agricultural Policy Analysis', Cambridge, Mass., April (mimeo).

Agel, C, and P. Thenevin (1984), *La Filière Arachide au Sénégal* (réactualisation 1983/4), Mission d' Evaluation, Ministère Français des Relations Extérieures, Paris, August.

BCEAO *Bulletin*, Dakar, various issues.

Benoit-Cattin, M. (1987), 'Hypothèses sur la Consommation de Riz dans le Bassin Arachidier du Sénégal', Montpelier, June (mimeo).

Braverman, A. and J.S. Hammer (1986), 'Multimarket Analysis of Agricultural Pricing Policies in Senegal', in I. Singh et al. (eds), *Agricultural Household Models, Extensions, Applications and Policy*, Baltimore, Johns Hopkins University Press.

Caswell, N. (1985), 'Peasants, Peanuts and Politics: State Marketing in Senegal 1966–80', in K. Arhim et al. (eds), *Marketing Boards in Tropical Africa*, London.

Delgado, C.L. (1987), 'The Role of Prices in the Shift of Rice and Wheat Consumption in Francophone West Africa,' Washington DC, IFPRI, July (mimeo).

—— and T.A. Reardon (1987), 'Policy Issues Raised by Changing Food Patterns in the Sahel', Washington DC, IFPRI, January (mimeo).

Duruflé, G. et al. (1985), *Déséquilibres Structurels et Programmes d'Ajustement au Sénégal*, Paris.

Gaye, M. (1987) 'Le Désengagement de l'Etat et la Problématique des Intrants Agricoles au Sénégal', Dakar, ISRA/ODI (mimeo).

Havard, Michael (1987), 'L' Incidence de la Politique Agricole sur la Mécanisation au Sénégal', Dakar, ISRA/ODI (mimeo).

Jammeh, Sidi (1985), *The Evolution of Marketing and Pricing Policy in Senegal*, MADIA draft study, Washington DC, World Bank, 6 September.

Jha, D. and P. Oram (1987), 'Patterns of Agricultural Resource Allocation in West Africa', Washington DC, IFPRI (mimeo).

Ly, H.M. (1986), 'Enquête – Sondage sur le Stockage de Sémences au Sénégal', Dakar, USAID (mimeo – 2 vols).

Martin, F. (1988), *Budgets de Culture au Sénégal*, Dakar, ISRA/BAME.

—— (1986) 'La Réforme de la Politique Céréalière dans le Sahel: Le Sénégal', Paris, OCDE/ CILSS, March (mimeo).

Matlon, P. (1987), 'Prospects for Improving Productivity in Sorghum and Pearl Millet Systems in West Africa', Stanford (mimeo).

Ministère du Développement Rural (1986), Plan Céréalier, Dakar, April.

Ndiame, Fadel (1986a), 'La Culture Attelée dans les Systèmes de Production de la Base Casamance: Aspects Techniques et Implications Socio-Economiques', Dakar, ISRA/BAME, (mimeo).

—— (1986b), 'Aspects Economiques de l'Utilisation de la Traction Bovine: Etude Préliminaire dans la Région de Ziquinchor', Dakar, ISRA/BAME, Dakar (mimeo).

—— (1987), 'Réflexions sur le Crédit Agricole au Sénégal' Expériences Récentes et Implications pour la Politique Agricole', Dakar, ISRA/ODI, (mimeo).

—— and I. Ouedrago (1987), 'Les Politiques d'Ajustement Structurel et leur Impact sur la Performance du Système Agricole au Sénégal', Dakar, ISRA/ODI (mimeo).

Ndoye, Ousseynou (1987), *Government Regulations and Cereal Marketing in Senegal*, Dakar, ISRA, July.

République du Sénégal (1985), *VII Plan de Développement Economique et Social 1985/89*, Dakar.

Shafik, Nemat (1986), 'Government Finance in Senegal', Dakar, USAID (mimeo).

SONED (1982), *Modélisation des prix agricoles, Rapport final*, Dakar.

Thioune, Assitan (1987), 'Calculation of price cross-elasticity of peanuts and millet/sorghum', USAID, 9 April (mimeo).

Tuck, Laura (1983), 'Formal and Informal Financial Markets in Rural Senegal,' Dakar, USAID (mimeo).

Waterbury, J. (1984), 'Agricultural Policy Making and Stagnation in Senegal: What is There to Explain?', Princeton (mimeo).

World Bank (1985), *Senegal – Structural Adjustment Loans and Credits (Loan 1931-SE/Credit 1084-SE) Program Performance Audit Report*, Washington DC, 21 May.

—— (1986), *Report of the President on a Proposed Development Credit to the Republic of Senegal for a Structural Adjustment Program*, Washington DC, 10 January.

—— (1987a), *Report of the President on a Proposed Development Credit to the Republic of Senegal for a Structural Adjustment Program (SAL III)*, Washington DC, 4 May.

—— (1987b), *Senegal: An Economy under Adjustment*, Washington DC, 13 February.

—— (1987c), *Senegal: A Review of the Three-Year Public Investment Program, 1987/88–1989/90*, Washington DC, 26 February.

—— (1987d), 'Agricultural Sector Strategy Brief', Washington DC, December (mimeo).

10

Morocco in the 1980s

David Seddon

ECONOMIC AND POLITICAL CONTEXT OF STRUCTURAL ADJUSTMENT

By the late 1970s, Morocco was seriously in debt, extensive foreign borrowing being required to cover a current account deficit amounting to 16.5 per cent of GDP. Comparable domestic imbalances had also emerged and the budget deficit comprised almost 16 per cent of GDP. These imbalances can largely be explained as a consequence of the major public investment programme of the previous five years, heavy expenditure on the war in the Sahara, and a growing oil import bill as well as the cost of food grain imports. Although in the 1950s Morocco was a net exporter of cereals, by the late 1970s between 40 and 50 per cent of the country's cereal requirements was imported.

In 1978, the government introduced a three-year stabilisation programme to attempt to redress the rapidly deteriorating financial situation, emphasising the need for stricter import controls and reductions in public expenditure. External 'shocks' – including the 1979 rise in oil prices, increasing international interest rates, a decline in revenues from the export of phosphates and from migrant workers' remittances – adversely affected this programme. Internal pressures also ensured that public expenditure remained relatively high and imports continued to grow. Moreover, by 1979 the war in the Sahara was estimated to cost between $2 and $5 million a day. 'Defence-related' expenditure may have accounted for no less than 40 per cent of the consolidated national budget. The agricultural sector failed to expand and value added in manufacturing actually declined. Food and other subsidies were maintained at heavy budgetary cost, but this failed to prevent strikes for higher wages by many different sections of the workforce during the early months of 1979.

By the early 1980s, the government faced growing pressure from its international creditors to implement more far-reaching measures to reduce public expenditure, encourage private investment and promote greater efficiency in the use of resources. However, the level of external borrowing remained high, allowing hard decisions regarding the introduction of domestically unpopular deflationary policies to be postponed, while opposition to such measures as had been adopted was also growing. The 1981–5 Development Plan attempted to achieve a compromise, aiming at substantial growth within the economy (6.5 per cent per annum) while at the same time cutting expenditure in selected 'non-productive' areas. But the economic and political crisis deepened.

Attempts during 1980 to cut public expenditure, particularly on education (which accounted for nearly 25 per cent of the current budget) and food subsidies, resulted in student strikes and more widespread social unrest. Price increases in a range of basic commodities (sugar, flour, butter and cooking oil) in June 1981 provoked a general strike organised by the Democratic Labour Federation that had been formed in 1978 to protest against price increases in staple goods. In Casablanca, several hundred people were killed over two days of violent clashes between demonstrators and the security forces. Faced with such opposition the government halted implementation of harsher austerity measures. Because of this, the IMF converted its three-year Extended Financing Facility into a one-year Stand-By in 1982. The World Bank also cancelled plans for a Structural Adjustment Loan (cf. World Bank, 1986b:2).

Early in 1983, emergency import controls and expenditure cuts were imposed and in September 1983, the IMF formally approved the government's economic stabilisation programme with a further 18-month Stand-by of SDR300m. Under the terms of the Stand-by, the Government undertook to devalue the currency – initially by 10 per cent – to effect severe cuts in public expenditure, and to impose fiscal and credit restraints and, particularly, cuts in subsidies involving price increases of between 20 and 35 per cent. The agreement also allowed for substantial external debt rescheduling. This was then linked to donor pledges.

Despite pledges of new money, servicing the foreign debt was estimated to absorb at least 40 per cent of Morocco's hard currency income, while the visible trade deficit – reduced by around 27 per cent during 1983, largely by restricting imports and stringent measures to reduce domestic demand (for investment as well as consumption purposes) – was expected to remain high. Official projections indicated that the 1984 budget would decline by roughly a third in comparison with the 1981–5 Development Plan projections and the 1985 level would be around 40 per cent below earlier projections. In order to reduce the budget deficit, the government initiated a second round of price increases affecting basic commodities in December 1983 and the draft budget for 1984 contained proposals to raise prices again during the year. These moves helped trigger off street demonstrations, particularly in the relatively disadvantaged regions of the south and north-east. After considerable violence, (as many as 400 killed in clashes with security forces), the government decided to suspend further price increases in January 1984 (for details, see Seddon, 1984).

In this context, both the IMF and the World Bank were increasingly concerned with determining the means for implementing policies that went beyond short-run deflationary measures and involved more far-reaching structural adjustment. In the World Bank framework such adjustment would involve a shift to outward-looking trade and exchange-rate policies, far-reaching reforms of price, credit, tax and regulatory policies to remove institutional and other obstacles to efficient mobilisation and use of resources in key productive sectors of the economy, improvements in the efficiency of government investment, more cost-effective methods and better targeting of social programmes, and a thorough overhaul of the public enterprise sector (cf. World Bank, 1986b:4).

The time horizon for such an adjustment process would reach, at the least, until the end of the decade, and would entail transitional social costs, resulting from severe demand restraint. This was likely to manifest itself in increased unemployment and some decline in real incomes, particularly for the urban population. However, it was argued that the cost of not undertaking 'the required economic adjustments' would be greater in the long run.

The government was thus caught in a dilemma. To implement a full adjustment programme risked worsening income distribution, increasing inequalities and provoking civil unrest. It also implied a severe cut-back in resources allocated to the war in the Sahara. However, without IMF and World bank support the government risked major difficulties with debt rescheduling in the near future. With these considerations in mind, it moved to curtail budgetary pressures, restricting public service recruitment and salary increases, raising the price of electricity, water, petroleum products and subsidised food stuffs, and cutting capital expenditures by a third. This adjustment process was supported by the World Bank, initially through an Industrial and Trade Policy Adjustment Loan (ITPA 1) in January 1984 aimed at improving the balance-of-payments situation with a package of measures to restructure Morocco's trade regime.

Parallel to trade reform was the emphasis on policy adjustment in the agricultural sector. The performance of the latter had not been impressive over the previous decade. To reverse these trends, the government initiated a five-year agricultural sector adjustment programme in 1984 which has been supported by the World Bank through a Sector Adjustment Loan in June 1985 as well as a large-scale irrigation improvement project loan in early 1986.

AGRICULTURE AND AGRICULTURAL POLICY

The first decade after Independence can be seen as falling into two parts: the first, between 1956 and 1960 marks a period of transition; the second, the consolidation of the power of the monarchy and the establishment of a weak form of state capitalism, in which private enterprise was encouraged and supported by state intervention. The first Five Year Plan drawn up after independence, under the leftist Ibrahim Government, would have led Morocco towards a more centrally directed economy. Agriculture was accorded relatively low priority but a far-reaching agrarian reform was advocated. Opposition from established interests resulted, however, in the dismissal, in 1960, of the Ibrahim government and the introduction of an inoffensive programme of agricultural reform; the primacy of private enterprise was reaffirmed and in 1962 the concept of agranian reform was eventually abandoned.

In terms of output it appears that while aggregate agricultural production rose by 11 per cent between 1960 and 1964, 'the production of cereals has not progressed significantly beyond the maximal levels of the 1930s' (Waterbury, 1971: 305). Per capita cereal production fell from an average of 330 kgs for the period 1945-55 to 220 kgs between 1956 and 1965 and the trade surplus in cereals slumped from an average of 335,000 tons per annum (between 1946 and 1959) to a mere 12,000 tons (between 1956 and 1965). The stagnation in cereal production was particularly serious, given the fact that, according to the 1960 census, some 71 per cent of the working population were involved in agriculture with around 80 per cent of the rural population involved in activities related to farming.

To address the problem of declining per capita output in the sector a new Plan, for the period 1965-7, was drawn up. This maintained the preference, established as early as 1960, of foreign donors for a policy towards agriculture which concentrated heavily on the construction and development of large irrigated areas (périmetres). USAID, for example, negotiated a loan for $23m. between 1959 and 1960 to construct an accumulation dam on the Moulouya river in the north-east and to develop irrigated agriculture in the region. The objective of such a policy was to expand rapidly the area under cash crops in order both to expand exports and to reduce the need for agricultural imports. The production of basic food grains was not an important feature of this conception of agricultural development; nor was the transformation of economic and social structures within the irrigated areas. It was largely on the insistence of USAID that a special state apparatus was established in 1961 to manage and direct the new areas under irrigation – the Office Nationale des Irrigations (ONI). In due course, this institution was restructured with primary responsibility passing, in 1967, to seven regional Offices de Mise en Valeur Agricole (ORMVAs), one for each major irrigation perimeter or scheme. The 'power-house' of agricultural development was to be the irrigated sector.

The dominance of the irrigated sector was also linked to the recomposition of the land holding structure post-Independence. In the decade between 1956 and 1965, some 300,000 to 500,000 hectares passed into Moroccan private ownership from European control; and it was essentially in the irrigated and irrigable areas, formerly under European ownership, that the new Moroccan agrarian bourgeoisie was expected to constitute itself.

It became increasingly apparent, however, that 'private enterprise' alone would be incapable of promoting agricultural development and modernisation on a sufficient scale. The expansion of the irrigated areas, supported by considerable public investment, resulted in a further 125,000 hectares equipped for irrigation between 1967 and 1972 to add to the existing 'stock' of around 190,000 irrigated hectares. The Code des Investissements Agricoles, which was introduced in 1969, provided the state with greater control within the irrigated perimeters, introducing new restrictions on inheritance and subdivision of agricultural holdings, with the ORMVAs providing not only the 'external' equipment (large-scale infrastructure) for irrigation but also equipping farm plots (small-scale infrastructure) and closely supervising the activities of individual farmers. This implied control over the cropping pattern and the allocation of farm inputs as well as the creation of 'appropriate' institutions, such as marketing co-operatives.

As the production of cash crops within the irrigated perimeters expanded, the need grew for efficient marketing structures. Here again, according to Waterbury (1971:130):

> despite the professed "liberalism" (i.e. the state's desire to limit its direct participation in the economy) of the regime, no group of Moroccan entrepreneurs was forthcoming to take over the organisation of the export of citrus fruit, artisanal produce and vegetables ... The state was obliged, as a result, to undertake this task itself through the Office de Commercialisation et d'Exportation (OCE).

For the next twenty years, the development of 'modern' capitalist agriculture and marketing essentially occurred under the auspices of the state, with very considerable direct state intervention and participation.

The performance of the agricultural sector as a whole from the mid-1960s through to the early 1970s was relatively strong. Growth exceeded 3 per cent per annum and accounted for 25 per cent of the total growth in GDP. This can largely be attributed to the policy of developing irrigated agriculture. Outside the irrigated areas productivity remained low, with a high proportion of production devoted to cereals for local consumption. Nevertheless, cereal output also grew appreciably up to the mid-1970s and in the five years up to 1972/3, aggregate agricultural output grew at an annual average of 6 per cent, far outstripping the forecast rate of 2.1 per cent.

Despite the improved performance of agriculture and a respectable overall growth rate, it was increasingly realised – both within the government and among the major aid donors – that structural inequalities, both social and spatial, had been increasing throughout the previous decade, creating the basis for future social and political instability. Moreover, the development of the irrigated areas, although certainly impressive, had not addressed the problems of the greater part of the rural sector. The question of how to achieve 'growth with equity' began increasingly to exercise the planners and the politicians. One outcome of this shift in emphasis was the Five Year Plan for 1973–7, which broke new ground by emphasising industrial expansion and, within agriculture, in addition to a continued expansion of the irrigated areas, a programme of investment in dryland farming. A three-fold increase in expenditure (up to 46 per cent of total agricultural development expenditure) on dryland farming was envisaged, with more importance also attached to livestock production. This strategy was endorsed by major donors, such as the World Bank and USAID.

The shift in policy implied by the Plan failed to take place. In 1974 the world price for phosphates rose rapidly and in response to this, and to the government's commitment from 1975 onwards to the war in the Sahara (cf. Seddon, 1987) the plan allocations were substantially revised. Agriculture's share of the total budget declined, while the allocation for 'administration and security' increased (from 9.9 to 22.3 per cent).

Until 1973, agricultural produce accounted for by far the largest proportion of total exports (59 per cent in the period 1969–73), but its relative importance dropped dramatically following the sharp increase in phosphate prices in 1974. In that year phosphates accounted for 55 per cent of Morocco's export revenue. The growing importance of labour migration from Morocco to Europe, in particular during the late 1960s and early 1970s, together with the earnings from phosphate exports, substantially improved the balance of payments, and in 1976 the value of remittances from abroad actually exceeded the value of the sale of phosphates. But the uncertainty surrounding both these major sources of foreign exchange during the late 1970s and early 1980s once again drew attention back to the performance of agriculture and industry. Over the 15 years from 1965 to 1980, agricultural output grew by 2.4 per cent a year, but during the latter part of the 1970s and in the early 1980s the growth rate fell to between 1 and 2 per cent – one of the lowest rates of growth among the so-called 'middle income countries'. Between 1974 and 1984, food imports, particularly cereals, rose sharply; domestic production of cereals actually declined (see Table 10.1).

In 1978, USAID in its country analysis stressed the need to pay greater attention to the poorer sections of the population and to cereal production, drawing attention to the rise in food imports, the stagnation of the non-irrigated sector of agriculture and the growing rural exodus, and arguing that policies which helped to stabilise the rural population would contribute to both economic and political stability.

However, the government's interim plan for 1978-80 once again emphasised the crucial importance of large-scale irrigation for agricultural development, with 57 per cent of the allocation to agriculture (18 per cent of public investment – about the same as in the 1973–7 Plan) going to investment in infrastructure and equipment for major irrigation projects. The World Bank, in its Memorandum on Morocco's Agricultural Sector published in May 1980, argued that (p. ii)

> an assessment of the current emphasis on large-scale irrigation compared to rainfed and poverty-oriented projects is now needed. . . greater priority should be given to rainfed agricultural projects, although ongoing irrigation projects should not be neglected.

The Bank's recommended strategy aimed at supporting (a) agricultural development in non-irrigated areas, (b) projects designed to increase the productivity and well-being of the rural poor, and (c) projects with a high economic rate of return –

Table 10.1: Morocco: cereal production and imports 1960–84 ('000 quintals)

Year	Wheat		Barley		Other Grains		All Grains	
	Production	Imports	Production	Imports	Production	Imports	Production	Imports
1960–64	14,474	2,345	15,025	568	5,927	7	35,425	2,920
1965–69	16,985	4,713	18,228	65	4,875	86	40,078	4,864
1970–74	19,153	6,208	21,265	155	4,736	166	45,154	6,529
1975–79	17,340	13,467	20,026	289	4,563	509	41,909	14,264
1980–84	17,693	19,453	16,429	974	3,588	1,605	37,711	22,033

Source: Banque Marocaine de Commerce Extérieure, (1986: 5).

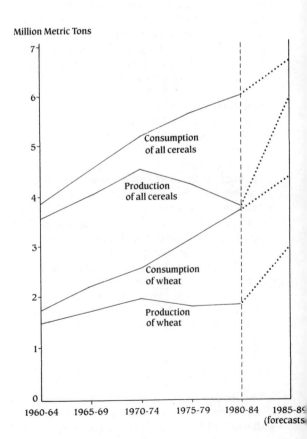

Figure 10.1: Morocco: production and consumption of cereals 1960–89 (five-year averages)

including export-oriented projects, agricultural credit programmes and irrigation rehabilitation. The Bank argued that rainfed agricultural projects in Morocco tended to show a higher economic rate of return than large-scale irrigation projects and concluded (p.6) that

> in terms of Morocco's food security objective, the deficit in cereals, vegetable oils and meat cannot be covered except by an intensification of agricultural production in rainfed areas.

Despite reluctance to commit itself to a major shift in policy, the government introduced substantial changes in its irrigation development policy in its 1981–5 Plan. With a total irrigated area of around 900,000 hectares, policy shifted towards emphasising improved efficiency. This was aimed at (a) ensuring optimal use of water through rehabilitation of existing schemes and more efficient operation and maintenance; (b) allocation of a larger share of investment to small- and medium-scale schemes because of their lower development cost per hectare; (c) favouring investments in those large irrigation scheme areas (now nine in number) served by existing dams; (d) increasing farmers' contribution to water management, partly through greater cost-recovery; and (e) establishing more effective extension services and water-saving technologies. At the same time, the Plan involved a significant reallocation of investment towards rainfed agriculture, livestock production and forestry. Proposed investments in dryland farming were almost doubled, while the share going to the large-scale irrigation schemes was reduced to 40 per cent.

These objectives were endorsed in the Agricultural Sector Adjustment Plan, agreed with the World Bank in 1984 and supported from 1985 onwards by an Agricultural Sector Adjustment Loan of $100m.

STRUCTURAL ADJUSTMENT AND AGRICULTURE

At present agriculture accounts for between 15 and 18 per cent of GDP, although it still provides between 40 and 50 per cent of employment. Agricultural exports have declined to around a third of total exports, while agricultural imports now account for about 25 per cent of all merchandise imports – about the same as petroleum imports. But, despite its declining relative importance in the national economy, agriculture remains of very considerable economic and social significance, and is a sector where major improvements are expected as a result of structural adjustment. It was hoped, for example, that one consequence of the changes under way would be a dramatic increase in cereal production (see Figure 10.1).

The programme of structural adjustment in agriculture began, in effect, as early as 1980. The 1981–5 Plan already envisaged a range of important changes, some of which have been mentioned above. As regards irrigated agriculture, improvements in the operation and maintenance of the large schemes have been made since 1980 as a result of the creation of separate Operation and Maintenance units in most ORMVAs, the appointment of skilled engineers and other technical personnel and the introduction of improved O and M methods. The objective of full cost recovery has been pursued, with a doubling of water charges in 1980, a further increase of 65 per cent in 1984, and the introduction of adequate pumping charges where applicable (these were updated in 1984). However, it was only in 1984 that the government formally developed and introduced a five-year agricultural sector adjustment programme. Its objectives were: (a) to re-structure the public expenditure and investment programme towards quick maturing and high return investments ; (b) to alter the prices and incentives framework to encourage 'economically sound' shifts in agricultural activities; (c) to strengthen the agricultural support services offered by the government, while rationalising the role of the public sector in the provision of commercially viable services, and improving cost recovery in other services; and (d) to build up institutional capacity for agricultural policy planning and analysis (cf. World Bank, 1986a: 12).

As regards public investment and expenditure, despite the formal commitment in the 1981–5 Plan to an increased allocation to dryland farming, only 37 per cent (as opposed to a planned 50 per cent) was spent in 1981–4 on programmes for rainfed agriculture. On the other hand, between 1982 and 1983 two large irrigation schemes in Loukkos and the Gharb were postponed, as were several medium-scale, high-cost irrigation schemes. In 1984 all budgetary appropriations for new projects (about 20 per cent of the 1984 budget) were frozen, while many other low priority activities and programmes (accounting for a further 20 per cent of the budget) were slowed down or halted. A core group of on-going priority projects and activities (for which 55 per cent of the budget was allocated) received over 70 per cent of investment. In 1985 a special Investment Budget was drawn up to continue these re-structuring and savings efforts. With regard to large irrigation schemes, priority was given to completing the equipment of those areas where the basic infrastructure was already in place, with the objective of rapidly reducing the backlog of an estimated 60,000 hectares waiting to be irrigated within existing perimeters. New investment was limited to developing the irrigation potential of low rainfall areas (an estimated 200,000 hectares, or 50 per cent of the total remaining potential). With regard to medium- and small-scale irrigation priority was accorded to the rehabilitation of 'traditional' schemes (involving about 30,000 hectares) with a high economic rate of return, rapid production build-up and greater cost recovery from the beneficiaries; new 'modern' medium-scale projects were postponed. With regard to livestock production, priority was given to production of vaccines and to making operational 38 existing milk collection centres rather than to building new ones. In agricultural extension, funds were primarily allocated to training.

As regards the second objective – to alter the price and incentives framework – several measures have been considered and some already initiated. The major thrust has been to reduce government subsidies on agricultural inputs and outputs, but also to adopt 'more realistic' exchange-rate policies to encourage exports. In fact, real effective exchange rates fell by a third between 1980 and 1986, thereby considerably improving the international competitiveness of Moroccan exports as against previous years. Overall, it was expected that exports would continue to grow spurred by the lower valued dirham as well as the government's export promotion policies, which have become less protectionist (cf. Lloyds Bank, 1985: 19).

Subsidies on specific consumer goods, notably flour, have also been cut so as to improve farm-gate prices. These measures have been taken for a number of reasons. First, about 70 per cent of subsidies on inputs to producers have benefitted farmers in irrigated areas which represent less than 10 per cent of the arable land and contribute about 45 per cent of value added in agriculture. Secondly, output subsidies, through price-support programmes, amounted in 1984 to around $95m. and also mostly benefitted irrigated farmers. Furthermore, it is argued (by the World Bank, for example) that the low level of consumer prices for flour (made possible by substantial subsidies, $170m. in 1984), together with the huge imported supply of food grains, tends to discourage domestic grain production. Although the level of official producer prices is close to the world market equivalents at official exchange rates, actual producer prices are 30–40 per cent below official prices in good years, and more generally between 20 and 30 per cent below world prices. Since the bulk of input subsidies go to irrigated farmers, rainfed cereal production has been consistently penalised over the past ten years. Estimates for 1984 suggest that dryland farmers faced a net negative protection of 30–45 per cent.

Improving incentives to cereal producers in rainfed areas under the structural adjustment programme has involved: (a) improving the effectiveness of the producer price support system for grains; (b) maintaining official flour prices high enough to induce production and marketable surpluses; (c) gradually reducing consumer subsidies on flour; and (d) making sure that imported animal feed is sold at or above the flour price. Official producer prices were raised by around 20 per cent in 1985. Another measure, intended to assist the dryland cereal producer to obtain higher prices for food grains, is the expansion of the private sector's role in domestic procurement of the marketable surplus of cereals so as to ensure the availability of minimum support prices at the farm level and to improve the co-ordination of imported and domestic cereal procurement.

As regards irrigated farmers, the gradual elimination of fertiliser subsidies by 1989/90 has been prominent. In addition, a fuller recovery of irrigation costs by higher water charges has been initiated, while the commercial and other services provided by the ORMVAs are to be charged at real cost. Finally, there is to be a phasing-out of price and distribution controls on animal feed. All these measures, which make greater demands on the relatively better-off farmers in the irrigated areas, are expected to have positive income distribution effects; as, indeed, are the measures adopted in support of the dryland cereal producers.

A third major objective of the structural adjustment programme is 'the restructuring of the role of the public sector'. Agricultural research was to be strengthened, primarily through the Institut National pour la Recherche Agricole (INRA) which was founded in 1981. The agricultural extension service was to be improved and strengthened, with a greater emphasis on training (through agricultural colleges) and better organisation and management. The ORMVAs, in particular, were to be subject to scrutiny and improvement. An agreement in early 1986 between the Government of Morocco and the World Bank, by which the latter would provide a loan of $46m. for a large-scale irrigation improvement project, included proposals for improving the efficiency and operations of the ORMVAs, particularly with reference to operation and maintenance, extension, research, cropping patterns, and irrigation cost recovery. The government also planned to: (a) reduce its administrative and financial controls over the ORMVAs; (b) establish a system of medium-term contracts with the ORMVAs; (c) improve their financial autonomy by introducing user charges and transferring, where feasible, certain services to the private sector or co-operatives; and (d) reduce the total budgetary support to the ORMVAs. The ORMVAs were also to have wider development responsibility for the rainfed areas surrounding their respective irrigation perimeters, in effect changing their role to that of regional centres for agricultural development, both irrigated and rainfed.

With regard to the reduction of avoidable costs to the public sector, various services for livestock (health services, breeding services and feed distribution) were to be handed over to the private sector, together with the provision of farm machinery for ploughing, harvesting, etc. The marketing of fertilisers was also to be progressively divested and the parastatal FERTIMA gradually withdrawn, once an adequate level of effective demand had developed in a given locality or region. This was deemed desirable on the grounds that

> the growth of FERTIMA since 1974 discouraged the private sector from developing a wide distribution network, created a shortage of storage downstream nearer the user, and left many farmers without assured and timely access to fertiliser (World Bank, 1986a).

With regard to the marketing of export crops, the Office de Commercialisation et d'Exportation (OCE) was no longer to have a monopoly (its monopoly was abolished in 1984), and export licensing was to be abolished for most agricultural commodities.

Most importantly, cereal marketing, where 36 per cent of volume was previously handled by the public sector, was to be integrated within a wider system of food policy and planning. The fact that during the early 1980s cereal producers were receiving well below the official floor prices (as much as 30–40 per cent below in many regions) was explained as the result of: (a) the prevailing subsidised food distribution systems; (b) the lack of coherence between price support objectives and actual programming of imported and domestic procurement; and (c) administrative rigidities in domestic trade regulations which prevented millers from buying wheat direct from farmers and traders, as well as a system of fixed margins for the domestic price support purchasing and processing services. These margins had not been revised since 1980 and had fallen to 15–50 per cent below cost for different cereals, while handling margins covered only half of estimated costs. Proposals to create a framework for encouraging more effective cereal production and marketing have included: (a) the establishment of a system for fixing producer support prices which takes into account not only production costs but also cost of imports and overall price movements; (b) the development of an integrated system of food policy and planning which treats imports, domestic procurement and storage as essential components of a food production and distribution system; (c) the encouragement of participation by private traders through allowing millers to buy direct; (d) the use of policies that encourage farmers to hold grain immediately after harvest, by providing credit for storage, etc; (e) investigation of the possibility of exporting or establishing a buffer stock in good years; and (f) bringing the procurement system closer to the farm by encouraging the formation of farmer co-operatives. Proposals under this general heading (of re-structuring the role of the public sector) have also included reconsideration of the role of the Caisse Nationale pour le Crédit Agricole (CNCA) and the encouragement of greater private sector participation in agricultural development through a heavier reliance on private investment by means of institutional credit and banking services.

The fourth objective was to 'build up institutional capacity for agricultural policy planning and analysis'. In 1981 a Directorate of Planning and Economic Affairs (DPAE) was established within the Ministry of Agriculture and Agrarian Reform. This was to be strengthened particularly in the areas of policy analysis, investment analysis and project monitoring and evaluation.

Finally, it was held that 'the potential for improvement of land structures and more rational land use in rainfed agriculture is substantial' and 'that the extension of the comprehensive land policy already developed for the irrigated areas into rainfed areas must be a priority' (World Bank, 1986a). Proposals included land registration, land consolidation and improved security of land tenure, to be implemented by a land agency for the rainfed areas.

The agricultural sector adjustment programme is designed to produce a set of interrelated positive effects (see World Bank, 1986a, final section). It is argued that the medium-term adjustment measures should have a favourable impact at the macro-economic and sectoral levels. At the macro level, the proposed resource mobilisation and subsidy reduction measures should translate into substantial public savings, while a positive impact on the balance of payments can be expected through price shifts favouring tradables supported by parallel steps in trade liberalisation and exchange-rate adjustments. At the sectoral level, adjustments in relative protection patterns between irrigated and non-irrigated farming should be achieved as a result of the reorientation of price policy and the strengthening of the floor price support programme for cereals. Positive structural effects with longer-term production impact can also be expected from the strengthening of essential private and public support services and the proposed land policy for the rainfed sector. Public savings should be achieved through (a) the gradual phasing out of fertiliser subsidies, (b) the increase in the water charge collection rates (c) the gradual withdrawal of the public sector from the provision of commercial services below real cost, (d) the gradual charging at real cost of services still provided by public entities, (e) the phasing-out of price controls in animal feed, and (f) the gradual phasing-out of unit subsidies on certified seed.

STRUCTURAL ADJUSTMENT IN THEORY AND PRACTICE

As regards the effects of stabilisation and structural adjustment since 1984–5, there is, as yet, very little empirical evidence and what evidence there is must be very carefully assessed.

The period 1983–5 was marked by the implementation of essentially deflationary policies: the rate of growth in GDP during 1983–4 averaged only 2 per cent per annum reflecting the impact of such policies on aggregate demand and two years of drought. The budget deficit was reduced from 12 per cent of GDP in 1982 to about 7 per cent in 1984, chiefly through a sharp reduction in investment outlays. Import growth was restrained by the reduction of domestic demand, while the share of exports and gross domestic savings rose appreciably. The current account of the balance of payments improved somewhat, but largely as a result of the debt relief obtained from official creditors. The net inflow of public medium- and long-term capital tended to decline over the two years.

Towards the end of 1985, Morocco seemed to be in a significantly more favourable position than during the previous two years: a bumper harvest and the continuing fall in oil prices had helped reduce the bill for imports. GDP grew by around 4 per cent, receipts from tourism had increased substantially, and the value of remittances from workers abroad had also risen. Successive currency devaluations had brought the real effective exchange rate down to 67 per cent of the 1980 rate. In September, the IMF agreed a new Stand-by whereby Morocco had access over the next 18 months to a facility worth some $230m. as well as a compensatory financing facility for cereal purchases worth about $130m. Agreement was then reached with the Paris Club for the rescheduling of $1 billion in medium- and long-term debts. However, the trade deficit worsened in 1985 and barely improved in 1986. Although exports grew during 1985–6, this was primarily for phosphates, with a weak response from manufactured and agricultural goods. Cereal imports stayed very high, and foreign reserves remained low – barely sufficient to cover one month's imports. The relatively high GDP growth in 1985 and 1986 depended to a substantial degree on two exceptionally good harvests associated with favourable weather conditions. The underlying weakness of the country's position was undeniable.

In January 1986, Morocco failed to make the first payment of $85m. due to foreign commercial creditors under the October 1985 agreement with the Paris Club, and was bailed out only by a loan from the Al Ubaf Bank in Bahrain. By June 1986, the IMF was pressing for a re-negotiation of the loan agreement reached in September 1985 on the grounds that Morocco had not succeeded in bridging its financial gap for 1986 and had failed to implement sufficiently rigorously the major elements of the IMF-prescribed package upon which the loan agreement was conditional. In addition to the country's fundamental weaknesses in industry, trade and agriculture, the IMF was concerned at the budget deficit (at 9.1/9.4 per cent of GDP well above the IMF target of 7 per cent), the failure to control the growth of credit and the corresponding expansion in the supply of money (at nearly 18 per cent, well over the IMF 10 per cent target), and the insufficient reduction in subsidies on basic foodstuffs. Under these circumstances, the IMF looked with extreme disfavour on the Moroccan Government's plans for economic expansion in the late 1980s, which include a 67 per cent increase in investment, a 30 per cent increase in military expenditure and a larger overall fiscal deficit.

As regards agriculture, one of the major objectives of the structural adjustment programme was to increase export crop output. Agricultural exports remain an important component of Morocco's total exports; in 1983 citrus fruit and canned vegetables alone accounted for nearly 10 per cent of the total value of exports. Exports of agricultural products in 1984 suffered largely because of the drought; citrus fruit exports could only manage a modest 5 per cent increase and preserved fruit exports actually declined in value by 20 per cent. Moreover, although export promotion has emerged as a government priority, growing protectionism abroad – particularly in the European Community which accounts for over 50 per cent of Morocco's exports and has in the past been a major customer for agricultural products – combined with the enlargement of the EEC, has increased difficulties in finding markets. Trade with France, which accounted for nearly 23 per cent of Moroccan exports and nearly 20 per cent of imports in 1984, declined in the first half of the 1980s by 2.2 and 5.2 per cent per annum respectively. Morocco is now attempting to diversify its trading partners, looking in particular towards the Middle East (including Turkey), India and Japan. But the European market remains particularly crucial for agricultural exports. Roughly 56 per cent of Morocco's citrus exports in 1984 went to the EEC, but this was 8 per cent down on the previous year and prospects here look uncertain. Such market constraints prompted Moroccan requests for further EEC concessions (since 1963 Morocco has benefitted from privileged access for agricultural products), culminating in an application to join the EEC in November 1984.

For domestic cereal crops, as also for cotton and sugar, output response has been positive, largely on account of weather conditions, but also in response to higher prices post-1984. Production figures for cereals during 1985 showed a dramatic increase. Wheat production, for example, exceeded production in any year over the previous quarter century with the exception of the extraordinarily good year of 1968; and barley production was higher than at any time during the previous decade. There was an even more dramatic result in 1986, with higher output of wheat and barley – both individually and combined – than in any of the previous twenty-five years (see Table 10.2).

Table 10.2: *Morocco: cereal production 1980–86 ('000 quintals)*

Year	Wheat	Barley	All Cereals	All Cereal Imports
1980	18,110	22,097	45,047	17,792
1981	8,921	10,390	21,218	26,582
1982	21,834	23,337	49,045	19,126
1983	19,703	12,277	35,734	19,437
1984	19,895	14,046	37,499	27,229
1985	23,582	25,414	53,005	21,369
1986	38,091	35,629	NA	NA

Source: Banque Marocaine de Commerce Extérieure (1986: 2, 5).

However, it is as yet difficult to identify the particular contribution of the measures adopted so far by the Moroccan Government, rather than climatic factors, in explaining this trend.

One significant change is in the area devoted to bread (soft) wheat – the major imported cereal. Between 1976 and 1986 the area devoted to soft wheat has doubled. Soft wheat – essentially a cash crop – has been cultivated to a greater extent than in the past in rainfed regions. It is not clear how far this increase represents a permanent rather than a temporary shift, but it is worth noting that the area devoted to basic subsistence cereal crops – hard wheat and barley – has remained constant over the past decade.

One result of the overall increase in cereal output has been that per capita food production rose by 13 per cent when comparing the period 1983/5 with 1979/81. This is striking when compared with the disastrous 5.1 per cent drop in 1981 and the decline of 2.1 and 1.8 per cent in 1983 and 1984 respectively.

Important though the increased cereal output of 1985 and 1986 undoubtedly is, it must be emphasised that most of the small farms that predominate in the rainfed areas – 75 per cent of the total land consists of farms of 5 hectares or less – have not been able to respond to the incentives provided by the government to produce more for the market. The vast majority are unable to produce sufficient even for their own subsistence and marketed releases are low. It is grossly misleading to say, as the World Bank does in its report concerning the proposal for a large-scale irrigation project loan (World Bank, 1986b:7)

> the real income of farmers, who constitute by far the poorest segment of the population, should rise as a result of increases in agricultural producer prices and improvements in support services and marketing institutions and infrastructure. This will be particularly true of farmers in rainfed areas.

Only a relatively small minority of landowners and farmers are able to benefit from these changes in the economic environment; the poorest segment of the rural population, by contrast, depends for its income, partly on its own limited cereal production for immediate consumption and partly on the sale of its labour. For such smallholders drought remains the principal problem. The government has had to promise tax exemption until the end of the century for poor farmers in drought-affected regions, even at the cost of a 10 per cent reduction in government revenue.

Moreover, a very significant proportion – perhaps as high as 30–40 per cent – of the rural population rely to a large extent on the market for their subsistence requirements, and the rural poor certainly do buy food, including grain and edible oil. Drought not only reduces the amount of cereal produced on a small farm, but tends to result in relatively inflated prices for grain on the market. In this way, the small rural producer and landless labourer (at least 50 per cent of the rural population) is doubly disadvantaged. Cuts in consumer subsidies on cereal products – flour, bread, etc – envisaged by the structural adjustment programme, and regarded by the World Bank as perhaps the crucial element in the programme for increasing cereal output, are certain to create economic and social difficulties for the rural poor, as well as for the urban poor.

The Moroccan Government is very well aware of the dangers inherent in the structural adjustment programme. The unemployment rate is currently around 30 per cent and effects the rural as well as the urban areas (partly explaining the substantial rural exodus). Direct government efforts to ease the problem have been frustrated by austerity measures. In 1984, out of a planned 44,000 jobs, only about half were actually created. And the age structure of the population, with 54 per cent under the age of

20, means that the problem is likely to worsen in the near future. Furthermore, the rising cost of living, particularly the increasing cost of basic commodities, resulting in large part from the measures adopted under the structural adjustment programme to cut subsidies and allow prices to rise, has affected urban and rural workers in both the private and government sectors. They have been subjected to strong downward pressure on their real wage, despite a 10 per cent rise in salaries and wages for industrial and agricultural workers and an extra 5 per cent for civil servants in 1985.

The latter attempt to mitigate the adverse impact on real incomes, combined with the announcement of an expansionary budget for 1986, led to the suspension of the IMF stabilisation programme in February 1986. In attempting, over the short term, to compensate for the effects of cuts in subsidies, particularly on cereals, by raising wages, the government is also concerned to explore alternatives. In 1985 it requested the World Bank to prepare a study on compensatory measures directed towards low-income groups for the period 1985–90. The proposals (World Bank, 1986c) centre on direct food assistance programmes, including 'food-for-work' programmes and rural development projects, for identified (and presumably means-tested) persons, with the marketing of new food products and the implementation of cost-reduction measures as complementary actions. The last of these (cost reduction) implies more extensive deregulation of trade in cereals and other foodstuffs and an improvement in the efficiency of production and processing of such items as sugar and edible oil. The proposal is thus in line with the general thrust of the structural adjustment programme for agriculture. But these recommendations of the Bank have yet to be implemented.

CONCLUSION

Moroccan agricultural policy since the early 1960s has been largely the outcome of a series of negotiated compromises between powerful foreign agencies (such as USAID, the IMF or the World Bank) and the Moroccan Government. While the former have been predominantly concerned with financial and economic performance, the latter has, understandably, also been concerned with the social and political implications of economic policy, in respect of agriculture as well as more generally, and with the pursuit of strategic objectives – such as the annexation of the Western Sahara.

The strikingly uneven implementation of recent IMF and World Bank recommended policies – supported by loans for stabilisation and structural adjustment – should be seen, therefore, partly in terms of the government's concern to minimise the risks of social and political unrest while at the same time improving economic performance, notably in agriculture. In part, however, it also results from a different perception and analysis of the contemporary structure and dynamic of Moroccan agriculture and/or the possible effects of specific policies. For example, while the World Bank clearly believes that major cuts in consumer subsidies on food grains would substantially improve productivity and output in cereal-growing areas across the board, the government recognises the high degree of differentiation among the rural and agri-cultural population and the fact that a significant proportion of small farmers (and, of course, agricultural labourers, rural artisans etc.,) rely heavily on food-grain purchases. As a result, it is more cautious regarding the likely consequences of eliminating consumer subsidies on cereals for the condition of the rural population as a whole and for cereal production more specifically. Furthermore, while external agencies have clearly shifted their priorities for rural and agricultural development from a focus on large-scale interventions through the construction of dams and the development of major irrigation schemes to an emphasis on rainfed agriculture and so-called 'small farmers', the government remains heavily committed to the irrigated perimeters.

The dilemma of the government, however, is acute. To implement the full adjustment programme as conceived by the World Bank risks worsening income distribution, increasing inequalities and provoking civil unrest; it also implies a severe cutback in resources allocated to public expenditure in areas where the government is strongly committed, and a possible loss of support domestically from those who have benefitted from the expansion in public expenditure over the years. However, it is now clear that if the government intends to pursue essentially expansionary policies, it risks withdrawal of support from the IMF and the World Bank. This is likely further to increase the country's economic and financial difficulties particularly in view of Morocco's very substantial foreign debt. It is probable, therefore, that the structural adjustment programme will be implemented – in agriculture as elsewhere – although certainly not as rapidly or as systematically as the World Bank and IMF would like. The government will continue to attempt to meet the demands of its creditors but only in so far as these do not seriously compromise its political authority within the country.

REFERENCES

Amin, S. (1965), *L'Economie du Maghreb*, Paris, Editions de Minuit.

—— (1971), *The Maghreb in the Modern World*, Harmondsworth, Penguin Books.

Banque Marocaine du Commerce Extérieure (1986), *Information Review*, No.57, September.

H.M.G. Morocco (1969), *Code des Investissements Agricoles*, Rabat, July.

—— (1964), Ministère du Plan, *Three Year Plan, 1965 - 1967*, Rabat.

Holt, R.T., D. Seddon et al. (1981), *An Assessment of the Lower Moulouya Irrigation Projects*, Washington DC, USAID/NE-C—1507, August.

Lloyds Bank (1985), *Morocco*, London, Lloyds Bank Group Economic Report.

Seddon, D. (1984),'Winter of Discontent. Economic Crisis in Tunisia and Morocco', *MERIP Reports* No. 127, October.

—— (1987), 'Morocco at war' in R. Lawless and L. Monahan (eds), *War and Refugees: the Western Sahara Conflict*, London, Pinter Publishers.

Waterbury, J. (1971), *The Commander of the Faithful: the Moroccan political elite, a study of segmented politics*, London, Weidenfeld and Nicolson.

World Bank (1980), *Memorandum on Morocco's Agricultural Sector: Identification of Issues and Bank Strategy*, Report 2667a-MOR, Washington DC, May.

—— (1986a), *Report and Recommendation of the President of the IBRD to the Executive Directors on a proposed loan in an amount equivalent to US $100.0 millon to the Kingdom of Morocco for an Agricultural Sector Adjustment Loan*, Report P-4032-MOR/CNR 2590-MOR, Washington DC, May.

—— (1986b), *Report and Recommendation of the President of the IBRD to the Executive Directors on a proposed loan amount equivalent to US $46.0 millon to the Kingdom of Morocco for a large-scale irrigation improvement project*. Report P-4171-MOR. Washington DC, January.

—— (1986c), *Morocco: Compensatory Programme for Reducing Food Subsidies*, Draft Report, Washington DC, February.

11

Colombia

1980–86

Vinod Thomas

Few people will disagree about the profound effects macroeconomic policy has at the sectoral level, and the critical implications sectoral initiatives can have for macroeconomic policy. For example, the profitability of agricultural production and exports can be influenced more by a country's exchange-rate policy than by incentives provided directly to the sector. Similarly, price and credit subsidies directed to a sector not only affect that sector's performance but also the fiscal situation of the country, monetary expansion and rural-urban resource flows. These policy variables are often central to the adjustment frameworks that are usually adopted. While recognised as important, however, the linkages among the variables are not usually incorporated into policy analysis and policy making. Such neglect risks excluding some important effects.

AN OVERVIEW OF POLICY LINKAGES

While far-reaching, the impact of macroeconomic policies on a particular sector is often unintended[1]. For instance, the objective of an overvalued exchange rate might be to keep domestic prices low, and of import restrictions to protect domestic production; but both policies can have the unintended – direct or indirect – effects of hurting exports. Viewed from the sectoral point of view, sectoral incentives to offset these macroeconomic effects on exports might be justified. Placing the discussion in the macroeconomic context, however, could reveal that it might be more efficient first to phase out the macroeconomic disincentives – for example, to depreciate the real exchange rate and lower import restrictions – before considering subsidies for a particular sector.

The degree of protection received is a sectoral issue that is frequently raised. Where industry receives a higher rate of effective protection than agriculture, there is a *prima facie* case for equalising these rates for the two sectors (Schuh, 1986). In the macroeconomic context, the benefits of lowering industry's effective protection might be first compared with those of raising agriculture's. Even if raising effective protection to agriculture is the right answer, consideration of macroeconomic instruments as opposed to special sectoral schemes might be warranted. For instance, a careful review of the public investment programme can highlight the case for correcting sectoral imbalances in the allocation of funds. Sometimes, improvements in the general economic environment, including infrastructure, credit and marketing, might address the incentive issue for agriculture more effectively than special sectoral policies such as input subsidies and price supports.

This is not to deny the fundamental contribution of sectoral policies to performance. Recent experience from the less developed countries has brought out the importance of sectoral policies and a sector's ability to respond to and take advantage of macro-economic reforms. An exchange-rate depreciation might be expected to favour, on balance, a heavily tradable sector such as agriculture. A reduction of the fiscal deficit can also benefit such a sector: the lower deficit can contribute to lower inflation, and thus to an improvement in the relative price and competitiveness of traded commodities. Taking full advantage of such policy improvements, however, might entail a variety of improvements at the sectoral level: improved credit availability, better design, marketing and information flows, for example, would be needed to sustain a production and export drive (see World Bank, 1982). Similarly, the translation of a more open import policy into lower agricultural costs and lower inflation requires several more steps. The increased availability of inputs should be accompanied by more efficient marketing, transportation and processing.

Sound sectoral policies are also needed to improve the ability to adjust efficiently to macroeconomic corrections. Fiscal austerity often requires reduced government expenditures. In such situations, greater efficiency would be needed at the sectoral level to protect high priority investments and the level of services provided, and to get more mileage from available resources. Concerning trade policy, an opening-up of the import regime may be expected to produce a more efficient and competitive economy, provided that the sectors adjust and lower their production costs.

To achieve greater efficiency requires, however, that producers are able to adjust and switch to more profitable avenues. More often than not, such automatic responses do not take place. It becomes important in the case of agriculture to provide assistance through better investment programming, research, extension, institutional improvements and the like.

Both the above-mentioned sets of macroeconomic and sectoral policies are usually picked up by Structural and Sector Adjustment Programmes. While desirable, it is not always practical, however, to establish all the macroeconomic-sectoral linkages in analysis, and much less in actual policy making. It should be possible, nevertheless, to identify the main policy connections and focus upon them. In a recent study of Colombian agriculture (Thomas, 1984), the sector's performance is linked not only to sectoral policies – price support, credit subsidy and investments – but also to exchange-rate management, import controls, fiscal and public expenditure policy. Colombia has recently been carrying out a stabilisation and adjustment programme improving the management of the above-mentioned macroeconomic policy variables: the World Bank provided support to this effort with a Trade Policy and Export Diversification Loan in 1985. In order to underpin the adjustment effort at the sectoral level, the government has been directing greater attention to the important, but relatively neglected, agricultural sector. In support of this task, the Bank has extended a further Trade and Agricultural Policy Loan in 1986. Recent Colombian experience illustrates the utility of addressing the links among macroeconomic and sectoral policies during a period of economic adjustment.

INFERENCES FROM THE COLOMBIAN EXPERIENCE

Recent economic policy making in Colombia has had to address the slowdown in performance during the first half of the 1980s, after a long period of rapid expansion, which was closely associated with a dynamic agricultural sector. Agricultural and other exports have yielded favourable external accounts in the past and have been a significant source of economic growth. At the same time, a proximate cause of the recent difficulties has been the setback in the external sector, particularly the performance of exports. For these reasons, a primary objective of policy is to consider ways and means of stabilising the external sector and revitalising growth, in particular by enlarging the net contribution of agriculture to foreign exchange.

While the list of interactive policy variables can be extensive, this chapter focuses on those that have been found crucial during Colombia's adjustment phase. Exchange-rate and fiscal deficit policies and their relation to coffee prospects, as well as agricultural price policies, figure prominently in the discussion. The chapter is mostly concerned with the policy implications for the adjustment phase covering the period 1984-6. In leading up to this point, however, it describes the problems emerging during the early 1980s, and brings out the factors behind them as they developed in the 1970s.

Macroeconomic Context

Since the latter half of the 1960s, Colombia has managed its economy with a well-integrated package of exchange-rate, fiscal, and export-incentive policies that have succeeded in promoting the development and growth of its exports. During the 1970s the performance of industry was more striking than that of agriculture, partly because it started from a smaller base. Nevertheless, agriculture maintained an average growth rate of about 4 per cent and the development of agricultural exports other than coffee was impressive. The economy steadily diversified into one that was more urban and more resilient to external shocks.

The policy package began to unravel, however, during the latter half of the 1970s, even as the country was enjoying a coffee boom (Table 11.1). The expansion in total non-coffee exports began to slow down, although between 1976 and 1980 it was hidden by the coffee boom. By the early 1980s, however, this was accompanied by a downturn in real coffee earnings, contributing to increasing deficits in the current account of the balance of payments. By 1982-3 this deficit amounted to more than 7 per cent of GDP. As in the mid-1960s, problems first emerged in the external sector and the situation was aggravated by growing capital-market constraints. The underlying domestic economic situation, however, remained far stronger than it had been twenty years earlier. Non-coffee exports from agriculture and the rest of the economy had established a high plateau of performance, and the real price of coffee was higher.

One way to correct the problems in the external sector would be to re-establish the previous basis for export development and growth. For this, restoration of agricultural incentives would be essential. At the macroeconomic level, however, new constraints have had to be addressed. The fiscal deficit grew during the early 1980s. Wage-rate and interest-rate expectations were also related to exchange-rate policy, making improvements in the real exchange rate more complex. Nevertheless, recent experience has shown solid, positive results in reversing these trends through careful macroeconomic management.

Coffee and Macroeconomic Policy

Policy decisions have been found to be especially difficult when the price of a major export commodity fluctuates sharply, as in the case of coffee in Colombia[2]. This arises from the uncertainty attached to assessments of the duration of price increases and, consequently, the degree of adjustment in macroeconomic variables that is required. During the coffee price boom of the second half of the 1970s, alternative means of stabilisation were pursued to varying degrees and effectiveness. To some extent, the increase in reserves was neutralised by the monetary policies adopted as well as by some increase in imports and appreciation of the real exchange rate.

Despite the coffee boom, a smaller appreciation of the currency might have been workable if it had been supported by a larger inflow of imports to absorb the increase in domestic demand and if borrowing had not increased sharply, as it did during 1978–82. It should be noted, however, that in general a major liberalisation in the face of an already appreciated currency could exacerbate the adjustment problems of import-competing domestic industries.Temporary protection for non-coffee exports in the form of special export incentives might be necessary for a short period and was, in fact, actually extended to a limited degree. Once the price boom has been diagnosed as transitory, however, a reversal of appreciation of the currency would normally be the right approach to take. In this respect, the adjustment of the Colombian economy in the early 1980s – in reducing inflation, improving the real exchange rate, and shifting resources into production of goods other than coffee – could perhaps have been more timely.

The difference between domestic and external inflation between 1975 and 1984 was large. Domestic prices, measured at the official exchange rate, rose by some 100 per cent while the increase in external prices was about 50 per cent (Table 11.1). Partly as a result, the producer prices of non-coffee tradables – which are strongly influenced by international prices – fell in relation to the price of domestic goods and services in this period. Since the share of tradables in agricultural output is greater than in the rest of the economy (including services) on average, this decline in relative producer prices has been especially adverse for the non-coffee sub-sector. Unfortunately, the shift of incentives in favour of non-tradables did not produce any significant output response; there has therefore been little ability to offset the losses in production and employment in the tradable goods sector.

Colombia began adopting significant measures for adjustment with growth during 1984–5. A programme for fiscal, monetary, and exchange-rate adjustments was put in place that would, among other things, improve the competitiveness of non-coffee tradables. The macroeconomic policy package concerns further reductions in the expenditure-revenue gap of the public sector, including a review of public sector investments and improvement in their effectiveness, postponement of large and long-gestating new projects, and maintenance of the prices of public utilities at appropriate levels; a slowdown in the expansion of credit to the government by the Central Bank; full correction of the overvaluation of the real exchange rate; liberalisation of imports that are needed for exports; a scaling-down of external borrowing targets; and policies to strengthen sectoral performance. Even as these policy improvements were under way, a new coffee boom was in the making in 1986, presenting a challenge once again for macroeconomic management in protecting the incentives for non-coffee production and exports.

Table 11.1: *Colombia: selected macroeconomic and agricultural variables 1970–86*

Year	Real Coffee Price (1975 = 100)	Growth of Money Base (%)	Central Government Balance as % of GDP[a]	Rate of Inflation[b] (%)	Real Exchange Rate[c] (1975 = 100)	Non-Coffee Exports[d] (1975 = 100)	Internal Relative Price Non-Coffee: Non-Coffee Agricultural Exports[e] (1975 = 100)	Agricultural Production[f] (1975 = 100)
1970	124.8	19.8	n.a.	6.7	81.1	68.3	132.5	92.8
1971	102.6	8.8	n.a.	11.6	83.1	67.8	93.5	93.9
1972	107.2	25.4	n.a.	13.8	86.4	73.3	110.8	97.4
1973	120.2	31.1	-1.2	22.0	89.3	83.6	117.0	105.1
1974	105.8	18.8	-1.5	25.2	94.7	106.0	122.5	106.8
1975	100.0	31.7	-0.5	23.6	100.0	100.0	100.0	100.0
1976	190.3	41.6	0.6	19.9	97.3	90.6	91.7	98.0
1977	263.8	40.1	0.5	34.7	83.4	83.6	101.4	103.4
1978	176.2	35.2	0.2	16.7	83.5	78.9	87.7	93.9
1979	154.1	30.4	-1.2	24.9	81.8	83.1	87.5	88.9
1980	137.4	28.8	-2.1	27.2	82.0	93.6	101.2	85.8
1981	97.4	21.8	-3.1	28.1	78.1	89.2	97.3	83.3
1982	109.9	17.7	-4.4	24.6	73.4	79.0	83.9	82.9
1983	104.8	13.5	-4.1	19.8	75.2	79.6	90.8	82.5
1984	111.5	18.3	-5.0	16.4	82.0	83.8	96.3	81.0
1985g	115.0	27.0	-2.8	24.0	100.0	n.a.	104.5	n.a.
1986g	155.0	28.0	-2.0	20.0	105.0	n.a.	n.a.	n.a.

[a] The consolidated public sector deficit, for which long-term data are not readily available, has been nearly double the Central Government's deficit during the 1980s.
[b] % changes in period average of the consumer price index: Blue collar workers.
[c] Annual average level, measured against a trade weighted basket of currencies.
[d] Ratio of implicit prices of exports to implicit GDP deflator.
[e] Ratio of non-coffee agricultural export price to that of all import prices.
[f] Gross value of output deflator for agriculture compared with that of non-agriculture.
[g] Preliminary estimate.

Source: International Finance Statistics, International Monetary Fund, Washington, DC (annual publication); Colombia's Central Bank, National Statistical Institute, and World Bank data.

Macroeconomic Policy and Agriculture

The effects of external factors – the OECD growth rate, the dollar interest rate, oil prices, trade barriers etc – have undoubtedly been significant for the agricultural and overall performance of developing countries under adjustment. In addition, domestic policy at the macroeconomic and sectoral levels has had a major impact. The interplay of macroeconomic and agricultural policies, however, is not all that well understood and is only now beginning to receive attention. It is often recognised that macroeconomic developments have been strongly influenced by the performance of agriculture in developing countries, and in the Colombian case, particularly by the principal export, coffee. In turn, agriculture's record is also substantially affected by macroeconomic policies, affected in part by the fortunes of coffee. Increases in coffee prices not only decrease the relative prices of non-coffee tradables vis-à-vis coffee but also with respect to non-tradables. The implied appreciation of the domestic currency may be aggravated by the increased spending and monetary–cum–inflationary effects of the coffee boom. If the currency is indeed allowed to appreciate and the boom is only temporary, the negative effects on non-coffee tradables woud become a major concern, and a revision of exchange-rate, fiscal and monetary policies would be called for.

The post-1975 agricultural expansion in Colombia has been in good measure based on coffee, a product for which only a modest increase in demand in world markets is projected for the long term. The principal macroeconomic constraints to more vigorous non-coffee expansion have comprised a high inflation rate, an overvalued exchange rate, and import restrictions, which impose a 'tax' on a heavily tradable sector such as agriculture (cf. Garcia-Garcia, 1981). The effects of such a macroeconomic policy may have been unintentional, but the net effect from the mid-1970s to 1984 on the relative prices of non-coffee agricultural tradables was negative. As shown in Table 11.1. the relative prices received by agriculture deteriorated steadily during this period. This trend was not matched by declines in agricultural production costs with the result that agricultural profitability, by many accounts, seems to have worsened relative to the rest of the economy. Through sectoral policies an attempt was made to increase the incentives for the relatively small group of mostly imported cereals – corn, sorghum, soya, wheat, barley and sesame – through high levels of protection and domestic price supports. In addition, credit subsidies to producers and storers, albeit moderate, provided some sectoral incentives. At the same time, however, agricultural investments by the public sector are estimated to have declined significantly in real terms since the mid-1970s. Research and extension suffered from neglect during the past decade. Insufficient rehabilitation of irrigation and infrastructure has also been a problem. High internal transport and port handling costs and inadequate marketing and credit facilities have contributed to high production and distribution costs in agriculture.

As in many other developing countries, the adoption of a more neutral macroeconomic policy posture[3] – as envisaged with the changes being made in Colombia – would be helpful, beginning with the elimination of overvaluation of the exchange rate, reduction of the fiscal deficit, rationalisation of the investment programme, liberalisation of imported inputs needed for exports, and strengthening of the financial sector. Depreciation of the real exchange rate began to take significant effect in 1984, and further substantial progress was recorded in 1985–6. Such necessary macroeconomic adjustments can also produce difficulties at financial and production levels which need to be addressed. Once the principal macroeconomic disincentives are eliminated, special sectoral incentives such as price supports and credit subsidies would be less justified. In view of the efficiency losses of the latter, they could be phased out gradually. On the other hand, there is a case to be made for supporting high-priority investments for irrigation, input supply, research, extension, and marketing.

Agricultural Incentives

Price intervention in coffee has meant a significant tax on coffee production through an elaborate pricing mechanism. This tax has been necessitated by the fact that external prices have been held up by agreements among world producers and consumers, with export quotas established to support the agreed prices. The translation of export prices to Colombian producers, however, would mean overproduction, given the export quota. Thus, what is in effect a coffee tax has meant more incentives in favour of non-coffee agriculture than otherwise. All things considered – technology, input supply, infrastructure, investments – however, the balance of overall incentives would still seem to benefit coffee production.

An important sectoral incentive for non-coffee agriculture is the price support offered by the government for rice, corn, sorghum, soya, wheat, barley, and sesame, all of which, except rice, are also imported. The domestic support price of these commodities exceeded the fob import price – unadjusted for special circumstances such as export subsidies abroad – by 50–100 per cent by 1983, although the rapid depreciation of the peso between 1984 and 1986 subsequently reduced this difference[4]. Despite the fact that the government has virtual monopoly profits from the sale of imports, the marketing board (IDEMA) has run a deficit on the whole on account of its price support operations. Apart from the fiscal issue, there is also the efficiency question of providing special incentives for crops, such as wheat, in which Colombia does not appear to have a comparative advantage. Technical analysis so far has pointed to potential net gains from phasing out the high protection for some grains.

The high price of inputs, particularly of fertiliser, is an often-mentioned sectoral disincentive. A sub-optimal use of fertiliser in most non-coffee commodities has resulted from high farm-gate prices for fertilisers. These are at twice the world market level, except in the case of coffee where the input price has been rather lower. These prices are to a modest extent caused by taxes and tariffs and, more significantly, by high port charges and domestic transport costs. Policies to reduce port and internal transport costs would therefore be highly beneficial to the sector. Fertiliser import and price policies themselves have been under government control with the pricing regime on balance providing protection for domestic production.

While subsidised credit has provided some special agricultural incentives, the present Colombian system reveals several inadequacies. An increasing share of agricultural credit has come through a system of compulsory allocations from the commercial banks at subsidised interest rates through the Central Bank's rediscounts. At the same time, the resources mobilised and lent by commercial and agricultural banks have declined, and growth in agricultural credit has been below the expansion in sectoral output. Furthermore, the present credit system favours short-term investments over long-term, larger farmers over smaller, and agricultural primary production over processing and marketing credit. The existing compulsory investment requirements need to be lowered gradually in order to reduce the gap between the free and subsidised credit markets. The proportion of loans refinanced by official financial funds needs to be reduced over time, and financial intermediation should be expected to contribute a larger share of term loan financing through deposit resources mobilised from savers.

While the greater part of agriculture-related investments are made by the private sector, it has been shown that public sector investments are significant in selected areas such as infrastructure development, including rural roads, storage facilities, rural electrification, irrigation, and land development, research and extension, provision of credit, and watershed management. During the past decade, public expenditures in the sector have decreased steadily and significantly. Although partly offset by greater private sector participation, the overall effects are notable in declining levels of research and extension and rising relative costs of agricultural production and marketing.

ESTABLISHING POLICY RELATIONS

A Framework for Further Analysis

The Colombian case suggests a way to organise policy analysis in cases where macroeconomic to sectoral linkages are important. In the case of agricultural policy, a common issue on which to focus would be the levels and changes in agricultural incentives. Measurement of incentives might proceed by observing:

i)   domestic price changes of agricultural commodity groups relative to those in the remaining traded and non-traded sectors;

ii)   production cost changes in agriculture as opposed to the rest of the traded and non-traded sectors; and

iii) level of public investment, including efforts in the areas of research, extension and technology.

In general, the relative profitability in agriculture is demonstrated by a comparison of agriculture's domestic prices net of exchange-rate effects, taxes and subsidies, less production costs resulting from the use of traded and non-traded inputs, with those of other sectors.

Policy variables affect all three factors listed above. Main policy areas for consideration in the Colombian case, with parallels in other countries as well, include:

a) *Macroeconomic policy*
  i)   Exchange rate and export incentives
  ii)   Import policy
  iii) Fiscal expansion and financing
  iv)   Monetary policy
  v)   External borrowing and overall public investment
b) *Coffee policy*
  i)   Import restrictions
  ii)   Coffee taxes
  iii) Input prices
  iv)   Investments
c) *Agricultural interventions*
  i)   Import restrictions
  ii)   Credit and interest-rate policy
  iii) Price support for importables
  iv)   Input pricing

d) *Non-coffee agricultural investment*
   i)   Infrastructure
   ii) Research and extension
   iii) Marketing

For tradable agricultural products, international prices, the exchange rate, export incentives and import restrictions ((a) above) determine the domestic prices. An exchange-rate depreciation and a more open import regime may be expected, *ceteris paribus*, to improve tradable agriculture's competitiveness. The prices of other products, including non-tradables, would be influenced by domestic inflation which, in turn, is affected by fiscal, monetary and borrowing policies. Inflationary policies might be expected to lower the relative prices of tradables including predominantly tradable agriculture. Relative product prices in agriculture are thus influenced by these macroeconomic variables.

In the case of a dominant commodity, such as coffee, its prices can have a special effect on the relative price of other commodities ((b) above). International coffee prices have been determined under special agreements among world producers and consumers, and domestic prices in Colombia are kept well below world prices to discourage domestic overproduction. Nevertheless, when external prices have risen sharply, as in the late 1970s, a decline in the relative prices of non-coffee tradables, including non-coffee agriculture, has occurred. First, increased foreign-exchange earnings lead to real exchange-rate appreciation. To the extent that the higher reserves are not stabilised by import and monetary policy, domestic credit and inflation expand, causing the real exchange rate to appreciate. Even in the absence of such a macroeconomic effect, the higher disposable incomes afforded by coffee increase spending on non-coffee tradables and non-tradables and, considering that the prices of the former are mostly dictated by international conditions, this lowers their relative prices.

Import controls and price supports ((c) above) are often provided to raise the domestic prices of import-competing commodities, as in the case of Colombia. While this policy can raise the incentives for the import-competing segment, its effect on overall agricultural incentives is questionable. In particular, it tilts incentives against the more competitive, exportable segment. Subsidies for credit and other inputs are often considered necessary to stimulate agriculture, particularly in view of the risks associated with farm production . While these policies are justified in terms of raising the sector's production incentives, their fiscal and efficiency costs for the economy as a whole and their efficiency in achieving sectoral goals have to be considered. On the other hand, policies to raise long-term yields through investment in infrastructure, technology and marketing can have high pay-offs ((d) above).

Netting Out Various Effects

It would be useful to consider the combined effects of the policy variables (a) to (d) on agricultural incentives, performance and efficiency. Performance is affected also by external factors. In order to keep the discussion manageable, focus might be placed for illustrative purposes on the 1975–83 period, and on the following agricultural commodities, drawing on the Colombian example.

i)   Coffee; 30 per cent of production.
ii) Non-coffee exports: cotton, sugar, bananas, cacao, tobacco, flowers, beans, sesame, rice, etc.; 30 per cent of production.
iii) Imports: wheat, barley, maize, sorghum, soya, etc.; 10 per cent of production.

iv) Non-traded: potato, cassava, brown sugar, yucca, plantain, etc.; 30 per cent production.
v)   Traded inputs: fertiliser, pesticides, herbicides, seeds.
vi) Domestic inputs: water, land, labour.

Table 11.2 attempts to summarise the possible effects of the policy variables a) to d) on categories (i) to (vi), thus providing implications for overall agricultural incentives. Panel A covers the changes in price incentives for the production of major output categories resulting from policy areas I-IV and external factors VI. Panel B does the same for the domestic production of input categories. The signs indicate the direction of change, a plus sign suggesting a positive effect, a minus a negative effect, and a zero little effect or irrelevance. Since the price of inputs determines the production cost of outputs, a plus sign in Panel B indicates a negative incentive effect for the production of output and *vice versa*.

During 1975–83, exchange-rate, fiscal and monetary policies, by and large, tilted price incentives against the production of non-coffee tradables, compared to non-tradables. The negative effects on agricultural exports and imports compared to

Table 11.2: *Colombia: effects of policies on changes in relative incentives in agriculture 1975–83*

		Panel A: Agricultural Production				Panel B: Input Production	
	Policy Area	Coffee	Exports	Imports	Non-Traded	Traded	Domestic
I.	Macroeconomic Policy						
	Exchange Rate	0	–	–	0	–	0
	Fiscal/Monetary	0	–	–	+	–	+
	Import Policy	0	–	+	–	+	–
II.	Coffee Policy						
	Domestic Price/ Taxes	–	+	+	+	0	0
	Input Price/ Investment	+	–	–	–	0	0
III.	Sectoral Policy						
	Import Restrictions	0	–	+	–	+	0
	Credit Subsidy	+	?	?	–	0	0
	Price Support	0	–	+	0	0	0
	Input Pricing	+	–	–	0	+	0
IV.	Investment/ Technology	+	+	0	–	0	0
V.	Possible Net Incentives	+	–	+	–	+	0
VI.	External Factors	+	–	–	0	–	0
VII.	Possible Total Net Incent. (V + VI)	+	–	+	–	small +	0
VIII.	Performance	+	small +	–	0	–	0

non-traded ones are indicated in the table. Coffee was largely unaffected by these macroeconomic policies because its incentives are determined by its own pricing arrangements. Overall import restrictions have been detrimental to agricultural production during the period as a whole, although there have been periods of import liberalisation (1978–82, for example).

One effect of the coffee pricing tax policy alone has been to improve the relative prices of non-coffee agriculture. On the other hand, coffee has been relatively favoured through more investment resources and better input supplies. Credit subsidies have also favoured coffee plantings. However, this appears not to have been the case for small farmers who generally lack access to such subsidised credit. Price and input policies also do not seem to have had much impact on small farmers who have tended to concentrate on the production of non-traded commodities.

Coffee has been able to gain from fertiliser subsidies until recently, whereas there are no special input price policies for the other products. The latter, in fact, have faced higher than world prices for imported inputs. As Panel B implies, import restrictions and pricing policies have provided protection to domestic input manufacturing. Although this policy benefits domestic production, it has raised the cost of these inputs for agricultural production, and in general the sector has been hurt by the protection thus afforded. On the whole, the above-mentioned policies have contained incentives for coffee, while raising those for import-competing products, lowering them relatively for exports, and producing little discernible effect on non-traded agriculture. Including the effect of external factors (world commodity prices), technology and investments, however, coffee incentives increased relative to the rest of agriculture between 1975 and 1983.

CONCLUSION

In the Colombian context, the relative prices received by non-coffee agricultural producers are determined by a combination of external factors and domestic policies. While world coffee prices have a major impact, domestic coffee prices are tempered, with varying effectiveness over time, by taxes on coffee. At the same time, domestic fiscal and monetary policies and inflation, and any resulting appreciation of the peso real exchange rate, can mean a worsening of the relative prices for non-coffee agricultural tradables. It is becoming increasingly apparent that these and other macroeconomic effects may have a larger bearing on agricultural price incentives than direct agricultural price policies[5]. If this is so, a major task of policy adjustment intended to promote trade will have to concern reductions of macroeconomic incentives that favour non-tradables, whether intentionally or otherwise.

Agricultural price policies often attempt to offset the disincentives to agricultural production. In Colombia the price supports and protection afforded to imports cover only a small part of agriculture and they have by and large been ineffective in eliciting a production response. Similarly credit subsidies have also not been effective, in addition to contributing to financial sector problems. Meanwhile potentially important, 'non-price' incentives to agriculture, such as investments in infrastructure, research and extension, marketing, etc, have been relatively neglected. Protection for domestic input production has aggravated the problem of high agricultural production costs.

It would seem that in such situations a combination of macroeconomic and sectoral price and non-price policies is called for. A more neutral macroeconomic framework, such as obtained between 1967 and 1975, that does not hurt exports would be essential.

If coffee booms are judged not to be permanent, which is usually the case, containment of the relative price of coffee domestically, and protection of incentives for diversification would constitute the needed direction. The effectiveness of agricultural price interventions must be evaluated carefully, and complemented by much needed non-price support.

NOTES

1 Some of these effects are examined in World Bank (1986).
2 For analysis of coffee booms and of the so-called Dutch disease in general see S. Edwards in Thomas (1985) and Corden and Neary (1982); Harberger (1983); and van Wijnbergen (1984).
3 On the effects of policy distortions in various countries, see Agarwala (1983).
4 In contrast to many other countries, price policies have meant that domestic prices of various food products are kept above world prices in Colombia. For discussions of other cases, see Schultz (1978).
5 For empirical discussion of this conclusion for Colombia and other countries, see Krueger et al., (forthcoming).

REFERENCES

Agarwala, Ramgopal (1983), *Price Distortions and Growth in Developing Countries*, World Bank Staff Working Paper No. 575, Washington DC, World Bank.

Corden, W. Max and J. Peter Neary (1982), 'Booming Sector and De-industrialization in a Small Open Economy', *Economic Journal*, Vol. 92, December.

Garcia-Garcia, Jorge (1981), *The Effects of Exchange Rates and Commercial Policy on Agricultural Incentives in Colombia: 1953–1978*, Report No. 24, Washington DC, International Food Policy Research Institute.

Harberger, A.C. (1983), 'Dutch Disease: How Much Sickness, How Much Boom?', *Resources and Energy*, Vol. 5, March.

Krueger, A.O., M. Schiff and A. Valdes (forthcoming), 'A Comparative Study of the Political Economy of Agricultural Pricing Policies', Washington DC, World Bank, (mimeo).

Schuh, Edward G. (1986), 'Agricultural Policy Reforms are High in the Bank's Agenda', *The Bank's World*, February.

Schultz, Theodore W. (1978), *Distortions of Agricultural Incentives*, Bloomington, Indiana University Press.

Thomas, Vinod (1985), *Linking Macroeconomic and Agricultural Policies for Adjustment with Growth: The Colombia Experience*, Baltimore, Johns Hopkins University Press.

World Bank (1982), *World Development Report 1982*, Oxford, Oxford University Press.

—— (1986), *World Development Report 1986*, Oxford, Oxford University Press.

van Wijnbergen, S. (1984), 'Dutch Disease: A Disease After All?', *Economic Journal*, Vol. 94, No. 373.

12

Brazil

1981–6

Gervasio Castro de Rezende

INTRODUCTION

Between 1981 and 1984 the Brazilian economy underwent a radical process of adjustment in response to a major balance-of-payments crisis. The impact of this adjustment process on the agricultural sector has not been adequately analysed, however, despite the fact that the economic policies pursued in this period may have crucially affected the sector's performance. In the first place, measures taken by the government to stimulate exports, as well as sugar cane production for biomass (the PROALCOOL programme), may have had a detrimental effect on the production of goods, particularly food, for the domestic market. This, in turn, depending upon the behaviour of food prices, may have aggravated the fall in the real incomes of the urban labour force. Such a disincentive to food production may also have had a detrimental impact on petty producers on account of the importance of home goods revenues in their total income.

Secondly, restrictive fiscal and monetary policies have affected agriculture, particularly through the reform of the rural credit system, one of the main instruments of Brazilian agricultural policy. Interest rates have been sharply increased and there has been a drastic reduction in loanable funds.

This chapter presents an overall perspective of agricultural performance in Brazil in the period 1981–6 with specific emphasis on evaluating the impact of the macroeconomic adjustment programme. The main questions of interest will be: (i) whether or not domestic food production has worsened as a result of the programme; (ii) the effects of the rural credit policy reform; and (iii) the programme's implications for rural employment and income, particularly with respect to petty producers.

AN OVERVIEW OF THE ADJUSTMENT PROCESS AND ITS IMPLICATIONS FOR AGRICULTURAL POLICY

Following the second oil price shock and the combination of rising international interest rates and an expansionist domestic economic policy, by 1979/80 the Brazilian economy was faced with rapid deterioration in the balance of payments and escalating debt obligations. This induced two attempts at stabilisation: in 1981–2 without an IMF agreement, while in 1983–4 such an agreement had been achieved. Table 12.1 summarises and compares the two programmes.

According to Carneiro (1986: 27)

> . . . though both programmes aimed at controlling external borrowing, it was believed in 1980 that there was still room for increased lending (on) the part of private banks. The diagnosis was then that, if the private sector could be induced to borrow, a mere show of fiscal austerity would be sufficient to bring bankers back into the game.

In order to provide this inducement the government adopted a restrictive monetary (and credit) policy in 1981, that caused a sharp increase in domestic interest rates. By 1982 the real interest rate exceeded 28 per cent per annum.

The sudden halt of voluntary lending in international financial markets that followed the Mexican moratorium of September 1982, however, set the stage for another round of orthodoxy, this time with an IMF agreement. As a result, fiscal policy was even more restrictive. Investment by state enterprises was especially hard hit, falling by 28.9 per cent in real terms in 1983. In addition, wage policy was changed in 1983, with a partial de-indexation of wages.

Finally, with the objective of improving the trade balance, in February 1983 the cruzeiro was devalued by 30 per cent. The higher domestic value of the dollar was kept intact throughout the period 1983–5 by full indexation to inflation (though the effective exchange rate fell in the first quarter of 1985 due to the appreciation of the dollar vis à vis other currencies); this policy was discontinued in 1986, however, in view of the freezing of the nominal exchange rate under the Cruzado Plan.

While the original function of maintaining high interest rates – financing the external deficit – no longer prevailed, the maintenance of restrictive monetary and credit policies, monitored by the IMF, was reinforced by further upward pressure on domestic interest rates, brought about by acute exchange-rate speculation (Carneiro, 1986: 32; also Arida and Resende, 1985).

Improvement in the external account initiated in 1983 and consolidated in 1984 by the growth of exports relieved the external constraint for the first time since 1980 and was the main factor behind the unexpected recovery of economic growth in 1984. Industrial output in the second quarter of 1984 was 14 per cent higher than in the second quarter of 1983, pulled by export growth and by the recovery of the rural sector's demand for industrial inputs, evidence of which will be presented later in this chapter.

From the second quarter of 1984 on, the multiplier effects of this economic recovery on the domestic market began to operate. On the other hand, at the end of the year economic policy itself became less restrictive; the 1983 wage law was modified and monetary policy was made more flexible.

The new government that took office in March 1985 further relaxed monetary and fiscal policies, and allowed for a general restructuring of wages. This did not impair the comfortable trade balance situation. In the period 1984–5 the current transactions account was balanced, notwithstanding net interest payments of US$19.8 billion.

It was in this context of external equilibrium but soaring domestic inflation that the monetary reform of February 1986 was instituted. This led to generalised excess demand throughout 1986 and, coupled with an overvalued exchange rate, brought back the trade deficit and loss of reserves – leaving the government with no other option but the moratorium of February 1987.

Table 12.1: *Brazil: two orthodox stabilisation programmes compared*

	1981/2		1983/4
Diagnosis:	(1) Excess demand due to monetary and fiscal laxity had led to both inflation acceleration and increase in current-account deficit; (2) Low interest rates and abundant domestic credit had led to excess consumpt on and discouraged private borrowing abroad; (3) Foreign bankers were unwilling to extend credit unless there was a convincing display of austerity to reduce consumption and induce export growth.	Diagnosis:	(1) Need to adjust the economy to the new situation in credit markets after the Mexican moratorium; (2) Control excessive domestic absorption to provide room for interest payments; (3) Public deficit as a symptom of the need to promote internal adjustment and control inflation;
Aims:	(1) Reduce demand to show control over the current-account deficit; (2) Display of austerity to bring foreign bankers back to finance long-run adjustment programme. (3) Induce private sector external borrowing.	Aims:	(1) Reduce the need for external credit; (2) Reduce inflation; (3) Increase exports.
Hidden objectives:	(1) Gain more time to permit investment projects directed to self-reliance objectives to mature; (2) Limit wage control to upper income groups to maintain control over trade unions and minimise 'social unrest'.	Instruments:	(1) Control PSBR, cutting it by 50% in nominal terms; (2) Control domestic credit of the monetary authorities; (3) Promote mild devaluation by accelerating mini-devaluations; (4) Liberalise trade.
Instruments:	(1) Liberalisation of interest rates; (2) Ceilings of 50% on the growth of the monetary base and M_1; (3) Ceiling on credit aggregates for non-priority sectors; (4) Reduction of public sector consumption spending in order to open room for the growth of private sector; (5) Definition of an import budget for state companies; (6) Tax incentives to manufactures exports;	Hidden Instrument:	(1) Reduction of wage indexation.

Source: Carneiro (1986), p. 26.

The adverse external shocks of 1979–80 followed hard on the crop failures of 1978 and 1979. This left the government with less room for manoeuvre to cope with the social unrest as well as the inflationary impact brought about by reduced domestic agricultural supply. The collapse of domestic reserves of agricultural commodities compelled the government to institute in 1979 a series of priority measures for the sector. Amongst these, a more effective minimum support price policy and the maintenance of relatively low interest rates on short-term credit to producers were the principal features.

However, as a direct result of IMF monitoring of fiscal and domestic credit targets, agricultural credit – including short-term credit – was sharply rationed in 1983 and 1984. Moreover, nominal interest rates started to be fully inflation-indexed in 1984. Attempts were made to offset these changes through adjustment of minimum prices. The impact of these policies on the agricultural sector will be the principal theme of this chapter.

Table 12.2: *Brazil: inflation and interest rates 1979–85*

Years	Inflation[a]	Agricultural prices[b]	Industrial prices[b]	Average nominal interest rates[c]
1979	77.2	80.5	78.8	41.2
1980	110.2	138.2	110.3	38.3
1981	95.2	70.7	99.6	90.7
1982	99.7	89.7	99.8	115.7
1983	211.0	335.8	200.5	170.1
1984	223.8	230.5	233.2	245.3
1985	235.1	267.7	221.1	248.2

Notes: [a] General Price Index (IGP–DI), December to December.
[b] Wholesale prices, December to December.
[c] Short-term (91 days) Government bills (LTNs), annual averages.

Source: Carneiro (1986) p. 30.

THE PERFORMANCE OF AGRICULTURE IN THE 1980s: AN EMPIRICAL ANALYSIS

Trends in crop and livestock production

Table 12.3 indicates annual growth rates for crop production for two periods 1973/80 and 1973/85. One aim of the table is to investigate to what extent (and in what direction) the period 1981–5 (the adjustment period) has had an impact on the longer-term trend rate for the period 1973/80. Growth rates are disaggregated by region, since Northeastern production has been affected by a five-year drought (1979/83), with adverse consequences for aggregate production of rice, beans, manioc, corn and cotton.

The results of this type of analysis are not conclusive. The statistical significance of the rates of growth in the majority of cases (especially for domestic market crops) is low, reflecting the high instability of yearly production for both periods. A closer inspection of the output data suggests, however, that the period since 1980, with the sole exception of 1983 (when floods hit the Centre-South), has been characterised by greater stability of production of major domestic crops, at higher than historical levels.

Table 12.3: *Brazil and regions: annual rates of growth[a] of production of selected crops 1973–80 and 1973–85*

Crops	Brazil		Center-South		Northeast	
	1973–80	1973–85	1973–80	1973–85	1973–80	1973–85
1 – DOMESTIC MARKET						
Rice	3.0[b]	1.6[b]	2.4[b]	1.7[b]	6.3[b]	0.7[b]
Irrigated (South)[c]			5.0	5.7		
Non-Irrigated (Center)[d]			1.2[b]	-0.6[b]		
Potatoes	5.3	2.4				
Beans	-1.1[b]	0.8[b]	0.9[b]	2.1[b]	-4.3[b]	-2.3[b]
Manioc	-1.1[b]	-1.4	-7.6	-4.9	2.9	-0.4[b]
Corn	2.5[b]	3.2	3.1[b]	3.7	-6.1[b]	-5.2[b]
2 – EXTERNAL MARKET						
Cotton	-3.2[b]	1.5[b]	-0.7[b]	3.8	-8.8	-4.5[b]
Cocoa	8.4	6.1				
Coffee	1.6[b]	5.0[b]				
Oranges	9.2	8.4				
Soybeans	10.8	7.7				
South[e]			9.2	4.5		
Center[f]			27.7	26.8		
3 – ADMINISTERED						
Sugar-Cane	7.6	8.8				
Wheat	3.5[b]	1.1[b]				

Notes: [a] OLS estimates of β_i in the regressions $Q_i = \alpha \, e^{\beta_i t}$, where Q_i are the respective quantities produced.
     [b] Not significantly different from zero at .05 level (two tailed t test).
     [c] States of Rio Grande do Sul and Santa Catarina.
     [d] Centre-South minus Rio Grande do Sul and Santa Catarina.
     [e] Rio Grande do Sul, Santa Catarina, Paraná and São Paulo.
     [f] Minas Gerais, Goiás, Mato Grosso do Sul, Mato Grosso and Bahia.

In the case of export and 'administered' crops, the most interesting facts are, first, the increase in cotton production, especially in the Centre-South; second, the sharp fall in the rate of growth of soybean production in Southern Brazil but a continuing high level of growth in Central Brazil; and, third, the great dynamism of sugar production in the 1981–5 period, as a result of the PROALCOOL incentives.

Turning now to the performance of livestock products, the most interesting fact to note is the unprecedented high level of net exports attained since the early 1980s. Net exports of beef cattle amounted to 22 per cent of total output in 1985, while for poultry this share rose to 25 per cent. In 1980, the corresponding figures were 5 and 18 per cent respectively. The rise in net beef exports between 1981 and 1985 can be explained, until 1983, by higher levels of slaughter, on the one hand, and declining domestic availability, on the other. In 1984 and 1985, however, domestic production fell from these peak levels, and net exports remained high, thanks to an additional fall in domestic availability.

The declining domestic availability of meat has not, however, led to any price inflation. This illustrates very well one major consequence of the adjustment programme, namely, the reduction in the demand for food. The increase in beef cattle slaughter in 1981–3, however, remains to be explained. It can possibly be attributed to cyclical factors: high prices in 1979–80, by inducing retention of calves and females, could have led to increased slaughter, and lower prices, in 1981–3. An alternative explanation, however, would stress the role of high interest rates from 1981 onwards. Livestock owners – following a behaviour pattern that seems to be very pervasive in the Brazilian economy – may have preferred lower livestock holdings, as against holding a greater share of financial assets. The latter hypothesis is strengthened by evidence that the de-indexation of financial assets in 1986, associated with the Cruzado Plan, was responsible for a greater retention of livestock and a sharp fall in slaughter rates and that the re-indexation of the financial system, in the wake of the failure of the Cruzado Plan, reversed the picture. Cattle slaughter increased and beef prices fell abruptly in early 1987.

The evolution of agricultural prices

Table 12.4 presents aggregate price indices for the period 1973–86 for both export and domestic market products. The picture that emerges is very clear. Prices for domestic products fell to significantly lower levels in the period 1982–6 than in the earlier period. The export crops' index has also shown a clear downward trend in the 1980s, apart from the sharp rise in 1984. The fall in domestic prices reflects a number of factors. First, the decline in food demand brought about by falling per-capita income and rising unemployment in the period 1981–4, a factor which was particularly relevant for animal products since the income elasticities of demand for rice, beans, manioc, potatoes (but not corn, due to its use as animal food) are low, perhaps even negative. For these crops, a second factor must be emphasised – the higher levels of domestic production in the period 1981–5.

A third factor may be relevant here, namely, as noted above in the analysis of beef cattle slaughter, a shift away from commodity stockholding in favour of financial assets as stores of value. This link between macroeconomic phenomena (high and accelerating inflation cum financial indexation and positive ex-ante real interest rates) and agriculture will be further discussed later.

Turning now to the downward trend in export prices, this derives from the fact that international commodity prices have been substantially lower in the 1980s than in the

Table 12.4: *Brazil: real indices[a] of prices received by farmers 1973–86*

Year	Home goods (crops)[b]	Home goods (animal products)[c]	Export goods[d] (excluding coffee)	Exports goods (including coffee)
1973	99	109	98	80
1974	101	122	89	73
1975	112	112	79	67
1976	117	98	76	80
1977	99	100	116	109
1978	105	108	91	81
1979	105	124	89	80
1980	119	117	78	69
1981	109	94	68	56
1982	85	82	66	55
1983	85	80	64	52
1984	95	92	101	79
1985	86	82	72	63
1986	91	94	68	78

Notes: [a] Calculated on the basis of monthly indices of producer prices and general price index, all with 1977 averages = 100;

[b] Rice, potatoes, beans, manioc and corn;

[c] Beef, pork, chicken, milk and eggs;

[d] Cotton, cocoa, oranges and soybeans.

1970s. This may explain the apparent loss of competitiveness of export crops vis à vis domestic crops in this period (as evidenced by the poor performance of soybeans relative to beans or corn, for instance), despite the incentives provided by exchange-rate devaluation and, implicitly, by the recession itself.[1]

Trends in agricultural exports and food imports

Table 12.5 shows that the value of exports of goods of agricultural origin – including processed goods such as orange juice and frozen meat – has not shown any upward trend from 1980 onwards. As a result, the contribution of agriculture to the total value of exports declined from 52 to 41 per cent. The table also shows, however, that this limited contribution of agriculture to the improved trade balance can be explained by the low level of export prices after 1980; in terms of volume, the growth of agricultural exports has been very significant. The last column of Table 12.5 confirms this fact: the value ratio of the crop content of agricultural exports to the total crop output (at constant 1962 prices) recouped, from 1980 onwards, the level it had reached before 1978 and 1979.

Additional evidence pointing to improved domestic food supply as a major feature of the period 1981–5 is the significant decline in food imports, other than wheat, since 1980. Imports, after having reached unprecedentedly high levels in the 1978–80 period, returned to their mid-1970s levels. The stabilisation of domestic production at a relatively high level (after two consecutive crop failures in 1978 and 1979) explains, more than declining food demand, this trend in food imports. However, wheat imports were kept high in the 1980s due to a high consumption subsidy and stagnant domestic production until 1984. Declining wheat imports in the period 1985 can be explained by the record levels of domestic wheat production in those years.

Table 12.5: *Brazil: total exports, agricultural exports, price and quantity indices of agricultural exports, and proportion of total crop output exported 1975–85*

Year	Total exports US$ 10⁶ fob	% of Total Exports	Index Numbers (1980 = 100) Value	Index Numbers (1980 = 100) Quantum	% of total crop output exported[b]
1975	8,670	60.9	53	86	20.8
1976	10,128	65.0	67	90	22.5
1977	12,120	67.1	81	79	20.7
1978	12,659	57.7	73	82	18.5
1979	15,244	52.7	79	82	16.8
1980	20,132	51.7	100	100	19.8
1981	23,293	45.9	103	120	23.0
1982	20,175	44.4	86	112	19.3
1983	21,200	45.8	97	126	20.8
1984	27,005	43.4	113	133	22.0
1985	25,639	40.9	101	134	19.9

Agricultural exports[a] spans the "% of Total Exports", the Index Numbers (Value, Quantum) columns.

Source: Agricultural exports, including the index numbers: Guimarães (1983 and 1987); last column: Barros and Manoel (1988).

[a] Includes unprocessed and processed goods of agricultural origin, except highly processed goods such as cloth and shoes.
[b] Aggregated value of crop content of agricultural exports – both *in natura* and in processed form – divided by the aggregated value of crop output. All values in constant 1962 prices.

It is tempting to connect this powerful wheat performance, in addition to other factors (such as technological innovations and price and credit incentives), to the loss of competitiveness of soybeans in the South. Wheat is grown in the winter, while soybeans are a summer crop. If substitutability, rather than complementarity, characterises the wheat-soybeans complex, then this argument is reasonable.

In order to complete the picture of the contribution of agriculture to the trade balance, account should also be taken of the decline in oil imports which became possible thanks to increased production of sugar-cane for energy use (alcohol). No less than 63 per cent of total sugar-cane produced in 1985 was destined for energy use, up from 30 per cent in 1979–80 (Barros and Manoel, 1988).

It can be seen, therefore, that agriculture's contribution to the external adjustment took the form of increased volumes of goods of agricultural origin not only for export but also to replace previous imports of food and oil. In view of the depressed external prices of commodities, the expansion of the sub-sectors geared to import substitution – including, in particular, crops for the domestic market – became highly consistent with the policy objectives of external adjustment.

Finally, it should be noted that there was a remarkable growth of non-wheat food imports in 1986. The government, in its attempt to keep prices frozen under the Cruzado Plan, over-reacted to the crop failure of that year, even at the cost of depleting foreign reserves. Export quotas were imposed and highly subsidised food imports, in excessive amounts, were authorised. As a result, the domestic food supply ended up surpassing domestic consumption, with the formation of large year-end stocks of agricultural products like rice and corn.

AGRICULTURAL PRODUCTION AND GOVERNMENT POLICY

The evidence presented so far all points to one basic conclusion. Crop production for the domestic market has performed much better in the adjustment period than might reasonably have been expected.[2] This can be attributed not only to better climatic conditions but also to trends in international commodity prices. In addition, the adverse conjuncture faced by livestock production – due to declining demand for meat and other animal products, and to high interest rates – must have strengthened the competitiveness of crops like beans, manioc, corn and even cotton, which has increasingly also become a domestic crop.

Minimum prices policy

The consolidation of domestic crop production has also been related to changes in the minimum prices policy that have occurred since 1980. In the wake of the domestic food shortages of 1978–80, the government decided in 1979 to change the old formula so that minimum prices were no longer constrained, as in the past, by credit ceilings. The two were now to be determined independently of each other.

The minimum prices policy underwent a second major reform in 1981. Up to then, minimum prices were fixed in nominal terms several months in advance; since inflation could (and usually did) differ from the official forecast, the farmer ended up facing great uncertainty regarding the actual real value of these minimum prices at harvest time. To circumvent this problem, the government instituted the so-called 'base-price' (*preco-base*) which was subject to indexation up to the beginning of the harvesting season (February for most crops) when it entered into operation as the minimum price. Available evidence suggests that since 1981–2 market prices have been strongly correlated with minimum prices and with a lower level of variance than prior to 1981. This has had the effect of reducing likely income variability and uncertainty, particularly for domestic crops.

It is also important to note that, associated with the correspondence of minimum and market prices, government intervention in the marketing of crops increased substantially after 1980. Under the Federal Government Acquisitions programme (AGF) and the Federal Government Loans programme (EGF), which financed private sector stocks, the government came to hold an increasing share of total marketed output. Since both the purchasing and the stockholding financing have been valued at minimum prices, this has strengthened the correspondence between minimum and market prices and also enhanced the attraction of selling to or seeking stockholding loans from the Federal Government.

It is clear that the combined effects of macroeconomic and sectoral policies served to reinforce the downward pressure on domestic agricultural prices that already derived from demand constraints and favourable climatic conditions. High and rising inflation, index-linking of financial assets and high positive real interest rates were obvious disincentives to speculative stockholding of agricultural output. Moreover, the lack of a marketing policy allowing for a seasonal price variation consistent with private storage also contributed to declining stockholding of agricultural commodities at harvest. The corrosion of the real value of the minimum prices, which resulted from high inflation and constant nominal minimum prices after February (up to 1984) or April (from 1985), left market prices virtually without a floor in the off-season. While this strengthened the government's power over agricultural price formation (mainly by means of selling stocks formed under the AGF programme) it also made private storage very risky.

Thus, in the adjustment period, agricultural producers have become increasingly dependent on government decisions relating to minimum prices and the volume of funds made available for crop marketing. The aggressive minimum prices policy pursued by the government since 1979 has thus stimulated domestic crop output.

The expansion of the small farm sector

The strong recent output trend for domestic goods appears to contrast with the pre-ceding period. In the 1970s growth rates for aggregate output and productivity of export crops were superior to those for crops destined for domestic consumption. In addition, studies have suggested that domestic food supply expanded less than demand, resulting in rising food prices. This divergence is commonly attributed to favourable conditions in the international markets, domestic policies of export promo-tion, and more rapid technical progress in the sub-sector, while relative lack of techni-cal progress, a higher apparent risk factor for yields and prices and official price controls held back domestic food production.

However, this earlier growth in the food supply gap has to be related to a number of developments linking agriculture with other sectors. Between 1968 and 1979 rapid overall growth in the economy was associated with a sharp increase in the demand for food and increased alternative income sources for petty producers. One consequence was a rising rural wage trend. The latter was further associated with increased rural migration towards the cities. Food output from the small farm sector – the major source of food items and migrants – consequently fell back (Rezende, 1986).

The changed economic context post-1980 has seen something of a reversal in these trends. High urban unemployment rates and falling real incomes have stemmed the flow of out-migration from agriculture. While the share of the labour force employed in agriculture declined from around 37 per cent in the mid-1970s to around 30 per cent by 1980, since then agriculture's share has stayed constant at around 29–30 per cent (IBGE, 1986). Within agriculture, moreover, there has been a significant increase in the number of small farms since 1980 across all regions. While most of the observed growth in agricultural employment in the 1970s took place in farms of over 10 hectares, in the 1980s this has been reversed. Most growth has been in the small farm sector and has taken the form of on-farm family employment. Amongst the larger farms there has been a retreat away from direct cultivation towards sharecropping and other tenancy contracts.

The renewed expansion of the small farm sector reflects the decreased attraction of the urban sectors, due to recession. In addition, 'push' factors have operated less strongly in the 1980s. It can be argued that with lower returns to soybean and livestock activity, the shift to food crops for the domestic market will have tended to favour the small farm sector. Furthermore, it appears that because of the minimum wage policy pursued between 1979 and 1983, rural wage rates have been more sticky downwards than returns to petty production. The declining availability of rural credit will likewise have acted most adversely on the medium and large farm sector, while falling land prices in the recent period will have encouraged the acquisition of land by landless workers.

Table 12.6: Brazilian regions: change in the number of farms and occupied personnel according to farm size groups – 1970–75, 1975–80 and 1980–85 (per cent)

Regions and farm size groups (in ha.)	1970/75		1975/80		1980/85	
	No. of farms	Occ. Personnel	No. of farms	Occ. Personnel	No. of farms	Occ. Personnel
NORTHEAST						
<10	9.4	19.5	0.8	-2.4	17.6	17.8
10 to 20	-0.2	10.8	12.1	9.4	3.8	4.4
20 to 50	1.4	10.4	12.4	13.1	5.7	4.9
50 to 100	2.8	11.7	12.6	20.4	6.3	3.1
100 to 200	4.7	14.4	7.7	21.2	3.1	1.5
200 to 500	2.6	10.5	7.7	32.2	0.3	-0.4
> 500	4.3	6.0	3.1	54.5	7.9	2.9
Total	5.9	15.8	3.9	6.8	13.4	11.1
SOUTHEAST						
< 10	-10.5	1.3	4.5	-0.3	23.5	23.1
10 to 20	-9.2	-1.1	2.1	-1.5	11.1	11.3
20 to 50	-4.4	3.8	-0.8	-1.9	7.0	6.0
50 to 100	-0.3	7.3	-2.1	0.8	4.6	4.9
100 to 200	3.1	11.0	-0.4	6.6	2.2	4.3
200 to 500	6.1	11.6	0.2	11.7	1.0	4.9
> 500	9.2	12.2	-0.4	26.6	-1.2	7.5
Total	-5.4	5.0	1.3	4.0	11.9	9.9

Regions and farm size groups (in ha.)	1970/75		1975/80		1980/85	
	No. of farms	Occ. Personnel	No. of farms	Occ. Personnel	No. of farms	Occ. Personnel
CENTRE-WEST						
< 10	12.6	44.8	-23.2	-21.9	28.5	12.4
10 to 20	0.8	25.5	-10.7	-11.9	17.5	9.4
20 to 50	-6.8	13.4	-0.9	-0.8	20.7	13.9
50 to 100	6.2	30.1	8.5	10.2	17.4	9.8
100 to 200	9.7	28.6	16.7	23.4	13.8	6.2
200 to 500	1.3	26.8	12.7	25.0	8.8	2.4
> 500	6.9	44.3	18.6	48.6	1.4	8.6
Total	6.7	31.2	-0.9	10.1	7.8	8.8
SOUTH						
< 10	-14.5	6.4	-1.9	-14.1	11.5	11.5
10 to 20	-9.2	12.9	-0.4	-10.9	2.3	-0.1
20 to 50	-5.5	18.8	-2.0	-10.7	-1.9	-5.4
50 to 100	3.2	31.5	0.4	-3.8	-0.3	-5.8
100 to 200	5.6	38.6	5.6	5.9	1.5	-3.7
200 to 500	5.6	40.2	8.3	10.1	3.7	-1.5
> 500	8.8	27.2	8.3	22.6	2.2	5.7
Total	-9.2	15.2	-0.9	-9.0	4.8	1.6

Source: Agricultural Census.

Rural credit policy, 1981-6

It has already been pointed out that one of the principal policy measures of the adjustment period was the curtailment of loanable funds and the raising of interest rates within the officially-sponsored rural credit system. Credit availability fell continuously from the peak 1979–80 levels, so that by 1984 rural credit availability was at least 60 per cent inferior to the 1980 level.

These trends have led many commentators to predict severe implications for the rate of growth of agricultural production. The government has attempted to dilute the possible adverse effects by raising minimum prices and by extending their indexing period.

It has been further agreed that the observed decline in the sales of modern inputs to farmers after 1980 can be attributed to these restrictive rural credit measures. As shown by Table 12.7, it is indeed true that apparent consumption of pesticides, fertilisers and tractors fell drastically after 1980; but it can also be seen that a significant recovery took place in 1984, precisely the year of lowest credit availability and the highest real interest rate.

Table 12.7: *Brazil: apparent consumption of farm inputs 1976–85*
(1975 = 100)

Year	Pesticides	Fertilisers	Tractors
1976	90	128	110
1977	113	162	84
1978	121	163	72
1979	127	180	85
1980	143	212	88
1981	111	139	49
1982	84	137	43
1983	74	122	39
1984	103	175	72
1985	93	162	71

Source: Barros and Manoel (1987).

However, it ought also to be noted that not all rural credit lines were curtailed after 1980. Short-term credit has been rationed only since 1982; in the 1979–82 period it actually remained at record levels (see Table 12.8). Consequently, changes in credit policy may perhaps explain the fall in tractor sales, but not in the current inputs sales.

An alternative explanation for the falling input demand after 1980 might be found in the behaviour of inputs prices relative to agricultural product prices. Inputs prices rose substantially post-1980, due not only to the oil price shock, but also to the government's decision to raise domestic prices closer to their border price equivalents as a means of reducing oil consumption and engendering a greater substitution of domestic sources of energy for imported oil. Moreover, in this period agricultural product prices fell significantly. As a result of these divergent price trends, shown in Table 12.9, the ratio of input prices to product prices shifted markedly in favour of the former.

As regards the recovery in input demand in 1984, the most likely explanation lies in the high net income generated by the 1984 crop and by expectations of continuing high prices for the 1985 crop. Producer prices in 1984 were high for a number of reasons, which included the crop failure in the summer of 1983, the substantial exchange rate

Table 12.8: *Brazil: yearly flows of rural credit loans by agricultural use 1977–86*
             (In Cz$ 10⁹ of March 1986)

Year	Total credit	Operational credit (custeio)	Investment credit	Marketing credit
1977	185.5	87.7	45.0	52.8
1978	188.7	90.0	47.1	51.6
1979	235.1	118.2	58.7	58.1
1980	224.8	127.2	42.2	55.4
1981	195.0	114.3	30.1	50.5
1982	188.8	121.5	24.7	42.6
1983	142.5	88.6	23.8	30.1
1984	87.1	61.4	10.7	15.0
1985	124.1	88.3	16.1	19.8
1986	179.8	99.7	59.3	20.7

Source: Central Bank.

Table 12.9: *Brazil real indices of prices received and of prices paid by farmers 1973–85*

Years	Index of prices[a] received by farmers (Crops)	Indices of prices paid by farmers			
		Machines & Equipment	Fertilisers	Fuel oil and Grease	Pesticides
1973	99	89	85	67	108
1974	96	98	164	87	133
1975	99	105	146	93	126
1976	101	99	112	101	105
1977	105	100	100	100	100
1978	99	101	95	102	101
1979	99	101	99	107	98
1980	103	99	129	120	116
1981	93	106	118	125	108
1982	78	110	103	121	103
1983	77	98	102	127	108
1984	97	108	112	119	114
1985	81	117	107	106	110

Source: FGV (for basic data used for building the index of prices received) and Secretary of
Agriculture of São Paulo (for the indices of prices paid).

[a] Calculated on the basis of monthly indices of producer prices and general price index, with
1977 as the base year. Note, however, that averages of real monthly producer price indices have
been calculated only for harvest months. Given different harvest periods, this results in real
price indices not necessarily equalling 100 for 1977.

devaluation of that year and a strong reserves constraint that held back the government's ability to import. The government, moreover, reinforced this trend by raising
minimum prices and extending the indexing period.

CONCLUSION

This chapter has argued that in the recent adjustment period domestic food crop production performed particularly well. This outcome can be attributed, at least in part, to favourable climatic conditions. However, a number of other factors can be cited, including more effective government support for domestic production through a revised minimum price support policy, and diminished competition from the export crop and livestock sub-sectors. One index of the increased relative profitability of the food-crop sector can be found in the expansion of the small farm sector and the reversal of the trends that had operated in the rural labour market during the preceding period.

The chapter has also demonstrated that in the case of rural credit policy reforms – a major feature of the adjustment process – the adverse effects on agricultural production, and even investment, appear to have been exaggerated. The government took care not to curtail short-term production credit until 1983, a strategy that contributed to agriculture's recovery from 1980; also when it was finally curtailed, not only had agricultural prices risen but farmers' expectations were also optimistic largely because of the government's stronger support through the minimum prices policy. The decline in input use between 1981 and 1985 can also be attributed to the shifting ratio of input to output prices.

In short, the chapter has argued that the adjustment period has seen a consolidation of production of goods for domestic consumption, as against export crops. This appears in part to run counter to a number of explicit rationalisations for key adjustment measures, including exchange-rate reform. However, it is important to note that the presence of a major balance-of-payments constraint would have limited the government's ability to have recourse to trade for closing the domestic food supply gap and, at the same time, controlling the price level. Major food imports – particularly of wheat – had become the norm in the 1970s. In a less favourable external environment, improved domestic supply has become a greater priority.

NOTES

1 It should be recalled that soybean expansion in the 1980s was restricted to Central Brazil, and resulted from the attractiveness of cheap lands (*cerrado*), opened up for soybean production thanks to technological innovations. In addition, this expansion was much more dependent on the minimum price policy than the earlier expansion in the 1970s in the South.
2 This conclusion differs from that of Homem de Melo (1985). For a critique of his empirical analysis, see Monteiro (1986).

REFERENCES

Arida, P. and A.L. Resende (1985) 'Recessão e Taxas de Juros: o Brasil nos primórdios da década de 1980', *Revista de Economia Política*, Vol. 5, No 1 (January-March).
Barros, J.R.M. and A. Manoel (1988) 'Insumos Agrícolas: Evolução Recente e Perspectivas' in

A.S. Brandão, Os Principais Problemas da Agricultura Brasileira: Análise e Sugestões. Rio de Janeiro,: IPEA/INPES.

Carneiro, D.D. (1986), 'Stabilization Policies and Adjustment: the Brazilian Economy in the Eighties', Rio de Janeiro, Department of Economics of Catholic University, Discussion Paper No. 138, October.

Cavalcanti, C. (1984), 'O Flagelo das Secas Nordestinas: Condições Sócio-Econômicas Observadas em 1979', in I.M.M. Carvalho and T.M.F. Haguette (eds), Trabalho e Condições de Vida no Nordeste Brasiliero. São Paulo, Editora Hucitec.

—— (1986), 'Natureza Econômica de uma Catástrofe Natural: Characterísticas e Impacto da Seca Nordestina de 1979–80', Revista de Economia Política, Vol. 6, No. 1 January–March.

Guimaraes, C.V. (1983), 'Balanço Mercantil de Divisas do Setor Agrícola, 1965–1982'. Brasilia, IPEA/IPLAN.

—— (1987), 'Comércio Agrícola, Saldo Comercial e Dívida Externa', in Dados Conjunturais da Agropecuária No. 142. Brasilia, IPEA/IPLAN, January.

Homem de Melo, F.B. (1983), O Problema Alimentar no Brasil. Rio de Janeiro, Paz e Terra.

—— (1985), Prioridade Agrícola: Sucesso ou Fracasso? São Paulo, Estudos Econômicos FIPE/Pioneira.

IBGE (1983), Metodologias das Pesquisas Agropecuárias Anuais – 1981, Rio de Janeiro, IBGE, Série Relatórios Metodológicos, vol. 3.

IPEA/INPES (1987), Perspectivas da Economia Brasileira – 1987. Rio de Janeiro, IPEA/INPES.

Johnson, D.G. (1950), 'The Nature of the Supply Function for Agricultural Products', American Economic Review, Vol. 40.

Monteiro, M.J.C. (1986), 'Prioridade Agrícola: Sucesso ou Fracasso? de Fernando H. de Melo (Review)', Pesquisa e Planejamento Econômico, Vol. 16, No. 2, August.

Mueller, C.C. (1987), 'Censos Agropecuários', Agroanalysis, Rio de Janeiro, Fundaçâo Getúlio Vargas, Vol. 11, No. 6, June.

Rezende, G.C. (1984a), 'Estocagem e Variação Estacional de Preços: uma Análise da Política de Crédito de Comercializaçâo Agrícola', Pesquisa e Planejamento Econômico, Vol. 14, No. 1.

—— (1984b), 'Crise Atual e Papel do Setor Agrícola', Conjuntura Econômica, Vol. 38, No. 6.

—— (1985), 'Interação entre Mercados de Trabalho e Razão entre Salários Rurais e Urbanos no Brasil', Estudos Econômicos, Vol. 15, No. 1.

—— (1987a), 'Inflaçâo, Preços Mínimos e Comercialização Agrícola: a Experiência dos Anos Oitenta', Rio de Janeiro: IPEA/INPES, Discussion Paper No. 110, April.

—— (1987b), Food Production, Income Distribution and Prices: Brazil 1960–80, Geneva, International Labour Office, Rural Employment Policy Research Programme, Working Paper WEP 10–6/WP89.

PART FOUR

An Overview of Adjustment Experience

13

The Reality of Structural Adjustment

A Sceptical Appraisal

Robert Bates

A major purpose of this chapter is to provoke, and I shall attempt to do so in three ways. I shall vigorously claim the vantage point of a professional 'outsider' and exercise the rights and privileges to which that position entitles me[1]. And I shall approach the problem of structural adjustment from a more political point of view than is normal among economists.

GENERAL POINTS

Paul Streeten's opening chapter argues cogently that we need to focus on such questions as adjustment 'for what', 'of what', and 'to what'. I wish to add to that list adjustment *'from* what' and, in that context, to define structural adjustment as the policy process by which countries adjust the domestic allocation of resources to prices prevailing in world markets. This framework would suggest that the phenomenon of structural adjustment is not a new one; it did not begin with the oil price shocks, or the debt crisis, or the recession of the 1980s. Rather, the processes we are now analysing represent a transition from a previous pattern of adjustment, in which governments sought to prescribe and enforce characteristic patterns of domestic resource allocation in the face of world prices.

The previous pattern of adjustment, especially as it pertained to agriculture, often exhibited highly unsatisfactory distributive effects; benefits accrued to the relatively prosperous at the expense of the poorest of the poor – commonly, the small peasant farmer. The previous pattern of adjustment often undermined growth. By undermining agricultural exports and reducing incentives for food production, for example, it generated present benefits at the expense of future prosperity. And the policies which marked the previous pattern of adjustment proved unsustainable; 'cheap food' policies, for example, could only be sustained by supporting disequilibrium prices either by importing food or by subsidising local production. Shortages of foreign exchange and the weakening creditworthiness of many developing country governments undermined the capacity to perpetuate such policy commitments; and these weaknesses proved fatal when the forces of international recession impacted upon these countries in the 1980s. The economic costs and benefits of the policies which are now being put in place in response to the events of the 1980s therefore must be evaluated against the economic costs and benefits of the previous policies.

The second implication is that by failing to take into account the previous pattern of adjustment we may make major analytical errors. One of the most serious may be the widely argued contention that present policies are aimed at the promotion of the private sector and the weakening of the public sector. The rhetoric of the debates over contemporary structural adjustment suggest that it is designed to unleash the private sector. But, taking past forms of adjustment into account, it seems much more likely that the real thrust of present-day attempts at structural adjustment is the revival of previous ways of doing business. This means restoring the health of governments by bringing their policies back into line with current economic realities.

There are three reasons for arguing this position. One is the recognition of the *status quo*. Governments have dominated the economic landscape; they continue to dominate the political landscape; and they therefore play a large role in the negotiation of any new set of policies. It is highly unlikely that they will direct change in economic policy into channels which depart sharply from their preferred way of conducting business. Secondly, the major international agencies which are involved in structural adjustment operate through governments. This is certainly true of the IMF; and despite its private sector rhetoric, the World Bank remains largely a banker to governments. The success of the programmes of both agencies depends upon the ability of these agencies to accommodate the interests of governments. Lastly, at least in the areas which involve markets, the reality is that economic adjustment had already taken place in the private sector; it took place years ago; and, indeed, in many respects it was the ability of the private sector to adjust which led to the crises which made 'structural adjustment' necessary.

THE MEANING OF STRUCTURAL ADJUSTMENT

This third point warrants further elaboration. In agriculture, many of the policies which characterised the 'old forms' of structural adjustment involved the implementation of disequilibrium prices. In Africa, for example, governments over-valued their currencies; alternatively, they administratively lowered the prices offered for agricultural exports. Private agents then responded. They did so by smuggling, as in the case of Ugandan coffee, which was then sold as 'Western Kenyan' coffee on the Nairobi auction floor, or as in the case of Ghanaian cocoa, which was marketed in the franc (CFAF) zone economies of Togo or Côte d'Ivoire. Alternatively, they responded by shifting out of the production of export crops, growing food crops instead. Or, more dramatically still, they shifted out of agriculture, quitting their farms for the cities, investing less in agriculture, or spending greater amounts of time in leisure. In the case of food crops, government attempts to alter prices resulted in extensive 'parallel markets'. Reginald Green's chapter in this book suggests that official food markets handle only about 7 per cent of the domestically produced food grains in Africa. And government attempts to institute price controls result in corruption and black markets, as essential commodities, such as foodstuffs, are sold privately at market clearing prices rather than at officially posted prices.

In all three cases, the private sector marches on. The major effect, then, is not to weaken or destroy the private sector. It is instead to render the public portion of the economy less important; people simply trade around it. And it is to leave public institutions starved of resources. Because of smuggling, for example, the central banks fail to get foreign exchange. It is also to leave them with mounting debts; food marketing parastatals may purchase grain at official prices, for example, but much of the food then gets sold by employees in the parallel market, resulting in lowered revenues. Or, more commonly, little food gets bought or sold at official prices, leading to the generation of low revenue by agencies with large fixed costs.

The impact of policy reforms, such as with pricing policy, will thus not be to promote the private sector or to lead to its expansion. It will be, rather, to move official policies in a direction which will enable public institutions to reclaim their place in the economy. The private sector has already adjusted. The reforms that are referred to as structural adjustment will lead to the revival of official economic institutions.

In connection with this point, it is interesting to note the domestic origins of the demands for structural adjustment. To use Hirschman's language, they originate from those economic agents who have been unable to exit, or to use the market option (Hirschman, 1970). The demand for reform, or 'voice', originates from the international agencies abroad and those unable or unwilling to use unofficial markets at home. One group would be the large firms, whose very visibility makes it difficult to transact at black market prices and who experience losses as a result. Another would be the public agencies, who find themselves increasingly irrelevant or bankrupt as economic activity shifts to the parallel markets. A last would be those who are offended by the increasing sense of loss in the public order and who resist doing what is individually rational at the expense of the public good. All seek a new set of policies which would revive and make sustainable a public order which has been eroded by the expansion of the private sector.

It is my deepest suspicion, then, that structural adjustment does not mean the expansion of the private sector and the retrenchment of governments. Rather, it may well mean the opposite, and represent an attempt by the public sector to revive an old order which proved unsustainable. An implication of this would be that many of the policies and programmes advocated under the name of structural adjustment would in fact have very little effect, in terms of fundamentally restructuring the political or economic order. Thus large-scale proposals for marketing reform in agriculture will probably result in market structures very similar to those which they were designed to replace, as in the case of Senegal or Kenya. Or rhetoric championing the cause of privatisation will lead to very little divestiture of state enterprises or the withdrawal of governments from farm input programmes. Or the food subsidy programmes are unlikely to continue to reach the poorest of the poor, and will instead be targeted at those with the political clout to make it in the interests of the governments to protect them. Many of the commentaries offered in the previous papers sustain these conjectures.

In the 1980s, the existing structures of power were crumbling in many developing countries; structural adjustment represents policy reform, conducted by governments; and it is therefore likely more to represent a reassertion and underpinning of the previous ways of doing business than any sort of fundamental reform.

STRUCTURAL ADJUSTMENT AND AGRICULTURE:

Having raised a number of issues relating to the larger sense of structural adjustment, the remainder of this chapter focuses on a set of specific agricultural sector issues; issues that are consistently raised in the preceding country studies.

Pricing policy

The commentaries in the preceding chapters often expressed scepticism about the capacity of changes in pricing policy to alter the performance of agriculture. It is my belief that those who make this argument have overstated their case.

It is clear that price reforms alone will do little good. If roads are impassable, transport immobile, or there is little to buy in rural shops, then clearly offering farmers higher prices will furnish little incentive for them to produce more output. But this is an argument not against the use of price incentives but rather against using them while not at the same time correcting deficiencies in macroeconomic policy, and, in particular, in exchange rates.

Research on farm production ranks along with that on migration and human capital formation as among the best social scientific work that has been conducted in the developing world. When conjoined with the fieldwork conducted by anthropologists in rural communities, this research strongly suggests that rural households respond positively and vigorously to financial incentives. It is interesting that the two papers in this volume – on Senegal and Ghana – which draw on field data tend to emphasise the extent to which local agricultural producers have adjusted to shifts in relative prices.

It remains a mystery as to why elites and those who work with them are so quick to back away from basic reforms in agricultural pricing policies. While perhaps correcting for an earlier excess of zeal, it may also be that this stance represents but another sign of the capacity of the old order to reassert itself.

Farm inputs

A number of chapters in this volume focus on the alteration of marketing arrangements and systems for the provision of farm inputs. A common theme is that there has been a very rocky transition to the use of private markets. The reasons for this are not always clear. In some cases, it may have been that the macro policy context was unfavourable; shortages of foreign exchange could have weakened the incentives for private agents to import farm inputs from abroad. Some mention a deficiency of rural credit. But the vast preponderance of detailed field data suggests that credit plays but a small, and often insignificant, part in explaining differential rates of use of off-farm inputs.

A possibility too little investigated is that private distributors and markets of farm inputs fear to invest heavily in researching the particular needs of particular crops in particular locations; in establishing a network of stockists and farm agents; and in accumulating inventories, because they fear that governments might once again move into the industry. Given their past ways of doing business in the developing world, governments promoting privatisation need means of convincingly pre-committing themselves to staying out of politically sensitive markets. Lacking visible and unambiguous ways of signifying such intentions, governments may find that private investors will remain reluctant to place themselves at risk by entering the marketplace.

This conjecture highlights an additional feature of the problem of privatisation: that private companies might not themselves prefer it. Investments in many developing countries are perceived as very risky; and in many cases, operating within public corporations provides a means of transferring the risks to governments. Among the greatest risks facing investors is that the government might subsequently move into an industry in which they have invested their capital. Because of this fear, private investors may well prefer to operate within the context of public corporations. By combining the interests of the goverment with their own, they seek ways of making it in the financial interests of governments to implement policies which guarantee a favourable rate of return to capital investments. Privatisation in the industries which provide farm inputs may therefore prove a slow process, if only because its supposed beneficiaries fear the increase in risks which it may create.

Farm products

Another set of policy reforms favoured by those advocating 'structural adjustment' involves the privatisation of commodity markets. Once again, as the preceding papers show, the overwhelming reality is that the *status quo* remains firmly in place, at least in the sense that governments continue to dominate and to structure agricultural markets.

It is important to comprehend why governments have been reluctant to allow private traders to take over. In some cases, it is because private traders represent unpopular minorities and governments fear the political repercussions of policy changes which would appear to favour such groups. In the case of export crops, governments also fear that less regulation will result in more smuggling or the failure of private traders to surrender their foreign exchange to the central banking authorities. (Needless to say, the adoption of more realistic exchange rates would curtail such behaviour.) Lastly, many governments fear the loss of tax revenues which would result from the privatisation of export markets.

As presently configured, many governments – particularly in Africa – purchase export crops at administratively set domestic prices and market them at prices prevailing in international markets, appropriating the difference in the form of tax revenues. To ask these governments to allow private traders to handle the export trade without providing them with alternative ways of raising public finances is to ask them to abandon a major component of their tax base. And with development programmes to pursue, and colonels to pay, they will be unwilling to do that.

An implication of this line of analysis is that an important part of any proposal to promote the role of private markets for the exportation of agricultural commodities must be a proposal to compensate the governments for their loss of public revenues. Tax reform will play an essential role in marketing reforms.

There are also compelling reasons why governments are reluctant to withdraw from the regulation and control of the market for food crops. As already noted, in Africa only about 7–10 per cent of the total production of food crops passes through state marketing agencies. It is also true that only about 7–10 per cent of Africa's population live in the cities. And it is very likely that the proportion of the cereals consumed in the cities which come from the state marketing agencies represents a very high figure indeed. The economic costs of subsidising the food consumption of the urban population are vividly detailed in the chapter on Zambia; the political costs of *not* providing such subsidies are alluded to in the chapter on Morocco. It is apparent that a major reason why governments are willing to bear the economic costs of remaining in the grain trade is that such costs represent payments on political insurance. To ask governments to abandon their political fortunes to private markets – in other words, to markets over which they exercise no control – is to ask them to incur a level of risk which no person would willingly assume.

A major implication is that the provision of assurances against food shortages should form an integral part of any policy proposals for the deregulation of food markets. The work of the World Food Programme offers one possible means of developing assurances against domestic food shortages. The provision of an international food bank provides another. Reformist governments would be entitled to claim deliveries from this bank when failures of the rain or runs on domestic stocks pass an agreed-upon trigger level.

There is another, perhaps less obvious, reason for governments to persist in the maintenance of monopsonistic grain marketing structures: the role played by 'single-channel' marketing agencies in underpinning rural credit markets. In many developing countries, land rights are defined in ways which make land an awkward form of collateral for loans. Being poor, most farmers possess few fixed assets which they can offer as collateral instead. And in this environment, lenders often use the crop itself as a form of security for loans. A major way of offering such security is by physically amassing the crop in a single marketing channel; the crop can then be appropriated by those who have experienced default on credit advanced to small farmers.

The implication is that if single-channel marketing agencies are replaced by private traders, the current basis for capital markets in small-farm areas will be disrupted. Governments which have been able to mobilise capital for seasonal loans or other forms of farm credit by maintaining control over the crop – and by exhibiting their control over the crop to private lenders as a form of security – will no longer be able to do that. And credit markets will have to find new forms of organisation in the rural sector.

In his opening chapter Paul Streeten challenges readers to think of what prescriptions they would offer a 'reform-minded leader'. Were the leader a member of the international development community and attempting to modify the domestic policies of governments, then the lesson to be learned from these remarks is: 'listen'. For while it is often pointed out that the institutions which regulate agricultural industries in the developing world impose major economic costs, the remarks offered here suggest that these institutions also provide major benefits, particularly to governments. They provide a source of public revenues; they provide political insurance to policy makers; and they underpin rural capital markets, lowering the costs of lending to small-scale farmers. To secure the alteration of these institutions, then, the concerns of governments about losing these benefits must be addressed. Policy prescriptions must be formulated which not only curb the pathologies introduced by the existing way of structuring rural economies but also compensate for the perceived loss of benefits on the part of policy-making elites.

Timing and sequence

It is clear that it will be extremely difficult to prescribe a single optimal sequence and pace of structural reform. In some cases, adjustments in the exchange rate must obviously precede the reform of marketing structures. Were the Ugandan Government, for example, to move to the private marketing of coffee prior to devaluing the Ugandan shilling, private agents would have every incentive to export coffee by smuggling it. The government's need for foreign exchange thus constrains the optimal sequence of reform measures.

In some cases, one must wonder why the best sequence was not chosen. In the Zambian case, for example, it would appear that, had the government devalued first, it could then have employed the flush of public revenues resulting from the enhanced profitability of the mines to finance a continuation of the food subsidies, at least in the short run. Organised labour would then have had less reason to veto the IMF package of reforms.

The major point, however, is not why the policy makers made the choices they did, but rather that the 'best sequence' of reforms must take into account the way in which they can attract political support and deflect political opposition. And as the configuration of organised political interests varies from country to country, the 'best sequence' should vary as well. In short, there is unlikely to be any one best prescription. As with any other form of political strategy, the pay-offs attached to a reform sequence will vary with the structure of the game.

NOTES

1 I am not an economist; I have not previously worked on this problem; and I have not served as a consultant for any of the international agencies who seek to implement structural adjustment programmes.

REFERENCES

Hirschman, Albert (1970), *Exit, Voice and Loyalty*, Cambridge, Mass., Harvard University Press.

14

Prices, Markets & Rigidities

African Agriculture 1980–88

Simon Commander

INTRODUCTION

The rapid growth in adjustment lending that has occurred over the past decade has been relatively widely diffused. At the outset, a major share of that lending was directed toward middle-income countries, particularly in Latin America, and was viewed largely in terms of balance-of-payments support. Increasingly, however, the concept and reality of adjustment have changed and both the definition and duration have become more protracted and elastic. Indeed, as narrower definitions focusing on the balance of payments recede, the concepts of adjustment and development appear to overlap to a great extent. This can partly be related to the growing awareness of the non-transitory nature of adjustment, not least because of an adverse global economic environment as well as the scale of imbalance present in a considerable number of developing country economies.

The presence of profound structural disequilibria is particularly obvious in the case of sub-Saharan Africa where a combination of unsatisfactory and unsustainable policies, civil strife and chronic inefficiencies in resource utilisation have generated very poor economic performance and in some cases outright retrogression. The adoption of classic IMF stabilisation programmes theoretically articulated to structural adjustment programmes can be seen as an attempt by both African governments and donors to reverse such trends. This reversal has, however, commonly implied major changes in country-level strategies for attaining higher growth and development. IMF and World Bank adjustment programmes emphasise a particular route to such goals, a route that has often carried a different set of emphases from those avowed by governments prior to the 1980s. Equally importantly, this divergence relates as much to the earlier lending strategies of some of the major donors, including the World Bank. And this is particularly the case with regard to the agricultural sector, where an earlier preference for parastatals and quasi-autonomous project entitities has now given way to a fairly generalised hostility to such institutions.

This concluding chapter aims to examine the degree to which adjustment lending (broadly defined here to include both demand- and supply-side measures, i.e. stabilisation and structural adjustment) has managed to raise economic performance in sub-Saharan Africa. Some key measures that feature implicitly or explicitly in adjustment programmes are analysed. It is demonstrated that on most counts, including those of growth and the balance of payments, improvements have been limited and patchy. The principal components of adjustment have been demand-reducing measures that have repressed consumption through public-expenditure and income reduction. Most SSA economies remain highly constrained by their weak ability to import. While it is generally argued that the agricultural sector remains the least import-intensive, this is less true in the case of SSA than for other regions. Basic inputs need to be imported and without greater fertiliser and technology adoption satisfactory productivity advances will not be generated in African agriculture. In the light of such longer-term developmental considerations, it is argued that the inability to generate better sustainable performance can, in part, be attributed to shortcomings in the policy frameworks proposed by donors. The second part of the chapter therefore aims to isolate the major design problems of adjustment programmes, emphasising, in particular, the limitations of price-based policies for, first, technical change and productivity growth and, second, the income distributional goals of many SSA adjustment programmes.

ADJUSTMENT LENDING, 1980-88: AN OVERVIEW

Adjustment lending is, for the most part, a phenomenon of the 1980s. In the case of the World Bank, adjustment lending accounted for only 3.3 per cent of total lending in 1980. By 1987 this share had risen to 25 per cent with the expectation that this level would be sustained over the next few years. The weight of such lending has been primarily directed toward sub-Saharan Africa, so that between 1980 and 1987 46 per cent of adjustment loans were directed to the region. However, in value terms they accounted for under 16 per cent of the total and around 24 per cent of total sectoral adjustment lending. The growth in sectoral adjustment lending has been primarily directed toward trade liberalisation measures and concentrated on a limited number of high-debt, middle-income countries, most of whom fall outside SSA. With specific regard to agricultural sector adjustment lending over this period, it should be noted that SSA accounted for around 6 per cent of total agricultural sector lending. This includes specific fertiliser import financing. Furthermore, over 40 per cent of that lending was accounted for by one fertiliser loan to Nigeria (World Bank, 1988).

Concentrating on sectoral adjustment lending alone would, however, ignore the fact that structural adjustment loans have contained significant explicit policy actions relating to agriculture. In over 80 per cent of such SALs for SSA agricultural pricing policy has been a major component, while institutional reform measures dealing with the sector have been a part of all such loans. In the former case, the main emphasis has been on subsidy reduction – primarily for inputs – with a lesser degree of emphasis on removal of price controls. SALs have also been concerned with questions of agricultural research, cost recovery, ownership transfer (divestiture) and the role and scale of public agricultural stock management. In addition – and perhaps most significantly – SALs have concentrated on trade and exchange-rate policy as well as the size and, to a lesser extent, the composition of public expenditures. Quite obviously, the role of macroeconomic policy remains critical in determining the structure of prices and the share of resources allocated to agriculture.

SUB-SAHARAN AFRICAN AGRICULTURE UNDER ADJUSTMENT: THE RECENT EXPERIENCE

Given the relatively limited duration of most adjustment programmes, assessment of their efficacy remains difficult. Nevertheless, available evidence indicates the emergence of a broad range of issues and problems. Apart from problems in implementation, due in part to the weaknesses of institutions in many developing economies as also to excessive concentration of policy changes, it is clear that basic indicators – for growth, output composition, current account and fiscal deficit – indicate a common pattern of response alongside considerable diversity in performance. However, using straightforward before and after comparisons as a means of assessment runs into the simple problem that adjustment occurred precisely because of the unsustainability of ex ante conditions. Hence, an implicit assumption that performance under adjustment can be evaluated in relation to this prior period does not hold. In addition, separating out the effect of other exogenous variables on overall performance adds further complications. Despite these problems, a number of important features do stand out.

Growth

In the first place, aggregate growth rates, though displaying considerable dispersion, have remained very depressed. Between 1970 and 1979 average annual GDP growth for SSA as a whole was 2.9 per cent. Between 1980 and 1985 negative growth has occurred (–0.7 per cent per annum). Per capita trends have been yet more strongly negative declining, in the case of the low-income countries, by just under 2 per cent per annum between 1980 and 1986. For sub-Saharan Africa as a whole per capita GDP (expressed in 1980 constant prices) was nearly 20 per cent lower in 1986 than in 1980. Both per capita GDP and consumption have declined consistently and significantly since 1981/2 (see Table 14.1). Secondly, despite a general emphasis on implementing policies designed to stimulate agricultural sector output and relative share in aggregate national product, the sector's growth rate has generally been disappointing. While output grew on average at 1.8 per cent per annum between 1970 and 1979, over the period 1980–86 growth declined to a rate of 0.9 per cent. For the low-income economies negative growth of – 1.2 per cent occurred. However, this disguises the fact of considerable variation in performance. For the twenty-six low-income countries for

Table 14.1: *Sub-Saharan Africa: basic indicator growth rates 1980–87*

Year	GDP	Agriculture	Industry	Exports	Imports	GDP per capita	Per capita consumption
1980	3.9	2.9	1.2	3.0	19.5	1.0	3.8
1981	–1.3	–2.5	–6.1	–21.0	6.7	–4.3	4.4
1982	–0.07	7.3	–3.2	–10.2	–4.9	–3.1	–1.7
1983	–1.3	–1.7	–2.2	–3.9	–19.1	–4.3	–5.0
1984	–1.8	–1.7	–3.6	10.3	–6.8	–4.8	–6.1
1985	1.6	2.6	2.8	8.1	–1.6	–1.2	–4.2
1986*	0.6	–	–	2.4	–9.5	–2.7	–
1987*	–0.5	–	–	–8.0	–3.8	–3.6	–

* projected
Source: World Bank.

which data are available, 18 experienced positive growth. The unweighted average tends to be dominated by the strongly negative performance of a number of countries – such as Mozambique, Sudan and Ethiopia – where civil war and other factors largely explain recent trends. Nevertheless, even excluding these particular cases, the fact remains that agricultural sector growth rates have remained very low and, when expressed in per capita terms, largely negative. Moreover, growth rates post-1980 have been generally several percentage points below trend rates over the prior fifteen-year period. In short, there has been no significant improvement at either aggregate or sectoral level.

Current Account

Recent trends in the balance of payments indicate the importance of, first, import reduction and, second and increasingly, long-term interest payments. For sub-Saharan Africa as a whole the current account deficit narrowed appreciably between 1982 and 1986 before widening again thereafter. Exports declined by around 14 per cent by 1986 when measured in constant 1980 prices. Much of this decline can be attributed to developments in the oil market and the impact on fuel-exporting countries. Import compression has also been particularly pronounced for the fuel-exporting countries. For those countries with adjustment programmes import volume fell by over 10 per cent between 1982 and 1986. This is likely to have had the most adverse implications primarily for the low-income economies where *ex ante* import levels were already depressed. By 1985 imports for this category had fallen by over 21 per cent from the 1980 level (1980 constant prices). When expressed as a share of GDP, imports fell from 25 per cent to 22 per cent between 1978 and 1985. Even for countries such as Ghana and Senegal that have generally been held up as successful examples of adjustment, imports have either risen slightly from a very weak base (in the case of Ghana) or remained constant. In the great majority of cases import capacity remains significantly sub-optimal. The fall in imports can be attributed not only to reduced aggregate absorption (at least over the short to medium term) but also to the effect of real exchange-rate depreciation and foreign-exchange rationing. At the same time relative price shifts that translate into compositional change in the structure of total output and factor allocation can affect the overall import profile. Thus it has been argued that agriculture has been and is the least direct import-intensive sector. While significant across-country variation exists regarding import/output composition effects, it has been estimated that a one per cent increase in agricultural growth holding aggregate growth constant would be associated with a median decrease in import growth of 0.3 per cent (Lopez and Thomas, 1988). However, it should be noted that, first, SSA has historically had far higher import/GDP ratios than other regions and that this has held true when decomposed at agricultural sector level. Second, with historical income elasticities of demand for imports commonly exceeding unity, for sustained GDP growth to occur there will have to be a significant increase in imports given recent post-1982 trends. Recent World Bank projections of 4 per cent GDP growth with 3 per cent import volume growth appear in this light to be unrealistic. Third, even if import growth can be held back through growth in agriculture's share of GDP resulting from policy reform, this ignores the fact that *ex ante* sectoral import levels have generally been very restricted, one direct reflection of which has been average productivity levels in African agriculture. A significant potential trade-off clearly exists.

A recent World Bank estimate indicates that, even with some debt relief and new money, the shortfall in external resources required to finance a basic level of imports exceeds $4 billion for the period 1988–90. Generation of satisfactory trade surpluses continues to be impaired by deteriorating external terms of trade and poor medium-term prospects for the major exportables of the region (see Table 14.2). Thus, even with some noticeable depreciation in the real effective exchange rate (in the case of the low-income countries), the positive effect on export revenues has been offset not only by restricted supply responses but by external market constraints. By 1986 merchandise exports were around 80 per cent of the 1980 level when expressed in 1980 constant prices.

Table 14.2: *Sub-Saharan Africa: external terms of trade (average annual percentage change) and commodity terms of trade (1980 = 100), 1980–86*

	1980	1981	1982	1983	1984	1985	1986
Sub-Saharan Africa	19.6	4.2	-3.3	-3.4	5.0	-2.9	-27.0
SSA-fuel exporters	49.8	13.5	-2.8	-9.4	0.8	-3.2	n.a.
SSA-non-fuel exporters	-8.5	-7.8	-3.8	2.1	8.4	-2.9	-3.1
Commodity terms of trade (1980 = 100)							
Cocoa	100	79	68	82	96	88	68
Coffee	100	69	76	87	99	85	88
Tea	100	90	87	108	163	92	76
Groundnut oil	100	120	68	85	124	109	58
Copper	100	79	68	75	66	67	55
Petroleum	100	111	102	95	9	91	39

Source: World Bank and IMF statistics.

Budget Deficits

In the standard IMF stabilisation framework the working assumption is that output capacity is fixed in the short run and that therefore emphasis has to be placed on manipulating demand-side variables. Addressing the imbalance between aggregate demand and supply then presupposes actions to control domestic credit creation; hence monetary restraint. Where financial systems are thin, as in sub-Saharan Africa, changes in the claims of the banking system normally correspond to manipulating the fiscal deficit. Reducing the money supply thus presupposes reducing the fiscal deficit and it is here that sectoral and distributional considerations enter. But, perhaps surprisingly, the composition and incidence of expenditure-reducing measures remains largely a *terra incognita* for the IMF.

The desirability of reducing substantial budget deficits is obviously not in dispute. Financing such a deficit through a combination of external borrowing, domestic borrowing and an inflation tax can have adverse implications not simply for debt and domestic inflation levels but also for future growth potential via the upward pressure on the interest rate and the general crowding-out effect. For most SSA economies, the external financing option no longer realistically exists.

Recent evidence regarding the level of fiscal deficit indicates considerable variation in performance under adjustment. For all SSA economies with adjustment programmes the fiscal deficit as a share of GDP increased slightly by around 1 per cent – when compared with the pre-adjustment period. However, in the case of eleven low-income countries for whom data are available, the budget deficit fell significantly in the 1980s, amounting, by 1985, to around 2 per cent of GDP. But it is important to note that this

Table 14.3: *International trade taxes as a share of total tax revenues 1975 and 1985*

	Low-income		Middle-income		Industrial	
	1975	1985	1975	1985	1975	1985
International Trade:	39	38	25	19	4	2
Imports:	25	28	20	17	4	2
Exports:	11	8	4	1	0	0

Source: World Bank, *World Development Report 1988.*

has largely been achieved through reductions in real expenditures and far less through revenue-side improvements.

The case of Senegal (Chapter 9) is a particularly clear example. The emphasis on expenditure reduction can be attributed to a number of factors, aside from the nature of the conditionalities imposed by external agencies. First, the elasticity of revenues remains low in most developing country economies and this is especially the case in SSA where administrative and institutional structures tend to be weak. Moreover, it is important to note that a major share of tax revenues derives from trade duties, particularly import duties, and these tend to decline, at least over the short and medium term, for most economies undergoing adjustment (see Table 14.3). To sustain revenues, governments have tended to have recourse to ad hoc taxation measures to compensate for the fall in import levels and hence import duties. Moreover, faced with adverse external terms of trade the possible offsetting effect through enhanced export duties has commonly been weaker than expected. It thus appears that improvement in the overall tax/GDP ratio has not generally occurred.

Second, fiscal deficit reduction has tended to yield low domestic investment rates with adverse longer-term implications. In Côte d'Ivoire, for example, where public expenditure fell from around 42 per cent of GDP in 1982 to around 36 per cent in 1986, capital expenditure collapsed from 15 per cent of GDP to just over 6 per cent in the same period. Similarly in Malawi capital outlays declined significantly, even though total public expenditure remained roughly constant as a share of GDP. Third, the composition of current expenditure reductions has been biased against supplies and materials – a factor of considerable significance for agricultural sector public agencies and field institutions. Operating efficiency has consequently been compromised.

Lastly – and of specific relevance for agriculture – shifts away from trade and producer price taxation have proved difficult. This can be attributed not simply to administrative problems but also to political difficulties in, say, moving to a graduated land tax or an improved system of personal income taxation in rural areas. Generally speaking – and particularly in the sub-Saharan African context – movement away from trade taxes will not be a feasible medium-term possibility, hence again raising, in a slightly different way, the question of the appropriate level of implicit taxation to be levied on agricultural producers in the absence of more suitable taxation methods.

Debt

In the context of declining external terms of trade and severely reduced access to private commercial finance, a critical issue concerns the external – and in the case of most SSA economies, concessional – finance that has become available through structural adjustment (including agreements with the IMF). In addition, the associated issue of the cost of borrowing and the debt burden then imposed has assumed major significance.

The release of external resources is critical primarily in terms of balance-of-payments support. As already mentioned, adjustment has largely occurred through import contraction and reduction in government expenditure. Available evidence indicates, moreover, that in recent years not only has there been a strong negative transfer of resources to private lenders but there has also been a net outflow of resources to the IMF. Indeed, the shift by that institution toward longer loan durations (as with the Structural Adjustment Facility) and easier terms can be attributed to this tightening liquidity squeeze and the growing outflow of resources. Table 14.4 shows very clearly, using data for low-income SSA economies, recent trends in net transfers. Apart from the sharp reversal in private financing, multilateral transfers declined between 1980 and 1985 in nominal terms and this trend has been yet more pronounced for bilateral lending.

The very restricted net transfer of resources to SSA has nevertheless run alongside a rapid accumulation in external debt. Between 1980 and 1986 total external debt for the region rose from around 30 per cent to 70 per cent of GNP and from 98 per cent to 313 per cent of exports of goods and services. In the same period the debt-service ratio climbed from just over 7 per cent to 19 per cent. For the low-income economies these trends have been yet more pronounced. Debt servicing on public and publicly guaranteed long-term debt and IMF credits rose from 14.4 per cent in 1980 to nearly

Table 14.4: *Low-income SSA: net transfers from official and private sources, 1980–86 (US$m)**

Year	Total	Multilateral Aggregate	IMF	Bilateral	Private
1980	3,519	1,305	309	1,380	835
1981	3,127	1,099	1,002	1,636	391
1982	2,646	1,074	338	1,306	266
1983	2,429	1,062	661	1,426	−59
1984	1,468	915	132	807	−255
1985	1,045	921	−127	437	−312
1986	1,696	1,390	−602	517	−212

* excludes Angola, Botswana, Cameroon, Congo, Côte d'Ivoire, Djibouti, Gabon, Mauritius, Nigeria, Seychelles, Swaziland and Zimbabwe.

27 per cent by 1986. For countries that have had extensive access to adjustment finance, the accumulation of debt has been even more startling. In the case of Ghana, where access to external borrowing was limited in the 1970s (hence making it distinct from countries such as Zaire, Côte d' Ivoire or Senegal), the debt-service ratio accelerated from under 18 per cent in 1981 to 47 per cent by 1986 and an estimated 70 per cent level in 1988.

While the accumulation of external debt, as in the Ghanaian example, may be one precondition for restoring the capacity to import, the available evidence suggests, first, that net resource transfers have remained inadequate, hence limiting the degree to which this constraint has been weakened, while, second, the capacity to service current debt levels, given the combination of both external demand and domestic supply constraints, is open to question. Adverse shifts in the external terms of trade, protectionism and weak demand on the part of the industrialised countries for the principal SSA exports are some of the major factors impinging directly on the ability to service such debt levels.

THE LIMITATIONS OF ADJUSTMENT

Assessment of the overall impact of adjustment programmes is obviously made complex not only by difficulties in separating out effects but also on account of their short duration. However, it is clear that such policies have as yet failed to have a widespread and significantly positive impact on economic performance and, more specifically, on agricultural sector growth. This suggests, among other factors, that the mix of policies pursued under adjustment has not itself been wholly adequate when placed in a growth perspective.

In the first place, few adjustment programmes in SSA have started systematically to address the more deeply embedded constraints on growth; in effect, largely supply-side phenomena. Rather, emphasis has almost exclusively fallen on policies for reducing effective demand. This has had major implications for the size and composition of public expenditure with direct and important implications for the agricultural sector.

Second, despite the fact that most adjustment programmes have largely concentrated on price reforms, including macro-prices such as the exchange and interest rate, the degree to which nominal price changes have been translated and sustained in real terms remains variable. Table 14.5 indicates some real depreciation since 1980 in the exchange rate but that this was preceded by sharp appreciation in 1984 and 1985. Moreover, while for an aggregate of low-income countries the exchange rate had depreciated by around 15 per cent by 1986, for the oil-exporting economies, this adjustment had only partially occurred. Again, in the case of members of the West African Currency Union, a sharp appreciation of the CFA occurred post-1986 that could not be countered through an active exchange-rate policy. Even when such a policy could be pursued, recent experience points to no clear or optimal means for exchange-rate management. Premature and uncontrolled movement to foreign-exchange auctions in Uganda and Zambia merely stimulated inflation and political dissent (see Chapter 8 in this volume).

Table 14.5: *Sub-Saharan Africa: real effective exchange rate indices (1980 = 100)*

| Country groups | Year | | | | | |
	1981	1982	1983	1984	1985	1986
Sub-Saharan Africa	110	112	117	139	129*	104*
Low-income SSA	112	115	110	101	98*	86*
Middle-income SSA	108	110	122	161	148*	114*
Oil exporters	110	112	127	175	159*	120*
Oil importers	100	101	93	92	87*	86*
Low-income with Adj. Programmes	119	131	123	103	98*	85*

* first half of 1985 and 1986.
Source: IMF.

Pricing Policy and Supply Responses

The strong emphasis placed by donors on price reforms obviously reflects the key importance of variables such as the exchange rate in determining sectoral performance. At the same time, it also reflects the view that one of the main factors restraining agricultural sector growth in SSA has been the use of price controls and output taxes as a method for redistributing income away from the sector.

Under adjustment, donors have strongly pressed governments pursuing output taxation to raise producer prices towards border prices, shifting the effective protection coefficient towards unity. Nevertheless, it is very evident that, while this may have been defined as a broadly desirable objective, other considerations have tended to predominate, leading to more ad-hoc outcomes. These include public finance considerations. Thus, where export taxes comprise a significant share of public revenues and where there is limited potential over the short or medium term for raising non-output taxes from the agricultural sector, this has restricted the scale of real farmgate price increments that governments have granted. Nevertheless – as Chapter 7 shows – producer prices of around 50 per cent of border price levels for the major exportable – cocoa – can still generate a significant up-turn in marketed releases, even if such increases can probably be best explained in terms of better capacity utilisation. The degree to which farmgate prices can be raised has also depended on international price trends. As international prices for Africa's principal primary commodity exports have fallen sharply, this has limited the room for manoeuvre. In Senegal, for example, declining groundnut prices have compromised the government's strategy of raising the producer price, necessitating a 23 per cent reduction in the domestic price in 1988.

The rationale for reductions in implicit taxation and for relative price changes is similar, relating to the incentive structure facing producers. The operating assumption is that real price increments will generate a significant supply response, particularly for tradables if expenditure-switching conditions are satisfied. Clearly this is not an unreasonable assumption, as Chapter 4 demonstrates. But the size of the response and, more particularly, the response at the level of marketed releases appears typically to be restricted in the SSA context. Positive supply elasticities of the order of 0.2–0.4 appear to obtain with long-run elasticities ranging between 0.6 and 1.8 (Bond, 1983). In the case of cocoa in Côte d'Ivoire the short-run elasticity was between 0.3/0.9 and the long-run 0.9–1.8 (Akiyama and Bowers, 1984). This level of supply response is likely to be higher than for many SSA economies, where non-price constraints are more significant. In such cases – as in Tanzania – price measures have tended to act only on a limited share of output, the remaining share of which may not be responsive to price changes in the presence of factors such as risk aversion, incomplete market liberalisation and bottlenecks in the supply of wage goods to the sector (Bevan et al., 1988). While relative price shifts may engender a set of area substitutions with added weight given to tradables, the aggregate supply response – perhaps the more appropriate dynamic measure of response – will tend to be considerably lower than for individual crops, particularly in the absence of complementary actions, such as infrastructural investment. Available evidence on the aggregate supply response for both Japan and India suggests, for example, that a one-period aggregate price elasticity does not exceed 0.2 with the long-run elasticity at around 0.4 (Krishna, 1982). Obviously this is not an argument for the irrelevance of prices but rather an indication of the combined role of price and other policy variables in raising output levels. In particular, an adequate price environment needs to be combined with investment in productivity-related shift variables, such as irrigation, education, capital formation and population density. In Indian wheat supply estimations, for example, the irrigation variable has been found to be at least 1.5 times that of the direct price elasticity (Krishna and Chhibber, 1983). Generally speaking, an equiproportionate change in a technology variable will yield a higher level of growth than through a straight price effect.

Technology, Institutions and Productivity Growth

Yet it is also evident that the rate of technical change will itself be – at least in part – price-driven. Indeed, it is this view that has supported the maintenance of significant input subsidies by a wide range of SSA governments. Despite such attempts to sustain direct price subsidies and, in some cases, maintain favourable input/output relative price relationships, most evidence from SSA points to low rates of technology adoption and perhaps more significantly very weak productivity effects. These factors, combined with budgetary considerations, have underpinned the widespread withdrawal of subsidies in SSA. While quantity rationing and inefficiencies in delivery systems can explain both the limited diffusion and the skewedness in that distribution toward larger farms (either intentionally, as in Malawi, or through classical ration-rental allocation systems, as in Ghana), the failure to register significant productivity advance has also to be attributed to a wider range of factors. These include inadequate levels of investment in technology itself, lack of complementary research and extension services and, in particular, a bias against non-exportable crops produced by the bulk of African smallholders. The importance of public inputs may be considered particularly marked in the SSA context where the combination of ecological, climatic and productive constraints alongside relatively low population densities has tended to impose quite severe limitations on the extent and pace of indigenous innovation and technological advance. To the extent that such advances have been made it is not clear that these have been translated into major, sustained productivity growth.

It is clear that to achieve the scale of productivity advance that has as yet eluded much of African small-holder agriculture will require greater public investment in and for the sector. Such investment implies not only improved infrastructure but also the production and distribution of suitable technological packages. Past experience suggests that, first, the share of agriculture in total public expenditure has been low. For a twelve-country sample for the period 1978–81 agriculture accounted for no more than 11 per cent of total public outlays, and in general its share in total investment expenditure has been substantially sub-optimal (Norton, 1987). A clear example relates to agricultural research expenditures. For West Africa, agricultural research expenditure in 1980 amounted to no more than 0.65 per cent of agricultural GDP in 1980, with traditional food crops attracting particularly low investment in terms of both value of output and consumption weights (Jha and Oram, 1987).

Achieving the necessary technical advances in SSA agriculture is thus likely to require not simply the provision of a facilitative pricing and taxation policy environment but also a more directed allocation of public resources. Until recently, the main emphasis of both governments and donors has been on establishing institutions capable of delivering a range of goods and services to the sector. These have ranged from credit (commonly at subsidised rates) to inputs and extension advice. In a majority of cases this was associated with the establishment of specific institutions – such as area development projects – which were characterised by a multiplicity of functions. These institutions have also tended, more unfortunately, to suffer from low efficiency and pervasive recurrent cost under-financing by governments. With donor reluctance to maintain long-term financing of these agencies and with the parallel pressure for fiscal contraction, the adjustment period has seen a widespread process of disengagement which, to varying extents, has led either to the liquidation of these institutions or to their selective dismantling. When combined with the retraction of budgetary subsidies for inputs, this has resulted not only in reduced demand for potentially productivity-enhancing inputs but also a reduction in the supply of complementary services, particularly extension. In the more extreme cases – such as Senegal or Sierra Leone – this has brought a growing absence of technical interventions in the sector in a context where private initiatives will tend, at best, to be a very incomplete and partial compensation.

The strong emphasis placed under adjustment lending on reducing the budgetary claims of both parastatals and projects obviously addresses only a partial subset of the relevant issues. It neglects, almost completely, the means for achieving the productivity effects that are a basic prerequisite for the agriculture-led growth that donors, in particular, have envisaged for the region as whole. Ironically, this emphasis runs strongly counter to the strategies that those donors had, until the end of the 1970s, urged upon African governments. In Senegal, for example, it is instructive to note that the World Bank played an active role in the propagation and support of the Integrated Area Development Projects that were designed to supplant the Ministry of Rural Development in the actual delivery of services to farmers. Justification for this approach was summarised as follows: 'the para-public sector, if well run, can be used, inter alia, to control key sectors of the economy ... encourage investment where private initiative is lacking, acquire new technology and managerial expertise, attract foreign financing from private and foreign official sources which might not otherwise come to the public administration, and develop an organizational form which is more flexible than Government's administrative services (World Bank, 1977). By 1980 these arguments were no longer acceptable to the major donors, the most obvious consequence of which was a rapid withdrawal of funding from the parastatal sector and subsequent disengagement by those agencies from a whole range of functions. Eight years after the adoption of the first adjustment measures, the Senegalese rural sector remains largely devoid of institutional supports to producers. The limited gains made through the diffusion of new technologies – particularly the introduction of animal traction – are, if anything, being reversed.

The priorities established under adjustment betray a clear bias towards reliance on price instruments. This has been justified largely on the assumption of flexible and integrated markets. Such assumptions – particularly in the SSA context – are not generally warranted. Further, addressing the sources of both domestic and external disequilibria has resulted in considerable emphasis being placed on reducing public expenditure. This has had a particularly marked impact on investment outlays and, in a number of countries, on the operating efficiency of rural sector institutions through reduction in recurrent cost budgeting. Quite obviously any sustained adjustment programme has to address the level of budget deficit, but available evidence from SSA indicates that concern with fiscal stabilisation has largely defined the framework of sectoral policy. Though the former may be a necessary condition, in the SSA context it is evident that it is not a sufficient condition for sectoral growth. More specifically, an ideological preference for the private sector and an emphasis on relatively rapid contractions in public outlays have resulted in the effective atrophy of rural sector institutions. Equally fundamental has been the reluctance of donors to face the likely public inputs that are required. This flies in the face of historical experience from other regions, let alone the basis on which donors had financed projects during the 1970s.

Adjustment and Income Distribution

It has normally been assumed that the combination of exchange-rate reform, domestic relative price shifts and explicit reductions in taxation levels for agricultural producers will raise aggregate welfare in the sector. This derives from the weight of tradables in total sectoral output and earlier biases against agricultural producers both through the prices they received and the direction of public resources.

The assumption of welfare gains in the sector largely derives from the apparent income effects that ought to be associated with a shift in the intersectoral terms of trade in favour of agriculture. Evidence from a number of countries indicates that such a shift has been a common consequence of adjustment programmes and an explicit design component (see Chapter 2). Yet the actual welfare effect will depend on the prior distributional features of the sector and, in particular, the relative balance between net buyers and sellers. At the same time, the relative weighting of traded and non-traded goods in consumption baskets will determine the more precise welfare outcome.

Mapping the distributional effects of an adjustment programme, as Chapters 5 and 6 demonstrate, is extremely difficult. Nevertheless, working from a standard dependent economy model the critical question turns not so much on the terms of trade, but the price of tradables relative to non-tradables. In this regard, exchange-rate policy is critical in achieving that switch. However, on the assumption that such switching occurs through real devaluations – itself a large assumption in the SSA context – further problems arise in isolating the distributional outcomes. For example, the degree to which the tradables/non-tradables distinction adequately identifies the basic characteristics of production systems may be problematic where, say, producers generate both outputs and where traded and non-traded sub-sectors are not exclusive.

Consider the more transparent distributional implications of an orthodox adjustment programme. In the short run, devaluation will improve the incomes of tradables

Table 14.6: *Short-run income effects (direction of change) associated with adjustment measures*

URBAN		RURAL	
Formal Sector:		*Large Farm Sector:*	
i) Government and public sector employees	–	i) Wage labour on plantations	+
ii) Private Sector		*Small Farm Sector*	
a. Exportable sub-sector	+	i) Owner-operators/tenants producing tradables	+
b. Home goods sub-sector	–	ii) Owner-operators/tenants producing home goods	–
Informal Sector		iii) Owner-operators/tenants: net food-purchasers	–
i) Wage Labour	–	iv) Subsistence producers	0
ii) Self-employed	–	v) Hired labour—tradables sub-sector	+
iii) Casual Labour	–	vi) Hired labour—non-tradables sub-sector	–
Unemployed	?		
		Non-agricultural workers	
		i) self-employed	
		a. tradables processing	+
		b. other	–
		ii) Wage labour	–

producers. The degree to which this is the case will depend on supply elasticities and the scale of non-price rigidities in the economy. On the assumption that factor mobility between sectors does not hold (a reasonable assumption over the short run), profits and wages will be higher for tradables producers than for non-tradables producers. The net welfare impact will then depend on the degree to which income gains in the former sector offset losses in the latter. In the SSA context, the likely gainers will be producers of foreign exchange, such as cocoa or coffee growers. Informal service-sector workers working in flex-price markets are likely to be significant losers. The degree to which formal public sector workers are likely to gain or lose will depend on the extent to which indexation and wage rigidity are present, one effect of which will be to erode any nominal relative price shift in favour of agricultural sector producers.

A crude attempt is made in Table 14.6 to summarise the likely short-to-medium-term direction of change in income terms where disaggregation is made on both a two-sector and sub-sectoral basis. Implicit in the representation is a price effect that favours tradable producers. This is, of course, not the same as a strict shift in the intersectoral terms of trade but may be viewed as achieving similar results, given the strong weight of agriculture in aggregate tradables output. The table shows a fairly wide range of possible income outcomes and provides some elementary key to mapping the differentiated impact of price changes associated with adjustment programmes. Unless full factor mobility is assumed and markets function without friction, such price measures generate within the agricultural sector unambiguous gainers and losers. While it is clear that both the real exchange rate and the agricultural terms of trade have a significant impact on the functional distribution of income, particularly if trade restrictions are present, the degree to which this occurs depends, in part, on whether farm households generate tradables output or can switch into such production and, second, whether those households are net sellers. For net purchasers and non-tradables producers – landed and landless – the net income effect, at least in the short run, is likely to be negative. Yet in much of SSA access to tradables production may be constrained by ecological factors, capital scarcity and effective labour market segmentation. Thus, poorer farmers who tend to be largely home goods producers may lack the ability to switch production.

In Malawi, for example, this outcome holds largely on account of land concentration and the direction of agricultural services. Preferential access to both land and factors of production results not only in higher productivity levels in the estate sector but also highly skewed income distribution within the agricultural sector. Even producer prices received from the monopsonistic marketing board by the estates have been significantly higher than for the smallholder sub-sector (Lele, 1987). Inability to switch production, partly on account of non-price factors, can thus result in a significant diminution in the overall welfare gains within the agricultural sector and a possible worsening in income distribution deriving from ex ante asset allocation and resource endowments.

The Ghana case study (Chapter 7) further indicates the restrictive welfare effects of expenditure switching. Relative price shifts towards the major exportable – cocoa – have tended to benefit the larger cocoa farms particularly in those areas where infrastructural constraints – particularly for marketing and transportation – have been less binding. But the poorer regions of the country, in which the bulk of low-income farm households are concentrated, are not suitable for cocoa production. While under adjustment the price of all goods (including home goods) will tend to rise relative to future goods, the exact income effect on non-tradable producers will depend on the degree to which households are buyers, their respective consumption weights and their ability to raise the level of marketed releases. If – as in Ghana –

there is market segmentation, let alone constraints on raising marketed output, then the general price increases for agricultural products will not necessarily translate into income gains through supply-side constraints while, in addition, the general dampening effects of expenditure reduction will hold down demand for home goods.

The degree to which these constraints are lifted will largely depend on the consumption and investment linkages that occur through the relative increase in tradables prices and, hence, producer incomes. Recent estimates indicate lower linkage effects than in Asia, with roughly 0.5 elasticity to agricultural income (Haggblade et al. 1987). Nevertheless, this can translate into a range of positive employment and income effects, assuming that real output price increases are sustained and that the net income effect of upward output and input price adjustments is positive. Non-tradables producers in economies marked by major labour market distortions, while not necessarily benefiting from improvement in the terms of trade, may, however, shield themselves by being predominantly subsistence producers. If simple reliance on two prices – the real exchange rate and the agricultural terms of trade – does not necessarily yield the positive welfare effects that are assumed in most adjustment programmes, more nuanced interventions may be more likely to achieve desired distributional goals. This can be seen in the case of Côte d'Ivoire where, as in Ghana, a significant share of poorer households are concentreated in areas unfit for producing the major tradables – coffee, cocoa and oil palm. Raising producer prices for these outputs would benefit only between 40 and 50 per cent of the poorer farm households. However, a greater share of the latter are cotton producers. Raising the cotton price would consequently benefit nearly 28 per cent of the poorest 10 per cent and 20 per cent of the poorest 30 per cent (Glewwe and de Tray, 1988). This indicates that if equity considerations are given some weighting in adjustment programmes, mere reliance on terms-of-trade effects will camouflage the highly differential impact within the sector of relative price movements.

CONCLUSION

Adjustment lending has now emerged centre-stage both for recipient governments and donors. Even as the emphasis now shifts more towards greater sectoral adjustment lending (at least in the case of the World Bank), the weight given to policy rather than project lending continues to grow. Yet, at least in SSA, the benefits are not readily visible. This is occasionally attributed to the root-and-branch nature of the reforms that adjustment lending imposes. In effect, it is an attempt to develop new structures and redefine existing ones. But the original objectives of such lending – the elimination of domestic and external imbalances – and the resumption of growth have as yet been only partially satisfied and in a very limited number of cases in SSA. Consequently, adjustment lending emerges as a continuing, longer-run phenomenon no longer ostensibly designed to correct for transitory disequilibria.

This chapter has shown that, apart from weak or non-existent improvement in basic indicators of economic performance, adjustment lending in the SSA context has rarely extended much beyond limited stabilisation objectives. The basic content of adjustment has been restraint of aggregate consumption, with consequent falls – often very pronounced – in personal disposable income levels and investment. This will tend to produce adverse longer-term growth implications as well as intended short-run effects.

Although it is widely recognised that the success of adjustment depends on the timing and depth of the supply response such measures engender, the evidence presented in this book points to generally weak and certainly patchy supply response from the key agricultural sector. The present chapter has argued that this can largely be attributed to the nature of the constraints – external (e.g. terms of trade) and domestic – that operate on the sector and, in addition, the limitations of the policy variables that have so far been given prominence in adjustment programmes. In particular, donors and governments have yet to deal adequately with the appropriate institutional structures required for stimulating productivity growth in agriculture. Too frequently, aversion to public agencies on both budgetary and straight ideological lines has masked reality. Apart from the question of expectations – including those regarding likely future behaviour by the government in price determination – the fact remains that in the majority of SSA economies the private sector is reluctant to assume certain public functions – such as provision of research, extension and inputs supply – on financial feasibility grounds (Commander and Killick, 1988). Historical experience, both in SSA itself and in other continents, strongly indicates that public inputs must necessarily play a prominent role. The search for greater fiscal balance and an impatience with the apparent failures of institutions established over the previous two decades appear to ignore these realities. This has been compounded by the limited focus on the composition and direction of public resources rather than on simple aggregates. Thus, while few would argue with the need for basic reforms or with the ordering of some of those reforms (the key role of the exchange rate, in particular), it is also very clear that stimulating agricultural growth in SSA requires the application of a basket of policies embracing institutional support, infrastructural development and appropriate pricing rules. To date, relatively little progress has been made in implementing such policies, in part a function of poor government, in part a consequence of donor myopia and the distance between the posited, desirable development strategy and the African reality.

REFERENCES

Akiyama, T. and A. Bowers (1984), *Supply Response of Cocoa in Major Producing Countries*, World Bank Working Paper, Washington, DC, April.

Bevan, D.L., P. Collier and J.W. Gunning (1988), *Trade Shocks in Controlled Economies: Theory and an Application to the East Africa Coffee Boom*, Oxford, Oxford University Press.

Bond, M. (1983) 'Agricultural Responses to Prices in Sub-Saharan African Countries', *IMF Staff Papers*, Vol. 30.

Commander, S. and T. Killick (1988) 'Privatisation in Developing Countries: A Survey of the Issues' in P. Cook and C. Kirkpatrick (eds), *Privatisation and Developing Countries*, Brighton, Harvester Press.

Glewwe, P. and P. de Tray (1988) *The Poor During Adjustment: A Case Study of Cote d' Ivoire*, World Bank, LSMS Working Paper 47, Washington DC.

Haggblade, S., P. Hazell, and J. Brown (1987), 'Farm-Nonfarm Linkages in Rural Sub-Saharan Africa'. Washington DC. World Bank, (mimeo).

Jha, D. and P. Oram (1987) 'Pattern of Agricultural Research Resume Allocation in West Africa'. Washington DC, IFPRI (mimeo).

Krishna, Raj (1982) 'Some Aspects of Agricultural Growth, Price Policy and Equity in Developing Countries.' *Food Research Institute Studies*, Vol. 18, No. 3.

—— and Ajay Chhibber (1983), *Policy Modeling of a Dual Grain Market: The Case of Wheat in India*, Washington DC, IFPRI.

Lele, Uma (1987) 'Structural Adjustment, Agricultural Development and the Poor: Some Observations on Malawi', Washington DC (mimeo).

Lopez, R. and V. Thomas (1988), *Imports and Growth in Africa*, World Bank, PPR Working Paper, Washington DC.

Norton, R.D. (1987) *Agricultural Issues in Structural Adjustment Programs*. Rome, FAO.

Sarris, A.H. (1987) *Agricultural Stabilization and Structural Adjustment Policies in Developing Countries*, Rome, FAO.

World Bank (1977) *Senegal: The Para-public Sector, Report 1619-SE*. Washington DC.

—— (1986) *Structural Adjustment Lending, A First Review of Experience*. Washington DC, 24 September.

—— (1988) *Interim Report on Adjustment Lending*. Washington DC, 25 January.

Index